D0811601

Introduction to IT Project Management

Introduction to IT Project Management

Cynthia Snyder
Frank Parth

MANAGEMENTCONCEPTS

MANAGEMENTCONCEPTS
8230 Leesburg Pike, Suite 800
Vienna, VA 22182
(703) 790-9595
Fax: (703) 790-1371
www.managementconcepts.com

Printed in the United States of America

Library of Congress Cataloging-in-Publication Data

Synder, Cynthia, 1962–
Introduction to IT project management / Cynthia Snyder, Frank Parth.
p. cm.
Includes bibliographical references and index.
ISBN 1-56726-178-7
1. Information technology projects—Management. I. Parth, Frank, 1949–
II. Title.

HD30.2S635 2007
658.4'038—dc22 2006046828

There are three people who help make my life a joy: my mother, my daughter, and my husband. Thank you, Mom, for your wicked sense of humor, your crone-like perspective, and your fabulous proofing skills. Thank you, Talaya, for your sweetness of your heart and your courage. Thank you, Michael, for making my life easy, and keeping it gooey, still.

— C.S.

This book is dedicated to my parents, Frank and Erna, who immigrated to the U.S. in 1952 with no money and unable to speak the language. Their years of hard work made everything else possible.

— F.P.

About the Authors

Cynthia Snyder, PMP, MBA, is a professional project management consultant, instructor, and author. She provides consulting and training services to government and private industry. Her consulting focuses on project management maturity, PMO startups, and positioning project management as a core competency for organizations.

Cyndi has experience in training in the corporate, public, and academic environment. Clients have included IBM, Kaiser, Toyota, and Southern California Edison. In an academic environment, she has taught online and in the classroom for UC Irvine, CalTech, and USC.

She has written two books on project management and has been the technical editor on many others.

Cyndi is an active volunteer with the Project Management Institute. She is the project manager for the 2008 editions of the *PMBOK® Guide* and the *Standard for Program Management.* In the past she has served on the Standards Member Advisory Group and was Chair of the Chapter Leadership Development and Excellence Committee for 2003–2005. She was President of the PMI® Orange County Chapter for 2001 and 2002. In 2002 she received the award for Outstanding Chapter President of the Year. Cyndi is a certified Project Management Professional (PMP) and earned her master's in business administration from Pepperdine University.

Frank Parth, MS, MSSM, MBA, PMP, is the President of Project Auditors, LLC, a project management consulting, training, and auditing company. After ending a career in aerospace as the assistant technical director on a $12 billion satellite program, he branched out in 1993 and began consulting in technology management to major U.S. companies, national governments, and the U.N. He was CTO for a small but successful e-commerce company, headed up systems engineering at TRW Information Systems during a major infrastructure upgrade, and created PMOs for several major corporations. He taught systems analysis and management at the Graduate School at the University of Southern California, has been an instructor at the University of California, Irvine PM Certificate program since 1994, and has taught at the Claremont Graduate School. Mr. Parth has undergraduate and graduate degrees in physics, a master's in systems management from USC, and an MBA from the Peter F. Drucker Graduate School of Management. He has published numerous papers on project management and systems engineering and is an international speaker. He has been in *Who's Who in the United States* and *Who's Who in the World* for many years. He is active in PMI®, serving on various committees both at the local and at the national level and is the 2006 Chair for PMI's Consulting SIG.

Contents

How to Use This Book

For the most part, this book is organized sequentially. We begin by giving an overview of how projects fit into an organization and how they assist an organization in meeting its strategic objectives. Then we talk about how projects are initiated and what should be done to properly initiate a project.

A huge amount of this book is spent on planning processes. Planning is where project success is made. Lack of proper planning is one of the key reasons why projects fail. Planning begins with project scope, and, in IT, requirements gathering is the key to developing and delivering project scope. After the scope is understood, a preliminary schedule and budget are developed. Notice we say preliminary. At this point, all schedule and resource information is an estimate. The necessary technical skills need to be defined, the availability of resources needs to be ascertained, and an analysis of the relevant risks needs to be completed before any kind of realistic final schedule or budget can be developed. As the project manager is elaborating the project scope, schedule, and resources, he or she is also defining the quality parameters and the communication needs of the stakeholders. These components define the planning process.

After we discuss planning, we spend some time looking at the actual execution of the project and how to monitor and control the project progress. This part of the book includes information on change management. We close the book with project audit and closure.

We are writing with IT project managers, team members, and those who aspire to be IT project managers in mind. Therefore, we use examples that are IT oriented. Many of the examples are of software application development, though we also include some examples of networks, relocations, and other types of projects that IT professionals may find themselves embroiled in.

This book is consistent with *A Guide to the Project Management Body of Knowledge (PMBOK® Guide),* 3rd Edition. The concepts are aligned with the processes and knowledge areas presented in the *PMBOK® Guide.*

Learning tools are placed throughout the book to help you absorb the information:

- *PM in Practice* sections are practical tasks and procedures that you can do on your own.
- *What Do You Think?* sections ask you to think about information presented in the chapter and form your own opinion.
- *Tips, Notes,* and *Warnings* are located throughout the book. These come from personal experience and are little pieces of information that will help you avoid problems or give you shortcuts we think are useful and interesting.
- *In Practice* sections are case study vignettes. These examples demonstrate information presented in the chapter or describe how something is done in organizations.
- Additionally, we insert some forms that should help you in your job.

At the end of each chapter, you will find a summary, key vocabulary terms, a key vocabulary quiz, and review questions to ensure that you understand the key concepts presented in the chapter.

Please note that an instructor's guide is available for text adopters. Call 703-270-4170 or email cfine@managementconcepts.com for additional information.

1 Projects and Operations

After reading this chapter, you will be able to:

- Define how projects and operations are different.
- Describe how IT projects differ from non-IT projects.
- Explain the value of project management for IT projects.
- Define key terms in project management.

Welcome to the world of information technology project management. In reading this book, you will find that managing IT projects can be highly rewarding and, often, equally frustrating. You will discover that project team members, project customers, and other project stakeholders can be very easy to work with and at the same time can be very challenging. It is not uncommon in project management to get a high-priority project from upper management one week and then find the next week that things have changed and a new project is the number one priority. You will almost never have enough resources to do the work and never have enough time to produce the best product possible. You will be told not to spend time planning the project but to just begin working, and you won't have enough time to gather the user requirements before you need to start development. Your resources will be working on three other projects as well as normal daily operations, while you're trying to get them to work on your project.

However, when the project is over you will have produced something that makes work easier for the other people in your organization, saves your organization a significant amount of money, keeps private data secure, or upgrades a legacy system into something much more effective and efficient. When all the work of the project is over, you will have made a real contribution to the organization.

WHAT IS PROJECT MANAGEMENT?

Project management is the application of skills, knowledge, and abilities to produce a unique product, service, or result. Three components that lead to successful projects are technical knowledge, general management abilities, and project management skills.

The project manager must have knowledge of the technical aspects of the project. Although some will debate this point, in IT projects particularly the project manager needs to know enough to detect when something is amiss and to understand the general principles of the project. He or she certainly does not need to be a subject matter expert in every facet, but some amount of knowledge is a necessity.

The project manager also needs some capability in the area of general management, including skills in budgeting, analysis, planning, and coordinating. Finally, the project manager must apply project management skills, tools, and techniques to make the project a success. This book focuses on the project management component while referencing technical knowledge and some general management abilities (see Figure 1-1).

Figure 1-1. Components for Successful Projects

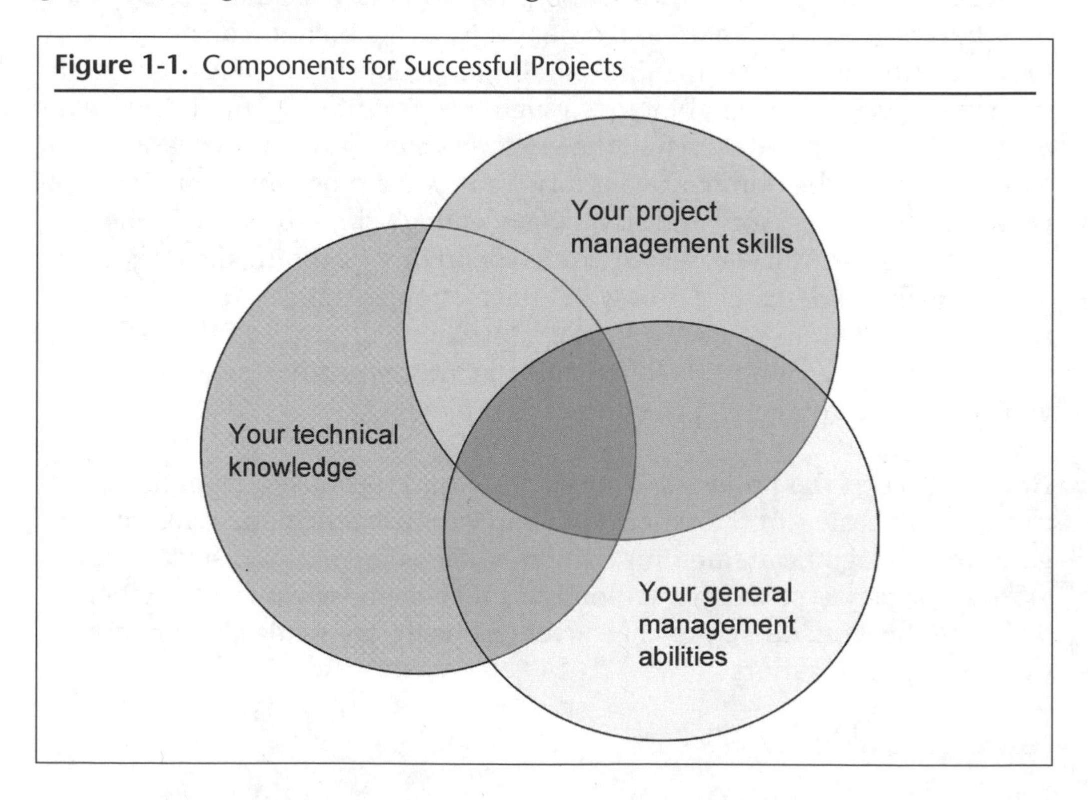

Managing IT projects is similar to managing other types of projects, such as projects in the fields of construction and pharmaceutical development. However, IT project management has unique aspects, including:

- Technical projects require team members with specific technical skills.
- For small projects, team members are typically working on multiple projects at the same time.
- Most team members have operational responsibilities as well as project responsibilities.
- Larger IT projects tend to form the very infrastructure of the organization, and failure can cost millions of dollars.
- Because of the pervasiveness of information systems, a simple IT project may become complex because of the number of other systems it touches.
- Technology is evolving so rapidly that software and hardware are almost always out-of-date before they are deployed.
- Technology requires continual upgrading, maintenance, and improvement.
- The changing nature of technology can make it difficult to estimate accurately or to learn from previous projects.

The differences inherent in IT projects create a need for specialized approaches to manage IT projects effectively. The basic methodology of project management continually advances as we learn what works under what conditions and what does not work. Although it is tempting to use a recipe approach to managing IT projects, the reality is that each organization must start with the basic principles of project management—which are presented in this book—and develop a detailed approach that works for its organizational structure, culture, and environment.

Project management practices and methods are evolving. As organizations change and evolve, the approaches needed to effectively manage projects also change and evolve. The largest professional organization dedicated to project management is the Project Management Institute (PMI®) with over 200,000 members worldwide at the time this book was written. PMI's book *A Guide to the Project Management Body of Knowledge (PMBOK® Guide)* was developed by practicing project managers, and it is the American national standard for project management.[1] This guide is continually evolving as new approaches and new practices are integrated into project management. However, it is not the only approach to managing IT projects. An approach called Projects in Controlled Environments (PRINCE2) was developed by the IT Directorate of the British Government. PRINCE2 places a heavy emphasis on creating a strong business case for IT projects and continually monitoring the project against the business case. The Information Systems Audit and Control Association (ISACA) has developed Control Objectives for Information and Related Technology (CoBIT), which emphasizes controlling and auditing IT projects.

WHY USE PROJECT MANAGEMENT?

Why are there so many approaches to managing IT projects? Because the failure rate of IT development work is high. The baseline study of IT project success is the *CHAOS Report* released by the Standish Group in 1995.[2] This report showed that 31 percent of projects were canceled before completion and 52.7 percent of projects cost over 189 percent of their original estimates.

Based on this research, the Standish Group estimated that in 1995 American companies and government agencies spent $81 billion for canceled software projects and had to pay an additional $59 billion for software projects that exceeded their planned schedules. It estimated that almost 80,000 projects were cancelled in 1995. Although large IT projects are always risky, many of these projects were as straightforward as a drivers' license database, a new accounting package, or an order entry system. This book will help you understand the unique aspects of managing IT projects and how to improve the success rate of your projects significantly.

This book is about how to manage IT projects. It is not a book on software project management and it is not a book on implementing enterprise-wide software applications. It is not a book on how to manage local area network (LAN) design and installation. All of these are types of IT projects, but IT is a much broader field than any one of those areas. We will use a working definition that IT project management is about managing projects where a significant portion of the product or result is dependent on some aspect of information technology. This book will give you a strong start towards managing those projects.

HOW IS PROJECT MANAGEMENT DIFFERENT FROM OPERATIONAL MANAGEMENT?

When most of us consider an organization, we think of a hierarchical assortment of departments that collectively produce some type of product or service. Most organizations have a marketing department, a finance department, a human resources department, some type of production or manufacturing department, and, of course, an IT department. These departments work more or less collaboratively to create something of value that the organization provides to its customers in order to sustain the organization. In the world of operations management, departments work towards company objectives.

For example, in operations management the goal could be to produce and sell the best widget for the least amount of money and to sustain those operations. At that point, production becomes repetitive and static. However, projects are not repetitive; projects are one-time events designed to produce specific results and then to end. The *PMBOK® Guide* defines a **project** as a temporary endeavor undertaken to create a unique product, service, or result.[3]

Although departmental operations tend to focus on the objectives that each department is working to achieve, projects focus on a client or business objective. Operations management is concerned primarily with keeping the lights on and ensuring that the company continues and grows. Projects produce a specific deliverable and then dissolve.

The structure of management is also different. Operational departments have managers and staff assigned full-time with well-established roles, responsibilities, and authority. Projects are temporary in nature; the project manager and team members are brought together for a short period, complete the work, and then disband. The project may be comprised of people at varying levels of skill, responsibility, and authority. Depending on the organization, project managers may have full authority or very little authority when it comes to making decisions and managing people and budgets. Although their level of authority varies, their level of responsibility does not—they are always fully accountable for bringing the project in on time and on budget and for satisfying all the requirements.

For projects, time, budget, and scope are constraints—limitations within which the project manager must work. By comparison, in production environments these constraints are incorporated into the process. For example, a production line produces 750 widgets each day, the staffing is sufficient to manufacture the widget, and material costs are negotiated upfront with a fixed percentage factored in for rework or failure.

Table 1-1 summarizes some of the primary differences between projects and ongoing operations.

Table 1-1. Differences between Projects and Operations

Projects	Ongoing Operations
Defined end date	Ongoing
Unique	Standardized
One time/new	Repetitive
Customer focus	Departmental focus
Drop-in project manager	Continuing manager
May lack formal authority	Defined authority
Temporary team	Permanent department
Complex communications	Everyday interactions
Scope may evolve	Well-established objectives
Scope/cost/time constraints	Constraints are factored into established processes
Generally have high risk	Most risks have been eliminated over time

Although this is a somewhat simplified version of operations, you can see that managing an outcome in the world of project management can be much more challenging than managing an outcome in an operations environment.

In Practice: Mergers

The merger between Hewlett-Packard and Compaq provides an example of how failure in IT projects can impact organizations and their profits. A major difficulty with the merger was the "bungled integration of separate HP and Compaq implementations of SAP AG's enterprise software."[4] Despite the fact that both companies were using the SAP enterprise resource planning (ERP) system, the problems with the integration cost the Americas division of HP's Enterprise Storage Group about $400 million in revenue and $275 million in operating profits.

SUCCESSFUL PROJECT MANAGEMENT

Now that we have provided a summary definition of successful projects and project management, let's take a closer look at project management. Project management includes identifying requirements; establishing clear and achievable objectives; balancing demands for quality, scope, time, and cost; and adapting the specifications, plans, and approach to the needs and concerns of various stakeholders. But this is just one aspect of what it takes to call the project a success.

Projects are usually performed by a team rather than by just one person, so a major component of being a successful project manager is managing people to achieve the project goals. Many new project managers mistakenly think that project management is just another task to be done on top of developing the product. As an IT project manager, you are primarily responsible for ensuring the work is done, not for doing it yourself. This is a difficult transition for many technical people to make. You are a manager now, not a technical person doing coding or designing a LAN.

What Do You Think?

- What aspects of projects make them more challenging than operations?
- What aspect of project management do you like the best?

Another common misconception is that if you have Microsoft Project or some other project software you can manage a project. There is an old saying in project management that having a copy of MS Project makes you a project manager to the same extent that having a copy of MS Word makes you an author. Managing schedules and using software are pieces of project management, but certainly do not, by themselves, lead to successful projects.

One of the most challenging jobs a project manager faces is defining and balancing the expectations of project stakeholders. If you meet the scope of the project, on time and within budget, but the customer is not satisfied, the project is not a success. Additionally, even if the customer is satisfied, if the project team is burned out—or worse, feels abused—the project should not be considered a success. One criteria of success can be whether the team would want to work with the project manager again. If the answer is no, then the project manager did not successfully manage the team.

So then, what is a successful project? One view says that a project is successful when all stakeholders are satisfied. For the most part that means that the customer's requirements were met in a timely fashion for the agreed upon budget. However, it also means that the project is a strategic success, is consistent with the organization's strategy (more on this in a later chapter), and meets the needs for which it was undertaken. It also means that the team members are satisfied. Sometimes the biggest challenge is how to meet tight deadlines without creating team burnout. Figure 1-2 shows the project management balancing act.

Figure 1-2. Project Management Balancing Act

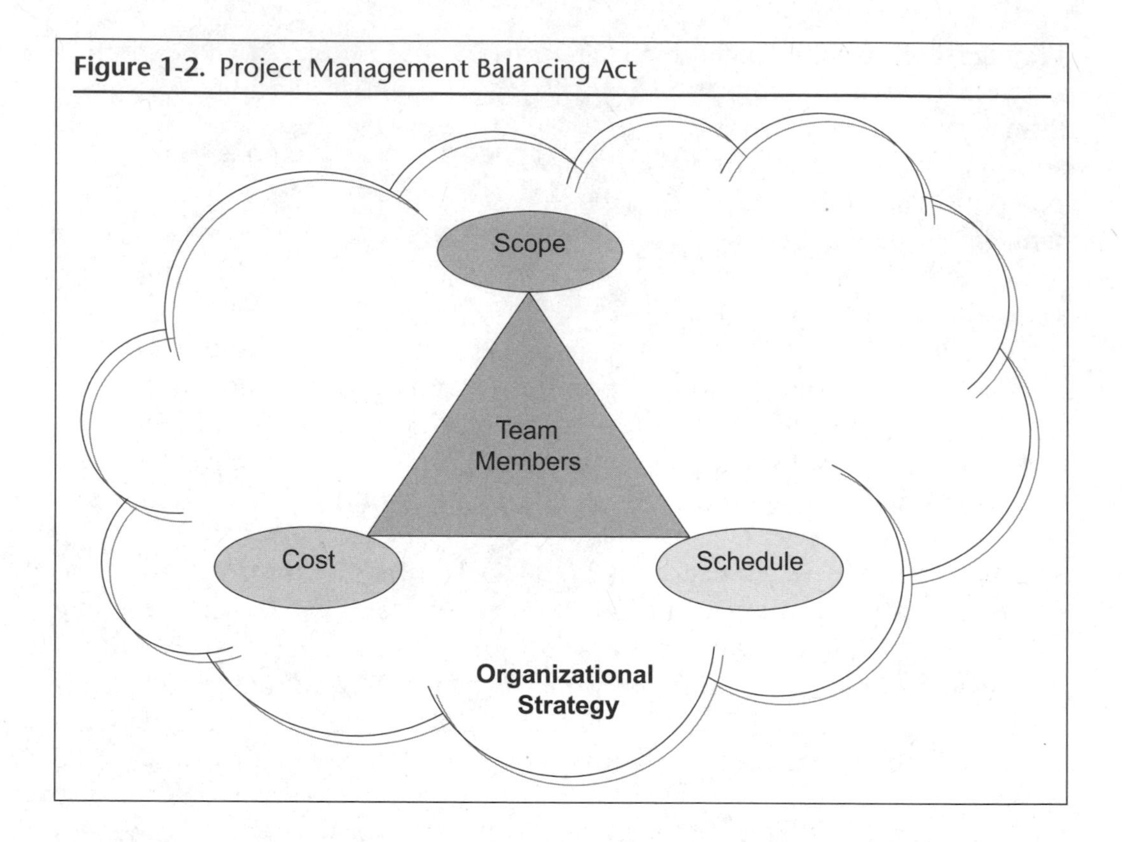

PROGRAMS AND PORTFOLIOS

Although this book will focus on projects and project management, understanding the context of projects in the bigger picture is useful. Some organizations do projects (sometimes many projects) that too often are not organized or prioritized in any particular manner. The entire suite of projects within a company or department is called the **project portfolio.**

Earlier we defined a project as a temporary endeavor undertaken to create a unique product or service. Some projects are so large that they have to be subdivided into multiple projects, each of which contributes to the accomplishment of the larger project. A project that consists of subprojects is called a **program.** Each of the smaller projects is managed separately, but

> ***What Do You Think?***
>
> - What are some of the areas where managing people is important to project success?
> - What do you think defines project success?

all of them have goals that support the program. An example of a program is a large corporate initiative such as installing an enterprise resource planning (ERP) system. Each department affected by this program may have a series of projects related to the program, such as requirements definition, process engineering, identifying the business rules, and so on.

A project portfolio is a collection of projects and/or programs managed as a single group to support organizational or departmental goals. The projects in a portfolio may be related, such as a portfolio of defense programs and projects or a portfolio of commercial programs and projects. They may be unrelated, such as when a portfolio is managed to ensure the proper balance among infrastructure projects, security projects, and business development projects. Figure 1-3 shows a possible project portfolio composed of various projects and programs.

Figure 1-3. Projects, Programs, and Portfolios

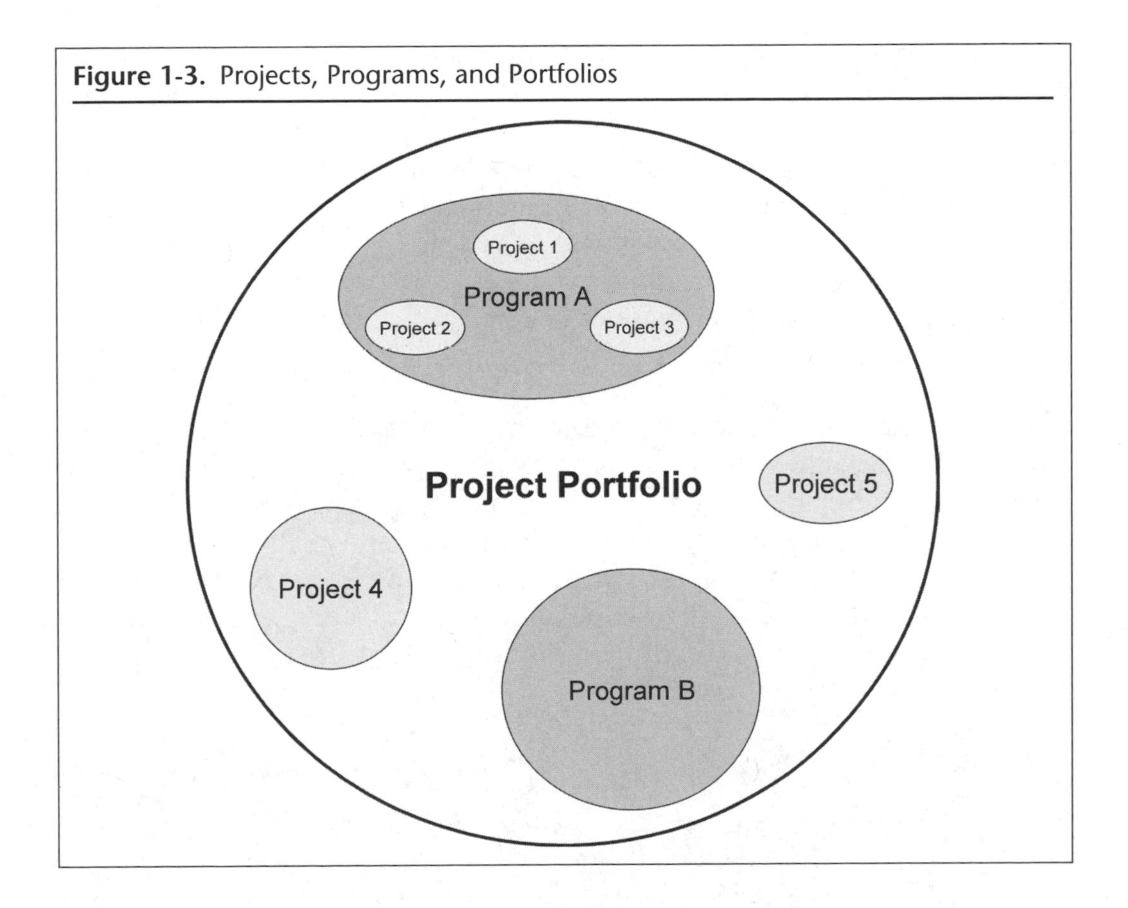

A BRIEF HISTORY OF IT PROJECT MANAGEMENT

Modern project management traces its roots back to the late 1950s when the Project Evaluation and Review Technique (PERT) and the Critical Path Method (CPM) were developed. These methods were created to handle projects that were growing increasingly complex. PERT was developed and used in the defense field and CPM in the construction field.

Projects from both of these fields shared common characteristics: they were large and complex, had significant technical risk associated with them, and had dedicated project managers and dedicated project teams. This environment existed for more than 20 years, and it worked very well. NASA's ability to develop large, complex, risky rockets and manned space systems under tight schedules during the 1960s was due to its strong project management skills.

Electrical machines have been able to perform calculations since the first large computer was wired together by hand. As mainframe computers grew, the field of software engineering also grew, and much of the development took place under government funding by NASA and the military. However, often these programming efforts were not managed as separate projects but as subsets of large programs. It was not until early in the 1980s that the practice of managing software development as a separate project began to mature in private industry. This development occurred as commercial applications grew in size and complexity.

For commercial applications, speed to market was the key to success and shortcuts, especially in testing, were common. The term *vaporware* began to appear as companies made promises about upcoming software to reduce sales to competitors. Over the course of the 1980s and 1990s; software grew increasingly large and complex, but speed to market remained the project driver. The need to balance the scope of the project against the time to market and to do so without bankrupting the company created the perfect environment for project management.

In Practice: Evolution of IT Complexity

In August of 1984, Bill Gates started a project to create Windows for Word, version 1.0, with a completion date of September 1985. At the time, Microsoft was also working on a version of Word for Apple computers that was released in July of

1985, so a project timeline of just over a year seemed reasonable. Yet WinWord turned out to be such a complex endeavor that it was finally released in November of 1989. Fifty-five man years of effort went into the development, a size that previously was associated with larger, more traditional types of projects.

Since then, the industry has developed huge application packages that are used to manage international corporations, packages that have many millions of lines of code. Both the development of these packages and their implementation must be managed as a project in order to have any possibility of success.

Challenges of IT Projects

Unlike the staff of traditional projects, where the team forms, develops, and releases the product, then dissolves and never interacts with the product again, IT people develop the product and, quite often, they maintain it after implementation (for internal IT projects) or fix problems that users identify. As a result, their time is split between daily operations and working on projects. This almost always leads to problems in prioritizing the work and in scheduling projects, since the availability of the resources is not known

Additionally, IT projects are usually much shorter in duration, with schedules measured in weeks or months rather than in months or years (the keyword is *usually*). IT projects have to share resources both with daily operations and with other projects. Working on multiple projects is a fact of life in the IT world, and being dedicated to a single project is a luxury for an IT project manager. Because IT projects tend to be shorter in duration than other types of projects, there is no ability to do traditional project team development.

Short timeframes and use of shared resources affect how IT projects are managed in a number of ways. Because daily operations have, or should have, priority, predicting exactly how much time each week is available for project work is difficult. Because people are working on multiple efforts, there is measurable reduction in productivity as team members jump from one effort to another. The daily schedules of many people are often driven by whoever talked to them last and asked when a particular project was going to be done.

Technology itself is a factor. Constantly increasing capabilities in both hardware and software pressure IT to incorporate the latest and greatest computer equipment.

Do these problems have solutions? Yes. A strong project management culture in the organization and a good project selection and prioritization process will help tremendously. We will talk about these solutions in the next chapters.

Table 1-2 summarizes the differences between non-technical projects and IT projects.

Figure 1-2. Differences between Non-Technical and IT Projects

Non-technical projects	IT projects
Usually have a dedicated team.	Project team is shared with other projects and with daily operations.
Are months and sometimes years long.	Are usually weeks long and occasionally months long, rarely years long.
Include team development.	Do not have enough time to do team development.
Have a well-defined priority.	Have multiple priorities that often change.
Technological risk is often constant during the course of the project.	Technological risk is different across different projects.
Team members work on predefined tasks in one project.	Team members must multitask across different projects as well as with daily operations.

THE VALUE OF IT PROJECT MANAGEMENT

Now that we have shown how projects are different from operations and how IT project management is different from non-technical project management, let's look at the value that IT project management provides to organizations. The Center for Business Practices does research and benchmarking and provides publications on project management and business practices. It performed a study with senior IT project management practitioners and found that using project management practices produced superior results compared to not using formalized project management practices.[6] The results were particularly compelling in the areas

What Do You Think?

- What is the most challenging aspect of IT projects, as opposed to non-technical projects?
- What is the most exciting aspect of IT projects, as opposed to non-technical projects?

of time to market, customer satisfaction, alignment to strategic goals, and meeting time, budget, and quality objectives.

In fact, 97.7 percent of the organizations surveyed said that implementing project management has added value to their IT organization. (Visit www.cbponline.com for more information.)

Earlier in this chapter, we mentioned the *CHAOS Report* from 1995. A more recent version shows that from 1995 to 2001, cost overruns decreased from 189 percent to 45 percent. Time overruns decreased from 222 percent to 63 percent.(For more information on the *CHAOS Report*, visit www.standishgroup.com.)

There are many reasons for this improvement. The most prominent are:

- Projects are smaller in scope.
- Projects are broken into discrete phases that are managed as separate projects, allowing subsequent phases to learn from previous ones.
- Better tools exist to estimate, monitor, and control project work. These allow better estimates upfront and allow project managers to detect baseline variations while there is still time to correct them.
- Having skilled project managers and better project management processes can significantly improve project success rates.

Chapter Summary

- Projects are one-time unique endeavors with defined starts and finishes. They are customer focused, have project managers with varying levels of authority, and use a temporary project team. Projects have scope, time, and cost constraints, and scope may evolve as the work is elaborated. Projects may be complex, involve outside stakeholders, and generally have more risk than operations.
- Operations are ongoing, standardized, and repetitive. The focus is on the goals of the department. Operations have a functional manager with full authority over permanent dedicated staff. Departments have established objectives, and constraints have been factored into the processes. Most risks have been accommodated or eliminated over time.

- A successful project is one that meets the triple constraints of scope, schedule, and cost. However, to be a success the project must be a strategic success, meeting the needs it was undertaken to address. Also, the team members should be satisfied with working on the project.
- IT projects are different from non-technical projects because the IT project team is usually working on several projects at one time as well as maintaining operations. The time span is shorter and priorities tend to shift. In technical projects, the technology itself is often a risk, and the risk on each project is different. Projects are shorter in duration, and there is no time for team development.
- Studies have shown that the use of project management increases customer satisfaction, quality, time and cost performance, alignment with strategic goals, and time to market. Significant improvements in project success have been made over the past ten years due to smaller projects; improvement in estimating, monitoring, and controlling processes; and improvement in project management skills and processes.

Key Terms

Project

Project management

Program

Project Portfolio

Key Term Quiz

Use terms from the key terms list to complete the sentences that follow. Don't use the same term more than once.

1. A ____________ is a temporary endeavor undertaken to produce a unique product, service, or result.

2. A _____________ is group of related projects managed in a coordinated way to obtain benefits and control not available from managing them individually.

3. The application of knowledge, skills, tools, and techniques to project activities to meet the project requirements is known as ______________________.

4. The term for a collection of projects and/or programs and other work grouped together to facilitate effective management of that work to meet strategic business objectives is ____________________.

Review Questions

1. What three constraints do projects have?

2. Do project managers have full authority over the resources on their projects?

3. List three components that make projects different from regular operations.

4. What makes a project successful?

5. Compare projects, programs, and portfolios

6. Describe three differences between IT projects and non-technical projects.

7. Studies have shown that using project management practices brings about improvement in many areas. Which five areas showed the most improvement according to the Center for Business Practices?

8. Which of the following is an example of a project?
   a. Month-end closing of the books
   b. Producing 1,000 widgets
   c. Shutting down production for retooling
   d. Researching a new product on the market

9. An IT applications director can categorize the projects in his or her shop as maintenance, new technology, upgrades and new releases, and business support. There may be many separate projects in each of these categories at any given time. However, each category is managed collectively in order to balance resources and smooth the schedule. This is an example of:

   a. Schedule-constrained allocation

   b. A portfolio of projects

   c. A superorganized director

   d. Project management

END NOTES

1. Project Management Institute (PMI®), *A Guide to the Project Management Body of Knowledge (PMBOK® Guide),* 3d ed., Project Management Institute, Newtown Square, PA, 2004.
2. The Standish Group, "The CHAOS Report," available at www. standishgroup.com, 1994.
3. Project Management Institute (PMI®), *A Guide to the Project Management Body of Knowledge (PMBOK® Guide),* 3d ed., page 5, Project Management Institute, Newtown Square, PA, 2004.
4. Renee Ferguson, "HP Still Working Out Compaq Kinks," *eWeek Magazine,* August 30, 2004.
5. Center for Business Practices, "Value of Project Management in IT Organizations," available at www.cbponline.com, 2001.

2 Organizational Structure and the Strategic Role of Project Management

After reading this chapter, you will be able to:

- Explain various corporate structures.
- Describe types of project offices.
- Define strategic management and key strategic terms.
- Describe how projects originate.

In Chapter 1, we developed some working definitions of operations, projects, and project management. We also looked at how IT project management differs from non-technical project management. In this chapter, we look at how organizations are structured, where project management fits in an organization, different types of project offices, and how projects can help organizations meet their strategic goals and objectives.

Company Organizational Structures

The way an organization is organized and the reporting structure it adopts significantly affect the way projects are done and the authority that a project manager has. We are going to look at three basic types of organizational structures: functional, project driven, and matrix. We will also explore some of the varying ways that organizations combine them and move along the continuum of the matrix-type environment. We will look at the role of the project manager and some of the pros and cons associated with each type of environment.

Functional

A **functional** environment is what we consider the traditional organizational structure. In a functional environment, various departments perform functions to support the company as a whole in meeting its objectives. Figure 2-1 shows a functional organization.

Figure 2-1. Functional Organization Structure

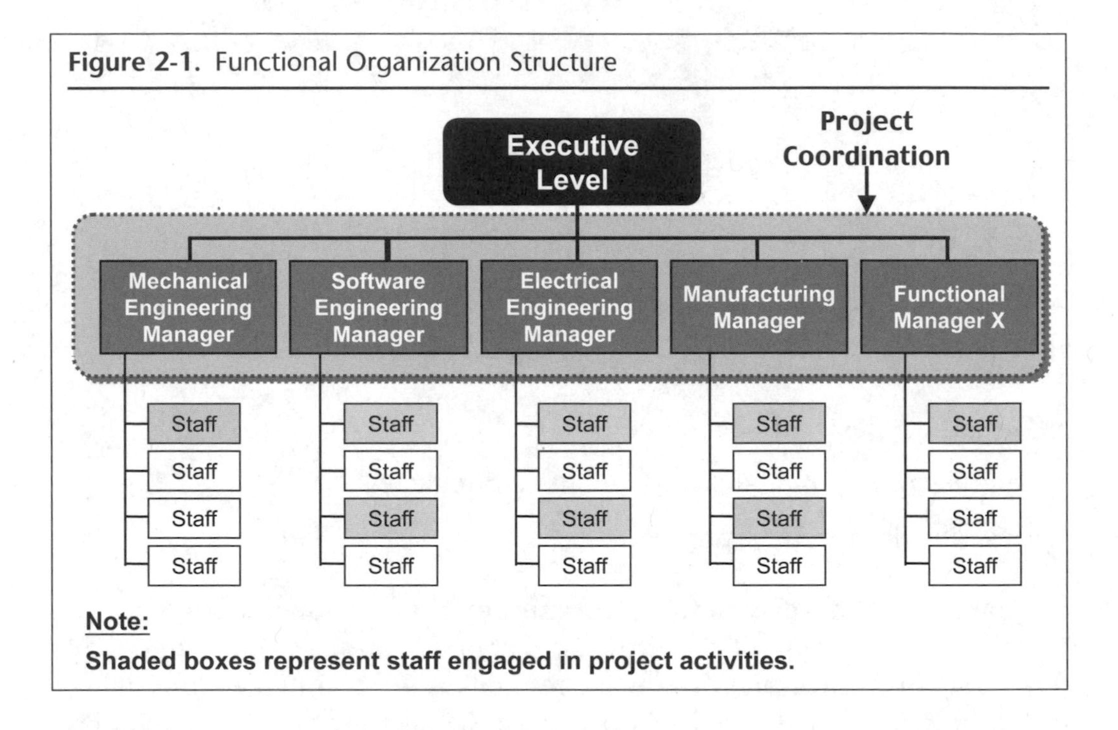

The advantage of a functional organization structure is that people with specific skill sets sit and work together and can support each other. The manager, whose responsibility it is to see that all work within the functional area is successfully accomplished, allocates their work. From an organizational standpoint, this is a very effective way to keep resources fully utilized.

In a true functional organization, there is often little coordination between functions. When there is a project or a new product to develop that involves more than one functional area, it takes longer to produce because there is little integration. A lack of integration results in miscommunication, rework, and not meeting the customer needs.

Here's a common scenario: The sales manager approaches the production department and tells it about a new product the market is demanding. Production relays the information to engineering. Given enough time, engineering designs a product that is both elegant and somewhat similar to what sales requested. Engineering turns over the design specs to manufacturing to produce. The line manager looks at the drawings and realizes that the production floor is not set up to produce this type of product. Manufacturing sends the drawings back to engineering for modifications. The drawings go back and forth for a while. Finally, production gets something usable and produces a large quantity of the product. Production proudly announces to sales that it has something that will delight the customer. The sales manager takes one look and states, "That is not at all what I asked for, and I can't sell it." You can see that in this type of environment no one is taking ownership of the timeliness, scope, cost, or ultimate success of the new product. There is a lack of coordination and communication across functional areas, and ultimately the needs of the customers (both internal and external customers) are not met.

Project Driven

On the other side of the spectrum is a **project-driven** organization. Virtually all work is accomplished by projects. This structure is common in aerospace companies, construction firms, engineering organizations, and consulting firms. In this structure, staff members are assigned to a specific project that they work on full-time through completion. There are some infrastructure departments, such as the legal and finance departments, that are not assigned to specific projects, but most of the employees are project oriented. In this situation, the project manager has full accountability for the success of the project. Figure 2-2 shows a project-driven organization.

Typical difficulties with project-driven organizations are that highly skilled and highly paid resources may be on a project whether needed now or not. The usual approach for a project manager in such an environment is to bring on the resources even if they are not utilized for several months in order to ensure that they are available when needed. Although this makes managing projects much simpler, it is an inefficient use of resources.

Figure 2-2. Project-Driven Organization Structure

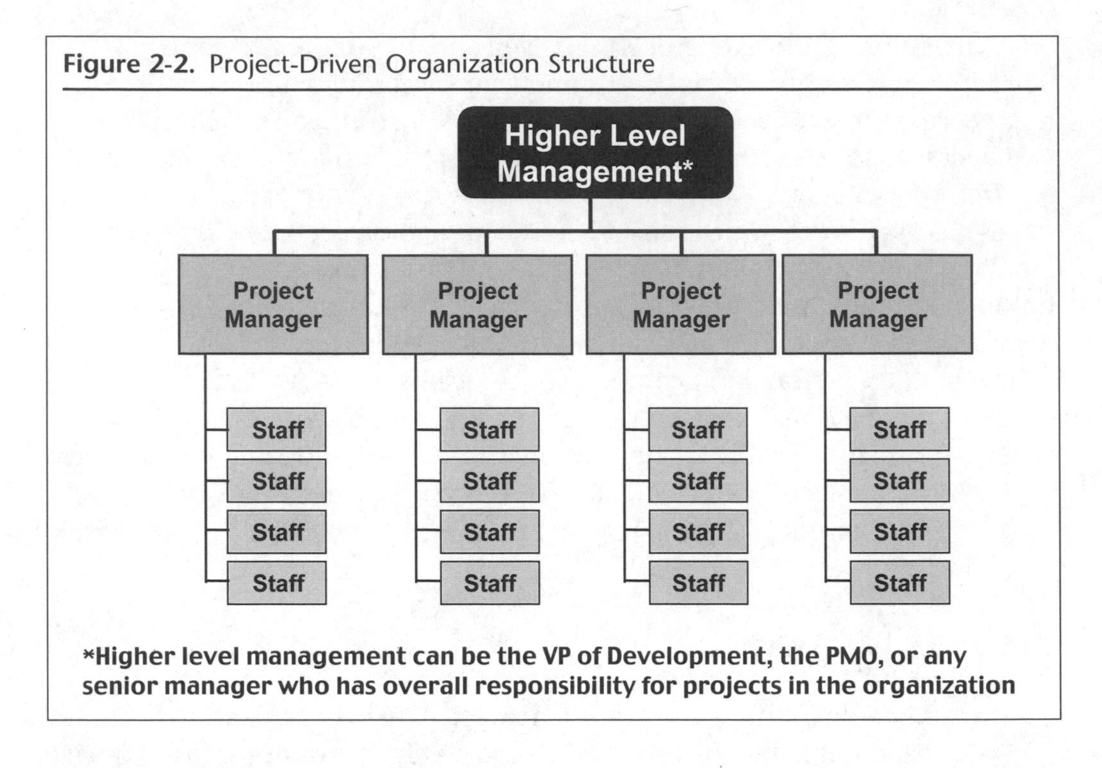

Matrix

A **matrix** environment is a blend of both functional and project-driven approaches. This usually means that there is a function in the organization called Project Management that manages projects using members from various functional areas. A matrix environment could also take the form of several functional areas having project managers on their staff to manage small- to medium-size projects. Figure 2-3 shows a matrix organization.

> ✱ ***NOTE***
> Sometimes a special project office is created on a temporary basis to manage a particularly large or strategic project, such as an ERP implementation or an acquisition. We will look at project offices in more detail in the next section of this chapter.

The matrix model evolved from the functional model in response to the need for faster implementation, better coordination among departments, and the need to satisfy customer requirements. In this model, the project manager is responsible for the successful implementation of the project. In some organizations, the project manager has staff and/or budget management. In some companies, the team members are temporarily moved to the project site, and they may not see their functional manager for as long as they are

Figure 2-3. Matrix Organization Structure

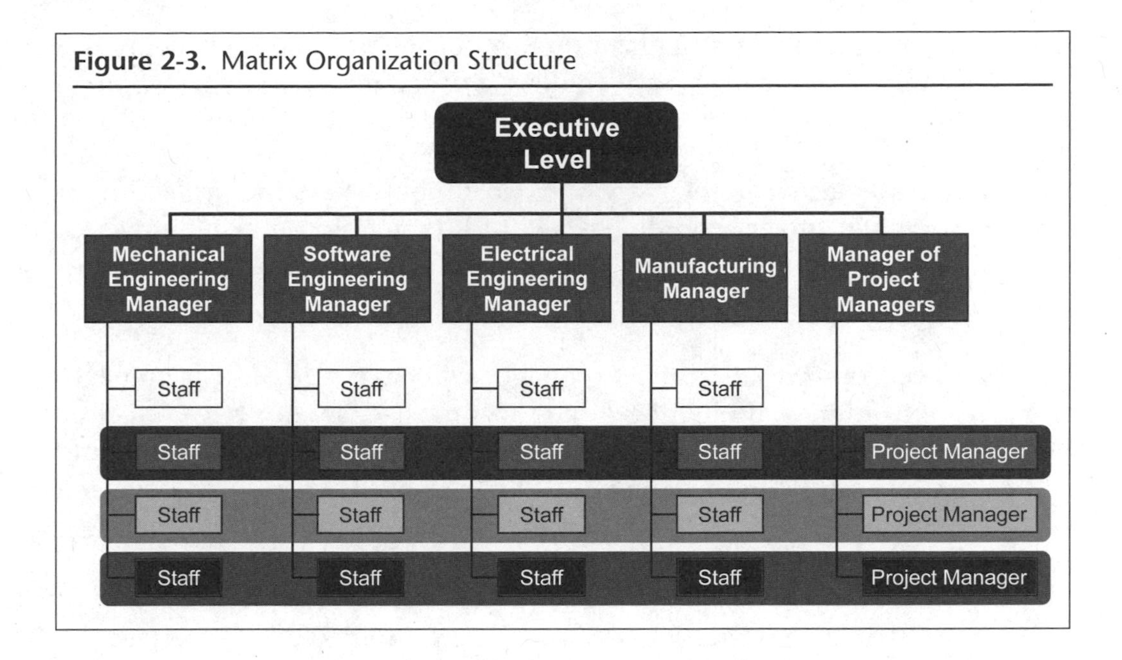

on the project. In other matrix situations, staff remain physically located in their functional areas and maintain some functional responsibilities. They may work on one project or several projects, depending on the organization and the size of the projects.

This organizational model presents some unique challenges. There may be conflict over scarce resources, such as when one person is on multiple projects. In addition, team members may feel like they have two bosses: their functional manager and their project manager. Moreover, even though team members pick up extra work on projects, their functional responsibilities rarely decrease significantly, which results in working longer hours.

Imagine that you're working on three projects and also have responsibility for supporting and maintaining a specific application. Project A has a major project review in three days and you have responsibility for a major piece of the presentation. Senior management will be reviewing the status of the project and making a recommendation on whether to continue or cancel it. You are also working on project B and have a deliverable due in five days. If you don't get it done, the rest of the project team will be waiting on you before they can move forward. Then your application goes awry, and you have 20 voicemails complaining that people's data is corrupted because of your application. Your manager is asking you what you plan to do about the situation. This type of conflict can occur in a matrix environment, where you have accountability to one or more projects and still report to your normal manager.

Sometimes matrix environments are referred to with a modifier, such as a *weak* matrix, a *strong* matrix, a *tight* matrix, a *balanced* matrix, or a *composite* matrix.

Generally, a **weak matrix** refers to an environment where the project manager is more of a project coordinator, with little decision-making power or control over the resources. Most of the power resides with the functional departments.

In a **balanced matrix,** the project manager will have true project management responsibilities, though he or she will most likely not have full-time staff on the projects. The project manager may have decision-making and budgetary responsibilities for the project. In real life, there is almost never a true balanced matrix: either the functional manager or the project manager will have primary control, depending on the organizational culture.

A **strong matrix** means that the balance of power tends to lean towards the project manager. He or she has full authority over project resources. It is more common to see program managers and project offices in this environment.

A **tight matrix** refers to a project team that is *collocated,* meaning the team is housed together for the duration of the project. Sometimes a strong matrix is also a tight matrix.

Lastly, a **composite matrix** is when an organization may have a mixture of the various organizational structures, depending on the project or department.

Often, whether a company has a strong matrix or a weak matrix depends on who you ask. Senior management may state that they have a strong matrix organization, but project managers may tell you that the reality is that the structure is a weak matrix, with functional managers pulling resources from projects as needed, sometimes without notifying the project managers.

PROJECT MANAGEMENT OFFICES

In organizations that have a matrix or project-driven structure, you may see something called a **project office (PO)**, or a **project management office (PMO)**. These two terms are used interchangeably. PMOs trace their history back to the earliest days of modern project management. When project management was just used for large, complex programs, the most effective way to manage the effort was to establish a central office to support the program manager with schedule management, financial tracking, and other administrative functions. In the past several years, POs have reappeared and taken on several different forms, functions, and structures. Before we look at the different types of PMOs, let's take a look at their recent background and evolution.

Background

During the late 1990s, when companies were performing assessments on how to update all their applications to move to the new millennium-numbering scheme of 2000 (Y2K) and undertaking activities to mitigate risks associated with Y2K, they discovered that establishing a central office to manage all of these projects was a good idea.

Although the PMOs established for Y2K have disappeared, many companies are now reestablishing PMOs to manage all of the projects they have in the works. Unfortunately, some executives mistakenly thought that just having a PMO would make all their projects run smoothly, so organizations spent hundreds of thousands of dollars to create them. Consulting companies were happy to sell a "PMO in a box"—just install their software and, voila, you had a PMO. Companies would put in policies, mentoring programs, and centers of excellence to do projects better, faster, and cheaper. Then, after about six months, when they did not see an immediate and amazing impact to the bottom line, they declared the PMO a failure and went back to business as usual.

In fact, there are several types of PMOs and the variations are as many as there are organizations that adopt PMOs. In the next section, we will look at some of the general types of PMOs and then we will talk briefly about some of the requirements needed to help make them successful.

Types of Project Management Offices

As mentioned earlier, the structure of a PMO is dependent on the organization that it operates within. Some offices are narrowly focused to meet one of the objectives below, and others are a blend. There is no right structure for a PMO; the best structure truly depends on the needs and culture of the organization. Below are five models that are common.

In Practice: PMOs in the Real World

The July 2, 2003, edition of *CIO Magazine* published a survey of 303 companies that have PMOs. Here are some of the results:

What do PMOs do?

- 43% of the respondents said their PMO is a support organization that supports multiple projects, primarily with administrative, time tracking, reporting, and other services.
- 12% of the respondents said the PMO is a project services organization managing several unrelated projects.
- Another 12% said their PMO manages a set of projects that are related.
- 5% reported that their PMO is responsible for business and technical management of a specific contract or program only.

Companies are finding that employing key practices like providing standard methodologies and linking projects to company strategy are helping the organization meet financial and strategic goals. 50% say that project success rates have increased as a result of having a PMO, on average by 46%.

Overall, the benefits are:

- 62% said implementing PM standards.
- 38% said increased internal customer satisfaction.
- 29% said increased employee productivity.
- 27% said lower costs.
- 25% said increased external customer satisfaction.

Center of Excellence Project Management Office

A **center of excellence PMO** is used for mentoring, training, and providing advice for project managers and other employees who find themselves managing a project. Some centers of excellence provide a project management–training curriculum for the organization. They may have certificate programs or provide project management basics for a wide audience.

Other centers of excellence have accomplished project managers who mentor new project managers on large and complex projects. They may help departments that don't normally have projects and find themselves needing to complete a project. They can provide on-the-job training, tools, or just be available in a pinch.

Another service these offices provide is giving expert advice. This may be advice on working with project software, developing a risk management plan, developing an estimate, or managing scope creep. Again, this can be offered at all levels of the organization. Generally, these types of offices are seen in a matrix or project-driven environment.

Administrative Project Management Office

An **administrative PMO** maintains the policies, procedures, processes, and forms that the organization uses to manage projects. This type of office may define categories of projects. Administrative POs may develop best practices that define the level of management required depending on the size, complexity, duration, or risk involved in the project. Frequently, this type of office serves as a repository for best practices, lessons learned, and knowledge management surrounding projects.

The administrative PO develops, revises, and keeps all policies and procedures regarding project management up-to-date. It also defines the processes and forms that should be used. The office will update and distribute forms as they are developed, changed, or become obsolete. This type of office is seen in a matrix-type environment or a project-driven environment.

Business Unit of Project Managers

Often this functional unit houses all project managers and project-related employees. It may house professional schedulers, estimators, and program managers as well as other project support personnel. The head of this unit will assign projects, track their progress, give advice and coaching to project managers, and provide administrative oversight.

This type of office collocates all project managers, which allows for mentoring among project managers, sharing of best practices, and professional development. Generally, all the project templates, forms, and records reside here as well. These types of PMOs are seen in a matrix environment.

Strategic Project Management Office

A **strategic project management office** is used to manage the organization's portfolio of projects. It is usually at the executive level and may be overseen by a chief project officer or a vice president of project management. The primary function of this type of office is to define the types of categories in the project portfolio, define the percentage of projects in each, allocate resources at a high level, and ensure that the portfolio is balanced per the direction of the organization. Often this office will review the initial business case or cost-benefit analysis for projects. This type of PMO is most often seen in organizations that are mature in project management. Organizations with this type of office will most likely be project driven or have a strong matrix environment.

Project-Specific Project Management Offices

A project-specific PMO may be opened in response to a large project. Perhaps an IT organization is looking to implement an ERP system, or an acquisition necessitates a PMO throughout the acquisition process. In these instances, the program manager, the project manager, and the key team members are collocated in an office. The functions of the PMO are to support the program manager in managing schedule and budget, managing the change control process and the risk management process, ensuring program quality, and performing other required functions. The PMO facilitates information sharing, decision-making, and expeditious handoffs. When the project is complete, staff return to their functional areas.

Organizational Location of Project Management Offices

PMOs can be line organizations or support organizations. In a line organization, the PMO has direct authority over the projects. All of the project managers report into the PMO as a functional department. It is the central location for all project activity in the business unit or the enterprise. A sample structure of a line organization is shown in Figure 2-4.

Figure 2-4. PMO in a Line Organization

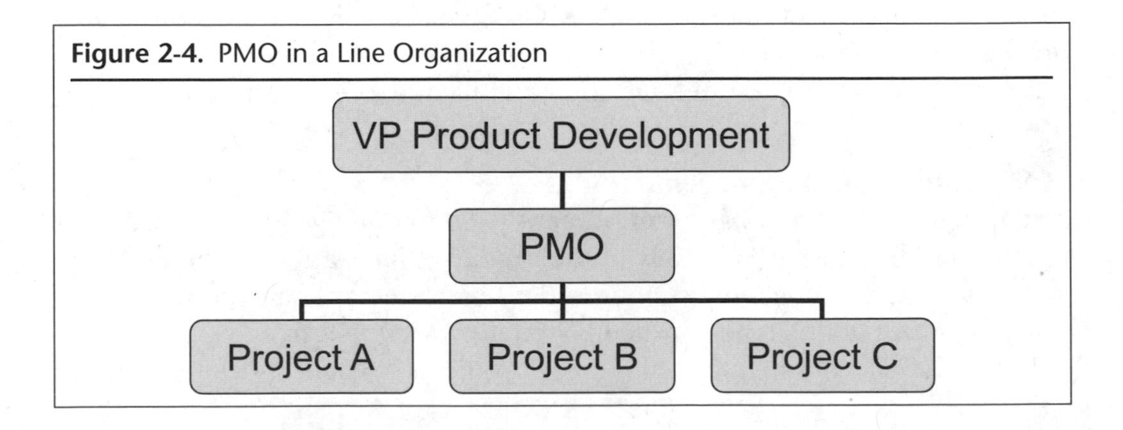

In a support organization, the PMO does not have direct authority over projects or project managers. It is purely a support organization to the project managers and to upper management. The project managers often report into other departments, and the PMO is there to centralize administrative work and perform other support functions. Figure 2-5 shows a representative organizational chart.

Figure 2-5. PMO in a Support Organization

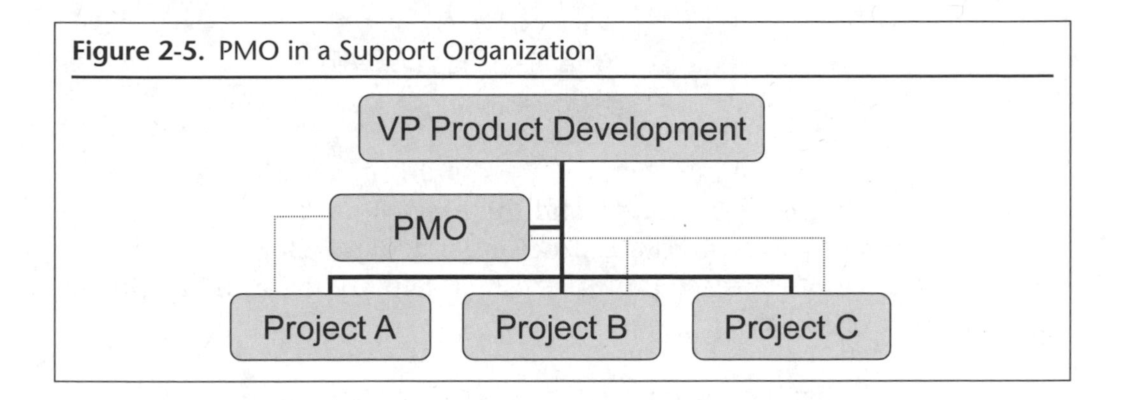

In both cases, the higher up the PMO reports, the more authority it has and the better it will work. Many project managers will resent having a PMO if they are not used to one. Rather than seeing the office as helpful, they often feel like it should be labeled the project police. Unfortunately, some PMOs behave like that, feeling that their job is to whip errant project managers back into line. However, a truly effective PMO is supportive to both the project managers and to the executives in the organization.

The best location for a PMO is wherever it will most effectively support the organization. Some PMOs have started as support organizations, and as their benefits have become clear, have become line organizations.

Criteria for Successful Project Offices

So, what is the best kind of PMO? It depends on the needs and level of project maturity of the organization. Paramount to success is to have clearly defined objectives for the PMO. Executive management must understand what it wants from the PMO. These expectations need to be written down in a charter format, with clear, measurable results attached to a timeline. That being said, the results and timeline should be reasonable and attainable.

It is not reasonable to expect a PMO to develop policies, procedures, and processes, and to train the entire organization to use them, along with mentoring project managers to produce stellar results on all projects, within six months or a year. The two main reasons that PMOs fail are the objectives are not clearly defined upfront, and therefore there is no criteria or roadmap for success, and the PMO is not given enough time to integrate into the organization's structure. It generally takes two to three years to start a PMO and see tangible results. The exception is the project specific office, of course.

> ***What Do You Think?***
>
> - What type of organizational structure would best help you perform your job: Functional? Matrix? Project driven?
> - What type of PMO would work best in your organization?
> - What PMO location would best help you perform your job?

An organization that is new to project management principles should operate within a matrix-type environment for a few years before taking on a PMO. It takes a certain amount of project management maturity and savvy to start and operate a PMO successfully. A brand-new organization, with no existing culture to have to change, should create a PMO and establish it as part of the organization at the very beginning.

A PMO can be a very expensive in terms of personnel. It can be hard to justify the creation of one, because many of its benefits are intangible and non-quantifiable. Some examples of failed PMOs include:

- A major health insurance provider attempted to create a PMO but failed because each project manager was used to doing things his or her own way and resisted having to subordinate a pet project to a central office.
- The PMO at the U.S. corporate headquarters of a major Japanese car manufacturer failed because the person put in charge didn't want to take expert advice and wanted to do things his way.

To create a successful PMO, it would be wise to spend several months planning and discussing the scope of the PMO before plunging in. A two- to three-year commitment also takes a significant budget. Therefore, the organization needs to be clear on its objectives and the person in charge of the office needs to do a good job of managing expectations from day one. Otherwise, the chance for success is significantly diminished.

Overview of Strategic Management

Now that we have discussed organizational structure and how project management fits within that structure, we will look at the importance of projects in organizations. At the highest levels of the organization, executives are concerned with strategy. To understand how projects contribute to strategy we first need to develop a common understanding of strategic management.

The definition of strategic management found on Wikipedia states that it is "the process of specifying an organization's objectives, developing policies and plans to achieve these objectives, and allocating resources so as to implement the plans."[1] Strategic management provides overall direction to the whole enterprise. An organization's strategy must be appropriate for its resources, circumstances, and objectives. The process involves matching the company's strategic advantages to the business environment the organization faces. A good corporate strategy should integrate an organization's goals, policies, and action sequences (tactics) into a cohesive whole, and must be based on business realities. Strategy must connect with vision, purpose, and likely future trends.

Key Strategic Terms

To discuss strategy, we first need to define some of the key terms used in strategic planning. Then we will show examples from some organizations of which you may have heard.

- **Mission:** The reason the organization exists. The mission describes the products or services the organization provides, the markets it serves, and, if relevant, the competitive advantage or the technology the company employs to provide the products and services. The mission may also address how the company serves various stakeholders, such as investors, employees, and customers.
- **Vision:** Aspirations for the future; a desired future state. The vision statement answers the question, what do we want to become?

> * ***NOTE***
> A vision should be inspiring. Consider Steve Jobs' vision to build an "insanely great" computer. Employees working on the first Macintosh computers surpassed what they thought was possible, in large part due to their commitment to their shared vision.

- **Values:** How a company treats its employees, how it treats its shareholders, how it behaves as a neighbor, and how it behaves with respect to its environment. Values describe what is important to it as a corporate entity. Values are used to help organizations make decisions and choices.
- **Goals:** Directions that the organization wants to head in to improve performance. These are generally qualitative in nature. They may address financial and nonfinancial measures.
- **Objectives:** Specific targets to be accomplished within a specified period. An organization may have one-year, three-year, and five-year objectives.
- **Strategy:** A general program of action. Strategic plans cover three to five years into the future. Strategies are broken down into more detailed objectives, which are then further broken down into quarterly action plans or tactics.

In thinking about these concepts, it's useful to imagine a pyramid, as shown in Figure 2-6, with strategies leading all the way up to vision.

Figure 2-6. Strategic Plan Hierarchy

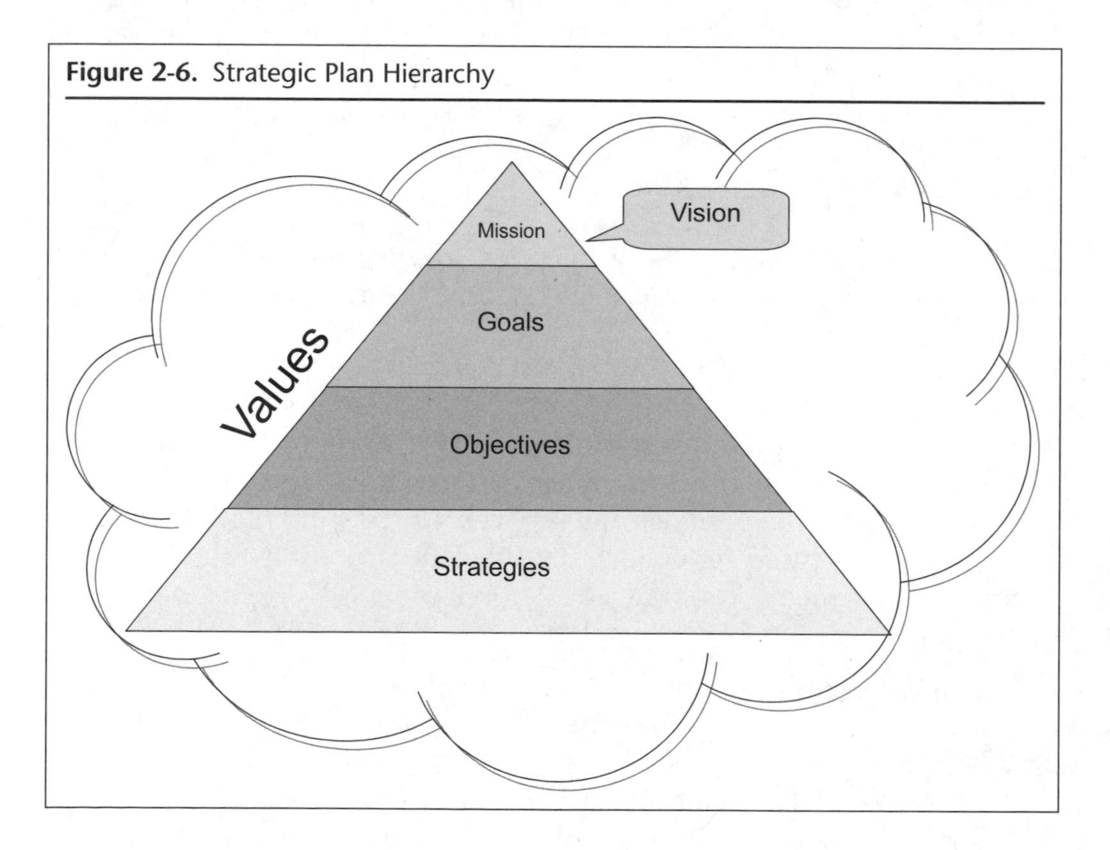

In Practice: Corporate Strategy

Below are some examples from various companies. We found these on the web, so they are only as up to date as the organization's web site was on the date we looked. They should give you a flavor of strategic statements.

Sample Vision Statement

Sun Microsystems

> Everything with a digital, electrical or biological heartbeat will be connected to the Network. With Auto ID-like technologies, assets of value will also be connected. This will create profound potential and challenges for enterprises, service providers and consumers. Technology, habits and governance will evolve and adapt to this new connected reality.

Sample Mission Statements

IBM

> At IBM, we strive to lead in the creation, development and manufacture of the industry's most advanced information technologies, including computer systems, software, networking systems, storage devices and microelectronics.
>
> We translate these advanced technologies into value for our customers through our professional solutions and services businesses worldwide.

Microsoft

> To enable people and businesses throughout the world to realize their full potential.

Intel

> Do a great job for our customers, employees and stockholders by being the preeminent building block supplier to the worldwide Internet economy.

PepsiCo

> Beat Coke.

Sample Values

PMI

> Knowledge
>
> Professionalism
>
> Community and Volunteerism
>
> Value of Project Management to Business

Intel

Customer Orientation

Results Orientation

Risk Taking

Great Place to Work

Quality

Discipline

Sample Goals

Goals are generally proprietary information, and thus they are not widely available to the public. Goals generally have to do with reducing costs or increasing revenue.

An example of cost reduction might be increasing employee efficiency through internal process improvement. This might translate into large projects such as an ERP implementation, consolidating legacy systems, or automating existing manual processes.

Examples of increasing revenue could include mergers, acquisitions, product development, and product line expansion. Almost all mergers and acquisitions entail large IT projects as part of the overall project.

Sample Objectives

Intel

Extend silicon leadership

Deliver architectural innovation for convergence

Pursue opportunities worldwide

Using Projects to Meet Organizational Needs

So where do projects fit with strategic management? Everywhere! First and foremost, every IT effort should be linked to one of the organization's goals or objectives. Most often, projects are used as the approach that organizations use to meet their objectives. Some organizations consider project management to be a core competency—one of the key operations that differentiate them in the marketplace. Because project management has proven to be such an effective approach, management by project is often used for consulting firms, research and development companies, and software development companies.

In addition to supporting a company's mission, goals, and objectives, projects should be executed consistent with organizational values. If one of the organization's values is high quality, the project should have sufficient testing built in and use high-grade components to create the product. Using untrained labor because it is less expensive or refurbished parts would be inconsistent with the company's values.

> ✱ ***NOTE***
> Because projects are used to meet an organization's strategic plan, if a project is not tied to an organizational goal or objective, it should not exist. Too often, we hear of projects that do not have a direct relationship (or even indirect relationship) with the annual goals or objectives. These projects tend to wither on the vine from lack of resources, since other projects take priority. In fact, they should never have been chartered at all.

Categorizing Projects

Projects come from many different sources. To provide some semblance of order it is useful to categorize both the ways that projects originate and the types of projects that organizations undertake.

Where Do Projects Come From?

Projects generally originate from one of the following:

- **Market demands:** The market may demand that new Internet connection software come with spam detection capabilities built in. Therefore, a project is created to retrofit all existing software with spam detection, to include spam detection in all new software, and to create a free download that past customers can access on the company web site.
- **Business needs:** The organization decides that it wants to expand its product line from cell phones to units that can perform cell phone/PDA/digital camera functions. This is a new product development project based on business needs.

- **Customer requests:** A client wants a customized software solution to capture all the hours that employees spend working on projects, tabulate the hours by project, and then total them by department. The solution should feed into both project management software and accounting system software.
- **Technological advances:** An underwriting system is two versions behind the current release, and the company that manufactures the software is going to discontinue support in 18 months. An organization will need to upgrade its systems to keep up-to-date with the latest advances in the software. Another impact of technological advances is that they create opportunities for new products. For example, the ability to download music from the Internet now exists. This has led to new projects in many companies, as they create systems to allow consumers to download music legally and block consumers from downloading it illegally.
- **Legal requirements:** The Health Insurance Portability and Accountability Act of 1996 (HIPAA) requires that organizations limit access to personal information. Healthcare companies need to create new levels of security for all users to make sure that personal information is secure.
- **Social needs:** Perhaps one of a company's values is to contribute to the communities where it is located. The local school needs upgraded computer equipment. The company opens a project to do a needs assessment, gather requirements, and propose a solution, which the company will help meet with in-kind donations.

Selecting Projects

One of the most critical aspects of successful project management is selecting the right projects.

Good ideas can come from anyone in the company. Yet, a company that starts too many projects quickly finds that it has more projects in the pipeline than it can reasonably accomplish. Too many projects means that many, if not most, will not get successfully completed on time and within budget, and that the people working on them will be burned out and frustrated. Remember the definition of project success? Scope, time, and costs are met; stakeholder objectives are met; the strategic intent of the project is realized; and the team members are satisfied. To accomplish this, world-class companies have fewer, more strategically oriented, projects.

To select the best projects, a company should encourage ideas from anyone in the organization and then set up a project selection process that filters out everything but the most beneficial projects. The final list is presented to a project selection committee, which then makes the final project selection.

Types of Projects

Three types of projects a company typically performs are:

- Mandatory projects
- Infrastructure upgrades
- Discretionary projects

Mandatory Projects

These are usually the projects that originate because of a legal or regulatory requirement. Typically, these regulatory changes come with a specific time limit within which the company must comply.

Any company that deals with private financial information must comply with both federal and state laws and regulations. Utility companies are regulated at the state level by public utility commissions. The U.S. federal government passed the Health Insurance Privacy and Portability Act (HIPPA) stating specific requirements for healthcare-related information. All hospitals, pharmacies, and health insurance companies had to comply with those changes.

Regulatory-driven projects are often called orange jumpsuit projects, because orange is a common color for jail uniforms, and the company's executives will go to jail if they do not comply with the regulations.

Infrastructure Upgrades

These projects are generally the result of technological improvements that can increase the efficiency of the organization. Infrastructure projects can be very high priority, but are not necessarily time-driven projects. An example would be a company upgrading its Windows 98 operating system to Windows XP. This could be a significant project if there are thousands or tens of thousands of desktop machines to be upgraded, but it does not have to be completed by a specific date.

Discretionary Projects

Discretionary projects are the result of a market demand, customer request, business need, some technical advances, or social needs. While they are called discretionary, that does not mean they are taken lightly. When a key customer wants a new product or service, it is not usually seen as a request that you will get around to when you have time. It is considered a high priority.

Internal process improvement projects are a special type of discretionary project. They may incorporate infrastructure upgrades. They are usually very complex because company processes often cross organizational boundaries, so impacts are made to several parts of the organization. These projects require a lot of analysis and coordination.

Project Selection

These days organizations find themselves with more projects than they have resources to complete. For many organizations, choosing projects is an informal process with various projects being started, delayed, discontinued, or killed. This has been called the "project of the week" approach. It leads to too many projects and projects that don't meet their objectives and come in late, over budget, and with a burned-out team. In other words, the projects tend not to meet the success criteria we defined earlier.

Organizations that have developed a more mature approach align their project selection process with the strategic needs of the organization. A project selection committee at the executive level of the organization defines the project portfolio categories, optimal weighting for each category, and a project scoring method (such as return on investment or a cost/benefit analysis). In this way, fewer projects are initiated, but those that are contribute to the strategic intent of the organization.

A detailed description of establishing and managing a project portfolio is outside the scope of this text. PMI has published a standard on project portfolio management and there are several other texts in the field that present a defined project portfolio methodology.

In Practice: Categorizing Projects

A recent article in *CIO Magazine*[2] suggested that discretionary projects be broken into the following categories:

- Category A projects are mission critical and provide a market advantage to the company.
- Category B projects are mission critical, but do not provide a market advantage.
- Category C projects are not mission critical, but provide a market advantage.
- Category D projects are neither mission critical nor provide a market advantage.

The article suggests that organizations should select all the Category A projects they have the resources to perform. Next in priority are the Category B and C projects, depending on the available resources. Ignore the Category D projects. They are not important enough to spend resources on.

Look at the categories we talked about in the previous pages. Do you see a correlation between mandatory, infrastructure, and discretionary projects and the categories denoted by *CIO Magazine*?

In Practice: Suggesting Projects

Toyota Financial Services USA developed an automated process (utilizing Lotus Notes) for new project suggestion and approval developing. Anyone in the company can log on and suggest a project. The requester identifies both what the benefits of the project are and which of Toyota's strategic goals the project supports. Toyota has four strategic objectives that center around the areas of Financial, Internal Processes, Customer Relationships, and Employees & Operations.

When the original requester fills out as much as he or she knows, the form is released and routed to different groups to complete other parts of the form. Most of the questions on the form are devoted to identifying specifically what the relationship is to the strategic objectives and to identifying financial impacts of the project.

At the end of the approval process, each question is scored. The scores are added up and the project is given an overall rating. Regulatory projects are given a very high rating automatically (with the specific number dependent on the timeframe for the project) to ensure they rank high in the final scoring. On a monthly basis, the rank-ordered list of new projects is presented to the Strategic Governance Committee, which selects the specific projects it feels need to be done.

> A further refinement of this process includes identifying each project's overall risk. This risk score becomes part of the selection process so that the project portfolio can be ranked with respect to risk as well as strategic benefit.

How to Choose a Project?

With all of these possible projects floating around, how do you choose the best projects to spend your time and resources on?

All potential projects are compared with all the others. Traditional approaches include cost/benefit analyses (CBA) or return on investment (ROI) analyses. Whatever method a company uses to select its projects, it needs to be done in a careful and objective manner. Research indicates that the best projects to choose are those that most support the strategic objectives of the company. Identifying these projects requires setting up a project selection process that provides the final decision-maker with the best information available. This is generally done at the portfolio management level by organization executives.

CHAPTER SUMMARY

- Companies have different organizational structures. The organizational structure affects the amount of authority a project manager has on a project. The three types of organizational structure are functional, matrix, and project-driven. A matrix environment may be a weak matrix, balanced matrix, or a strong matrix. A collocated team is called a tight matrix. An organization that mixes structures based on its needs has a composite organization.
- Some organizations have POs. There is no right kind of PO. Each organization should build a PO to meet its needs. Five of the more common types of POs are center of excellence, administrative, strategic, business unit, and project specific. POs can be line POs or support POs. To implement a successful PO requires time to understand the requirements, gather input from stakeholders, and manage expectations, much like managing a project.
- Organizations use strategic planning to stay competitive in today's environment. Some of the key aspects of strategic management include vision and mission statements, values, goals, and objectives

- Projects are one of the ways that organizations turn strategic plans into reality. All projects should tie into the strategic plan.
- Projects can come from six different sources: market demand, business needs, customer requests, technological advances, legal requirements, and social needs.
- Because there are usually more projects than there are resources, organizations need a project selection strategy. A selection strategy can break up the projects into three categories: mandatory projects, infrastructure projects, and discretionary projects.

Key Terms

Matrix organization	Administrative project office
Project-driven organization	Center of excellence project office
Functional organization	Tight matrix
Strategic project office	Balanced matrix
Vision	Weak matrix
Mission	Strong matrix
Values	Composite organization
Goals	Project office
Objectives	Project management office
Strategy	

Key Term Quiz

Use terms from the key terms list to complete the sentences that follow. Don't use the same term more than once. Not all terms will be used.

1. A matrix organization that has characteristics of a functional organization, with the project manager's role being more of an expediter or coordinator, is called a ________________________.

2. A project office that manages an organization's portfolio of projects is a __________ project office.

3. The ________________ defines the reason an organization exists.

4. A ________________ is an organizational structure that has various structures, depending on the needs.

5. The ________________ is a set of intentions that are broad, forward thinking, and all inclusive. It generally refers to a desired future state.

6. A project office that maintains the policies, procedures, processes, and forms that the organization uses to manage projects is called a(n) ______ ________________.

7. A ________________ organizational structure has project managers that have full authority over their project, including staff, budget, decisions, and allocation or resources.

8. Which vocabulary term describes specific targets to accomplish within a specified timeframe?

9. A ________________ is any organization in which the project managers share responsibility with the functional managers for assigning priorities and for directing the work of persons assigned to the project

10. Which type of project office has accomplished project managers that mentor new project managers or project managers on large and complex projects?

Review Questions

1. In which type of organizational structure would the project manager have the most amount of authority?

   a. Strong matrix

   b. Tight matrix

   c. Functional

   d. Balanced matrix

2. In which type of organizational structure would the project manager have the least amount of authority?
   a. Strong matrix
   b. Tight matrix
   c. Functional
   d. Balanced matrix

3. In which type of organizational structure are project team members most likely to feel they have two bosses?
   a. Composite
   b. Matrix
   c. Project-driven
   d. Functional

4. Which type of project office is used predominately for mentoring, training, and providing advice on projects and project management?
   a. Administrative
   b. Strategic
   c. Business unit of project managers
   d. Center of excellence

5. Which type of office is used predominately to develop and manage processes, policies, and procedures?
   a. Administrative
   b. Strategic
   c. Business unit of project managers
   d. Center of excellence

6. Which of the following is a description of a mission statement?
   a. Aspirations for the future
   b. The reason the organization exists
   c. An enduring preference for a mode of conduct
   d. Specific targets to be accomplished within a specified timeframe

7. When planning for implementation of a PMO, what should you include?

8. What is one of the pitfalls of project-driven organizations?

9. Describe the difference between objectives and goals.

10. All projects should be tied to an organization's _______________.

11. What role do an organization's values play?

12. Projects come from many different sources. Which of the following is an example of a project that is required to meet legal requirements?

    a. A virus detection software upgrade.

    b. One of your customers, a municipality, has asked your organization to install software that can detect attempts to hack into the system.

    c. Sarbanes-Oxley requirements necessitate upgraded software.

    d. Giving all directors PDAs.

13. Which of the following is an example of a project that is due to a customer request?

    a. A virus detection software upgrade.

    b. One of your customers, a municipality, has asked your organization to install software that can detect attempts to hack into the system.

    c. Sarbanes-Oxley requirements necessitate upgraded software.

    d. Giving all directors PDAs.

14. Considering the project priorities discussed in the chapter, which of the following is the right sequence of priority for these projects:

    a. 1) Developing a new product 2) upgrading your computer operating system 3) complying with a new state law that requires your company to report quarterly its income sources

    b. 1) Improving your own internal processes 2) developing a new product that marketing has asked for 3) complying with a new regulation from the SEC requiring a list of your shareholders

c. 1) Complying with a new state regulation that requires your company to upgrade your security software 2) completing an upgrade to a financial package that your CFO needs 3) making an improvement to an internal process

d. 1) Creating a new product that will increase your company visibility but provide no additional income 2) completing an upgrade from MS Office 2000 to Office 2003 3) installing a new software package that makes it easier to do financial reports

15. Why do projects have to be prioritized?

    a. Because there are limited resources to do all of them

    b. Because only marketing should be able to choose which projects to do

    c. Because all projects should be the Number 1 priority

    d. Because the CEO said to

END NOTE:

1. *Wikipedia, The Free Encyclopedia,* accessed 6-23-06.
2. Lafe Low. "First Things First." *CIO Magazine,* March 15, 2004.

3 *Project Processes, Phases, and Life Cycles*

After reading this chapter, you will be able to:

- Understand what the appropriate processes are for an IT project.
- Be able to define the project phases for an IT project.
- Discuss different types of project life cycles.

When you are first given a project, it can seem a little overwhelming. There's an old saying in project management: "How do you eat an elephant? One bite at a time." In project management, we divide the project into phases and concentrate on managing each phase. Each phase is composed of a set of processes that guide us in starting the phase, planning it out, monitoring and managing it, and closing it out to move onto the next phase. The full set of all the phases on the project is called the project life cycle.

Not every project requires the same amount of project management, and every project will have different needs for documentation, planning, and control. It is the responsibility of the project manager to identify how to successfully complete his or her particular project in the most efficient manner by selecting the right combination of processes, tools, and techniques. This chapter will address project management processes and various life cycles for IT projects.

The programmer may think, "Why should we go through all this? We know what to do. We don't need this bureaucracy. Let's just start working and the code will come out all right." Watts Humphrey, in his seminal work *Managing the Software Process,* said: "The software graveyard is strewn with the carcasses of partially completed projects that were three to five times larger than anyone dreamed. No responsible builder would contract for a house without reviewing the plans and specs."[1]

PROJECT MANAGEMENT PROCESSES

A **process** is a series of activities that takes an input and brings about a result or output. Why use processes to manage a project? Why not just jump in and start working? Shouldn't we just know what to do?

Processes guide us step-by-step in what we have to do during our project. But processes don't guide just one project. Processes ensure that all projects we do are performed consistently, time after time. By applying the appropriate project management processes—not too many, not too few, and appropriate to the type of project being done—the team will have a much higher rate of success. Jumping in and starting the work causes many projects to fail because the project manager and the team are not necessarily doing the right things. They are just doing whatever makes sense at the moment. Project processes define the project management activities that are carried out during the project.

According to the *PMBOK® Guide*, 3rd Edition, Chapter 3, there are five **project management process groups** used to manage a project—initiating processes, planning processes, executing processes, controlling processes, and closing processes. They can be viewed as shown in Figure 3-1.

Figure 3-1. The Five Project Management Processes

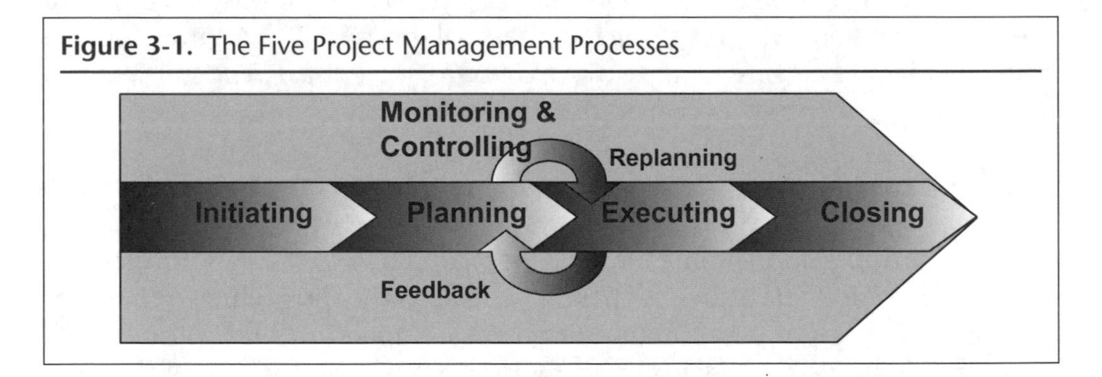

These processes are followed from the very beginning of a project until it is closed out. But more than that, these processes are used for each phase within the project as well. The team initiates a phase, plans how to accomplish the work, executes and controls the work, and finally closes out the phase and moves into the next phase.

These processes are not performed in isolation. They interact with each other, as shown in Figure 3-1.

Initiating Processes

Initiating processes are used to start up the project or the phase. Initiating the project can consist of things like developing the business case, getting approval to start, getting the team together, writing the initial documentation, and so on.

Initiating a phase may consist of reviewing lessons learned from the last phase so as not to repeat mistakes, initiating new team members, and having a kickoff meeting for the phase.

Planning Processes

Planning processes are processes used to think through and plan out what has to happen in the project or the phase. How many people are needed? What skill sets are necessary? How long will it take? How much money will it cost? What risks might happen? The planning process is iterative in nature and occurs throughout the project as it progresses. As information about the project is more clearly defined through the planning process, the team will go back and update information, which in turn can cause other information to change. In planning, the team is essentially attempting to influence the outcome of the project. Though even the best laid plans can't guarantee a successful project, lack of planning can certainly increase the chances of failure.

During the execution and control processes the team may find that it needs to come back and replan if things don't go according to the original plan, and they almost never do. A guiding principle is "Plan well, but don't get attached to the plan. It will change."

The start of a new phase is a good time to replan, since information gained from the previous phase can be used to better plan the current phase. For example, more information may be known about potential project risks, or the project manager may have learned from experience how to improve duration estimates for some activities. On large projects, a concept called **rolling wave planning** is used. That is where the near-term work is planned out in detail and the far-term work is left at a high level. Establishing the detailed planning at the start of a project phase is an example of rolling wave planning.

Executing Processes

Executing processes are those where the actual work to produce the product is performed. This is where the project team involvement is heaviest. Indeed, this is typically where most of the resources are involved and the costs of the project are rising most rapidly. Typical project management activities include status meetings, stakeholder management, issue resolution, and lots of communication!

Controlling Processes

Throughout the project, the project manager uses **controlling processes** to monitor and manage the work. This set of processes includes collecting status information, comparing it to plan, and making adjustments as needed. It is the information gained in the controlling processes that may cause replanning.

Closing Processes

Finally, the **closing processes** are those used to complete all the documentation, deliver the product to the customer or put it into the production environment, close out contracts, conduct a lessons learned session, and so on. Whether closing out a phase or a project, the closing processes are the same. It is the scope of activities that is different.

NOTE

In the PRINCE2 methodology that was designed specifically for IT projects, the project processes look like this:

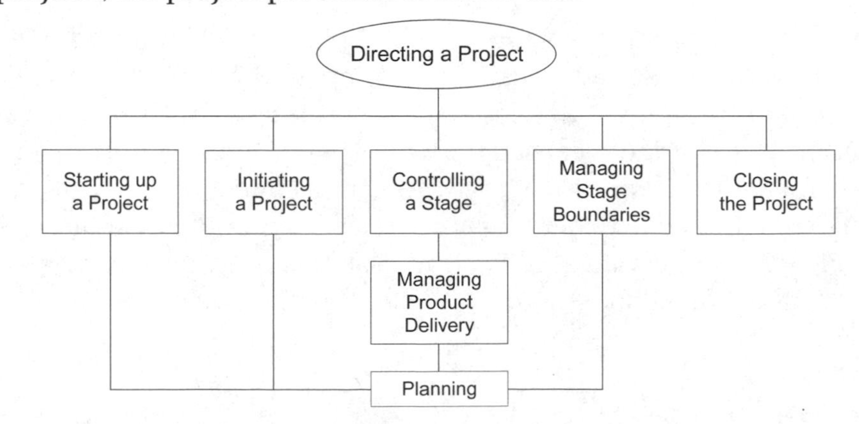

Just as in the PMI framework, there are activities associated with the processes shown in the figure. In PRINCE2, these activities include the business case, change and configuration control, quality, risk management, controlling the project, project management plans, and project roles and responsibilities.

In Practice: CMM and CMMI

Some of the processes we use in IT project management can get very sophisticated. A good example is the Capability Maturity Model (CMM) developed by the Software Engineering Institute (SEI). Watts Humphrey's book, mentioned earlier in this chapter, was the starting point for this effort. The CMM was developed during the early 1990s as a five-level model to measure the maturity of the software project management approach. Each level has a specific set of processes associated with it that will improve the ability of the company to successfully deliver projects. Research has shown that for every level an organization moves up in the model, it has a 15% improvement in productivity. In the past four years SEI has stopped supporting the CMM model and has moved to the CMMI (CMM Integrated) model, which incorporates processes beyond pure software project management.

Project Phases

The project processes we just discussed are used in each phase of the project. A **phase** is a segment of the project that occurs in a sequential order. At the completion of all of the phases, the project will be complete. There are multiple possible phases that can be used, depending on the type of project, the industry segment, and the organization. Typical phases used in the construction industry are very different from those used by a major aerospace contractor or by a pharmaceutical development company. In general, almost all IT projects follow some variation of these basic phases: planning, requirements, architecture/design, development or construction, test and integration, and implementation.

For example, typical phases for a software project would be:

- Project planning
- Requirements analysis
- Architecture and preliminary design

- Design and coding
- Test and integration
- Implementation

John J. Rakos, in his 1990 book *Software Project Management for Small to Medium Sized Projects,* recommends the following phases for software projects:[2]

- Definition
- Analysis
- Design
- Programming
- System test
- Acceptance
- Operations

Regardless of the industry, each phase requires inputs before it can be started, each phase has a set of activities unique to that phase, and each phase produces deliverables. These deliverables are often the inputs to the following phase. Figure 3-2 shows typical phases for an IT department's projects.

The conclusion of each phase is marked as a **milestone,** i.e. the completion of a significant event, on your schedule. At these end-of-phase milestones you should have phase end review meetings, which are sometimes referred to as stage gates. At these meetings you:

- Review how the work went during the previous phase.
- Assess what could have been done better and what went well.
- Make a go/no-go decision to move to the next phase.

These phase-end reviews are management control points where management decides whether the project should continue or not.

> ✻ ***NOTE***
> A milestone marks the end of something significant in the project. You can have milestones that are not associated with the end of a phase. For example, for a complex LAN development effort, the ap-

proval of the requirements document might be significant enough that it can be considered a milestone. Having several milestones within each phase of the project is not uncommon.

Remember that for each phase, we use each of the process groups. We plan out the phase, we initiate it, we monitor and control it as it is being executed, and finally we close out the phase and move on to the next phase.

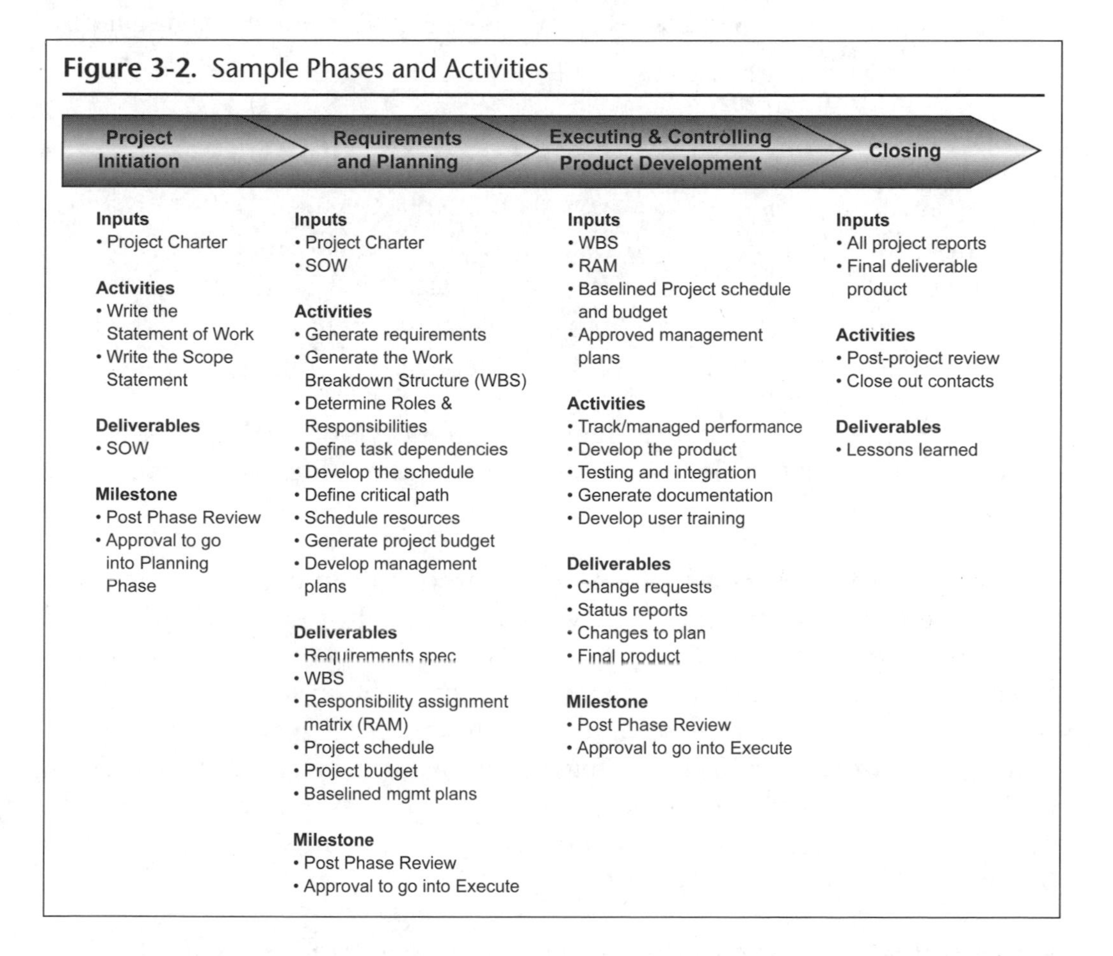

Figure 3-2. Sample Phases and Activities

PM in Action!

Imagine you have contracted with a builder to create your dream home. This evening, you're going to sit down with the builder and define how the project will go. List the phases you will want to use and define some key deliverables for each phase.

PROJECT LIFE CYCLES

As we have said, to manage a project effectively, a project manager divides the project into phases and performs the phases in sequential order. The **project life cycle** is the full set of those phases.

Why divide a project into smaller pieces? Because it is far easier to plan, manage, and control small pieces than it is one giant project. Having a predefined life cycle with well-planned-out steps makes the effort of managing a project much easier. The project life cycle starts defining the project with phases.

When we talk about life cycles, we have to be careful to clarify the context. There are actually three levels of life cycles—product life cycle, project life cycle, and system development life cycle (commonly abbreviated SDLC).

What Do You Think?

1. What are the phases used in your organization? Are they formal or informal?
2. In your organization, how do you see the project management processes interacting with the life cycle phases?

The **product life cycle** covers the product through its initial conception, the first version, and later upgrades and variations until the product is retired and a new product comes to take its place. This is the area that product owners (who may be in the marketing department) care about. As shown in Figure 3-3, project management is used to develop the initial product and its upgrades, but the product life cycle begins before any project, extends through multiple projects, and ends after the company decides to retire the product. The initial development, each upgrade, and each new version of the product is a project by itself.

Similarly, there is a relationship between the project life cycle and the systems development life cycle, as shown Figure 3-4.

In the May 14, 2002 edition of *ComputerWorld* magazine, a **system development life cycle (SDLC)** was defined as the overall process of developing information systems through a multistep process, from investigation of initial requirements through analysis, design, implementation, and maintenance. There are many different models and methodologies, but each generally consists of a series of defined steps or stages.

Figure 3-3. Product Life Cycle

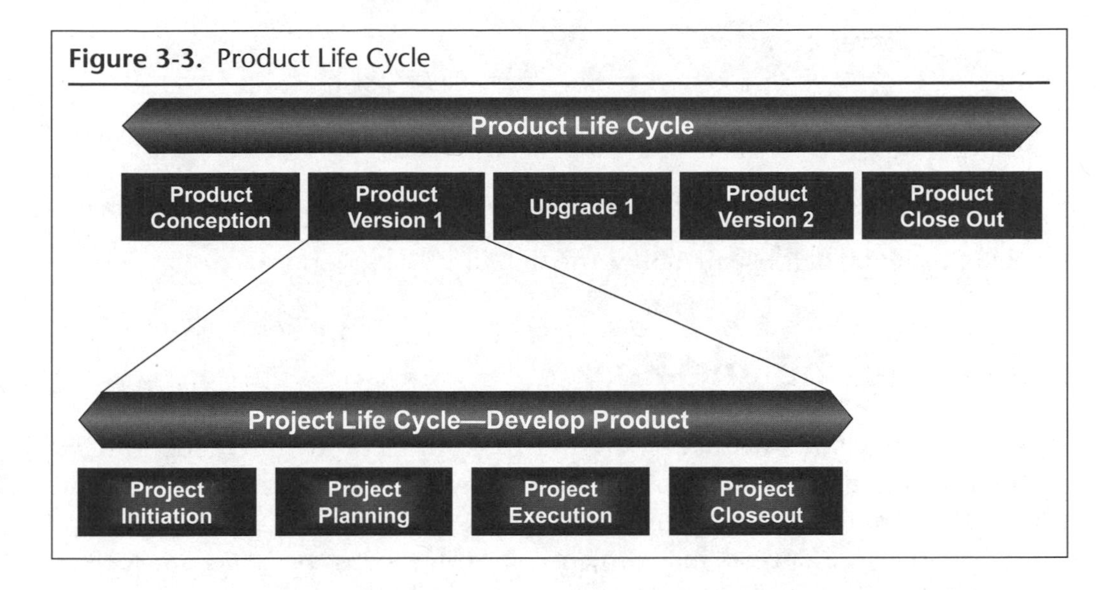

Figure 3-4. Project Life Cycle

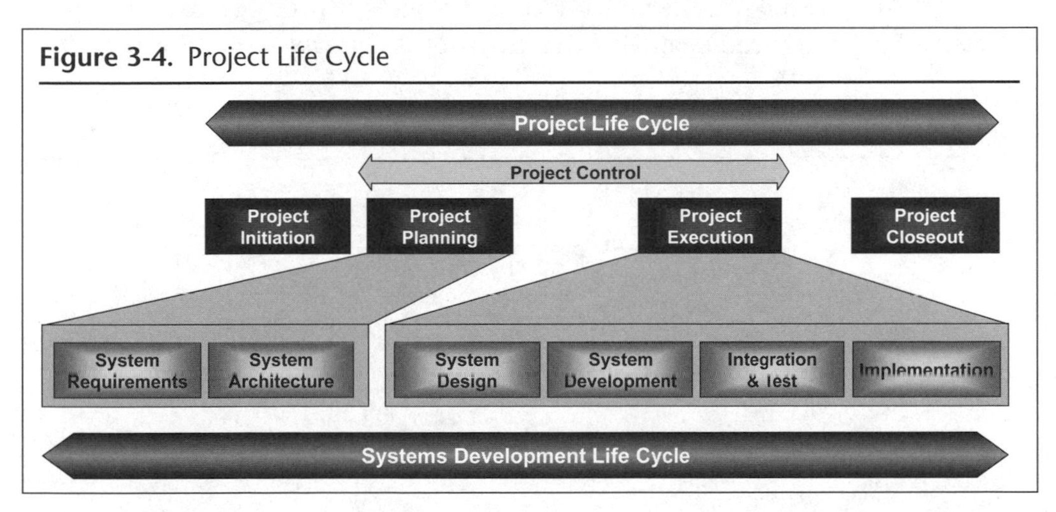

Many different SDLC models exist. The best one to use depends on the type of product you're developing. If you're developing a product where the user requirements are poorly defined, choose one of the approaches that puts the product in front of the user as often as possible, such as an iterative approach. If your project has little user interface or the user interface is well-defined, you can choose a more classic waterfall methodology.

Common IT life cycle approaches include:

- Ad hoc/code-and-fix
- Waterfall

- Iterative/incremental
- Spiral
- Prototyping
- Light life cycles, such as agile development

Let's look at each of these in a bit more detail.

Ad Hoc/Code-and-Fix

Figure 3-5 shows the ad hoc/code-and-fix approach. **Ad hoc/code-and-fix** is the most unstructured approach and is sometimes referred to as hack and patch. No formal design documentation and no specifications exist. This approach works only for very small projects. The downsides are that it is very risky and high cost (in the long term), and the products it produces often require extensive maintenance because of the unstructured development approach.

Figure 3-5. Ad Hoc/Code-and-Fix Approach

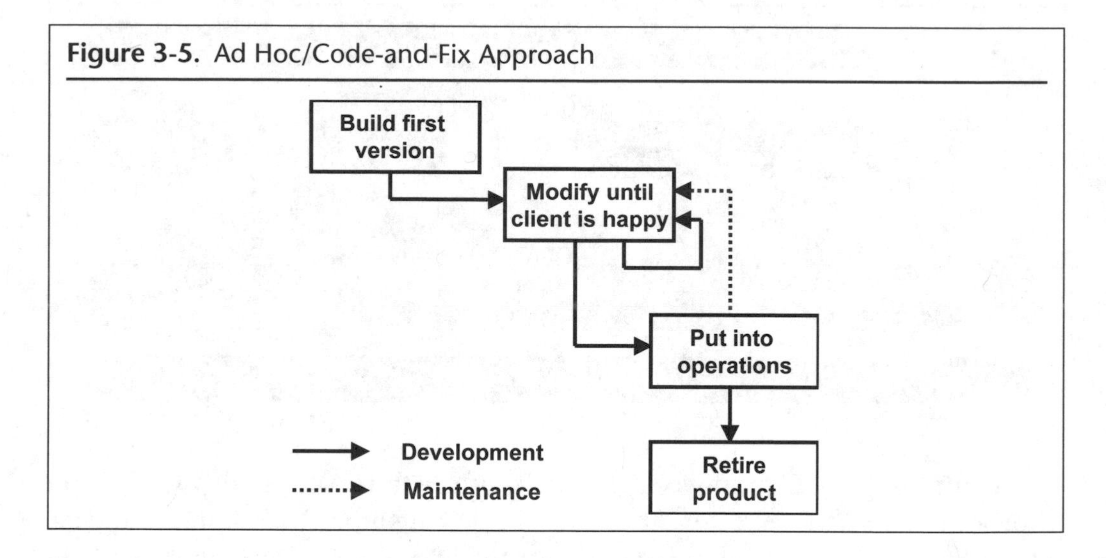

One version of this approach, called extreme programming (XP), is a more structured version of a very unstructured approach. It calls for the team to gather minimal requirements from the user or the client, then break up into groups of two. Each group generates what it thinks the client wants and then shows the resulting functionality to the client. If the result is what the client wanted, the team picks another piece of functionality and generates it the same way. If none of the results are what the client wants, the team throws out the code and writes new code that it thinks satisfies the requirements.

Because of the lack of planning or requirements development, and because of the high percentage of discarded code, from a project management approach XP is generally not recommended for anything other than small software projects.

Waterfall

The **waterfall** approach is the most commonly used and recognized life cycle. Figure 3-6 provides an example.

Figure 3-6. Waterfall Approach

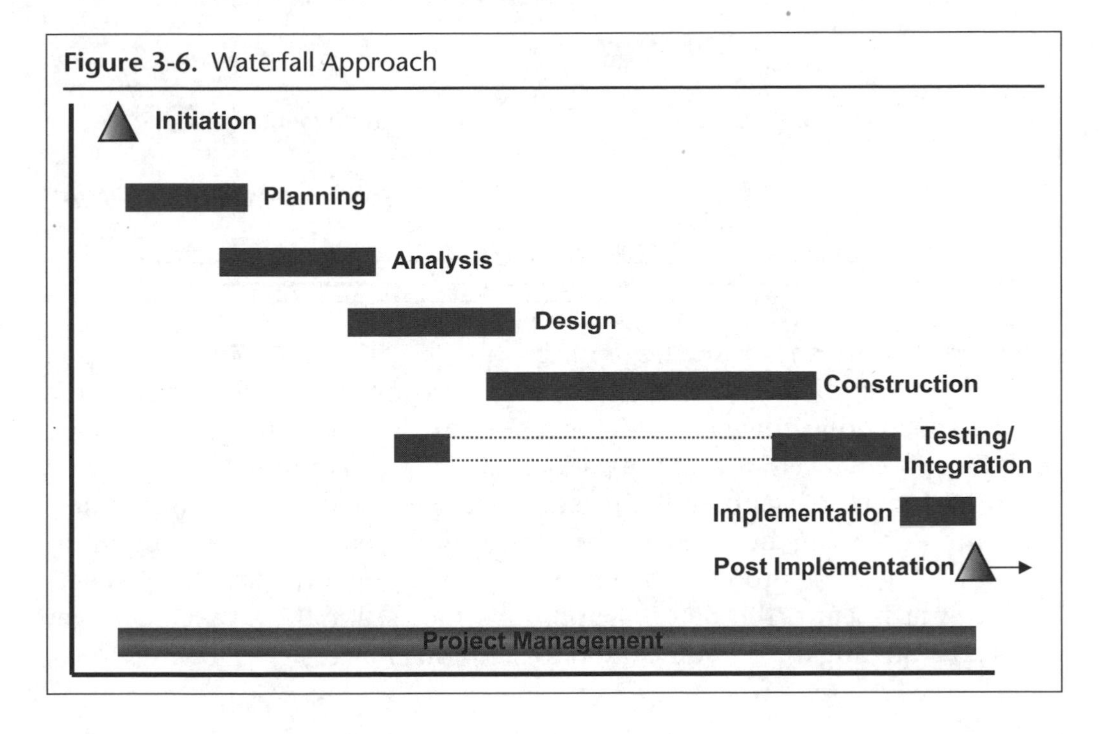

Why is it called a waterfall? When a project is behind but the end date doesn't move, activities are crammed onto the right side of the schedule. The schedule ends up looking like a waterfall, as shown in Figure 3-7.

The waterfall approach is a very linear approach to managing projects. Everything is planned out ahead of time and everything is documented. It emphasizes completing one phase of the development before proceeding to the next phase.

The waterfall approach has several advantages: it's easy to follow, the team gets approval for the design before moving into development, and manage-

Figure 3-7. Waterfall Approach, Version Two

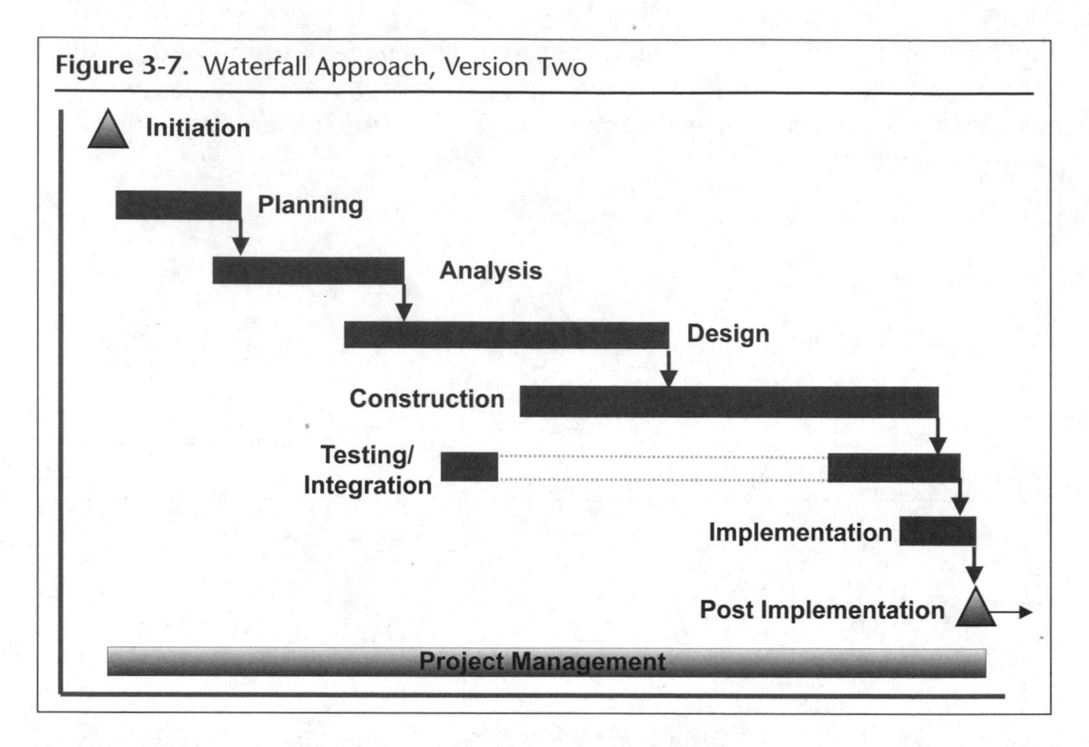

ment understands from the beginning what activities are going to happen and when. The difficulties with it are that it assumes that all requirements can be specified in advance (which usually isn't the case); the end users are only heavily involved during the early analysis and requirements gathering steps, and then not again until the user acceptance test; and it requires planning and budgeting the entire project early, often before there is enough information to do a thorough job of planning and budgeting. Real life projects are rarely as linear as the waterfall approach shows, and the project manager ends up adjusting the schedule often to factor in changes.

Iterative/Incremental

An **iterative** (or **incremental**) approach is one which goes through the development cycle more than once, adding additional functionality to the product each time. Figure 3-8 shows the iterative approach. The advantage to the approach is that it produces usable subparts that can be tested and delivered earlier in the process. The iterative approach is a good choice if the product has a heavy user interface and the customer or user is readily accessible. A part of the product can be developed, the user can be shown the part and provide input to the design, and then the next part can be developed.

One variation on the approach has been dubbed the Rational Unified Process by Rational Software (now a part of IBM). Rational Unified Process is more commonly referred to as RUP.

Figure 3-8. Iterative/Incremental Approach

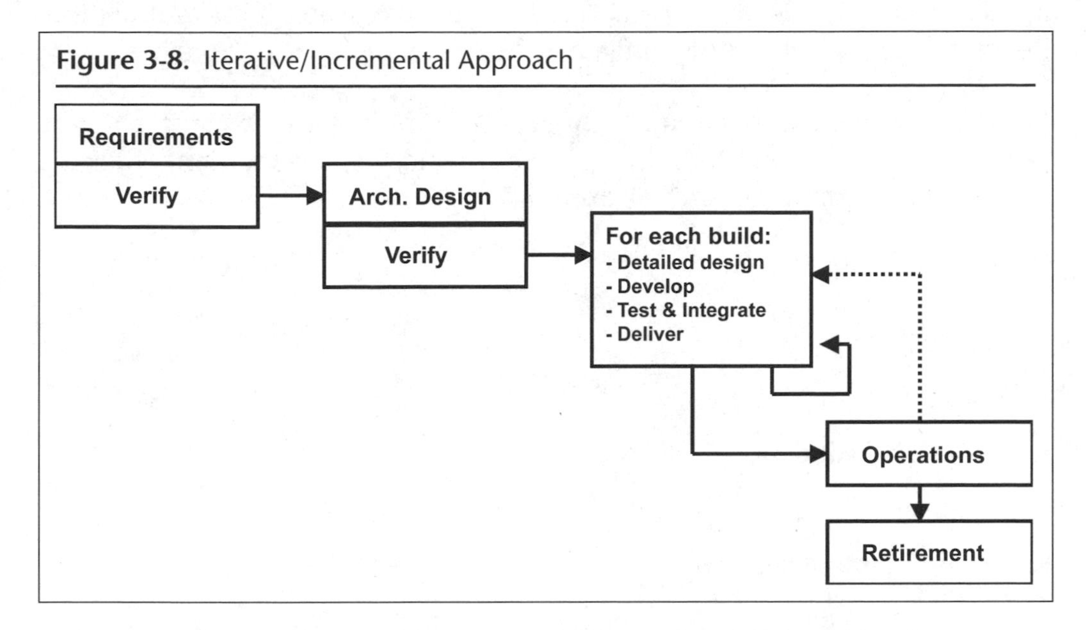

While there are advantages to using the iterative approach, there are also difficulties: the approach requires well-defined interfaces to all subparts; often, the most difficult parts are moved to the end so that management sees progress on the simplest parts; and formal reviews and audits are more difficult to implement on only parts of a complete system. When would you use it? David Whitgift, in his book *Methods and Tools of Software Configuration Management,* says that "If it's too risky to develop the whole system at once, then the incremental development should be considered."[3]

Spiral Approach

The **spiral** model created by Barry Boehm in 1985 is one example of an iterative approach to software development. Each cycle of the spiral begins by identifying:

- The objectives of the portion of the product being elaborated
- Alternative means of implementing this portion of the product
- Constraints imposed by cost, schedule, interfaces, and so forth

The second step is to identify alternatives relative to the objectives and constraints, along with identifying areas of uncertainty that are sources of project risk. If risk areas are identified, a cost-effective strategy for resolving the sources of risk is developed. This may involve prototyping, simulation, benchmarking, analytic modeling, or other risk reduction approaches.

Once a low-risk approach is identified, development can begin for a core portion of the product. Both the steps above and the development effort are managed as traditional waterfall approaches.

Typical cycles include

- Risk analysis
- Prototype
- Design and validation
- Planning
- Identification of alternatives

As each portion is developed, it is approved by the customer or user and additional functionality is added to it during the next phase. The original expectation was that each cycle would last between six months and two years—long enough for the customer or user to work with the functionality that is developed in each phase and to develop the requirements for the next phase's development work.

An important feature of the model is that each cycle is completed by a stakeholder review that covers all products developed during the cycle and includes the plans for the next cycle. The goal of the review is to ensure that all stakeholders are committed to the next phase. So at each phase of the approach, a portion of the final product is developed, shown to the users, and used as the basis for later development.

The disadvantages of the spiral approach are that if the users are not responsible for the schedule or the budget, executive control can be difficult; the approach requires significant risk assessment expertise to succeed; and the project can just keep going in circles, adding "just one more feature," or run out of time and money. Unless the project manager manages the scope tightly, scope creep can turn into scope gallop!

Prototyping

Prototyping is the development approach that builds a less functional version of the product just to show the user and see if the prototype is what the user wants. Because it can show the user an early version of what the user is actually getting, prototyping is best used when the user requirements are difficult to determine. In the basic prototyping approach, called rapid prototyping or evolutionary prototyping, the main phases are:

- Gathering the requirements
- Making a quick design
- Building a prototype
- Submitting the prototype for customer evaluation
- Refining the prototype—iterate the previous two steps
- Engineering the product

As shown in Figure 3-9, there's a lot of feedback during the prototype development. The feedback is necessary to prevent too much effort being placed into developing something the user will not be happy with.

Figure 3-9. Prototyping

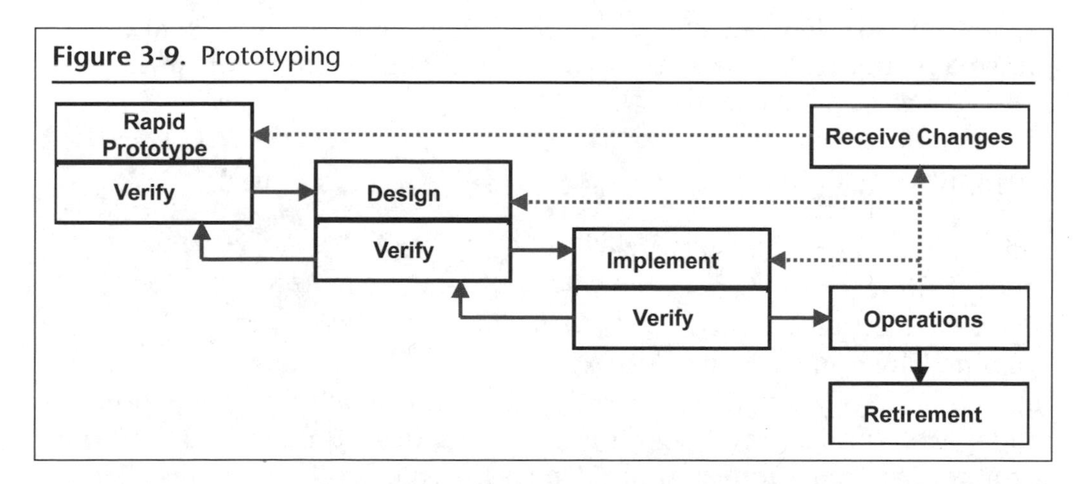

The advantages of prototyping are that it helps define the user requirements by producing something the user can touch and feel, provides a working version of the product, reduces downstream design activities, and simplifies the implementation effort.

Disadvantages to this approach are that the process is not particularly well structured; specifications keep changing as new requirements are discovered; it leads to premature design decisions that may turn out later to be wrong; the prototype itself may become the final product without going through the required QA and testing processes; and documentation tends to be poor. Probably the most difficult part of this approach is managing it. When is it finished? When is it right?

A variation on prototyping is called incremental prototyping or structured prototyping. This is a combination of rapid prototyping and a waterfall life cycle model. To use this approach, you create a prototype at each phase (feasibility, requirements, design, and coding) and test them. The product is developed in functional increments. Difficulties with this approach are that no long-term planning exists and falling into a code-and-fix model is very tempting.

Light Processes

In the field of software development, a number of **light project management** approaches have recently appeared. These approaches are attempts to overcome the limitations of the traditional waterfall approach in software development. They work most effectively when the project size is not too large and not too small. They emphasize strong client focus and involvement, strong software development team members, and flexibility in the project organization.

> ### *What Do You Think?*
>
> What would be the most effective system development life cycle to use on a typical project in your organization?

One of the more widely used of these newer processes is called agile development. The emphasis in this methodology is to divide larger projects into smaller, shorter, and more manageable projects and to put a heavy emphasis on continual interface with the client or customer. Another focus for agile development is seeking to overcome organizations' habits of overworking their staff by setting up project management plans to develop a work pace that can be maintained for long periods of time. Agile development is an evolving project management approach for software development.

In Practice: How Life Cycles, Phases, and Processes Interact

- Projects are divided into phases to help define and manage the work. The project manager and the project team should define the appropriate phases for the project.
- Projects have project management processes to initiate, plan, execute, control, and close the phases and the projects.
- A system development life cycle is used to define the steps necessary to develop the product of the project.
- The development of the product, product upgrades, and new releases are projects that occur within the product life cycle.

CHAPTER SUMMARY

- Different industries have different product life cycles. A product life cycle includes everything from conception to final product retirement, including development and maintenance.
- Projects are completed by using project management processes. The five processes are initiating, planning, executing, controlling, and closing. These processes are used throughout the life cycle of the project.
- The system development life cycle (SDLC) contains phases that include a multistep process from investigation of initial requirements through analysis, design, implementation, and maintenance.
- There are several basic life cycle approaches. Some of the better known ones are:

  — Ad hoc/code-and-fix

  — Waterfall

  — Iterative/incremental

  — Spiral

  — Prototyping

Key Terms

Life cycle
Process
Milestone
Product life cycle
Initiating processes
Executing processes
Project life cycle
Closing processes
Waterfall
Spiral
Phase
Project management process groups
Rolling wave planning
System development life cycle
Planning processes
Controlling processes
Light project management
Ad hoc/code-and-fix
Iterative/incremental
Prototyping

Key Term Quiz

1. Process
2. Phase
3. Life cycle
4. Product life cycle
5. System development life cycle
6. Initiating processes

A. Processes used to complete all the documentation, deliver the product to the customer or put it into the production environment, close out contracts, and so on

B. Processes used to start up the project or the phase

C. Processes to monitor and manage the work

D. Processes used to do the actual work to produce the product

E. Processes in which we think through and plan out what has to happen in the project or the phase

F. A series of steps that complete the project when done in sequence

7. Planning processes
8. Executing processes
9. Controlling processes
10. Closing processes

G. A series of actions that bring about a result or output

H. Covers the product from its initial conception, through the first version, later upgrades, and variations until the product is retired and a new product comes to take its place

I. The overall process of developing information systems through a multistep process, from investigation of initial requirements through analysis, design, implementation, and maintenance

J. Segment of the project that occurs in a sequential order

Chapter Review Questions

1. Where in the project life cycle is the need for project management the greatest?

2. A life cycle is:

   a. A series of steps that will complete all parts of the project when done in sequence

   b. The set of activities we do in a project

   c. What the project team does while we manage the project

   d. The steps needed to start the project

3. The most common project life cycle approach is the:

   a. Spiral model

   b. Pilot development

   c. The waterfall model

   d. Iterative approach

4. Which life cycle approach should only be used for very small projects?
   a. Iterative approach
   b. Waterfall approach
   c. Extreme programming
   d. Spiral model

5. At the end-of-phase reviews, which of these following activities would you not typically do:
   a. Review how the work went during the previous phase.
   b. Tell the project sponsor that you're over budget and need more money.
   c. Determine whether the project is ready to go onto the next phase.
   d. Make a go/no-go decision to move to the next phase.

6. The most effective development life cycle to choose is one that:
   a. Gets the majority of the product to the customer the fastest
   b. Puts the least stress on the project team
   c. Costs the least for the project
   d. Makes the most effective use of resources while satisfying the product requirements

END NOTES

1. Watts Humphrey, *Managing the Software Process,* Addison-Wesley Publishing, New York, 1990, page 58.
2. John J. Rakos, *Software Project Management for Small to Medium Size Projects,* Prentice-Hall, New Jersey, 1990
3. David Whitgift, *Methods and Tools of Software Configuration Management,* John Wiley and Sons, New York, 1991

4 Project Management Plan Elements

After reading this chapter, you will be able to:

- Describe the elements of a project management plan.
- Assess the amount of project management needed based on project category.

Like most things in life, projects require paperwork. The most important paperwork for a project is the **project management plan,** also known as a **project plan.** The project management plan is a series of documents that defines and describes how the project will be planned, executed, monitored, controlled, and closed out. It is essentially a road map for the management of the project.

The project management plan is composed of many separate documents. For ease of presentation, we break thesc into three types of documents: management documents, planning documents, and project logs.

Note: All of these documents are addressed in later chapters of this book. They are presented here as a summary overview.

Management Documents

Management documents include the information on how the project manager will manage specific areas of the project. A scope management plan, a change management plan, and a configuration management plan are all examples of management documents. These documents also define the product life cycle, phase gates, and acceptance criteria. The following table shows a representative example of the types of management documents you may need on a project.

NOTE

Because each project and organization is different, you may not need each of these documents, or the issue that would normally require a whole document may be addressed in a single paragraph in a summary document. Also, this table is not a comprehensive list. You must determine the types of management documents you need for your project.

Plan	*Content*
Scope management plan	• Process for preparing a detailed project scope statement • Process for preparing the WBS and WBS dictionary • Criteria for obtaining formal acceptance and verification of project deliverables • Process for controlling changes to the project scope statement
Schedule management plan	• Criteria for developing and controlling the project schedule
Cost management plan	• Precision level of estimates • Cost variance thresholds • Criteria for controlling changes to the project budget and cost estimates
Staffing management plan	• Information on acquiring team members, such as policies for outsourcing and virtual versus co-located team processes • Information on bringing new people onto the team and information on releasing team members that are no longer needed • Team member availability, often depicted with a resource histogram
Quality management plan	• How the quality policy will be implemented

Plan	*Content*
Communications management plan	• Stakeholder analysis • Description of the types of information that will be distributed, including level of detail, format, content, etc. • Distribution structure that includes who will get information and the format that they will receive it in • Glossary of terminology
Risk management plan	• Methodology • Risk categories • Definitions of probability and impact • Probability and impact matrix • Reporting and tracking process
Configuration management plan	• Processes for submitting change requests • Systems to review submitted change requests • Levels of authority for approving changes • Process for validating approved changes • Procedures for documenting characteristics of product components • Procedures to report changes to product components • Audit procedures

Planning Documents

The following table shows some of the planning documents you may need to use on a project.

Plan	*Content*
Project scope statement	A detailed description of the project objectives, deliverables, and the work necessary to create those deliverables. It may incorporate project and/or business requirements, acceptance criteria, project

Plan	*Content*
	constraints, and other high level project information. It is a key document that assists the team in understanding the project. Other project documents will be compared to the project scope statement to ensure compliance with the project objectives. Frequently, this document includes information on what is excluded from the project.
Work breakdown structure (WBS)	A hierarchical depiction of all the work necessary to deliver on the project objectives. It starts at the project level and decomposes the project into deliverables.
Cost estimates	Estimates for labor, materials, supplies, equipment, travel, and all other costs necessary to complete the project work.
Cost baseline	A time-phased budget that is used to track, monitor, and control the project's cost performance.
Schedule baseline	Contains the start and finish dates for project activities. It includes the activities necessary to fulfill the project objectives, the relationship between activities, the duration estimates for activities, and the resources needed to complete activities. It may be presented at a milestone level or at a more detailed level. The schedule baseline will be used to track, monitor, and control the project's schedule performance.
Responsibility assignment matrix	A document that ties each deliverable in the WBS to an accountable party. It usually includes the level of responsibility or accountability that each party has for particular deliverables.
Risk register	Lists each project risk, an analysis of the risk, and the identified response to the risk.

Project Logs

Project logs are documents that are used to collect, organize, and maintain specific aspects of the project. They are tools used to carry out the guidelines established in the management plans and the planning documents. The following table contains some examples. Remember that you may not need each of these on every project, and you can add others as needed.

Plan	*Content*
Assumption log	**Assumptions** are statements that are considered true but that are not validated or verified. It is common to have uncertainty around the decisions made about the project and product. The team usually makes an assumption about the area of uncertainty and acts upon that assumption. The log is used to document, track, and validate assumptions about the project, product, resources, the market—basically anything that can impact the project or the approach to managing the project.
Issue log	**Issues** are items that need to be dealt with in order for the project to move forward. They include decisions that need to be made, information that needs to be acquired, or anything that needs to be resolved to move the project forward.
Action item log	This log is used to track action items that have been assigned to team members or other stakeholders. It contains information on the action item assigned, who it was assigned to, and the due date.

Projects are filled with assumptions, issues, and action items. The project manager can't possibly carry around all this information in his or her head. Logs are a structured approach to document assumptions, issues, and action items.

TIP

One of the easiest ways to start a project is get two three-ring binders. Fill the first binder with templates for the project management plan documents that must be written. You can use the templates to generate the management plans. In the second binder, put in tabs for everything you are expected to keep up-to-date on a weekly basis: schedule updates, budget updates, the risk log, the issues log, an action item list, the assumptions log, change request log, and so on. This two-binder approach provides a structure for keeping project management on track from the beginning.

TIP

What you don't understand you can't control. The best way to understand what is going on is to write it down. Keep your project logs up to date, and you will save yourself a lot of wasted time trying to remember why you made a decision or to whom an action item was assigned.

PM in Action

If you were assigned a project to upgrade your organization's operating system, what assumptions would you make? Create an assumption log with at least 15 assumptions.

How Much Documentation Do I Really Need?

Are all of the documents listed on the previous pages necessary on all projects? It depends on the project. For large projects, you will need to write a separate management plan for each component. These management plans will tell upper management and the client how the project will be managed.

For small projects, the level of effort to write these plans far exceeds their benefit. Remember, we said earlier that you should apply just enough project management to ensure the project is successfully completed, and no more. Writing a separate plan for each of these areas is overkill. Instead, you should take one of the initial project documents, such as the project scope plan, and write a paragraph or two on each of these areas. This is sufficiently detailed to make management comfortable that you will have the project under control.

> ## *What Do You Think*
>
> 1. Can you think of a time when having assumptions recorded in an assumption log would have helped you?
> 2. Can you think of a time when having an issue log or risk log would have helped you?

What about medium-size projects? For those projects that lie in the grey area between small projects and large projects, we recommend that you write a separate management document with a section on each of these areas, incorporating just enough detail to show you have thought through what is necessary but are not going to micromanage the project.

Figures Figure 4-1 and Figure 4-2 on the following pages are document checklists that will help you define the project documentation for your projects. For small projects, you only need to produce the documents shown on the small project checklist. For large projects, all the documents shown need to be developed. You can make the template more useful by adding columns for who is responsible for the document and when it is scheduled to be produced.

TIP

We highly recommend that you develop project management plan templates, and have your management approve them, so that you do not have to recreate documents from scratch for each project.

How Much Project Management Is Enough?

After looking at the previous section on the project management plan, you might be saying, "But if I do all that, I'll spend more time managing the paperwork than managing the project!" Rest assured that the documentation in the project management plan should only take up a small proportion of your time. Most of your time should be spent actively managing the scope, schedule, cost, quality, risk, issues, and all the other things that must be managed to keep the project on track.

Figure 4-1. Small Project Checklist

Project Phase	Deliverables	Planned Date	Completed Date	Sponsor/User/ Client Sign-Off
Planning	❑ Project Charter & Management Plan			
	❑ Project Scope Document/WBS			
	❑ Project Schedule			
	❑ Project Resources (people, budget and equipment)			
Analysis & Design	❑ Requirements Document			
	❑ Project Schedule & Budget			
	❑ System Design Specification			
	❑ System Integration Plan			
Development	(Most documentation in this phase consists of status updates, change requests, etc.)			
	❑ Development Deliverables			
	❑ Training Documentation			
	❑ User Manuals			
	❑ Post-Phase Review			
Test & Integration	❑ Completed Test Plan and Log			
	❑ System Test Results			
	❑ User Acceptance Test			
	❑ User Acceptance Sign-Off			
	❑ Post-Phase Review			
Implementation	❑ Implementation Plan			
	❑ Production Maintenance Doc.			
	❑ Operations Documentation			
	❑ Post-Phase Review			
Project Closeout	❑ Project Completion Report			
	❑ Project Binder			
	❑ Project Lessons Learned			

You don't want to spend so much time managing that your team members feel that they're being micromanaged. You also don't want to spend so little time that you lose control over the project. You want to manage just enough to understand and control what's happening.

By definition, all projects are unique. Each project has its own blend of scope, duration, budget, resource requirements, visibility, etc. Some projects involve new technology that is unfamiliar to the team, and thus carry technology risk. Other projects have complex interactions or are particularly critical to the organization.

Figure 4-2. Large Project Document Checklist

Project Phase	Deliverables	Planned Date	Completed Date	Sponsor/User/ Client Sign-Off
Initiation and Planning Phase	❑ Scope Management Plan			
	❑ Schedule Management Plan			
	❑ Budget Management Plan			
	❑ Quality Management Plan			
	❑ Risk Management Plan			
	❑ Communications Mgmt Plan			
	❑ Resource Management Plan			
	❑ Procurement Management Plan			
	❑ Project Charter			
	❑ Project Scope Statement			
	❑ Work Breakdown Structure			
	❑ Issue Logs			
	❑ Assumption Logs			
	❑ Configuration Management Plan			
	❑ Post-Phase Review			
Analysis Phase	❑ Requirements Document			
	❑ Baselined Project Schedule			
	❑ Baselined Project Budget			
	❑ Post-Phase Review			
Design Phase	❑ System Architecture			
	❑ Process Change Spec.			
	❑ Design Specification			
	❑ System Test & Integration Plan			
	❑ Post-Phase Review			
Development Phase	(Most documentation in this phase consists of status updates, change requests, etc.)			
	❑ Development Deliverables			
	❑ Training Documentation			
	❑ User Manuals			
	❑ Post-Phase Review			
Test & Integration Phase	❑ Completed Test Plan and Log			
	❑ System Test Results			
	❑ User Acceptance Test			
	❑ User Acceptance Sign-Off			
	❑ Post-Phase Review			
Implementation Phase	❑ Implementation Plan			
	❑ Production Maintenance Doc.			
	❑ Operations Documentation			
	❑ Post-Phase Review			
Project Closeout	❑ Project Completion Report			
	❑ Project Binder			
	❑ Project Lessons Learned			

These characteristics can help you create categories of projects. The categories, in turn, help you define how much project management you need on a particular project and what types of tools can be most helpful. In project management, one size does not fit all. Rolling out a version upgrade of software requires much less project management than implementing an ERP system.

Project size is a relative matter. "Big" and "small" depend on what is normal for your organization. In IT in general, rarely is anything less than 100 hours of work considered a project; the task is just folded into normal operations. At the other extreme, hardly any IT projects require over 10,000 hours of work (the exceptions are implementations of large packages such as ERP or CRM systems). As an initial guideline, we might consider any project that requires between 500 and 1,000 hours to be a small project, anything between 1,000 and 3,000 hours to be a medium-size project, and anything over that to be a large project. Why is size important? As we'll see in this next section, different levels of documentation and of oversight are required for the different sizes and categories of projects.

Project Categories

The project management axiom is to apply only the amount of project management necessary to ensure a successful project. In other words, not every project needs every project management tool and technique. At a certain point, the payoff in efficiency is outweighed by the investment in time and energy. The trick is to find the correct balance point on each project. As a rule of thumb, about 10 to 15 percent of the overall effort should be spent in project management activities, with more effort spent for complex projects and projects that the organization has never done, and less effort for more routine types of projects. To assist you in finding the balance point for your projects, you can look at certain variables to help define the amount of project management necessary to deliver a successful project. These variables are:

- Duration
- Budget
- Resource usage
- Criticality

- Risk
- Complexity
- Communications requirements

Projects can be divided into three categories based on these variables. Category A projects are long, complex, risky, and require the most amount of project management effort. Category B projects are smaller, less complex, and may require either a full-time project manager or a part-time project manager. Category C projects are small, routine, and often have part-time project managers as well as part-time team members.

We will look at each of these variables separately, and then we will present a table that can serve as a guideline to follow when setting up the infrastructure of your project.

Duration

Duration is rather obvious. A project that lasts four weeks requires a significantly different amount of project management than a project that lasts two years. Think of the communication requirements alone! A two-year project will have multiple milestones, perhaps several critical and near critical paths, many phase gates, and will require variance analysis and reporting on a predetermined schedule. Most likely, a four-week project will not be tracked past start, finish, and maybe a couple of tasks, depending on the level of detail needed.

Budget

Budget is also obvious. The amount of tracking, estimating, and reporting you will need to do for a $12,000 project is much less than for a $2,000,000 project. Variance reports have wider bands, approval levels are higher in the organization, and the tracking systems for larger projects are far more detailed than for smaller ones.

Resource Usage

Resource usage includes the size and makeup of the team as well as resources such as equipment and supplies. It includes resources that are available internally and resources that need to be procured from an outside source. Consider team members: the more team members and stakeholders involved in a project, the more coordination and communication you need to do. If you have a four-person team, you can use informal e-mail communications and informal hallway conversations to get things done. An initial kickoff and occasional status meetings will assist in keeping things on track. Additionally, much of the information needed is in, and can stay in, people's heads (barring high-risk or high-complexity tasks). However, when you get into projects with larger teams of, say, 15 to 20, and you have people of various levels on the team, such as directors, external customers, and outside consultants, the amounts and types of communication and coordination grow significantly. Consequently, the amount of project management needed is greater.

Now let's look at equipment and supplies. An IT project that requires significant amounts of hardware, such as servers, routers, switches, data circuits, and workstations, requires more project management planning and control than a project that does not require such equipment. Projects that require extensive resources generally need to procure these resources from external vendors. This then brings in the additional requirement of solicitation, procurement, contracts, and the like.

Risk

Risk is also a defining factor in the amount and type of project management you will need. Business risks can have an upside (opportunity) or a downside. For our purposes, we will only consider negative impacts. An upgrade or equipment replacement carries minimal risk. However, if you have a project that requires you to define requirements and build, install, and test equipment in a hospital emergency room, you have some very high risk involved. The amount of requirements definition, validation, testing, risk management, and quality control will be significant given that lives are at stake.

Complexity

Many projects are relatively simple and do not interact across an enterprise. They are basically stand-alone projects that can be done, if not in isolation, then at least without major integration, system, and regression testing. Other projects seem to have spider-like tendrils that stretch everywhere. They affect the business processes of multiple departments, alter reports, cross multiple platforms, and change business rules. These are **complex projects.** This type of project requires a lot more facilitation, documentation, communication, risk management, testing, and patience!

Criticality

Criticality in a project refers to its impact on the business. Critical projects may be the mandatory projects we talked about in Chapter 2 or they may be projects that are critical for business reasons, such as developing a new product. Most regulatory projects are very critical, and thus require stringent application of project management processes. Often new product development is critical, as time to market can mean the difference between cornering a market and losing market share by being an also-ran competitor. Project management decisions on balancing the costs and benefits of crashing schedules, adding resources, shortening testing cycles, and so forth are paramount to this type of project.

Communications Requirements

Reporting requirements can run the gamut from a high-level scope statement, schedule, and budget, to a detailed and comprehensive set of reports that covers everything from procurement to quality and risk. The higher the priority and visibility of the project, the more important is frequent and thorough communications. If the project has stakeholders outside the company, then a strong communications management plan should be developed to include them.

Category A, B, and C Projects

The following tables summarize one method you can use to categorize projects based on their different aspects. Keep in mind that this is only a guideline, and that projects, by nature, are unique. So, use these tables as tools to guide you, not as constraints to dictate what you must do!

The first table shows projects that require the most effort in managing. These are called Category A projects. Although not all aspects of the project may require such detail, generally, large projects are large across the board—a big budget generally means a long duration, many team members, higher risk, etc. These types of projects require a full-time senior-level project or program manager. They may require additional project managers to manage subprojects.

Note: These lists cannot be all-inclusive due to the variability of project environments. They should be used as guidance to start the thought process of how projects of different size and complexity should be managed.

Category A Projects		
Aspect	***Threshold***	***Tools and processes***
Duration	12+ months 3,000+ hours	• Earned value project management • Milestones/dependencies/critical path identified • Phase gates • Buffer or contingency in schedule • Critical chain management (as appropriate)
Budget	$1M+	• Feasibility study and strong business case • ROI or benefit/cost analysis • Payback period • Detailed capital and labor expenses • Depreciation report (as needed) • Currency exchange rates (as needed) • Contingency funds and management reserve
Resource usage	Internal and external resources 15–20+	• Resource calendars • Dedicated resources • Skill set lists • Formal organizational chart • Responsibility matrix • Vendor management plan • Model contracts • Equipment and materials lead time estimates
Risk	High	• Risk management plan • Risk register • Risk categories • Probability and impact analysis • Risk triggers • Risk owners • Risk response plans
Complexity	High	• Gap analysis • Robust communication plan

Aspect	*Threshold*	*Tools and processes*
		• Training plan • Redundancy and business interruption needs
Criticality	High, strategic	• Sr. management sponsor • Robust risk management strategy
Reporting documentation requirements	Complete—stand alone versions of all project management documentation	• Project charter • Full project scope document • WBS • Critical success factors • Technical specifications –Complete hardware, software, and interface specifications –Technical design documents –Overall architecture documents –Business requirement documents • Configuration management plan • Issue log • Assumption log • Fully developed and baselined schedule • Integrated and baselined budget • Communication plan • Quality plan • Status reporting processes (earned value, weekly and monthly status reports) • Vendor specs and management plan as applicable • Risk management plan • Regular coordination meetings • Meetings –Monthly team meetings –Monthly sponsor meeting

Category B projects require significant project management, but less so than Category A projects. These projects generally have a dedicated full-time project manager, but IT team members may be full-time or part-time.

Category B Projects		
Aspect	***Threshold***	***Tools and processes***
Duration	4–9 months 500–2,000 hours	• Milestones • Dependencies • Critical path identified • Phase gates • Buffer or contingency in schedule as needed
Budget	$200K–1M	• Feasibility study • Cost benefit analysis • Quantitative analysis • Qualitative analysis • ROI • Payback period • Capital expenses • Labor expense • Depreciation report as needed • Contingency funds and management reserve as needed
Resource usages	5–10, may include vendor	• Skill set availability • Vendor management • Equipment lead time • Shared resources
Risk	Medium or high	• Risk register • Probability and impact analysis • Risk categories (used as appropriate) • Risk triggers • Risk owners • Risk response plans—fall back plans, contingency plans, and funds
Complexity	Medium	• Training plan • Communication plan • Redundancy and business interruption needs
Criticality	Medium–high	• Management sponsor • Risk management strategy

Aspect	*Threshold*	*Tools and processes*
Communications	Weekly status	• Project charter • Full project scope document • WBS • Technical documentation • Configuration management plan • Issue log • Assumption log • Integrated schedule • Budget • Communication plan • Quality plan –Quality parameters for project –Critical success factors –Key metrics as appropriate • Reporting requirements –Weekly status report –Monthly risk assessment • Vendor specs and management plan as applicable • Risk updates • Weekly/monthly status meetings with team and with sponsor or client

Category C projects may have a full or part time project manager. The project manager may be managing other projects or may have more of a team lead position in the organization. The team itself is likely to be working on other projects or performing operational work in addition to this project.

Category C Projects		
Aspect	*Threshold*	*Tools and processes*
Duration	1–4 months 100–500 hours	• Schedule with milestones, critical path, and dependencies • Phase gates
Budget	$25K–200K	• Feasibility study as needed • ROI as needed • Payback period as needed • Capital and labor expenses

Aspect	*Threshold*	*Tools and processes*
Resource usage	1–4	• Skill set availability • Equipment lead time • Shared resources
Risk	Low	• Identify any major risks and triggers • Identify risk owners as appropriate • Develop risk response plans as needed
Complexity	Low	• Redundancy and business interruption needs
Criticality	Low–high	• Department manager sponsor
Reporting requirements	Status only	• Project charter with integrated, abbreviated scope document • Technical documentation • Milestone schedule • Budget • Quality of service testing and documentation • Communication plan as needed • Quality parameters for project • Weekly status report • Vendor specs as applicable • Risk management plan –Identification –Risk response plans • Meetings –Team kickoff meeting

Generally, the need for project management activities will be highest in the beginning and end of the project, and fairly even in the middle. This means that the time spent initiating, planning, and closing is very important to the overall success of the project.

What Do You Think?

1. Think about projects you have worked on. Which ones were Category A projects? Category B? Category C?
2. How do you make a decision as to what category a project is in when some of the aspects are in one category and some in another?

Chapter Summary

- The documents used to plan, monitor, control, and document the project are collectively called a project management plan. The project management plan documents will vary based on the needs of the project. The project management plan contains documents to manage the project, planning documents, and project logs.
- Not all projects need the same amount or the same kind of project management. Large, complex, risky, and critical projects require a significant amount of planning, monitoring, controlling, and documentation. These are Category A projects. Category B projects require a moderate amount of planning, monitoring, controlling, and documentation. Category C projects are low risk, smaller projects that are not too complex or critical.
- For Category A projects, separate plans that describe how you will manage each aspect of the project, such as a scope management plan and a communication management plan, are used. For Category B projects, one management plan document that covers all of the elements at once is sufficient.

Key Terms

Project management plan

Complex projects

Assumption

Issue

Project logs

Criticality

Risk

Key Term Quiz

1. ____________________ are items that need to be dealt with in order for the project to move forward. They include acquiring information, making decisions, or resolving situations.

2. A ________________________ is a series of documents that describes how the project manager will plan, execute, monitor, control, and close the project.

3. ____________________ are used to collect, organize, and maintain specific aspects of the project.

4. A(n) _______________ is something that is considered true but that is not validated or verified.

5. _______________________ refers to the impact a project can have on the business.

Chapter Review Questions

1. List three of the variables that help define the category of a project.
2. When we refer to the impact of the project on the business, what variable in project categorization are we referring to?
3. What category is a project to upgrade 20 network printers to printer/scanners?
4. True or False: All projects require the same set of documents to manage them.
5. Where in the project life cycle is the need for project management the greatest?
6. List five items that can be found in a project management plan.
7. Give an example of two types of logs that you might find on a project.

5 Initiating and Planning Project Scope

After reading this chapter, you will be able to:

- Describe the elements and purpose of a project charter.
- Define the elements that go into a project scope statement.
- Gather requirements for your project.

In Chapter 2, we talked about how to select projects when the demand for projects is high, but the resources available are low. We looked at a project selection method and noted that all projects should relate to the organization's strategic intent. After a project is selected, the CEO does not just find an available project manager and say, okay, here is what I want you to do, when do you think it will be done? At least we hope that is not what happens.

Project selection begins the initiation process. The initiation process is complete when the project charter has been signed. At that point, the project manager begins the detailed requirements gathering process.

The Project Charter

The completed **project charter** is often considered the official start of the project. This document authorizes the project and allows the project manager to apply organizational resources. As such, it should be developed by management rather than the project manager. In this context, management may be the project sponsor, the requesting functional manager, or—in the case of a Category A project—a member of the executive team. Generally, the larger the project, the higher up the ladder the author of the project charter. In many organizations, upper management is often too busy to write the project charter. In this case, the task may be delegated to the project manager, with upper management having approval and sign-off authority. This approach has the advantage of getting the project manager involved earlier in the project and going through some of the upfront analysis that is necessary to plan the project.

What Goes into the Project Charter

A few things must go into the project charter. The project charter identifies the high-level requirements necessary to satisfy customer, sponsor, or stakeholder needs. It describes the business needs that the project was undertaken to address, which provides a justification for the project. The project charter also includes a tie to the organization's strategic objectives. Whether the project is a means of improving efficiency, increasing market share, reducing costs, or aiding some other aspect of an organization's strategic plan, the information should be spelled out in the project charter. The charter also provides a high-level description of the project and the product.

The project charter must also prioritize the triple constraints of scope, schedule, and cost for the project. Is it more important to deliver full product functionality with cost and schedule being secondary? Is meeting the delivery date important, even if functionality has to be sacrificed? Is the priority to keep costs as low as possible? The primary driver should be clearly stated in the project charter so that the project manager knows what to emphasize during the execution phase of the project, when tradeoffs have to be made. Knowing what is most important to the client or sponsor will allow the project manager to meet those expectations.

In some organizations, the project charter also contains additional information. This includes a high-level milestone schedule, a rough order of magnitude (ROM) budget, and the initial project organization. Sometimes the roles and responsibilities of key project staff, including the project manager, project sponsor, and key team positions are described. This description may take the form of a responsibility matrix with high-level roles and responsibilities, showing who the primary stakeholders are and their roles on the project, or it may just provide the titles and summary of responsibilities. The initial project assumptions and constraints are frequently part of the charter, either by being directly integrated or through the charter's including a reference to outside documents such as assumptions logs and risk logs.

Sometimes a business case is summarized or referenced in a project charter. An initial business case may have been developed that includes market research, ROI or other financial models, prototype information, and legal or regulatory information. Stakeholder influences may be listed as part of the business case or integrated into the charter. For instance, if a regulatory agency has input or signs off as part of the project, this stakeholder influence is mentioned in the charter.

In summary, a project charter always addresses the following:

- High-level requirements that satisfy customer, sponsor, or stakeholder needs
- Business needs, high-level project description, product requirements
- Project purpose or justification that ties to a strategic need
- A high-level description of the product and the project
- Prioritization of the triple constraints

And a project charter may also include the following:

- Business case justifying the project, including ROI
- Summary milestone schedule
- Summary budget
- Initial project organization
- Assumptions
- Constraints
- Known risks and issues
- Stakeholder influences
- Assigned project manager and authority level

In the case of a consulting firm or an organization that bids for business, the information for the project charter may come from a contract or a statement of work. If the project is internally generated, the information may come from within the organization or from external environmental factors such as market demand, regulatory requirements, technology advances, customer requests, or social needs.

Figure 5-1 shows a sample project charter.

Figure 5-1. MegaNews Project Charter

<table>
<tr><th colspan="2">Project Name: MegaNews Infrastructure</th><th>Date</th></tr>
<tr><th colspan="2">Project Sponsor: B. Ware</th><th>Project Manager</th></tr>
<tr><td>Project Description</td><td colspan="2">Provide the IT component for opening up new offices in downtown Los Angeles for 1,000 new employees, including 50 executives, 25 secretaries, and ~925 staff. Offices will be located in three different leased office buildings in a campus type setting.</td></tr>
<tr><td>Business Alignment</td><td colspan="2">• Increase advertising revenue by 20% in 3 years
• Increase the subscription base by 15% in 3 years</td></tr>
<tr><td>Project and Product Requirements</td><td colspan="2">1. Backup requirements:
a. We need to do full backups, both within each facility as well as having hot backup off site that covers all facilities.
b. Daily backup to corporate HQ is run each night for the HR and the financial data
2. Each person gets their own desktop, except the reporters who get laptops with a docking station.
3. Basic systems need to be compatible with corporate systems. Therefore the basic desktop suite is Microsoft Office, the DB is DB2, the HR systems will be a PeopleSoft implementation.
4. Two groups, human resources and news, need some custom software development for programs that are unique to them. These are moderate size programs, 150 function points, which tie in-house software to external systems such as payroll processing. They should take no longer than 2,000 man-hours each to develop.
5. Develop and host the corporate web page for MegaNews International. The site does not have any e-commerce capability but will have a registration DB. It must be live 3 weeks prior to the office opening to create name recognition and it will tie into the marketing campaign.
6. In order to make maintenance operations simple after the office goes live, a full set of design and configuration documentation will be developed, consistent with company policy.</td></tr>
<tr><td rowspan="3">Roles and Responsibilities</td><td>Project Sponsor</td><td>• Champion the project within the organization.
• Provide business support for major project decision and direction setting.
• Approve the project plan, cost, and schedule
• Support the Change Control Board meetings</td></tr>
<tr><td>Project Manager</td><td>• Develop the project plans and schedules
• Manage all aspects of project delivery in the areas of scope, time, cost, quality, resources, communication and risk.
• Direct and coordinate the activities of the project team.
• Assure the meeting of Business Sponsor's objectives for the project.
• Lead the Change Control Board meetings</td></tr>
<tr><td>Business Analyist</td><td>• Gather and document business requirements.
• Support gathering and documentation of functional and technical requirements.
• Support the project plan development
• Design and document new business processes.
• Support the Change Control Board meetings</td></tr>
</table>

Figure 5-1. MegaNews Project Charter (continued)

	System Engineer	• Lead the decomposition of the business requirements into the functional and technical requirements • Manage the requirements and assess the impact of changes to the requirements • Identify external interfaces, ensure they are verified • Ensure the testing and integration program verifies all requirements • Support the Change Control Board meetings
	IT Lead	• Lead the design effort and write the design specs • Ensure that all requirements are covered by the design • Design external interfaces in accordance with the specifications • Support the Change Control Board meetings
Initial Project	Betty Ware—Sponsor ... Overall PM └── IT Project Manager ······ (dotted line to Overall PM) Business Analyst, System Engineer, IT Specialists	
Major milestones and deliverables	**Milestone**	**Deliverables**
	Project Plan Baselined	Project management plans, project schedule, and cost
	Requirements Approved	Sponsor signoff on project requirements document
	Design Approved	Design specifications
	LAN Implementation Completed	Completion of LAN and desktop machine installation
	Approval of Custom S/W	Custom software completed and approved through User Acceptance Test
	Backup Site Approved	Hot backup site completed and tested
	Go Live Approval	UAT completed Corporate is ready to turn link on
ROM Budget	**N/A**	
Constraints	Go Live date in 6 months Must have web site up 3 weeks prior to go live Do not have access to server room until 1 month prior to go live All technology must interface with existing systems	
Assumptions	1. The server room will be ready for move in 1 month prior to go live. 2. MegaNews will be responsible for its own system maintenance. 3. Each facility already has a T3 link (high speed, high bandwidth link). 4. The offsite data storage will be through an outside vendor. You will have to manage that procurement process as part of this project. 5. The Director of Corporate IT will sign off on all documentation for the project.	
Known risks	1. We don't have a server room until 1 month prior to go live. Therefore, all development work on custom programs and the web site must be done off site and then transitioned to the new location once it is up.	
Prioritization	*Schedule, Scope, Cost*	
Other		

PM in Action!

Assume that you have been asked to upgrade all the computers at your company to the newest release of your operating system. The CTO is the sponsor and she has asked you to create a project charter for her to review tomorrow afternoon. Making assumptions about areas you don't have the information for, create a project charter for this project.

Value of the Project Charter

The project charter is the link from senior management to the project and the project manager. One of the main reasons that projects fail is lack of senior management support. The charter is management's visibility into the project, its commitment of organizational resources, and its communication to the project manager and the organization of what it wants. The charter also ensures that each project is tied to a strategic need. Therefore, when decisions have to be made that involve trade-offs or resource allocation, management can look at the project charter, note the contribution the project is making to the company, and use this information to make a wise decision. The project charter also helps the project manager with authority when he or she is dealing with functional managers. The charter is management's statement to the organization that management supports the project and the project manager.

The Kickoff Meeting

Usually, once the project charter is created, a kickoff meeting is called. Every project should have a kickoff meeting. The purpose of the kickoff meeting is to introduce the team to the project and to each other and to generate some excitement about the project. Starting the kickoff meeting by going around the room and doing introductions is a good idea if the team has not worked together before. If everyone has worked together, you can launch right into the project charter.

The purpose of the meeting is to make the objectives clear and to ask the team members if they have any questions. At the meeting, the scope of the project should be reviewed along with the milestones, key deliverables, and the team organization. At the end of the meeting, everyone should understand the scope of the project, their role in the project, how the project relates to the company's strategy, and the next steps. The project charter can be used to facilitate all the discussions held at the kickoff meeting.

> ***PM in Action!***
>
> Using the example of updating your operating system and the charter you previously developed, create an agenda for a kickoff meeting.

The Project Scope Statement

The project charter is focused on how the project relates to the organization in terms of resources, strategy, and stakeholders. It also includes high-level information about scope, schedule, and cost. The project scope statement, meanwhile, is focused on the scope of the project *and* the product. Developing the scope is an evolutionary process, just as developing the schedule and budget are. The **project scope statement** helps define what is being developed and raises the questions necessary to accurately define what will and will not be included as part of the project.

Notice that **project scope** is different from **product scope.** The product scope defines only the end deliverable and its components. The project scope defines the work necessary to deliver the product scope. For example, part of the requirements may call for an end-to-end testing suite where a robust user acceptance test can be administered. This is part of the project, but it is not part of the product. Therefore, the project manager must clearly define both the work needed for the product and the work needed for the project.

In developing the project scope statement, the project manager will reference the project charter as well as any other additional information that is available. Developing the scope statement generally requires a number of interviews and meetings with the client, team members, the sponsor, and other stakeholders. Many of the decisions that affect the final product are made in this stage. This is where the work of defining the product and the project management approach begins.

What Goes into the Project Scope Statement

So, what is included in the project scope statement? Like most things in project management, it depends on the product, the organization, and the external environmental factors. However, here is a list you can use as a guideline:

- Project objectives
- Product or services requirements and characteristics (including any technology requirements)
- Project requirements and deliverables
- Product acceptance criteria
- Project boundaries
- Initial WBS
- Configuration management requirements
- Updates to information from the charter, such as project milestones, budget estimates, etc.

Let's look at these in a bit more detail, and then we will look at a sample template (see Figure 5-2).

Project objectives are the specific measurable results that the organization is looking for the product to meet. Some possible project objectives are:

- Reduce turnaround time from 20 days to 17 days.
- Reduce waste from 3 percent to 1.5 percent.
- Save 12 percent on manufacturing costs in the next calendar year.
- Eliminate two FTE positions.

Project objectives are tied to the business justification identified in the project charter. Project objectives give the project manager and the sponsor a way to measure the success of the project—to see if the project delivers what was intended. The objectives will also be used as a guideline in making project decisions. When evaluating the approaches to a project, using the project objectives is a good way to select the best approach. Objectives also keep the project focused. Particularly with IT projects, scope tends to get out of con-

Figure 5-2. MegaNews Project Scope Statement

Project Name: MegaNews Infrastructure	Date
Project Sponsor: B. Ware	**Project Manager**
Project Description	Provide the IT component for opening up new offices in downtown Los Angeles for 1,000 new employees, including 50 executives, 25 secretaries, and ~925 staff. Offices will be located in three different leased office buildings in a campus type setting.
Business Alignment	• Increase advertising revenue by 20% in 3 years • Increase the subscription base by 15% in 3 years
	1. Backup requirements: a. We need to do full backups, both within each facility as well as having a hot backup off-site that covers all facilities. b. Daily backup to corporate HQ is run each night for the HR and the financial data 2. Each person gets their own desktop, except the reporters who get laptops with a docking station. 3. Basic systems need to be compatible with corporate systems. Therefore the basic desktop suite is Microsoft Office, the DB is DB2, the HR systems will be a PeopleSoft implementation. 4. Two groups, human resources and news, need some custom software development for programs that are unique to them. These are moderate size programs, 150 function points, which tie in-house software to external systems such as payroll processing. They should take no longer than 2,000 man-hours each to develop. 5. We will develop and host the corporate web page for MegaNews International. The site does not have any e-commerce capability but will have a registration DB. It must be live 3 weeks prior to the office opening to create name recognition and it will tie into the marketing campaign. 6. In order to make maintenance operations simple after the office goes live, a full set of design and configuration documentation will be developed, consistent with company policy.
Project Objectives	The quantifiable criteria that must be met for the project to be considered successful. Project objectives must include at least cost, schedule, and quality measures.
Cost Objectives (quantify)	N/A
Schedule Objectives	Entire project complete in 6 months. Web site up 3 weeks prior to go live. Hot backup completed and tested prior to go live. Access to server room in 5 months.
Scope/quality Objectives	Quality must be consistent with company standards. Start up on Day 1 with no glitches.
Project Deliverables	*A list of the summary-level sub products whose full and satisfactory delivery marks completion of the project. Should include product and project deliverables.*
Deliverable A	Web site with registration database
Deliverable B	System design documents
Deliverable C	Network connectivity including switches, routers, circuits, and servers
Deliverable D	All hardware connected including desktops, laptops, printers, scanners, etc.
Deliverable E	HR custom software

Figure 5-2. MegaNews Project Scope Statement

Deliverable F	News custom software
Deliverable G	Contract for off-site data backup
Deliverable H	Design and configuration documentation
Initial WBS	1. IT Infrastructure 1.1. Web Site 1.2. Network 1.3. Software 1.4. Back Up 1.5. Project Management
Project Boundaries	Blackberry beta test Anything outside IT for overall project Any ongoing IT operations
Acceptance Criteria	All systems tested and signed off 2 weeks prior to go live Web site operational 1 month prior to go live All software fully functional by go live Documentation signed off by Director of IT Back up operations tested and functional
Configuration Management	Per company policy
Change Management	Per company policy

trol. A wise project manager will use the project objectives and scope statement to keep a tight reign on scope.

Product or service requirements might include compatibility with existing systems, regulatory requirements, or certain functionalities. These requirements should be clearly documented, as they will be used to verify completion. If there are quality measurements that need to be met as part of the product, those should be documented as well. We will discuss requirements in more detail later in the chapter.

Project requirements and deliverables address how the product requirements will be met. This may include information on testing, alternative approaches, life cycle or phase gates, training and documentation requirements, and any other aspect that affects the product scope but may not be part of the end product.

Product acceptance criteria define measurements, performance, objectives, and metrics that need to be met in order for the client to accept the product. Information from product and project deliverables, requirements, and objectives will provide information for this section.

Project boundaries define what is in scope and what is out of scope for the project. Project boundaries can be the project manager's best friend when it comes to controlling scope creep. It is a given that the customer will assume that if something is not specifically excluded, it is included. Project managers assume that if something is not explicitly included, it is excluded. Therefore, be very clear on what is included in the project and what is excluded. We also suggest that the project manager form a method for addressing conflicts and uncertainties in project scope. This may be a project change-control board or a project advisory committee.

For anything other than a small project, incorporating a section on what the project will *not* do is critical. For example, if the project is to upgrade the operating system in the company's computers, stating exactly what interfaces the project will test and which ones it will not is important. This will prevent any confusion about whether that critical piece of software on the CFO's machine will work with the new operating system.

An initial work breakdown structure (WBS) is necessary to start to chunk the work. Work may be chunked by phase (such as life cycle), by major component, by geography, or in any other way that makes sense. We will talk more about WBSs shortly.

Configuration management may be included in the scope statement, as well on certain projects. Configuration management addresses how versions, updates, materials, and changes will be incorporated into the product and the project. It may address materials, documentation, progressive elaboration, and iterative planning.

In addition to the above, the project scope statement may contain updates. One of the realities of project management is what we call progressive elaboration. This means that the entire project isn't planned in detail in one sitting. Rather, it is increasingly elaborated, planned, and made clear over time. As product requirements are defined, the resources requirements can be refined, the schedule gets a lower level of detail, and the budget is flushed out. This is ongoing throughout the planning and even during the executing and control processes. Therefore, updating project documentation on an ongoing basis is important.

As part of preparing the project scope statement, the project manager may find that he or she can update the initial milestone schedule and the initial rough order of magnitude (ROM) budget. In starting to define the product and project requirements and the objectives, the project team will make certain assumptions and uncover risks. These need to be added to the various project logs.

Value of the Project Scope Statement

In addition to poor requirements gathering, two other main reasons for project failure are insufficient planning and lack of customer participation. The scope statement is the planning link between the customer and the project manager. It is how the project manager knows that there is clear communication between the customer's needs, wants, expectations, and the end product the project manager is helping to create. It helps the project manager organize the project management process and creates a context for the planning process.

The list of deliverables and the top-level WBS communicate what is being developed and how it will be developed. Getting client input into the WBS (or at least client sign-off), assures that the client and the team are heading in the same direction. The acknowledgment of project boundaries in the beginning of the project can save scope creep or having to explain later why the team is not going to add the growing list of requests for the product. The project objectives help the project manager and other stakeholders make choices about alternatives by clearly listing what is expected from the project. The acceptance criteria assist the project manager in better defining the target and help in the close out. Most project managers have been on a never-ending project at one time or another. By clearly defining the acceptance criteria, the project manager can effectively box the project and define the end point where the product is transitioned to the customer or to operations.

ALL ABOUT REQUIREMENTS

Requirements are the foundations of projects. They are defined at a high level in the project charter and elaborated in the project scope statement. In projects with an extensive set of complex requirements, the project manager usually keeps a separate requirements document that is subject to configuration control.

Note: More projects have run into severe problems because of missing or poorly stated requirements than any other single cause. In *Effective Require-*

ments Practices, Ralph Young states that studies show that up to 85 percent of the defects in developed software begin in the requirements.[1]

Introduction to Requirements

What are requirements? Everyone knows what they are, but everyone's understanding of them is different. When you tell the marketing person that you need the requirements for the new product she's asking for, she'll be happy to tell you what she wants in the product. What she gives you is virtually always very high level and is totally concerned with the user's experience with the new product. When you ask the identical question of someone in engineering, he will be happy to give you an answer, but the requirements he gives you will be so detailed that the marketing person will look at them as if they are from another planet and say, "What does that mean?"

They are both giving you requirements, but from different levels of detail. What, then, is a requirement? A **requirement** is a clear statement of a need, sufficiently detailed so that there is no question about what is being asked. The International Institute of Business Analysts (IIBA) defines a requirement as a necessary attribute in a system. Requirements are statements that identify a capability, characteristic, or quality factor of a system in order for it to have value and utility to a user.

One of the more significant challenges is to collect clear, concise, and correct requirements. All new products or services start with someone's needs. These needs are translated into requirements, and the requirements form the scope of the product. The success of your project depends on how well you deliver what the user expects. That is, on how well you meet the requirements.

But let's face it: gathering requirements is not much fun. To do it right can require interviewing stakeholders, doing business process analysis, reading the documentation you have, making some best guesses as to what is wanted, documenting it all, and then walking through it with the stakeholders to verify that it truly is what they want. However, if you do it right, you can manage the rest of the project with full confidence that you *know* you understand what the stakeholders want. Without it, you will spend the rest of the project swallowing heartburn medicine and worrying about whether you are building the right thing.

WARNING

The major indicator of a project that is headed for trouble is that the requirements change constantly.

We said in the introduction that the success rate of IT projects is poor. Multiple surveys say that 85 percent of IT projects fail to deliver the full scope within cost and within schedule. The two primary causes of this high failure rate are inadequate planning and not having a good understanding of the requirements.

How do requirements fit into our overall project? The flowchart in Figure 5-3 should give you a good indication of where they fit.

In Practice

A study conducted by Frederick T. Sheldon showed the following about the sources of software bugs in a complex Air Force project.[2]

- 41% due to requirements errors
- 28% due to logic errors in design
- 6% interface errors
- 6% data errors
- 5% environment
- 5% human errors
- 2% documentation
- 6% other

Figure 5-3. Requirements Hierarchy

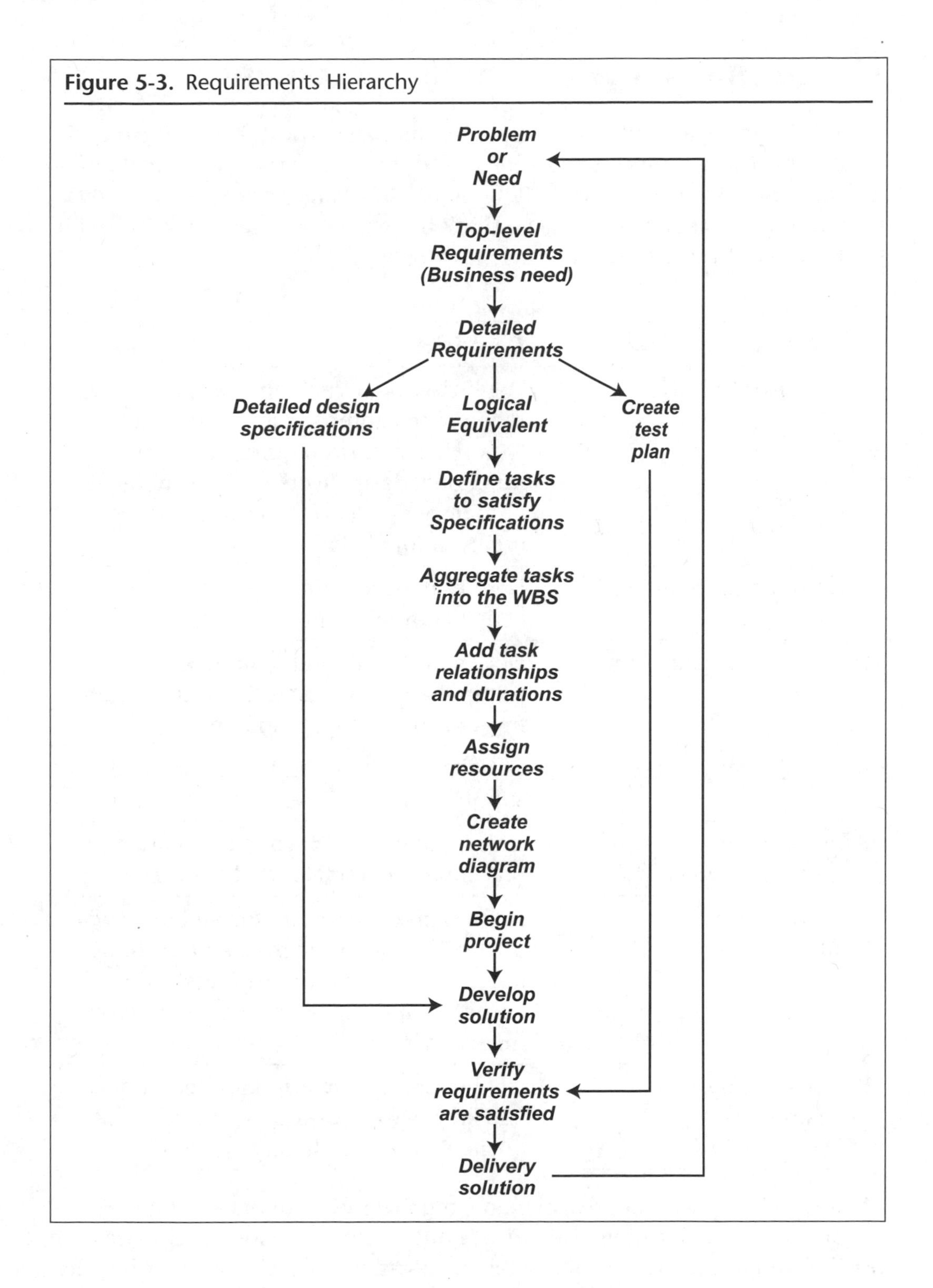

The Business Analyst and Requirements

A good business analyst can be a project manager's best friend. Frequently, it is the business analyst who gathers, analyzes, manages, and tests requirements. The IIBA has developed a body of knowledge for business analysts that focuses on requirements. The IIBA's body of knowledge is comprised of the knowledge areas shown in the following table.

IIBA Knowledge Areas	*Description*
Enterprise analysis	Defines activities and approaches required to capture necessary business views that support requirements and functional design work on a given initiative or to develop an overall enterprise or organizational plan.
Requirements planning and managing	Defines requirements, project life cycle activities, and requirements deliverables.
Requirements gathering	Defines activities and approaches required to capture business solution requirements from the project stakeholders.
Requirements analysis	Defines how business, functional, and supplemental requirements are analyzed.
Requirements communication	Defines requirements documentation and presentation practices and policies.
Requirements implementation	Defines tasks necessary to validate how the business solution meets stakeholder objectives, ensures appropriate test coverage, and supports requirements management and administration.
Business analysis fundamentals	Defines competencies, skills, techniques, and knowledge needed to perform business analysis effectively.

The project manager focuses on managing the project management processes, or initiating, planning, executing, controlling, and closing, whereas the business analyst is focused on the technical aspects of the project scope, such as requirements gathering, analysis, and implementation. Figure 5-4 shows how the SDLC, the project management process, and the requirements processes work together.

For more information on the IIBA, visit www.iiba.com.

Types of Requirements

Requirements are hierarchical, starting with top-level user or business needs that determine what this project is. A top-level need might be "E-mails from our customers are taking much too long to get through our system. We want them to show up at their destination within two minutes after they arrive." When the problem is a business need, the best people to gather these requirements are business analysts. Their job is to understand the business processes and the business strengths and weaknesses.

We take those top-level needs and decompose them into more detailed system needs. We now start thinking about the details of the solution. We consider how the end product may be designed and developed. These are system requirements and include **functional requirements** (what the product has to do) and **performance requirements** (how well it has to do it).

Figure 5-4. IIBA and Project Management Process Integration

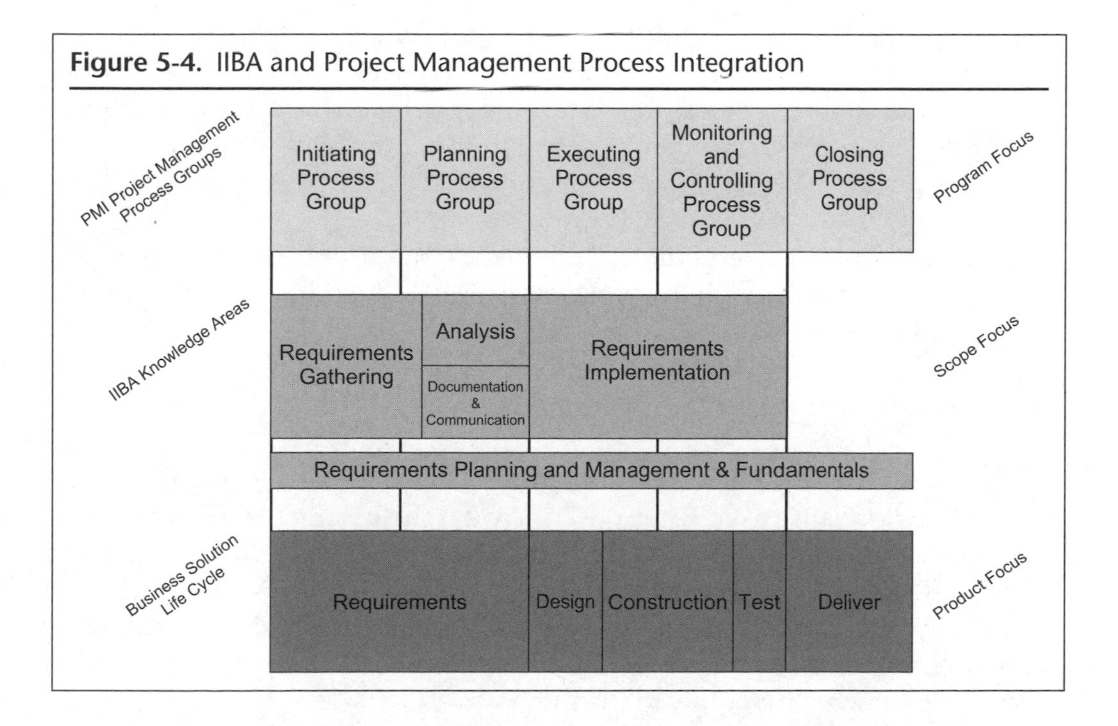

The technical gurus take those system requirements and decompose them even further, into detailed **technical requirements.** This is where the marketing people usually get lost; this level is too detailed for them. They cannot picture the final product from reading a stack of technical design specifications.

All of these requirements flow from the original need for the product. Unfortunately, that is not the only source of requirements. Other requirements are imposed on us by regulatory needs, industry best practices, testing needs, and other sources. Nevertheless, the product-derived requirements are the core starting point.

The following are the types of product requirements that you will find on IT projects:

Functional requirements are defined by the source of the project need. Functional requirements are specifically what the product must do. These are taken from the business needs or the client's needs.

Performance requirements are also defined by the source of the project need. This is how fast, how safely, and how securely the product must perform. When you gather requirements, you have to be careful that the performance requirements do not contradict the functionality requirements.

Interface requirements come in two types: internal interface requirements and external interface requirements. Internal interfaces are how the different modules or pieces of the product interact with each other. External interfaces are how the product will fit into the environment for which it is designed.

Look-and-feel requirements are defined by the user. They describe how the user will interact with the product. This can be as simple as the graphical user interface (GUI) of a computer program or as complex as the pilot interface in a new passenger jet. The old name for these requirements was man/machine interface (MMI).

Operational requirements describe the operational aspects of the product when it is being used. They describe what the product will do and what the operators will do. In a satellite system, for example, careful trade-offs are made between what the satellites can do and what decisions need to be made by the ground operations crew. Operational requirements are often dictated by business rules that derive from how the company operates or from regulations that apply to the industry.

Verification requirements describe how the system will be tested. In computer circuits, test points may be designed in to allow calibration and testing of the completed circuit. In software applications, "hooks" may be inserted into the code that a tester can access to see the result of a test at different levels of the application.

Implementation requirements dictate how the final product will be implemented. If the product is a hardware product, implementation requirements can dictate how the hardware will be rolled out to the user. If it is a software product, implementation requirements can dictate how it will be installed into the final production environment.

Security, legal, and privacy requirements are a relatively new category of requirements. These are dictated partially by regulation and partially by the need to keep out viruses, Trojan horses, and spam from our systems. For example, in the medical field many new regulatory requirements have been dictated by the Health Insurance Privacy and Portability Act (HIPPA).

Finally, we have the generic category of requirements called **"ilities"**—reliability, maintainability, upgradeability, manufacturability, and so on. Figure 5-5 shows a breakdown of the types of requirements.

In Practice: Achmed the Engineer

While the 777 jet was being designed, almost as much work was put into designing and developing the maintenance program as was put into the jet itself. During this project, Boeing created a fictional maintenance engineer by the name of Achmed. Achmed was born in the Middle East, raised in China, currently lives in Africa, and does not speak English. The design requirement was to develop a maintenance system that Achmed could understand.

Properties of Requirements

Because the entire project depends on having a thorough understanding of what the product will be, that is, of the requirements, you want to take requirements very seriously. Individual requirements must be clearly written so that there is no misunderstanding of what the requirement says. The full set of requirements must be complete and thorough. There must be no missing requirements and no contradictions among the requirements.

Requirements are like fish—they swim alone but they also form schools. Individual requirements and sets of requirements each have criteria they must meet.

Figure 5-5. Requirements Breakdown

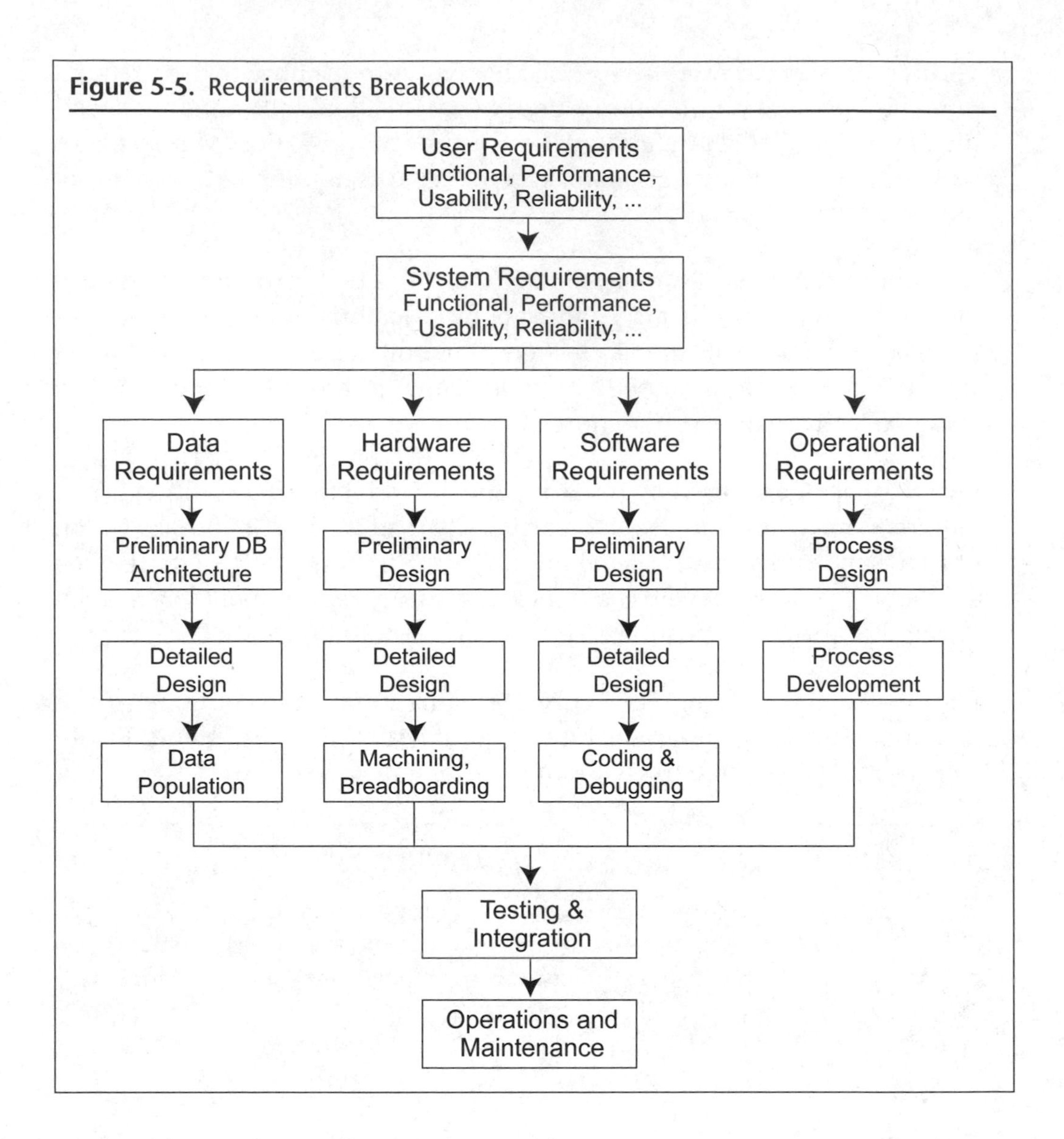

Individual Requirements

Individual requirements must satisfy the following set of criteria.

The requirement must be necessary. The stated requirement is an essential capability, physical characteristic, or quality factor of the product or process. If it is removed or deleted, a deficiency will exist that cannot be fulfilled by other capabilities of the product or process.

The requirement must be concisely stated. The requirement statement includes only one requirement stating what must be done, and only what must be done, simply and clearly. The old rule in aerospace contracting was that you only stated one requirement per paragraph and that every paragraph was numbered. This allowed you to develop requirements tracking systems.

The requirement must be free of any implementation bias. The requirement states what is required, not how the requirement should be met. A requirement statement should not reflect a design or implementation nor should it describe an operation. (The treatment of interface requirements is generally an exception.)

The requirement must be feasible. The stated requirement can be achieved by one or more developed system concepts at an affordable cost. Barry Boehm, one of the software field's leading management gurus, has been quoted as saying a requirement must be affordable, or it is not a true requirement.[3]

The requirement must be complete by itself. The stated requirement is complete and does not need further amplification.

The requirement must be consistent. The requirement neither contradicts other requirements nor is a duplicate of another requirement. The requirement makes sense within the context of the product.

The requirement must be unambiguous. Each requirement must have one and only one interpretation. The words used in the statement must not leave a doubt in the reader's mind as to what is meant.

The requirement must be verifiable. The requirement is stated in such a way that it can be verified or tested.

In general, requirements must be relevant, affordable, implementable, and apply specifically to the product under development. A requirement statement should never define the solution; it simply states the need. The solution comes from the analysis effort. If requirements are written using the *SMARTT Requirements* format, they will be clear, unambiguous, and understandable:

Specific:	No ambiguity, no fuzzy descriptions
Measurable:	Quantifiable to the extent possible

Agreed to:	By the stakeholder
Realistic:	Achievable within constraints
Traceable:	Full up and down traceability
Testable:	Be able to prove you met it

When you write requirements, you want to avoid using words that are vague or subject to interpretation (or argument). Words that should be avoided include: "flexible," "fault tolerant," "high fidelity," "adaptable," "rapid" or "fast," "adequate," "user friendly," "support," "maximize," and "minimize." (A sure sign that someone has been trained in consultant-speak is that he or she will string together combinations of these words to make the product sound fantastic.)

Sets of Requirements

Just as we said individual requirements had to meet criteria, the full set of requirements taken as a whole also has criteria it must meet.

Completeness. The set of requirements is complete and does not need further requirements. The requirements address all categories and cover all aspects of the product.

Consistency. The set of requirements does not include some requirements that contradict other requirements.

Sources of Requirements

So, where do we get these requirements? There are a number of sources for them. The top-level requirements often come from early project documentation, such as the project charter, the project scope statement, the statement of work (SOW), or a request for proposal (RFP) from a client. They can also come from business process analyses on existing processes, from the business rules, and most importantly, from the future users and other stakeholders.

Technical requirements can be derived by decomposing the top-level requirements and by doing simulations, running scenarios, or by using specific requirements-gathering techniques such as use cases.

PM in Action!

The Atlantic Systems Guild has developed an excellent process it calls Volere. Go to the Volere web site, www.volere.co.uk/index.htm, and download the shareware. Academic institutions and students are exempt from the shareware fee. Use this template to develop a set of requirements for a PDA for yourself.

Your most important source of requirements for most projects will be the project **stakeholders.** By definition, a stakeholder is any person or organization who:

- Is directly involved in the project
- Has oversight or some authority over the project
- Uses the project's end product
- Has work affected by the project

The *PMBOK® Guide* defines stakeholders as individuals or organizations actively involved in the project or those whose interests may be affected (positively or negatively) by project execution or project completion.[4] Stakeholders may also exert influence over the project and its results.

Most projects have more stakeholders than the project manager wants to think about. They always seem to be getting in the way and interfering with how the project is run. Yet, stakeholders are core to the project because it is their requirements that we are trying to satisfy. We speak about stakeholders as being only people, but from a system engineering perspective, stakeholders can also be an external system that interfaces with ours, an organization, a database, standards, bodies, and anything else that might impose requirements or constraints on our project.

Stakeholders come in multiple flavors and sizes. Examples include:

- End users who will actually interact with the product on a daily basis
- Power users who need advanced features in the product
- The people who have to maintain it (e.g., the help desk and infrastructure support)

- The boss and his or her peers
- Team members who will design and create the product
- The client who is paying for the product

Stakeholder Categories

In order to bring some sanity to this zoo of stakeholders, we can divide stakeholders into active stakeholders and passive stakeholders. An active stakeholder is someone who will interact with the product once it is deployed and operational. Passive stakeholders include groups such as procurement personnel, standards bodies, and everyone else who is not an active stakeholder.

We can also distinguish a product stakeholder from a project stakeholder. A product stakeholder is someone such as an end user or client who needs, uses, and interacts with the product the project is developing. A project stakeholder is someone who cares about how the project is managed. This category of stakeholders has little or no input to the requirements. We will discuss stakeholders in more detail in Chapter 9.

Everyone's input is important when you are gathering requirements. However, not everyone's input has equal weight. You must clarify the importance of stakeholders to the project and to the product while you are getting their input on requirements. This can be managed by setting up a priority process for categorizing requirements. Be able to identify which requirements are critical to the final product, which are less critical, and which are just "desirements" rather than design requirements.

> **NOTE**
> With due respect to George Orwell:
>
> *All stakeholders are equal. Some stakeholders are more equal than others.*

Once you've gathered your requirements, document them in a requirements document. This document forms the basis for developing the detailed specifications and the test plans. For each requirement, you want to identify where the requirement came from, what type of requirement it is, what test case will test it, and be able to track any change requests against it. If you use the rule mentioned earlier about only writing one requirement per paragraph and then numbering your paragraphs, you will have a built-in tracking system for your requirements.

Gathering Requirements

Asking users for requirements is like offering to give them an appendectomy. It is easier for them to write their needs down and assume you will design what is in their minds. Generally, they do not know how to express what they want in terms a designer can understand.

People are our best source of requirements for many projects, and there are a number of ways to gather the requirements—individual user interviews (you will get great requirements, but it is very time-consuming), group sessions (just avoid having one or two people dominate the requirements), joint application development (JAD) sessions, or e-mail surveys and questionnaires. If your project involves business processes, then you might start by doing business process analysis or examining the concept of operations (ConOps).

Interviews

Interviewing users, either in a group or individually, is tricky. If you ask users "What do you need," quite often they will not give you a requirement, but will state a solution:

- "I need a 25-inch monitor to display all my charts."
- "I need an Excel spreadsheet to calculate my total sales to date."
- "I need a convertible to go to work."

These are solutions, not requirements.

The group that will be doing the interviews should design the questions for requirements gathering carefully. It is important to understand the psychology of how people answer when you ask them a question. Open-ended questions, where people are free to express themselves, are likely to give you more information than closed-ended questions where you give them a limited choice of how to answer.

Examples of some questions are:

- What are your top needs for this product?
- What are the minimal things the product needs to do?
- If the product could provide more features, what would be most useful?
- If you use this product, how quickly should it respond to your inputs?
- How often do you think you would use this product?
- Would you like to be able to customize the product?
- Is the color of the product important to you?

When someone walks into a hardware store and says they want to buy a quarter-inch drill bit, what is the requirement? It is *not* to buy a quarter-inch drill bit for the sake of buying a drill bit. The need is for a quarter-inch hole. The drill bit is the solution. It is up to the questioner to ascertain the real need and not to settle for a description of a solution.

Here are some interviewing hints:

- Interview every type of user.
- Take them seriously.
- Document the interviews and have the interviewees review them.
- Quickly compile the interviews into requirements, and review the requirements again with the users.
- Make the users aware that the requirements will shape the system.
- Don't be judgmental about user requirements.

Joint Application Development Sessions (JAD)

A JAD is a facilitated meeting where all key business users participate in identifying the business requirements. At the beginning of the meeting, you will want to have a working document that contains the high-level requirements of the application to be developed. This is used as a guide to stimulate user participation and discussion throughout the session. A JAD session, when run well, can result in better discussion and synergy than individual meetings and is far more efficient.

Other Approaches

In her paper "What a Project Manager Really Needs to Know about Requirements" Rosemary Hossenlopp defines these additional methods of gathering requirements:[5]

Brainstorming: Generating ideas, approaches, issues, and gaining consensus on a reduction of ideas that are documented for further project action.

Survey: Administration of a written set of questions to the stakeholders to determine information on customers, work practices, and attitudes. Responses are analyzed for requirements, supplemental requirements, and stakeholder interests and positions. This can also include a review of customer-support user problems and product failure data.

Documentation review: Review of the existing system, business policy, and contractual documentation. This can include a review of project lessons learned.

Interface analysis: Review of system, people, and process linkages with the proposed business solution. System interfaces define system interactions, which systems provide input, which ones require output, and what medium is used.

Supplemental requirements analysis (non-functional requirements): Review of end-user business solutions quality expectations that constrain the development of the requirements.

The key to project success is making sure you are using the appropriate requirements gathering process for your project. The more complex the project, the more conversations the business analyst will need with your stakeholders to ensure understanding of their needs.

In Practice: ISO Guidelines

The following is an excerpt from ISO guidelines on the development, supply, and maintenance of software:

ISO-9000-3, Guidelines for the Application of ISO 9001 to the Development, Supply, and Maintenance of Software, Subpart 5.3.1: "In order to proceed with software development, the supplier should have a complete, unambiguous set of functional requirements. In addition, these requirements should include all aspects necessary to satisfy the purchaser's need. These may include, but are not limited to, the following: performance, safety, reliability, security, and privacy. These requirements should be stated precisely enough so as to allow validation during product acceptance."

Go to www.iso.org for more information.

CHAPTER SUMMARY

- A project charter is the document that officially recognizes that a project exists. It is issued by a manager outside the project. It gives the project manager the authority to apply organizational resources.
- The value of the project charter is that it is management's statement to the organization that management supports the project and the project manager.
- Every project should have a kickoff meeting to introduce the project to the team and the team members to each other. At the end of the meeting, the team members should understand the scope of the project, their role in the project, how the project relates to the company's strategy, the planning process, and the next steps.
- The scope statement is the planning link between the customer and the project manager. It is how the project manager knows that there is clear communication between the customer's needs, wants, and expectations and the end product that the project manager is helping to create. It helps the project manager organize the project management process and creates a context for the planning process.
- A requirement is a clear statement of a need, sufficiently detailed that there is no question about what is being asked. Many different kinds of requirements exist, such as functional, technical, performance, interface, look-and-feel, operational, verification, "ilities," implementation, security, legal, and privacy requirements.
- Requirements come from stakeholders. It is best to meet with the stakeholders in person and interview them to help define requirements. This can be done one-on-one or in a group meeting, such as a JAD session.

Key Terms

Stakeholder
Project scope statement
Project scope
Project boundaries
Functional requirements
Technical requirements
Look-and-feel requirements
Verification requirements
Project charter
Product scope
Project objectives
Requirement
Performance requirements
Interface requirements
Operational requirements
Implementation requirements

Key Term Quiz

1. ________________ define what the product must do.

2. ________________ define how fast, how safely, how securely, etc. the product must operate.

3. A ____________ is defined as individuals or organizations that are actively involved in the project, or whose interests may be positively or negatively affected as a result of project execution or project completion.

4. The ________________ is often considered the official start of the project. It is the document that authorizes the project and allows the project manager to apply organizational resources.

5. ____________________ define what is in scope for the project and what is out of scope.

6. ______________ are the specific measurable results that the organization is looking for the product to meet.

7. The ________________ defines only the end deliverable and its components.

8. The ________________ defines the work necessary to deliver the product scope.

9. The ____________________ helps define what is being developed, and starts to raise the questions necessary to accurately define what will and won't be included as part of the project.

Chapter Review Questions

1. Which document is used to officially recognize that a project exists?

2. What is the purpose of the kickoff meeting?

3. At the end of the kickoff meeting, the team should have a clear understanding of what?

4. List five items you might find in a project charter.

5. List five items you might find in a project scope statement.

6. Describe the difference between the project charter and the project scope statement.

7. Describe the difference in product scope and project scope.

8. What is the success rate of IT projects, based on survey results?

   a. 85%

   b. 50%

   c. 15%

   d. 67%

9. You are asking a client about an IT requirement, and the client responds by telling you that it needs 25-inch monitors to display all its charts. The client is giving you:

   a. A valid requirement that you need to document

   b. Their feeling about what they need

   c. A solution, not a requirement

   d. The brushoff

10. You are asking a client about an IT requirement, and the client responds by telling you that it needs 25-inch monitors to display all its charts. The true requirement is:
    a. The client wants to display all its charts
    b. A 25-inch monitor
    c. Unknown
    d. Irrelevant, since the solution has already been determined
11. The best source of requirements for an internal process improvement project will be:
    a. The CEO
    b. The project sponsor
    c. The people who will be affected by the process change
    d. All of the above
12. Which of the following is not part of the definition of SMARTT requirements?
    a. Specific
    b. Measurable
    c. Affordable
    d. Realistic
    e. Testable

END NOTES:

1. Ralph Young, *Effective Requirements Practices,* Pearson Education 2001.
2. Sheldon, F. et al., "Reliability Measurement from Theory to Practice," *IEEE Software,* July 1992
3. B. Boehm, W. Brown, L. Huang, D. Port, "The Schedule as Independent Variable Process for Acquisition of Software-Intensive Systems," INCOSE International Conference, Toulouse, France, June 2004.
4. Project Management Institute (PMI®), *A Guide to the Project Management Body of Knowledge (PMBOK® Guide),* 3d ed., page 376, Project Management Institute, Newtown Square, PA, 2004).
5. Rosemary Hossenlopp, "What a Project Manager Really Needs to Know About Requirements," PMI Global Congress Proceedings, Toronto, Canada, 2005.

6 Creating the Work Breakdown Structures and Project Schedule

After reading this chapter, you will be able to:

- Develop scope using a work breakdown structure (WBS).
- Define activities necessary to deliver project scope.
- Identify resources needed to deliver project scope.
- Establish the sequence of activities.
- Estimate activity durations.
- Estimate project costs.

In Chapter 5, we talked about using a project charter and a project scope statement to define the work of the project. In this chapter, we will start to bring more detail to the project scope by using a WBS to decompose the project scope into deliverables. The next steps are to turn those deliverables into activities, identify what resources will be needed to carry them out, define the sequence in which they occur, estimate their durations, and finally, estimate project costs.

Once the project charter is approved and the scope statement is created, the team needs to do more detailed planning so that everyone understands the size and complexity of the project. At this point in the project, the team is still working with rough estimates. These estimates will probably change as the project continues to be elaborated, as resources are confirmed or changed, and as risks are taken into consideration. That's why we will revisit and finalize our schedule and budget later in the book.

THE WORK BREAKDOWN STRUCTURE

Now that you have used a scope statement to clarify your project and product scope and you have defined your requirements (all of which is explained in Chapter 5), it's time to take the requirements and deliverables and break them down into manageable chunks of work. The tool used to do that is called a **work breakdown structure (WBS).** According to the *PMBOK® Guide,* a WBS is a deliverable-oriented hierarchical decomposition of the work to be executed by the project team.[1] Work not in the WBS is outside the scope of the project.

Organizing the Work Breakdown Structure

The WBS is one of the most important tools in planning and managing your product and project scope. It will help define activities for the schedule, assign resources, develop time and cost estimates, identify risks, and assess make-or-buy decisions for project components. Therefore, great care should be taken in organizing the WBS.

Some rules of thumb for the various levels are:

Level 1 is your project.

Level 2 is the way the project manager will organize and manage the project.

Level 3 contains the main components or deliverables of your project.

Level 4 breaks down the main components into constituent components or subdeliverables.

Often in IT project management, level 2 is represented by the project life cycles that we talked about in Chapter 3. Figure 6-1 shows an example of a WBS.

One of the questions many new project management practitioners have is, "How low do I go?" Unlike dancing the limbo, lower is not necessarily better. You should continue decomposing the work until the lowest level is broken into activities on the schedule. However, do not put activities on your WBS—it is for deliverables only!

Figure 6-1. Levels of a WBS

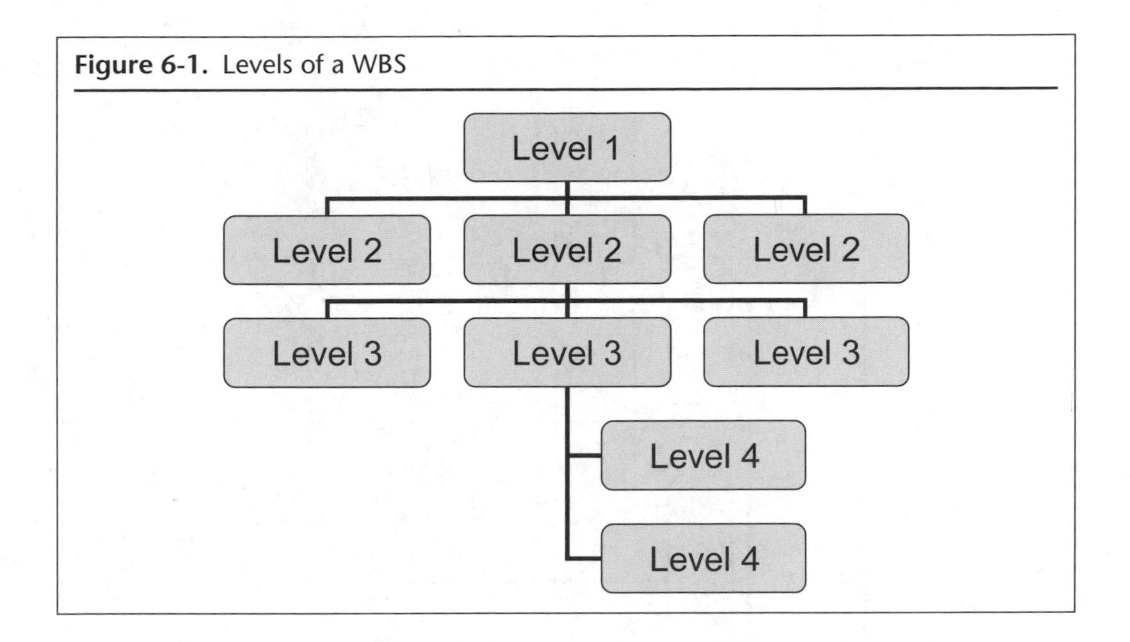

The lowest level of the WBS is a **work package.** A work package is a deliverable that can be measured, scheduled, budgeted, and has an accountable party assigned to it. After you have decomposed your WBS into work packages, the work packages are transferred onto the schedule for further decomposition into the activities necessary to produce the deliverables.

There is no right or wrong way to set up a WBS. Arrange the WBS however you like, unless your company has a relevant policy or you are working with a contract that dictates how you arrange it. The WBS is your tool for your project, and it should reflect the way you will manage the project.

Figures 6-2 and 6-3 are samples of a WBS for an application development project and a network implementation project, respectively.

> *** *NOTE***
>
> Some companies have WBS templates. The good news is templates make your job easier when you fill in the WBS. The bad news is that templates pretty much dictate the way you will organize and run your project.

Figure 6-2. Application Development WBS

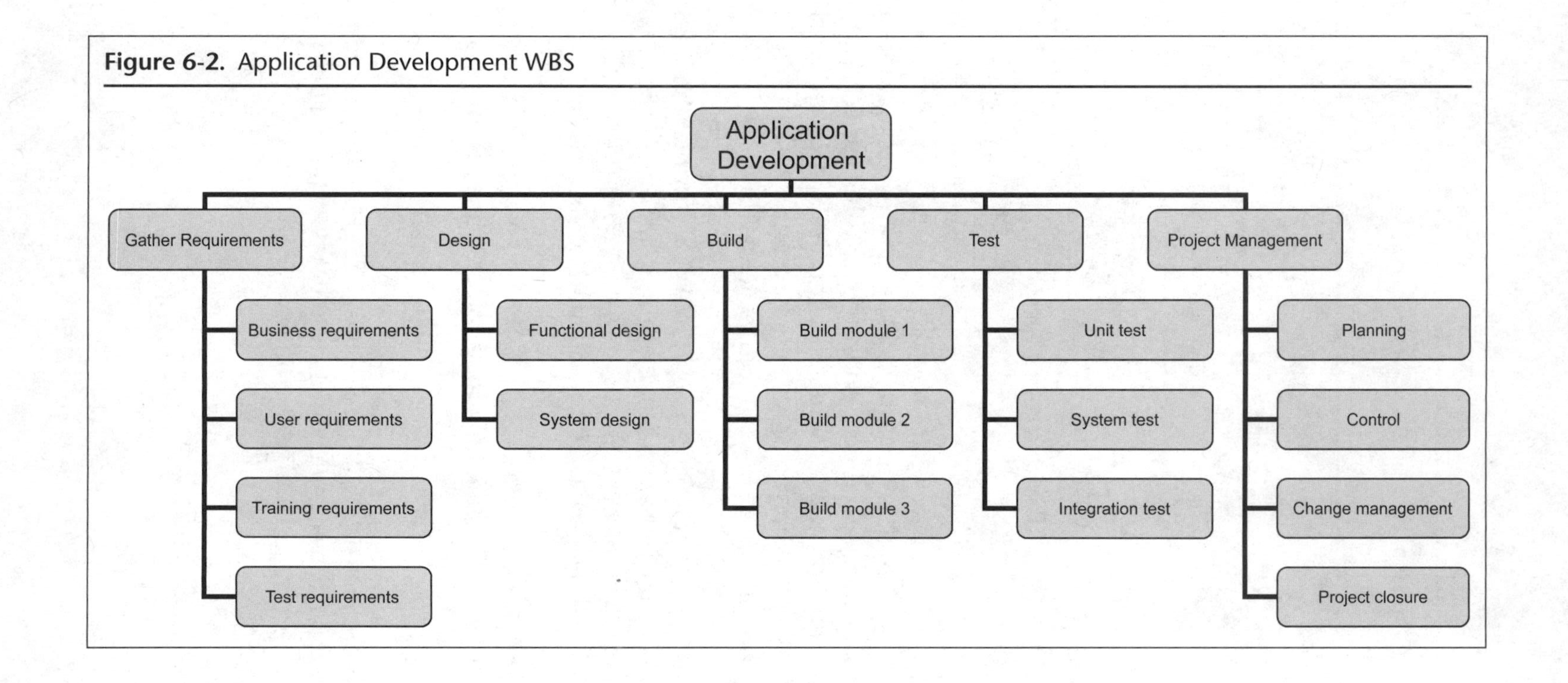

Figure 6-3. WBS for Establishing a Network

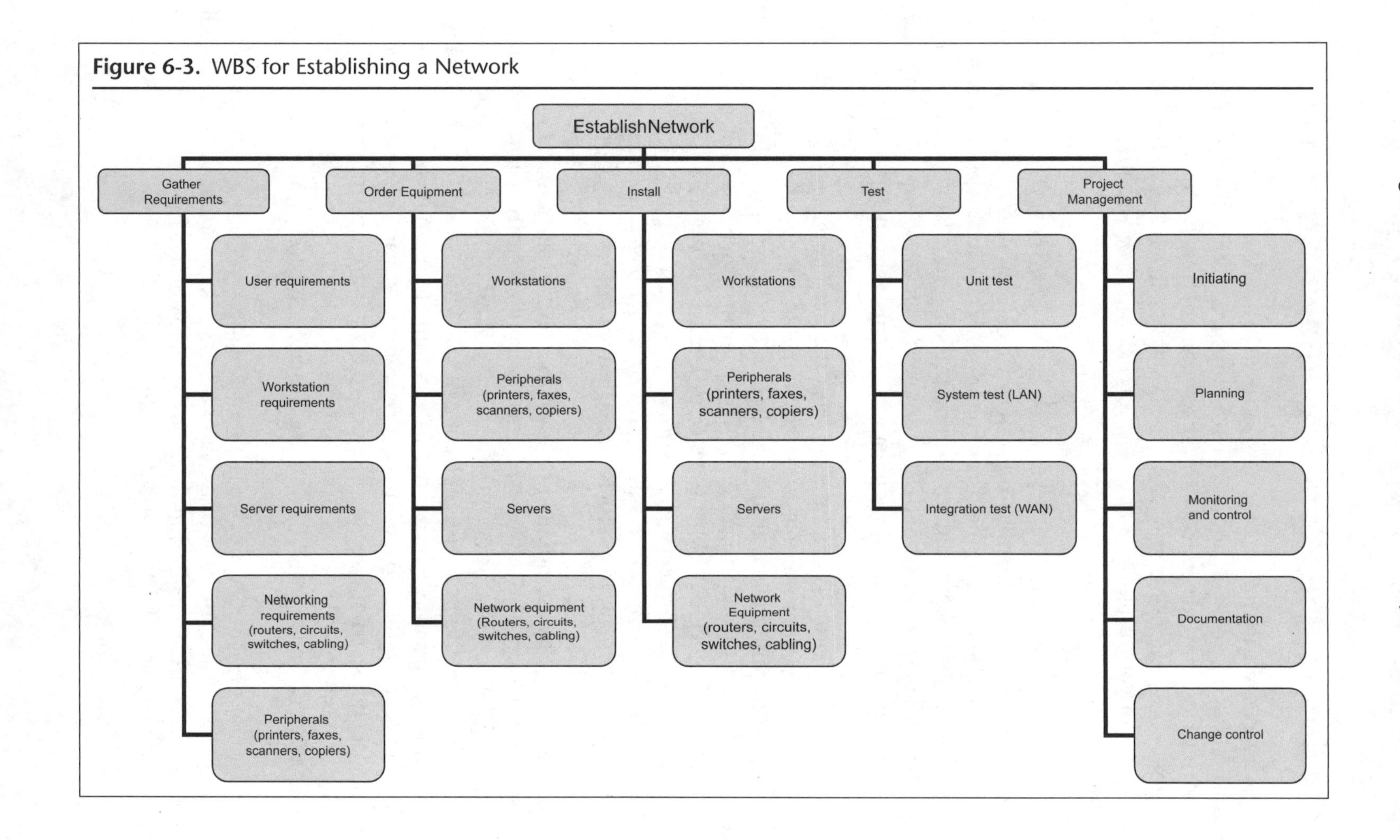

Developing the Work Breakdown Structure

One way to develop work breakdown structures is a process called **decomposition.** In decomposition, you start with the end product and decompose the work until you have discrete deliverables that can be scheduled, costed, and assigned to a responsible party. Think of a WBS as an organizational chart for the work on your project. Decomposition is a top-down approach to developing a WBS.

Another way of building a WBS is to start at the bottom and work up. Oddly enough, this is called a **bottom-up process.** It actually starts with the deliverable at the top, but then all the components and constituent pieces needed to get to the finished deliverable are brainstormed. Eventually, when all lower-level deliverables are identified, they are then logically grouped, and the upper-levels emerge based on whatever logic seems appropriate.

The bottom-up process can be used with the project team to help develop the WBS. It provides a good opportunity to get team member input, thereby ensuring that nothing is left out, and it can help in team building since the team is creating the WBS together. The bottom-up process is also good to use for a type of project that hasn't been done before. Let's face it: if you've done several networking projects, you're pretty clear on how you will manage the next one. However, if you are starting with a blank page, then brainstorming the components to build a WBS is a great way to define the scope.

Because most software application–development projects use a system development life cycle (SDLC) to organize and manage their projects, many times the WBS follows the development life cycle. In these cases, each phase of the life cycle is represented in level 2 of the WBS. Levels that are beneath level 2 break the phases down into the components and deliverables for each phase. This is considered a best practice in many organizations. However, if a life cycle doesn't make sense for your project, you may want to use geography, stakeholders, or major components as your level 2s. Figure 6-2 shows an application development WBS and is a generic sample.

One thing we learn very quickly in managing projects is that there is almost always more than one way to develop a WBS that will take us to our goal. What is most important is that the primary deliverables have been captured, not that they're put in any particular order.

Many people forget to account for project management in their WBS. You should always have a placeholder at level 2 for project management. Generically, you may fill in level 3 with the various project management processes, such as initiating, planning, controlling, and closing. Notice that executing was left off the list. This is because the rest of the WBS is the executing part. Another approach to putting project management into the WBS is to list the deliverables from project management, such as requirements document, project schedule, budget, risk plan, communication plan, and so on. The important thing is that project management is clearly represented in the WBS.

Work Breakdown Structure Display

We have shown you a couple WBS examples that are in the format of an organizational chart. This format provides a nice visual display of the work. However, it is not the only way to create a WBS. You can also use a simple outline format. The following outline is the same WBS as is shown in Figure 6-3, it is just presented differently.

1. Establish network
    a. Gather requirements
        i. User requirements
        ii. Workstation requirements
        iii. Server requirements
        iv. Networking requirements
            1. Routers
            2. Switches
            3. Circuits
            4. Cabling
        v. Peripherals
            1. Printers
            2. Faxes
            3. Scanners
            4. Copiers
    b. Order equipment
        i. Workstations
        ii. Servers
        iii. Network equipment
            1. Routers
            2. Switches
            3. Circuits
            4. Cabling

    iv. Peripherals
        1. Printers
        2. Faxes
        3. Scanners
        4. Copiers
c. Install equipment
    i. Workstations
    ii. Servers
    iii. Network equipment
        1. Routers
        2. Switches
        3. Circuits
        4. Cabling
    iv. Peripherals
        1. Printers
        2. Faxes
        3. Scanners
        4. Copiers
d. Test
    i. Unit Test
    ii. System test (LAN)
    iii. Integration test (WAN)
e. Project Management
    i. Initiating
    ii. Planning
    iii. Monitoring and control
    iv. Documentation
    v. Change control

This WBS could also be laid out with the following organization:

1. Establish Network
    a. Workstations
        i. Gather requirements
        ii. Order equipment
        iii. Install
        iv. Test
    b. Servers
        i. Gather requirements
        ii. Order equipment
        iii. Install
        iv. Test

c. Networking
   i. Gather requirements
   ii. Order equipment
   iii. Install
   iv. Test
d. Peripherals
   i. Gather requirements
   ii. Order equipment
   iii. Install
   iv. Test
e. Project Management
   i. Initiating
   ii. Planning
   iii. Monitoring and control
   iv. Documentation
   v. Change control

To summarize, the WBS is a deliverable oriented depiction of all the work in the project. You should set it up to reflect the way you will manage the project. Only go as low as you need to in order to assign resources, establish duration, and assign a responsible party.

> ***NOTE***
> Recent versions of MS Office Project and MS Visio have an interface that allows the user to import a WBS created in either of the programs into the other program.

> ***PM in Action!***
>
> Using the information from the MegaNews Case Study in Chapter 5, create a WBS with at least 25 elements.

Activity Definition

An activity is a component of work performed during the course of the project.[2] Activities are the backbone of the project schedule. We begin to define activities by taking work packages from the WBS and entering them into our project management software. For this book, we will assume that software is Microsoft Office Project (MS Project), although many other programs are available. For small projects, you can use MS Word, MS Excel, or even MS Visio.

Note that sometimes the word "task" is used instead of "activity," and "activity" is considered a grouping of tasks. The specific terminology used depends on the industry and your company's usual practices. For this book, we will use "activity" to describe the lowest level of effort.

For IT projects, the WBS is decomposed into a much more detailed list of activities. How detailed should that list be? That's one of those good questions that has no precise answer. It should be detailed enough to allow you to manage the project—no more detailed and certainly no less detailed. If a project manager is going to upgrade the OS for an office of 100 users, a WBS with 500 tasks in it is much too detailed. If a project manager is going to implement PeopleSoft (Oracle human resources and financial software) in an international organization with $10 billion in U.S. sales, a WBS with 500 activities is not nearly detailed enough to allow the project manager to manage the project.

Let's look at an example of how deliverables are decomposed into activities. Assume that our project is to upgrade 300 systems with the newest version of MS Project. The following assumptions are in place:

1. Three sites need to be upgraded and there are 25 remote users. The sites are Pine Grove with 150 users, Palm View with 75 users, and Whispering Springs with 50 users.

2. Pine Grove and Palm View can be upgraded via server as the users log on. However, Whispering Springs will need to have the application loaded manually onto each workstation. Remote users will need to get their laptops to one of the three sites for the upgrade.

3. The project includes four hours of total training: three hours of best practices for the software and one hour on the new functionality of the latest version.

4. The project, including training, must be complete by May 1.

5. Five IT staff members have to maintain help desk service levels and ensure the proper installation of the new software.

6. The training department has a senior and a junior staff member who are available halftime to develop and deliver the training and testing. Training will be held at all three sites. Each training suite can accommodate 15 users.

7. As remote users come in for training, their laptops can be upgraded.

8. Our criteria for success is that every user has the application installed, has gone through training, and has passed an online test on the new functionality within 30 days.

9. Subject matter experts (SMEs), identified by the sponsor, will work with the training department on developing content, testing, and mentoring those who do not pass the first time.

The first step is to develop a WBS for the project. Some activities, such as user training, need to be done for all sites. Some activities, such as communicating to users that the upgrade is coming so they can back up critical data, need to be done before the project starts.

A well-managed IT department will have an independent development and test environment that mirrors (to a great extent) the production system. This environment is used to test new software, upgrades, and patches to ensure the software will not conflict with existing software before rolling it out to the rest of the company.

For this project, we suggest the following WBS:

1. Install MS Office Project on 300 work stations
    - 1.1. Installation
        - 1.1.1. Pine Grove
        - 1.1.2. Palm View
        - 1.1.3. Whispering Springs
    - 1.2. Training
        - 1.2.1. Define user training requirements
        - 1.2.2. Develop training
        - 1.2.3. Develop proficiency testing
        - 1.2.4. Deliver training
        - 1.2.5. Remedial train and test
    - 1.3. Project Management
        - 1.3.1. Planning
        - 1.3.2. Executing and control
        - 1.3.3. Close out

After being entered into MS Project using the task and WBS columns, the information is displayed as shown in Figure 6-4.

Figure 6-4. MS Office Project Install WBS

ID	WBS	Task Name	Duration
1	**1**	**Install MS Office Project on 300 workstations**	**1 day?**
2	**1.1**	**Installation**	**1 day?**
3	1.1.1	Pine Grove	1 day?
4	1.1.2	Palm View	1 day?
5	1.1.3	Whispering Springs	1 day?
6	**1.2**	**Training**	**1 day?**
7	1.2.1	Define user training requirements	1 day?
8	1.2.2	Develop training	1 day?
9	1.2.3	Develop testing	1 day?
10	1.2.4	Deliver training	1 day?
11	1.2.5	Remedial train and test	1 day?
12	**1.3**	**Project management**	**1 day?**
13	1.3.1	Planning	1 day?
14	1.3.2	Communications	1 day?
15	1.3.3	Executing and Control	1 day?
16	1.3.4	Close out	1 day?

Now that we have a WBS, the next step is to define detailed activities for each of these areas. Let's work with the deliverables listed under training to start defining the activities necessary to provide the training.

PM in Action!

Using Microsoft Office Project, create the WBS as shown above for the project to install 300 upgrades. Then define the tasks you think are appropriate for the training section. You can enter the tasks in MS Office Project by highlighting a task on the WBS and inserting a new task from the toolbar, or by selecting *Insert* from the menu and then choosing new task, or simply by pressing the insert button on your keyboard. The inserted task will show up *above* the task you have highlighted. Use the bold green arrows on the toolbar to indent or outdent your activities as appropriate.

After you have defined your training activities per the PM in Action! section, your project schedule should look something like Figure 6-5.

Of course, your activities may be a bit different from what is shown in the figure. Each project manager thinks a little differently, but the output should be similar to the example shown.

Figure 6-5. Activity Definition for MS Office Project Installation

6	**1.2**	**Training**	**1 day?**
7	**1.2.1**	**Define user training requirements**	**1 day?**
8	1.2.1.1	Identify subject matter experts (SMEs) to interview	1 day?
9	1.2.1.2	Interview SMEs for content needs	1 day?
10	**1.2.2**	**Develop training**	**1 day?**
11	1.2.2.1	First draft of training content	1 day?
12	1.2.2.2	Validate content with users	1 day?
13	1.2.2.3	Finalize content	1 day?
14	1.2.2.4	Put content into workbooks	1 day?
15	1.2.2.5	Develop presentation	1 day?
16	**1.2.3**	**Develop testing**	**1 day?**
17	1.2.3.1	Create test questions	1 day?
18	1.2.3.2	Create test case scenarios	1 day?
19	1.2.3.3	Validate questions with SMEs	1 day?
20	1.2.3.4	Validate scenarios with SMEs	1 day?
21	1.2.3.5	Finalize test questions	1 day?
22	1.2.3.6	Finalize scenarios	1 day?
23	**1.2.4**	**Deliver training**	**1 day?**
24	1.2.4.1	Pine Grove	1 day?
25	1.2.4.2	Palm View	1 day?
26	1.2.4.3	Whispering Springs	1 day?
27	**1.2.5**	**Remedial train and test**	**1 day?**
28	1.2.5.1	Identify users who did not meet 80% on exam	1 day?
29	1.2.5.2	Establish mentoring session with SME on class	1 day?
20	1.2.5.3	Retest	1 day?

For most projects, the project manager (along with the team) defines the major components of the project and the team members define the activities needed to produce those components. Therefore, your job as a project manager is to facilitate the development of the WBS, then assign an accountable party for each work package. That accountable party will define the activities or tasks necessary to produce the deliverable. Once the accountable parties define the tasks, they send them to you to enter into the project schedule.

The next steps in the development of the project are to identify the resources necessary to complete the tasks and to put the tasks in the appropriate sequence. Let's look at resource planning first.

✓ TIP

MS Project, like all tools, will do exactly what you want, but understanding how the tool works will save you much frustration. MS Project has three types of task setups—fixed resource, fixed work, and fixed duration.

- A fixed-resource task (called fixed units) is a task in which the assigned resources are a fixed value, and any changes to the amount of work or to the task's duration do not affect the task's resource usage. This is the default setup for tasks within MS Project.
- A fixed-work task is a task in which the amount of work is fixed, and any changes to the task's duration or resources do not affect the amount of work.
- A fixed-duration task is a task in which the task duration is fixed, and any changes to the amount of work or the number of resources do not affect the duration. For example, a project kickoff meeting might be scheduled for one day, regardless of how many resources come to the meeting.

Rather than automatically using the fixed-resource default, use the following table to identify how you want your tasks set up.

Task Type	*If you change resources:*	*If you change duration:*	*If you change the amount of work:*
Fixed resources (units)	Duration is recalculated	Work is recalculated	Duration is recalculated
Fixed work	Duration is recalculated	Resources are recalculated	Duration is recalculated
Fixed duration	Work is recalculated	Work is recalculated	Resources are recalculated

RESOURCE PLANNING

Once activities are defined, the project team can determine the resources necessary to complete the activities. Resource planning is concerned with establishing all the resources necessary to complete the project scope: people, equipment, supplies, facilities, and money. It also establishes the grade and quantity of resources needed.

Defining Resources

Some projects require a senior-level system engineer with 10-plus years of experience. On others, an entry-level programmer will suffice. Some projects require state-of-the-art equipment. Others can make do with an off-the-shelf, bargain basement functionality. To define the types of resources needed, the project manager can ask the following types of questions:

- What equipment do I need and how much?
- What skills/experience/knowledge does each activity need?
- When do I need the resource? How long will I need it?
- Do I need any special permits, licenses, or certifications?
- Do I have the equipment/skills in-house, or will I have to outsource?
- Do I have the right type and location of facilities?
- Should I buy, lease, or rent?
- What other parts of the IT infrastructure do I need?
- What other parts of the organization need to be involved?

Like the information on activities, this information should come from the people who will be doing the work. The project manager collects this information, compiles it, and uses it to establish cost estimates. Cost estimates are a little further along in the book. First, let's look at just the people aspect of estimating resources.

To continue with our scenario about installing 300 upgrades to MS Project, the following assumptions have surfaced after speaking with the training department:

1. The senior trainer will ultimately be accountable for all training. She has decided to deliver the training at Pine Grove and use the junior trainer at the other locations.

2. The junior trainer will be responsible for interviewing the subject matter experts (SMEs) and developing the draft of the training.

3. The senior trainer will edit and sign off on the training.

4. The senior trainer will develop all testing materials.

5. The junior trainer will develop the presentation.

6. Any makeup and remedial work will be the responsibility of the senior trainer, who will identify candidates, and will be delivered by the junior trainer.

7. The project sponsor wants to be informed when the training and remedial training are complete.

Additionally, the IT manager confirmed that each site has a training suite with at least 15 machines, so no new hardware will have to be purchased for the training aspect of this project.

> ***PM in Action!***
>
> Using the seven additional assumptions we just listed, insert a column into your project schedule that lists resource names and enter the position accountable for each of the tasks identified for training new users on MS Project.

Project managers generally have a good idea who the highly skilled resources are and who to avoid having on the project. But having this information requires experience in the organization, and if you have been hired in as a contractor project manager or are new to the company, you won't know the personnel. Asking people who have more experience in the organization to recommend people for the project can help. Keep in mind that every project manager wants the best resources, so you will have to negotiate for them or even rearrange your project schedule around when they're available.

Some organizations maintain skill matrices that list resources by name and the skills required in the organization, and give each resource a rating—typically from zero to ten—showing how much experience that resource has in that skill.

Work through the PM in Action! exercise to see how resource estimates are established and integrated into a project schedule. After you have entered your resources, your project schedule should look like Figure 6-6.

Figure 6-6. Resource planning for MS Office Project Installation

ID	WBS	Task Name	Resource Names
6	**1.2**	**Training**	
7	**1.2.1**	**Define user training requirements**	
8	1.2.1.1	Identify subject matter experts (SMEs) to interview	Sponsor
9	1.2.1.2	Interview SMEs for content needs	Jr. Trainer
10	**1.2.2**	**Develop training**	
11	1.2.2.1	First draft of training content	Jr. Trainer
12	1.2.2.2	Validate content with SMEs	SMEs
13	1.2.2.3	Finalize content	Sr. Trainer
14	1.2.2.4	Put content into workbooks	Jr. Trainer
15	1.2.2.5	Develop presentation	Jr. Trainer
16	**1.2.3**	**Develop testing**	
17	1.2.3.1	Create test questions	Sr. Trainer
18	1.2.3.2	Create test case scenarios	Sr. Trainer
19	1.2.3.3	Validate questions with SMEs	Sr. Trainer
20	1.2.3.4	Validate scenarios with SMEs	Sr. Trainer
21	1.2.3.5	Finalize test questions	Sr. Trainer
22	1.2.3.6	Finalize scenarios	Sr. Trainer
23	**1.2.4**	**Deliver training**	
24	1.2.4.1	Pine Grove	Sr. Trainer
25	1.2.4.2	Palm View	Jr. Trainer
26	1.2.4.3	Whispering Springs	Jr. Trainer
27	**1.2.5**	**Remedial train and test**	
28	1.2.5.1	Identify users who did not meet 80% on exam and scenarios	Sr. Trainer
29	1.2.5.2	Establish mentoring session with SME on class content	Jr. Trainer
30	1.2.5.3	Retest	Jr. Trainer

Defining Roles and Responsibilities

Another aspect of planning your human resources is defining the roles and responsibilities of the various stakeholders. One of the tools that we use to clarify roles on a project is called a responsibility assignment matrix (RAM). A RAM can be developed at any level of the project to whatever amount of detail is needed. During the preliminary planning stages, a project manager might use a RAM at the deliverable level of the WBS.

Although it might seem like unnecessary work, creating a good RAM is a very helpful thing to do at this stage of the project. The RAM should include all the major activities on the project and determine the assignment for each primary stakeholder. When you publish a high-level RAM in the project charter, it serves as a strong communications tool to inform everyone of what is expected of them. It can be especially useful for clarifying potentially overlapping roles. For example, there should be a clear delineation of what the project manager does and what the business analyst does. The RAM can help clarify those roles.

In the training example, there is a deliverable of training materials. For this deliverable, the junior trainer is responsible for developing the materials with the participation and input of the SMEs. The senior trainer will sign off on the materials. To build a RAM, create a table with the deliverables down the left side, and the various resources across the top, as follows.

	Sr. Trainer	***Jr. Trainer***	***Sponsor***	***SMEs***
Define user training requirements				
Develop training				
Develop testing				
Deliver training				
Deliver remedial training				

Next, define the various types of roles and responsibilities you will have on your project. As a working definition, consider that a *role* is a job title or position and a *responsibility* is who does the work. Accountability belongs to the person who is ultimately responsible for the work being accomplished. For many projects, you can assume the following:

- One, and only one, person is accountable for each task.
- Separate from, or in addition to, the accountable party, several people may be responsible for getting the work done.
- Some people may need to be informed about the status or completion of the task.
- Some tasks require sign off or approval before they are considered complete.

We will use these assumptions for our project responsibility matrix. We can abbreviate the various roles and responsibilities so that:

A = accountable

R = responsible

I = informed

S = sign off

If you followed the assumptions, you should end up with a project RAM that looks like the following:

	Sr. Trainer	*Jr. Trainer*	*Sponsor*	*SMEs*
Define user training requirements		A		R
Develop training	S	A		
Develop testing	A			
Deliver training	A	R	I	
Deliver remedial training	A	R	I	R

PM in Action!

Using the information above, complete a RAM for the entire training section of the project to upgrade MS Project.

Activity Sequencing

The purpose of activity sequencing is to define the order in which you should do activities. The outcome of this is called a **network diagram.** The network diagram is a graphic display of the sequence of the project events. The WBS arranges tasks logically, while the network diagram arranges them sequentially. The sequencing of activities is based on the logical relationships. Logical relationships are called **dependencies** and describe the precedence among activities.

Types of Dependencies

Some activities are linked in a particular order based on the nature of the activities. For example, in software development the code must be written before it can be tested. Dependencies of this kind are referred to as **mandatory dependencies.**

Another type of dependency is called a **discretionary dependency.** Discretionary dependencies may be linked in a particular order because having the particular sequential link is considered a best practice. For example, it's preferable to completely test the program before developing training materials. If something doesn't work as planned and a component needs to be reworked, some of the training may need revision, creating unnecessary work and rework. However, in a time crunch, testing and developing training material sometimes overlap.

Another common cause of discretionary dependencies is having the same resource assigned to different tasks at the same time. By moving one of the tasks, the resource is no longer overallocated.

Still other tasks are linked based on external influences. For example, a customer who is external to the organization may need to sign off at a phase gate before additional work can continue. This is an example of an **external dependency.**

All of these dependencies affect the sequencing of activities.

Types of Relationships

Task sequencing is concerned with the types of dependencies, such as mandatory, discretionary, and external, and the types of precedence. In other words, what happens first, what happens at the same time, and what happens next?

Most project schedules start with all tasks set up based on one task finishing and then the next task starting. This is called a **finish-to-start** precedence. However, there are instances when it is better to set up tasks so that they finish at the same time or start at the same time. In our example, it would be best if the development of the test questions for the proficiency tests and the development of the test scenarios finished at the same time so that we could give them to the reviewers at the same time. This type of precedence is called a **finish-to-finish** precedence. Another type of precedence is a **start-to-start** precedence. We might start finalizing the test questions and start finalizing the scenarios at the same time—after we received the feedback from the SMEs, we could start both tasks simultaneously. Although many types of precedence relationships are possible, the one used most often is the simple finish-to-start relationship.

After the task dependencies have been established and the types of precedence are identified, the information is entered into the schedule to create the network logic. The schematic display of the logic is the network diagram for the project.

*

NOTE

Most project management software programs use the following abbreviations:

- Finish-to-start = FS. This is the default precedence, so you don't have to enter anything for an FS dependency.
- Start-to-start = SS.
- Finish-to-finish = FF.

PM in Action!

Return to your project schedule for the training example. Insert a column for predecessors. Enter the dependencies based on your best assumptions and the information provided above. Do not enter or change durations at this point—that will come next.

TIP

You can link (establish precedence) tasks in two ways:

- You can select the two tasks and click on the chain icon on the tool bar.
- You can key in the number of the task that is the predecessor task.

When you are entering in an SS or FF dependency, first type the number of the task it is dependent on and then enter SS or FF. Do not insert a space. For example, if task 8 has a finish-to-finish relationship with task 7, in the predecessor column for task 8, enter 7FF.

After you have finished the PM in Action! exercise, your project schedule should resemble Figure 6-7.

Figure 6-7. Activity Sequencing for MS Office Project Installation

ID	WBS	Task Name	Resource Names	Predecessors
6	**1.2**	**Training**		
7	**1.2.1**	**Define user training requirements**		
8	1.2.1.1	Identify subject matter experts (SMEs) to interview	Sponsor	
9	1.2.1.2	Interview SMEs for content needs	Jr. Trainer	8
10	**1.2.2**	**Develop training**		
11	1.2.2.1	First draft of training content	Jr. Trainer	9
12	1.2.2.2	Validate content with SMEs	SMEs	11
13	1.2.2.3	Finalize content	Sr. Trainer	12
14	1.2.2.4	Put content into workbooks	Jr. Trainer	13
15	1.2.2.5	Develop presentation	Jr. Trainer	13SS
16	**1.2.3**	**Develop testing**		
17	1.2.3.1	Create test questions	Sr. Trainer	13
18	1.2.3.2	Create test case scenarios	Sr. Trainer	17FF
19	1.2.3.3	Validate questions with SMEs	Sr. Trainer	18
20	1.2.3.4	Validate scenarios with SMEs	Sr. Trainer	18
21	1.2.3.5	Finalize test questions	Sr. Trainer	19
22	1.2.3.6	Finalize scenarios	Sr. Trainer	21SS
23	**1.2.4**	**Deliver training**		
24	1.2.4.1	Pine Grove	Sr. Trainer	22
25	1.2.4.2	Palm View	Jr. Trainer	22
26	1.2.4.3	Whispering Springs	Jr. Trainer	22
27	**1.2.5**	**Remedial train and test**		
28	1.2.5.1	Identify users who did not meet 80% on exam and scenarios	Sr. Trainer	24, 25, 26
29	1.2.5.2	Establish mentoring session with SME on class content	Jr. Trainer	28
30	1.2.5.3	Retest	Jr. Trainer	29

DURATION ESTIMATING

After the dependencies are entered, the project manager can start to plug in the durations to develop a preliminary schedule. It's a funny thing with estimates—duration or cost—that even when you say, "This is only a preliminary estimate, the final duration or cost will probably be different," the only thing that people hear is the number you give them. This doesn't mean that you shouldn't give estimates; it is just a warning so that you know that, at some point, someone will say, "But you said. . . ." This also doesn't mean that you should pad your estimates to be safe. Remember Parkinson's Law: "Work expands to fill the time allotted."

Effort and Duration

Duration estimates are best developed by the people who will be doing the work. They are the experts. They understand the complexity of the work, the other work they have to do as they are working on the project, and, hopefully, the other variables that can affect the duration of the work involved.

Generally, when developing a schedule, the duration estimate (the number of days or weeks it will take to finish the activity) is the number that the project manager is interested in. In other words, how long will it take to get the activity accomplished from start to finish? If more than one person is assigned to the activity, the duration will be affected by the number of resources at work on it. The project manager may also be interested in the amount of effort it will take to accomplish the work because adding more people to complete an activity with a fixed amount of effort shortens the duration.

Here's an example. You are on a project that requires the development of 1,000 lines of code. Assume it is fairly simple code. You estimate that your programmer can develop about 100 lines of code per eight-hour day. Therefore, the effort is 80 hours. This is two weeks in duration if you're allocating 40 hours per week for tasks. But let's say that you have two people working on this. It is still 80 hours worth of effort, but the duration is now only one week. On the other hand, what if it's one person, but he or she is only available 50 percent of the time? Then it is four weeks in duration (but still only 80 hours of effort).

When asking for an estimate, you need to be very specific about what you're asking for. Are you asking when an activity will be done? Are you asking how much labor it will take? The more precise you are in your request, the better information you will get. Of course, this assumes that you have a well-defined scope. If the scope is not well-defined, there is no chance that your estimates can be considered accurate.

Fred Brooks, in his book *The Mythical Man-Month,* talks about the concept of partitionable tasks.[3] A fully partitionable task is one that reduces in duration as more resources are put on it as long as the work does not require any communications among the workers. For example, think of painting a room.

A single painter can paint all four walls and the ceiling in 20 hours if he averages four hours per surface. However, if we put five painters in the room, each painting a surface, then we can finish the job in four hours.

The opposite type of task is a task that is non-partitionable. This task will take the same amount of time no matter how many people are working on it. For example, think of testing a software string. The test does not go any faster if we put more testers on it.

Complex tasks, such as most tasks in the IT world, are neither fully partitionable nor fully non-partitionable. Their duration can be reduced, but only to a point. After that point, adding more people does not make the duration lower but may in fact make the duration longer by increasing the communications needs. Think of coding a large and complex software module. One coder could do it, but it would take a long time. If four coders were put on it, the duration would be reduced. If six coders were working on the module, they would start getting in each other's way, writing over each other's code, and needing more time to communicate and coordinate. In this example, there is an optimum number of people who could be assigned to the task. The result is that there is an optimal size for the project team—too few and the work is not done as fast as it could be, too many and there is increased management complexity and communications. The optimal size is not a specific number. Rather, it is a range. As long as the number of people working on the project is within that range, there is probably the correct number of people on the project.

Types of Estimates

What should the project manager do if the scope is not well-defined? What type of estimate can he or she use to move forward? There are a couple of things to consider. The first is the accuracy of the estimate. The other is the estimate's level of certainty.

If the project scope is not well-defined, then the estimates will not be well-defined. In reality, even if the scope is well-defined the estimates may still not be well-defined. In this case, the project manager might give a best case, worst case, and most likely case estimate. This is called a **probabilistic estimate;** the project manager is estimating a duration based on probability. Here is how it works.

Sarah, our project manager, is given a charter to deploy an off-the-shelf software program that does asset management for computer networks. It will keep an inventory of hardware and also do a periodic scan of the software that is on each machine and the amount it is being used. After some preliminary investigation, Sarah determines that the software will need to interface with three other applications, and it will be rolled out to 500 machines. The sponsor asks Sarah for a preliminary estimate of how long the project will take.

At this point, she hasn't done a requirements document, a configuration plan, a deployment plan—nothing. Sarah decides to meet with the core team members to go into their collective intellectual archives and review documentation from similar projects. The team establishes that if all resources remain dedicated to this project, there are no problems, and the scope remains stable, the project could take as little as four months. However, if the software is not compatible with the current applications and the team needs to do significant modification, or if resources are taken off the project to work on other projects, or if there is scope creep, then the project will take up to eight months. However, given the team's collective experience on this type of project, the team members estimate that it will most likely take five-and-a-half months.

Depending on how accurate the estimate needs to be, Sarah can report that it will take five-and-a-half months, or she can develop a statistical estimate by taking an average of the best, worst, and most likely scenarios. This is called a **triangular estimate,** and it would look like this: (4m + 5.5m + 8m) / 3 = 5.83 months. Alternatively, she can weight the most likely estimate and come up with a beta distribution estimate that would look like this: (4m + 4(5.5m) + 8m) / 6 = 5.67 months. Research shows that either one of these estimates will give Sarah a more accurate project duration than a simple, one-number estimate.

For a very simple project, the effort of going through this type of calculation outweighs the benefit of the improved accuracy. For these projects, the project manager can take the most likely estimates and document the assumptions that led him or her to that estimate. If the project has any complexity or risk associated with it, the increased time to get the additional two numbers (best case and worst case durations) is well worthwhile.

Down the hall from Sarah, Walt has a very well-defined deliverable. He is estimating the time it will take for Steve, a staff technical writer, to develop the technical documentation on the asset management software that has been deployed. Steve is familiar with the environment, understands the scope of work, has done this type of work for many years, and has a strong technical background. In this case, Steve can provide a fairly certain estimate. He may say something to the effect of, "I can have it done in three weeks, give or take two days." Or he may say, "I am 90 percent certain that it can be completed in three weeks." This is called a **deterministic estimate;** the estimate can be determined with some high amount of certainty.

Methods of Developing Estimates

There are basically three ways to develop estimates—analogous estimating, parametric modeling, and bottom-up estimating. **Analogous estimating** compares the existing project to a similar project and then accounts for the dissimilarities. For instance, go back to our technical documentation estimate. Perhaps Steve looked at the scope of the work and said, "Oh, this is similar to the inventory control system that went into the accounting offices last year. The only difference is that the interfaces are different, and we are inventorying hardware and software instead of warehoused materials. That one took two weeks. This one should be a little more complex because of the additional interfaces and the technical nature of the application, so I should be able to do it with 50 percent more time." Steve drew an analogy to a similar project to come up with his estimate.

Another type of estimate is a **parametric estimate**. This type of estimate follows a mathematical equation. Referring back to the example of the 1,000 lines of code that was estimated at 100 lines per day, the estimator might refine the estimate by saying, if the requirements are complex, 70 lines of code per day; if the requirements are average, 100 lines per day; and if they are simple, then 120 lines per day. The equation could further be refined by estimating the skill levels of the team members. The estimate could reduced by 15 percent for skilled members, kept the same for an average worker, and increased by 20 percent for workers with less than six months experience. Parametric measurements are good only for things that are measurable and scalable.

A **bottom-up estimate** is the most accurate and the most time-consuming estimate to produce. This estimate demands that the scope be well-defined and that the WBS is complete and thorough. In this situation, the project manager is looking for an estimate activity-by-activity and person-by-person. This type of estimate is not appropriate in the beginning phases of a project, but once the full scope of the project is understood, this is the most accurate method of determining the duration of the project. In addition, the people who are developing the estimate (usually the team members) buy into the estimate rather than having to work on estimates developed by someone who is not familiar with the project.

Factors that Affect Estimates

The tricky thing about estimates is that so many factors influence them. In addition to the certainty level in the scope and the effort and duration factors, the project manager also needs to keep in mind that resources may not be available 100 percent of the time. This applies not just to team members, but also to resources like a testing environment that is only available during a certain window of time, or perhaps a training suite that is booked when the project manager wants it. These factors affect the duration of activities as well.

Other factors also need to be kept in mind. Not everyone works at the same speed or with the same level of accuracy. Estimates can be affected by the skill level, the experience level, the accuracy and quality of the work, and the familiarity of the work. This last item is sometimes referred to as the learning curve. The more familiarity someone has with the environment, the type of work, and the actual repetition of performing the work, the faster and better the outcome tends to be. A newly hired college graduate, no matter how skilled, cannot give estimates with the same level of accuracy as someone who has been in the company for several years, knows how things operate, and knows that it can take two weeks to get management sign-off on a document. The experienced person builds management sign-off into the estimates, but the inexperienced person does not.

What Do You Think?

1. If you are bidding on a fixed-price project for a customer, what type of estimate do you want to develop?
2. For what types of IT projects can you use parametric estimates?
3. In the concept phase of a project, what is the best type of estimate to develop?

Given all the variables that affect estimates, the types of estimates, and the accuracy needed for an estimate, it is important to document the basis of the estimates so that if a given resource is not available, the duration can be modified as appropriate. The assumption log is a good place to document the basis of the estimates. A task note in MS Project can also work.

Keep in mind these common sources of errors when developing estimates:

- Making overly optimistic assumptions of participants' skill levels
- Underestimating the impact of interruptions
- Not including wait times for approvals
- Underestimating travel time
- Assuming team members are willing to put in extra hours
- Discovering new tasks
- Not factoring in reduced productivity due to multitasking

COST ESTIMATING

We've discussed scope and schedule; now it is time to talk about cost. Developing the project budget is not a one-time effort. It is, as stated earlier, part of the progressive elaboration of the project. Early in the project, the project manager is often asked for a rough cost estimate, traditionally called a **rough order of magnitude (ROM)** estimate. This is a quick calculation with the intent to provide just enough information to allow an intelligent decision as to whether the project should be approved.

A ROM is supposed to be a quick and dirty estimate and can vary by 50 percent or more from the final cost number. Speed of estimating is more important than high accuracy. The ROM just needs to be accurate enough to allow decision-makers to decide if the project is justifiable from a cost standpoint. Remember, senior management has to weigh the benefits and costs of a project against other projects to make sure the organization is making the best use of limited resources. You may want to use an analogous form of estimating to get the ROM, or if it is hardware intensive, perhaps some kind of parametric estimate.

If the project is approved, there will be another cycle of cost and schedule estimating. Effort will go into developing numbers that are more accurate. These numbers will require more information to develop, such as some analysis of the high-level requirements, the architecture, and sizing estimates. The result should be accurate within plus or minus 15 to 20 percent.

Often a third round of estimating is done, resulting in cost numbers that are expected to be just a few percentage points from the actual costs. These numbers are often called a **definitive budget** or an **engineering budget.** This type of estimate is developed using bottom-up estimating. At this point, the project budget is baselined and the project manager manages to those budget numbers. In order to develop this high level of accuracy, the requirements analysis should be substantially completed so that a thorough understanding of the final product is available.

Before the project manager can even begin to provide cost numbers, he or she has to ask management exactly what number management is looking for: basic project costs or life cycle costs. The basic project costs include personnel costs, purchased items, special equipment costs, and maybe facilities costs. If management wants a life cycle cost, the project manager includes costs for ongoing maintenance, help desk support, and upgrade costs to the basic project costs. The difference between the two costs is significant, so project managers should understand which costs they are being asked to develop.

Developing a Rough Order of Magnitude Cost Estimate

To develop a ROM estimate, the project manager will need to estimate the costs of any purchased materials and equipment. This might include the costs of servers, storage, cabling, application software, operating systems, and desktop machines. If the project includes buying a large custom off-the-shelf (COTS) package such as SAP, the cost depends on the number of seats that are being purchased, i.e., on how many people will need to have access to the system. If the project calls for buying a major database such as IBM's DB2 or Oracle, the pricing can vary considerably depending on whether the organization is buying a license by the seat or by the number of CPUs.

In some organizations, the project manager will also need to estimate the expected labor costs. This could include internal staff as well as any leased or temporary staff. Frequently, salary or grade information is considered confidential, and the project manager will need to get average rates from the human resources department. In some organizations, project managers are not asked for the internal labor projections in the budgeting. To develop labor estimates, start by estimating the number of team members by skill set and the duration that they will be needed. Then multiply the total hours per job level by the average rate for that position.

Although developing a cost estimate for a new project may appear overwhelming at first, there are guidelines that can make it less daunting. For starters, do not try to guess at the cost of the entire project as a single cost. Break it down into project phases, and then break the phases down by group or department. This makes the effort much more manageable. The more detail, the more accurate the resulting numbers. The trade-off is the amount of time to develop the detail and the numbers. A ROM is supposed to be quick and very rough, so this estimate can be developed by defining the equipment and labor for phase and department.

For example, let's say Larry wants to develop a ROM for a project to install a new LAN into a recently expanded building. His CIO asks, "How much is the project going to cost? Just give me a rough figure until we decide whether we want to do it ourselves or outsource it."

Rather than guess at the cost for the entire project, Larry can break the costs down into more detail, as follows:

Hardware/software costs:

- Cost of desktops:
  - OS cost/desktop
  - Application suite/desktop
  - Machines and monitors
- Number of printers
- LAN costs:
  - Data storage units
  - Print servers
  - Application servers
  - Routers
  - Internet accesses
- Cabling costs

Labor:

- Cost/desktop
- Cost/cable drop
- Cost/server

This already sounds easier, doesn't it? However, Larry can make estimating accurately even simpler by using the above categories and estimating them by project phase. Figure 6-8 gives an example of a simple chart that can be used to develop a ROM estimate.

Figure 6-8. ROM Cost Estimate

Category	Requirements	Architecture	Detailed Design	Implementation	Testing
Cost of Desktops					
O/S cost each					
Application suite each					
Machines and monitors					
Printers					
LAN costs					
Data storage units					
Print servers					
Application servers					
Routers					
Internet access					
Cabling costs					
Labor					
Cost/desktop					
Cost/cable drop					
Cost/server					

Using a matrix like this, Larry can parcel out the work to the different groups involved and have them estimate their particular areas. This not only gives him faster responses, but it also spreads out the work. An alternative to doing it by project phase is to do it by department. The numbers will be slightly different, but either way the numbers will be within ROM accuracy limits.

What is needed to provide an estimate? The project manager, team members, and anyone else who might have insight into costs, such as a finance person. These resources can use information from previous projects, industry data on cost standards, or even external consultants.

Challenges of Accurate Costing within IT

Estimating costs is more challenging in IT than it is in some other project management fields. For one thing, the technology itself keeps changing. A program upgrade in 2007 is totally different from one that was done in 2003.

The technology used to test the upgrade will be different, the machines that are using the information will be different, and the software the upgrade interacts with will be different.

Another thing to keep in mind is variation in productivity between different IT departments. There is wide variation in the types of work that an IT project may entail—there may be some COTS integration, there may be some LAN development, and there is often some custom programming. If a software portion of the project is outsourced, there is a much stronger need for solid requirements definition and testing than if the work is done in-house. If the COTS being installed are mission critical, the need for thorough testing is much greater.

IT projects rarely rely on only one discipline. Usually, a mix of skills is needed for the different aspects of the project. Because many IT projects affect other parts of the enterprise, one skill set is often overlooked that is very valuable: the skill set that the business analyst (BA) brings to the table. The BA has a thorough understanding of the business processes and goals and can be invaluable in defining the business needs and priorities for the project.

There is one other aspect of IT costing, and that is the uncertainty of testing. Although testing is necessary to ensure things work the way they should in the final product, specific tests are hard to justify because it is difficult to predict exactly what problems the testing will capture. We will explore this topic in more detail in a later chapter.

CHAPTER SUMMARY

- A WBS is a hierarchical decomposition of the work to be executed by the project team to accomplish the project objectives and create the required deliverables. It is an instrumental piece in defining the scope of the project. A WBS is developed using decomposition. The WBS is decomposed into work packages. Work packages are transferred to the schedule for further decomposition into activities.
- Activities are defined by taking deliverables from the WBS and entering them into project management software in enough detail to allow the project manager to manage the project.

- Resource planning is concerned with establishing all the resources needed to complete the project scope. Resources include people, equipment, supplies, and facilities. Resource planning also establishes the grade and quantity of resources needed.
- An aspect of resource planning is defining the roles and responsibilities of the various stakeholders. One of the tools used to clarify roles on a project is a responsibility assignment matrix (RAM). A RAM can be developed at any level of the project, to whatever amount of detail is needed.
- The purpose of activity sequencing is to define the order in which activities should be accomplished.
- The dependencies among activities may be external, mandatory, or discretionary.
- Activities may be sequenced as finish-to-start, finish-to-finish, or start-to-start.
- Generally, when developing a schedule, the project manager is interested in the duration estimate. Sometimes the duration is affected by the number of resources working on the task. The project manager may also be interested in the effort it will take to accomplish the task.
- Probabilistic estimates are used if the estimates lacks certainty. If scope is certain, a deterministic estimate can be generated.
- Estimates can be developed in three ways: analogous estimating, parametric modeling, and bottom-up estimating. Analogous estimating compares the existing project to a similar project and then accounts for the dissimilarities. Parametric models are developed using a mathematical, or quantitative, method. A bottom-up estimate is the most accurate and the most time-consuming estimate to produce.
- Early in the project, the project manager is often asked for a rough cost estimate, traditionally called a ROM estimate. This is a quick calculation with the intent to provide just enough information to allow an intelligent decision as to whether the project should be approved.
- Estimating costs is more challenging in IT than it is in some other project management fields. Factors that affect IT estimating include the nature of the changing technology, the variation in productivity among IT departments, the fact that IT projects rarely have only one discipline that is required, and the uncertainty of testing.

Key Terms

Work breakdown structure (WBS)

Work package

Decomposition

Network diagram

Responsibility Assignment Matrix (RAM)

Mandatory dependency

Discretionary dependency

External dependency

Finish-to-start

Finish-to-finish

Start-to-start

Traingular estimate

Probabilistic estimate

Deterministic estimate

Analogous estimate

Parametric estimate

Bottom-up estimate

Rough order of magnitude

Definitive budget

Engineering budget

Key Term Quiz

1. A ______ is a hierarchical decomposition of the work to be executed by the project team to accomplish the project objectives and create the required deliverables.

2. The type of estimate with the widest range of outcomes is a __________ ____________ estimate.

3. A(n)________________ estimate is used when developing an estimate by comparing the work to be done to a similar project.

4. If task A must finish before task B can finish, this is an example of a _____ ______________ precedence.

5. A(n) ________________ is one that comes from outside the project or performing organization.

6. ______________ are used because they are considered a preferred way of performing the work.

7. To define who is accountable for a deliverable, who is responsible for doing the work, and who should be informed, you would use a ________ ______________

8. A ______________ estimate can be used if the scope is well-known and the estimator has experience performing the type of work being estimated.

9. A(n) ______________ estimate is used to provide a detailed assessment of the work to be done.

10. __________________ are based on the nature of the work.

Chapter Review Questions

1. True or False: There is a right way to build a WBS.

2. What are the two ways to build a WBS?

3. True or False: In IT projects, level 2 of a WBS is often the system development life cycle.

4. What type of precedence would you use to describe the relationship between finishing placing all the computers and then laying the cable?

5. What type of precedence would you use to describe the relationship between finishing programming before finishing documenting the software?

6. List the accuracy of estimates from the most specific to the least specific.

7. What are the benefits of a rough order of magnitude estimate?

8. What are the benefits of a bottom-up estimate?

9. Which type of estimate has to be scalable?

10. What tool would you use to make sure that everyone knows their accountability on the project?

11. What is the difference between mandatory and discretionary dependencies?

12. The city has to sign off on the wiring before you can close up the walls and begin painting. This is an example of what type of dependency?

13. If you are not certain of the duration of a particular task, and you want to give a range of possibilities from best case to worst case, what type of estimate would you give?

14. You have a best case duration scenario of four weeks, a worst case duration of eight weeks, and a most likely duration of five weeks. What is the duration based on a triangular average? What is the beta distribution?

15. The purpose of performing a ROM is to:

    a. Decide whether to do the project in-house or outsource.

    b. Let the managers know which of their people will be involved in the project.

    c. Give the decision-makers enough information to decide if the project should be approved.

    d. Inform the organization that we're going to do this project.

END NOTES:

1. Project Management Institute (PMI®), *A Guide to the Project Management Body of Knowledge (PMBOK® Guide),* 3d ed., page 112, Project Management Institute, Newtown Square, PA, 2004.
2. Project Management Institute (PMI®), *A Guide to the Project Management Body of Knowledge (PMBOK® Guide),* 3d ed., page 350, Project Management Institute, Newtown Square, PA, 2004.
3. Frederick P. Brooks., *The Mythical Man-Month: Essays on Software Engineering,* 20th Anniversary Edition, New York, Addison-Wesley, 1995.

7 Developing the Project Team

After reading this chapter, you will be able to:

- Define the roles of the project manager, project sponsor, team members, and functional managers.
- List the skills, abilities, and traits of effective project managers.
- Discuss project teams, team building, and techniques for leading project teams.
- Discuss some of the difficulties in managing virtual teams.
- Define common areas of conflict on projects and explain different methods of resolving project conflicts.

In order for projects to successful, everyone must know their role and their specific responsibility for the project. In the last chapter, we talked about a responsibility assignment matrix (RAM) that could be used to define the accountabilities and responsibilities for a specific project. In this chapter, we speak in more general terms. We examine the skills and traits of effective project managers, what a sponsor should do to support a project, what, in general, team members are responsible for, the role that the functional manager plays in projects, and also examine other key roles.

The Project Manager

No book on project management would be complete without talking about the project manager. What makes a good project manager? What makes a *great* project manager? How do you know if you have what it takes to be great? This section looks at the skills, abilities, and traits that influence project management competency.

Managers, by definition, get work done through other people. They do not do it themselves. This is a critical distinction and is sometimes lost in IT, where so many project managers have risen to become managers as a result of doing a good job as technical people. The management role is very different from the technical role, and the project manager must clearly understand this.

Project management has two aspects: management and leadership. We are going to look at skills, abilities, and traits in the context of management and leadership. In other words, what are the necessary management skills, abilities, and traits? What are the necessary leadership skills, abilities, and traits?

Project Manager Skills and Abilities

The distinction between a skill and an ability can be fuzzy. We have combined the concepts, as the subtle distinctions are not necessary for this book. In this section we present the skills and abilities necessary to manage and lead projects.

Project Management

The skills and abilities necessary to manage a project successfully include:

Proficiency with project management methods: To successfully manage a project, a person should have an understanding of the basic project management processes, such as planning, executing, and controlling. If the organization has project management policies or methodologies, using them is considered a skill as well.

Proficiency with project management tools: Although they are similar to project management methods, project management tools are specific items such as a RAM, a WBS, a schedule, and other instruments that the organization or the individual can use to organize and provide structure to the project. Although software tools are not necessary for simple projects, they can significantly reduce the amount of effort required to manage projects.

Technical skills: These are industry skills. For instance, in IT they could be software development, networking, systems, or engineering skills.

Business skills: Business skills include budgeting, developing presentations and reports, monitoring performance, and other general business duties that the project manager needs to be competent at in order to function effectively in an organization.

Communications skills: It has been said that 90 percent of a project manager's job is communication. Effective communication skills are probably the most critical of all skills. For project management, we are focused particularly on verbal and written, formal and informal communication.

In the technology sector, many complex problems have to be solved. These problems need to be explained to various audiences, including senior management, team members, and (sometimes) outside consultants. Effective project managers have the ability to describe complex information in ways that different audiences can grasp and understand.

Synthesis and analysis: Synthesis and analysis are thinking skills. A project manager must be able to synthesize information—collecting disparate information and arranging it into a meaningful whole. A project manager must be able to see patterns in information and derive meaning from distinct pieces of data. Analysis is the skill of breaking a whole into component parts, much like decomposing work into a WBS.

Balancing stakeholder expectations: This entails balancing the various needs of the customer, end user, sponsor, team members, and other stakeholders. Most often, the needs and desires of these stakeholders are not aligned. It takes a skillful project manager to keep all stakeholders satisfied. We list this under skills and abilities, but we could just as easily call it an art!

Balancing priorities: Sometimes balancing priorities feels more like juggling plates. There is always the need to balance the project constraints of scope, schedule, and budget. However, there is also the need to balance priorities among multiple stakeholders, multiple projects, and day-to-day operations.

Holistic thinking: People who think holistically look at the whole project, its fit with other projects, its fit in the organization, and its fit in the marketplace. They take into account the whole picture, not just a piece of the project. This is sometimes called *systems thinking*.

Negotiation skills: Negotiation skills give you the ability to obtain the resources and priorities you need when other projects or functional managers want the same resources. Being able to obtain critical items for your project and give up non-critical items is highly useful in a dynamic environment.

Project Leadership

In addition to managing the many components of a project, great project managers have the ability to lead their project teams to successful project completion. The following are some leadership skills.

Leadership ability: Leadership is that quality in a person that makes people want to follow him or her. It is a combination of having a vision for the project, communicating it in a compelling fashion, establishing rapport with the team members, and encouraging each individual to support the team. So much has been written about leadership that going into detail here would be futile, so we'll just say that we think it is a very important ability for project managers to have.

Team skills: To be successful we need to understand how to work in a team environment. Some people are more comfortable working on their own, and they have to learn to work well in a group environment.

People skills: This refers to working with people one-on-one. It includes giving and receiving positive and negative feedback as well as setting expectations. It indicates that a project manager can work with people in a constructive manner. In many projects, there are conflicts—disagreements about the right technical solution—or personality conflicts. Being able to resolve these situations can be critical to keeping the team motivated and involved.

Team building skills: Team building is the act of taking the people in a newly formed group and assisting them in developing trust, communication, and an effective working relationship.

Team motivation skills: Being able to motivate a team to work (sometimes under less than optimal circumstances, and sometimes on less than thrilling projects) is an ability that distinguishes very good project managers from merely competent project managers. In today's IT environment, many project managers must be able to motivate team members who work in other parts of the world.

Being able to balance the style to the situation: Good project managers know when they need to be adamant about meeting deadlines and requirements and when they can back off. They understand that in some circumstances they should take the lead and in some circumstances they should allow the team to come up with its own solutions. It generally takes many years to have the confidence to know which style should be used in various situations.

Cross-cultural communication skills: On any given day, an IT project manager may speak with team members, managers, senior management, consultants, peers, or superiors—and sometimes all of them at once. To be effective, the project manager must be able to speak the language of the audience he or she is talking to. A programmer thinks and speaks differently than a chief financial officer. The project manager must be able to speak about the business and system requirements to the programmer and about the cash flow projections and cost variances to the chief financial officer. It goes without saying that cross-cultural communication skills apply when speaking to team members from different countries and backgrounds as well.

Project Manager Traits

A trait is a feature of a person's character. It is an enduring aspect of a person. Generally, a person either has a particular trait or doesn't have it.

It's important to distinguish between traits and skills because if people don't have a particular trait, they are usually uncomfortable adapting the behavior associated with that trait. Traits can be developed, but developing or changing a trait usually takes a long time. Skills, on the other hand, are easier to develop.

Project Management

The management traits that we most often see in effective project managers are:

A willingness to address tough issues head-on: The worst thing a project manager can do is be aware of a potential problem or risk and hope that it will go away if it's ignored. Effective project managers address potential problems and risks head-on—and in a levelheaded fashion.

Being a problem solver: We have all known people who see the glass as half empty. They can always find a reason why something will not work. One of the traits good project managers have is that they are problem solvers. They are always looking for ways to make things work.

Being able to say no!: One of the most difficult things to learn in project management is when and how to say no. Saying no comes in very handy when avoiding scope creep. However, there are ways to say no that don't create problems, such as, "We would be happy to add that to the project. I will get back to you with the additional time, money, and resources needed. Then we can put this through the change control board for approval." That will usually take care of most of the "good ideas" people have for your project.

Being able to delegate: One of the most common problems we see with new project managers who come up through the IT ranks is that they still try and do things themselves, especially when they think they can do them better. Do not do this. Your job is to manage results, not to create them!

Project Leadership

Project leadership traits of project managers include:

Being supportive: Sometimes being supportive means being encouraging to someone. However, being supportive can also mean letting a person know that the result was not exactly what you were hoping for, but that you know he or she can improve the work to get it where it needs to be.

Being a risk taker: Project managers tend to be calculated risk takers. Projects are by their nature risky, because they have not been done before. A project manager has to be comfortable with a certain number of unknowns and a certain amount of risk.

Being assertive: Project managers are assertive. You will not find many wallflowers in the group!

Being confident: Confidence is a key factor. Sometimes it is only the confidence and assuredness of the project manager that lets the team members find a way to overcome an obstacle.

Being optimistic: Have a strong belief that your project will be successful. Since most projects go through hard times during their development, believing that your project will be successful helps sustain you and the team members.

Being facilitative: In order to be effective, a project manager needs all the expertise of his or her team. Project managers cannot come up with solutions and approaches on their own. They facilitate discussions and meetings to get the knowledge and options out on the table. They facilitate the conversation so that it moves forward to find a solution to the situation.

Being flexible/adaptable: In projects, one thing is for certain: Things will change. Project managers need to know when to let go of one approach and be flexible in selecting alternative approaches. As the project environment changes, they need to be able to adapt to the new requirements, team members, customer requests, and all the other day-to-day changes that happen on a project.

Being open-minded: Often, a team member will have solutions and ideas that are completely different from those of the project manager. A wise project manager will listen to different, new, or innovative ideas and consider them with an open mind.

Being slow to panic: To lead a team effectively, the project manager MUST remain calm, especially in a crisis. The team members, and even management, sometimes take their cues from the project manager. Although other people are losing their cool, the project manager needs to remain calm and steady. The project manager has to be the rational voice in the midst of upset. This sets the tone for others to settle down and focus on the situation at hand rather than escalate into a doom and gloom scenario.

Figure 7-1 shows a list of project management and project leadership skills, abilities, and traits.

Figure 7-1. Project Management and Leadership Skills, Abilities, and Traits

Skills and Abilities	Traits
Project Management	
Project management methods	Address tough issues head on
Project management tools	Problem solver
Technical skills	Say no!
Business skills	Delegate, don't do!
Synthesis and analysis	
Balancing stakeholder expectations	
Balancing priorities	
Holistic thinking	
Explain complex things in simple terms	
Project Leadership	
Leadership	Being supportive
Team skills	Risk taker
People skills	Assertive
Team building	Confident
Team motivation	Facilitative
Balance style to the situation	Flexible, adaptable
Communication	Open minded
Cross-culture communication	Don't panic

PM in Action!

Go on the web and look up "project management competency." Read a few of the articles and see what the common themes are.

OTHER PROJECT ROLES

The project manager is central to the project, but other individuals play key roles as well, including the project sponsor, the business analyst, team members, and functional managers.

The Project Sponsor

The **sponsor** is usually the project manager's link to the executive offices. On larger projects, a project sponsor will be someone at a corporate level with a title such as chief technology officer, vice president of information services, or chief operating officer. For smaller projects, the sponsor may be a manager, a functional manager who is looking for IT to assist in making his or her job easier, or an IT operations manager. Regardless of the size of the project or the sponsor's title, the sponsor's role is to provide executive oversight and support to the project.

During the initiation process, the project sponsor is usually actively involved in developing the business case for the project. This may take the form of presenting the information to a project selection committee, providing a business justification for the project, or developing a compelling reason to initiate a project. Developing the business case frequently requires performing a return-on-investment (ROI) analysis or a cost/benefit analysis. The project is then compared to all other projects being reviewed by the project selection committee with regard to its financial benefits and to its inherent risks. As we pointed out in the last chapter, at this time any cost numbers are likely to be a rough order of magnitude estimates and will be refined during the initial project planning process.

What Do You Think?

1. What traits that aren't listed on the previous pages do you think are important in order to be an effective project manager?
2. What are some skills that aren't listed that you think are important in order to be an effective project manager?

After the project is approved, the sponsor will generally meet with the assigned project manager and outline the objectives for the project, provide a high-level overview, and review any documentation that has been gathered to date. The sponsor may work with the project manager in developing the project charter, or he or she may sign off on a charter that is completed by the project manager.

During the planning process, the sponsor will provide strategic direction for the project manager. The sponsor will approve the scope and schedule baselines and assist in securing the appropriate resources. Resources may include people, money, or equipment. Generally, the sponsor is accountable for the project investment, especially large investments, so he or she is quite likely to be involved in developing the budget for large-scale projects.

During the project execution processes, the sponsor will monitor the project environment and keep the project manager apprised of changes to project prioritization, funding, resource allocation, and changes to other organizational factors outside the project manager's control. If there is uncertainty or conflict in the organization regarding the project, the sponsor is the buffer for the project manager and protects him or her from the conflict. The sponsor will also meet with the project manager on a regular basis to assess the project progress. A sponsor may provide strategic insight into situations that arise and assist in making decisions that are outside the project manager's scope of authority. Additionally, if there are conflicts that the project manager is unable to resolve because of political or other reasons, the sponsor steps in to assist in conflict resolution.

In controlling the project, the sponsor approves major changes to the product or project scope as well as the schedule, requirements, and budget. Major risks are also reviewed and monitored at the sponsor level. The project sponsor should be one of the voting members of the project's change control board (CCB) that reviews and approves changes to the project.

At the close of the project, the sponsor will review the completed product and sign off on its correctness and completeness. In some organizations, a sponsor will have input into the project manager's annual appraisal as well.

In Practice: Burning the Midnight Oil

A good project sponsor can do wonders in maintaining project team morale. One example occurred on a short-term, high-intensity project that consisted of responding to a large and complex request for proposal (RFP). The project duration was three weeks and the team consisted of 20 team members and 4 writers. For most of the project the team and the writers were working 18-hour days. Most of the writing work was done between 6:00 at night and 2:00 in the morning. One of the key factors that kept the team going strong, in spite of the grueling hours, was the level of sponsor involvement.

The sponsor, James, was key in identifying the critical points that needed to be made in the proposal. He managed most of the senior-level participation, ensuring that it was consistent with the strategic objectives for the proposal. He also kept upper-level conflict and uncertainty out of the head and hands of the project manager so she could focus on managing the rest of the team and the tight deadlines. Because this was a critical piece of business for the organization, James was able to marshal any needed resources, whether they were equipment, temporary help, food, or additional subject matter experts.

Many nights James would come by at 7:00 or 8:00 to check on progress and buy the writing team dinner. He was usually the last to sign off at night, frequently sending updates at 1:00 and 2:00 in the morning. The final day he was with the writing team from early morning until he signed off on the proposal when it went to the post office.

The results were very positive. In fact, the proposal was the best that had ever been produced by the organization. As part of the lessons learned, the process for responding to large RFPs was benchmarked off of this example. And most importantly, the proposal won the business!

The Business Analyst

For projects internal to the business, the business analyst (BA) can play a vital role in the success of the project. The primary function of the BA is to understand the business—the priorities, the business processes, and the business needs. The BA forms a major part of the interface between the business and the project. At the beginning of the project, the BA takes a lead role in identifying business requirements and identifying how the business will be affected by the project. Once the project is baselined, the BA can serve on the CCB and help identify impacts to the business resulting from changes to the project. Towards the end of the project, the BA gets involved in testing and integration to ensure that what is being delivered to the business by the project will actually meet the business requirements.

Team Members

Team members are the muscle in the project team. Having great team members makes managing a project an enjoyable experience. However, having the wrong type of team member, or team members without the right skills, can make managing a project little better than having an ingrown toenail. So, what makes a good team member?

Obviously, the person has to have the proper skills and experience to complete the assigned tasks. Ideally, the person should also have experience working on project teams, so that he or she understands the inherent time conflicts between operations and projects.

Another important attribute is being a team player. This means being supportive of other team members. It means contributing ideas to solve project issues and being open to suggestions to improve an approach to an issue. Sometimes the most brilliant technical people do not play well with others. Although they may be able to perform the tasks competently, they can be a detriment to the team. Personally, we would rather have someone with average skills who works well on a team than a technically brilliant person with no people skills.

Good team members have a global perspective. In other words, they look for what is best for the project and the organization, not just their piece of the project. They are solution oriented, not problem focused.

In working with the project manager, a good team member communicates proactively. He or she comes to the project manager before an issue becomes a problem. If he or she is going to have trouble meeting a deadline, it's communicated beforehand.

In Practice: Outstanding Employees

In an article published in *Harvard Business Review* in July/August 1993, Janet Caplan and Robert Kelly studied the highly skilled workforce within Bell Labs. What they found was that a set of nine qualities distinguished the outstanding employees from average employees. Those qualities are:

1. Taking initiative—doing work above and beyond your specific job requirements
2. Networking—maintaining an active network of other team members who can help you and who you help when they need it
3. Self-management—regulating your own time commitments and working on the high priority items first
4. Teamwork effectiveness—being able to work as a strong team member
5. Leadership—taking charge of an effort when you are the best person to do so
6. Followership—being a strong follower when someone else is leading
7. Keeping perspective—keeping your work effort in its proper perspective and not letting it take over your life
8. Communications skills—being able to communicate effectively verbally, in writing, and in giving presentations
9. Organizational savvy—understanding the organization you work in, how it operates, and how to navigate among the competing interests

Functional Managers

Although functional managers are not usually on a project team, they are stakeholders and they can affect a project positively or negatively. The primary role of the functional manager is to provide resources (team members) for the project. For project planning purposes, a team member may be responsible for a specific deliverable (the what), but the approach to create that deliverable is not defined (the how). The team member will often consult with the functional manager to develop the best approach for the deliverable. Func-

What Do You Think?

As a project manager, would you rather have a highly competent team member with less-than-stellar communication skills or a person with average technical abilities but good communication skills?

tional managers may be involved in developing the estimates for durations and costs for the deliverables as well.

During project execution, team members will often consult with their functional managers to gain assistance in resolving a technical issue. Additionally, the functional managers may identify risks associated with the technical approach, any resource constraints, and integration with other functions.

Often, functional managers find themselves in the unenviable position of having too few resources on too many projects. Their job is to balance their limited resources between the demands of business operations and project needs. They do this by allocating resources based on project prioritization. If projects are not officially prioritized, then allocation is usually based on who is yelling the loudest.

Project Teams

Working with a group of individuals on a project is not the same as working with a team. For some short-term projects, working with a group of individuals is appropriate. The requirements, time, and criticality of the project may not require a tight, cohesive team, and the time necessary to build such a team may not be time well spent. However, on long-term or critical projects, spending the time to build the synergy that a strong team exhibits will definitely benefit the project.

> ***What Do You Think?***
>
> As a project manager, how would you handle a situation where a functional manager, without telling you, pulled resources away from a project when something that was higher priority for the functional manager arose?

For our discussion about teams, we discuss the team development life cycle, followed by a brief conversation about team building tools, then look into the characteristics of teams and techniques for leading teams. We conclude by talking about some of the challenges involved with managing virtual teams.

Team Development Life Cycle

Teams go through a development life cycle. Sometimes the stages are obvious and other times they are subtle. The classic description of a team life cycle is the forming, storming, norming, and performing model developed by Bruce Tuckman in 1965.[1] Tuckman's model explains that as the team develops maturity and ability, relationships become established among the team members and the leader changes leadership style. The leader starts with a directing style, then moves to coaching, then participating, and then finally uses a delegating style.

Forming—Stage 1

In the first stage, there is a high dependence on the project manager for guidance and direction. The project manager must be prepared to answer many questions about the team's purpose, objectives, and external relationships. Individual roles and responsibilities are unclear. The forming stage is usually seen in the initiation and early planning stages of the project life cycle. The project kickoff meeting and the project charter are two tools that the project manager can use to address many of the concerns in the forming stage. A directing style is most effective in this stage.

Storming—Stage 2

As the objectives, scope, and requirements are progressively elaborated, team members may vie for position as they attempt to establish themselves in relation to other team members and to the project manager. It is usual for the project manager to receive challenges from team members. Cliques and factions may form, and power struggles may occur. Decisions do not come easily within the group at this point. The project manager should focus the team on its goals to avoid becoming distracted by relationships and emotional issues. Some compromises may be required to enable progress. Storming is usually worked through in the planning phase of the project life cycle. Many team building seminars and articles have been written about how to get through this stage as quickly as possible. Coaching is the best form of leadership here.

WARNING

Even though the storming phase can be uncomfortable and a bit trying, it is an important stage to go through. The project manager who tries to bury conflicts will find them erupting later at less opportune times. The wise project manager allows the conflicts to bubble up in the beginning so they can be worked through completely.

Norming—Stage 3

By the time the team has moved into the execution stage of the project, it is generally in the norming stage of team development. Agreement and consensus have formed among the team. Roles and responsibilities are clear and accepted. Big decisions are made by group agreement. Smaller decisions may be delegated to individuals or small teams within the group. Commitment and unity are strong. The team may even engage in fun and social activities. The team discusses and develops its processes and working style. There is general respect for the leader, and the team shares some of the leadership. The project manager must create an environment where all team members feel free to contribute and ensure that the team is not dominated by a small group. The project manager facilitates and enables the team to perform but does not need to engage in a directive or even coaching style very often.

Performing—Stage 4

At this point, the team has a high amount of autonomy with little participation from the project manager. The team makes most of the decisions, using criteria agreed upon with the leader. Disagreements occur, but now they are resolved positively within the team. Necessary changes to processes and structure are made by the team. The team is able to work towards achieving the goal and to attend to relationship styles and process issues along the way. Team members look after each other. Team members might ask for assistance from the leader with personal and interpersonal development. The project manager delegates and oversees the project progress but rarely needs to intervene. On a short-term project, a team may not attain the performing stage. It usually takes a while for the team to become more strategically aware and have a shared vision.

Project teams that have worked together before can move more quickly through these four stages. Sometimes they fall right into a performing mode. Other times teams will become stuck in one of the development stages for a lengthy period. Knowing the indicators of each phase of the life cycle will help you understand team behaviors and how best to work with the team in each stage.

Team-Building Tools

Team building for IT projects is different from normal team building because many IT projects are short-term. However, some team building can be done even for short-term and temporary teams. Here are some simple ways to help people feel like they're part of a team instead of just one person in a group of individuals:

- At the kickoff meeting, discuss the team's objectives, roles, processes, and resources.
- Schedule some joint coffee break times to get to know one another more informally.
- Establish learning lunches on topics relevant to the project. Have various team members share their expertise and knowledge.
- At team meetings, acknowledge team members for recent successes.

Of course, for a long-term project of a year or more, more extensive team building may be appropriate and should be planned and budgeted for. A quick search on the web will return plenty of information on consulting groups that can assist in team-building activities. When selecting team-building activities of a more formal type, you should look for activities that have the following outcomes:

- The team is clear about goals and establishes targets.
- Team members' roles are defined.
- A high level of interdependence exists among team members.
- A relaxed climate for communication exists.
- Team members develop a mutual trust.
- The team and individuals are prepared to take risks.
- Team members know how to examine team and individual errors without personal attacks.
- The team has the capacity to create new ideas.
- Each team member knows he or she can influence the team agenda.

The enemies of team building are:

- The need to be right
- The need to look good in front of others
- The need to be perfect

- The need to protect our egos
- The need to judge
- Group think

In most cases, because of the nature of project teams, it is productive to train people on the skills and traits they need to be effective team members. The next section looks at some characteristics of effective teams.

Team Characteristics

Obviously, groups and teams share some characteristics, such as having multiple people from various disciplines working towards an agreed-upon result. However, the atmosphere of a team is quite different from that of a group. A team operates in a supportive environment, an environment that supports getting the job done and building and maintaining the relationships on the team. Some of the aspects of effective teams include good communication, trust, participation, shared leadership and accountability, and a focus on the team itself.

Communication

Team members engage in honest, open communication without being critical or judgmental. For instance, if the team needs to resolve a situation, the team members may engage in discussions with many suggestions, comments, and even disagreements. However, the intention is grounded in maintaining a problem-solving and helpful demeanor, not in criticism and ego-based judgments. As such, differences in opinions are resolved openly and conflicts are not considered negative. In fact, some conflict is considered favorable, because conflict creates the opportunity to see things differently and to come up with well-rounded, effective solutions.

Strong teams have members who listen to one another. Each person's opinion is valued and no one holds back from contributing. Each person knows that he or she will be listened to with respect.

Trust

Team members develop a high sense of trust in one another. Team members can speak freely and openly, and there are no hidden agendas or repercussions for voicing opinions. Trust also allows team members to give and receive positive and negative feedback that is based on being helpful and improving the team's performance.

Participation

Effective teams have balanced participation by all members. That is not to say that everyone contributes to the same extent. Extroverts will still participate more than introverts. However, we do tend to see more of a balance in participation. Team members participate in discussions as well as decision-making and even share team leadership.

Shared Leadership and Accountability

In many team environments, the leadership role is shared and changes depending on the situation and the position of the project in the project life cycle. Team members are comfortable in both a leading and a following position. For example, if an issue requires technical understanding, the leadership role may fall to the person with the greatest understanding of the situation. The issue is not who is in control. Rather, it's how the team can make the best decisions and get the job accomplished.

Teams share accountability and responsibility for the result. Team members use roles and responsibilities to get the job done, but they are also accountable for the whole. If one area of the team is not performing, the team addresses the problem rather than backing away with an "it's not my job" mentality.

Reflection on the Team Process

Many teams actually take time from the project to consider their team process. They ask questions such as "How are we operating as a team?" "What can we do better?" and "Is the process working?"

Teams tend to have a higher level of morale than groups. In addition, there is more creativity and risk-taking in a team. When things do not go as planned with a creative solution or a risk, it's treated as a learning situation rather than an opportunity for punishment. As such, teams also tend to see greater productivity and better results.

Team Leadership

What can a project manager do to be an effective team leader? Several techniques and tools can be used, some of which have to do with attitude and some of which have to do with behavior.

Leadership Attitude

Good leaders have several traits in common. They approach situations with a positive attitude. When confronted with a problem or issue, they look at it as a problem-solving opportunity. Good leaders include the team in the problem-solving process. Rather than come up with a solution themselves, they facilitate the team process for developing a solution. Where possible, team leaders look for a consensus resolution rather than a majority resolution. In team meetings, they are nonjudgmental and accepting of alternative points of view. Good team leaders are motivational and empowering. They help team members find ways to resolve issues and empower them to make decisions and develop new skills. Most of all, the team leader trusts the team and the team process to develop a good approach to the project.

> ***What Do You Think?***
>
> Think about teams you have been a member of. What characteristics distinguish a well-functioning team from a mediocre team?

Leadership Behavior

Leadership behavior is exhibited right from the start of a project. Leaders take the time upfront to establish the vision and goals for the project. They make sure that everyone understands his or her role on the project. They allow time for questions and clarification, as well as time for discussion about possible approaches for the project. They tend to ask questions and spend their time listening rather than being directive and coming up with their own solutions. As such, they are also comfortable sharing the leadership as appropriate. Team leaders also assess the team process throughout the project and vary their leadership style based on the current needs of the project and the project team members.

Leadership Tasks

How can project managers demonstrate leadership? They can ask for input into the meeting agenda. Then they can start each meeting with clear objectives and manage the timeline and the agenda to make sure everything is accomplished that need to be accomplished. This often includes managing conversations to make sure that they are productive and on track. They keep the team from getting sidetracked and bogged down in negativity or too much detail.

What Do You Think?

Think about people you have worked with. Not everyone in a leadership position is a leader, and leaders can appear at lower levels of the organization. What are the characteristics that made someone a leader even if he or she wasn't in a formal leadership position?

Team leaders initiate conversations, articulate the situation, summarize information, and encourage balanced participation by team participants. They synthesize information, seeking to find common ground, and assist the team in finding a consensual solution. This may involve managing conflict as it arises to make sure that the conflict is productive and not destructive. They address tension that arises and find a way to restore harmony to the team. They also observe the process and seek feedback about the leadership and the team performance.

Obviously, leaders also demonstrate good management skills, such as tracking progress against the stated vision and project objectives. They address progress discrepancies, reward good results, and facilitate the team in developing strategies to get back on track.

In Practice: Project Leadership

Don, a senior manager, had recently been hired to turn a major internal IT project around. The project was a complete replacement of a multi-terabyte database that the company used to sell consumer information to credit granters. When Don was brought on board, the company had already tried twice to replace the database and failed both times after spending many millions of dollars. These past failures were evident in the team's motivation. Not only was the database technology new, but there were millions of lines of new code that had to be written to access the data and to present it in a deliverable form after passing through several thousand business rules.

Don's first move was to create a project to manage the effort of the 150-plus developers and testers over the three-year development effort. As part of his $50 million budget, he allocated money for personnel development and motivational awards. Because of the technical challenges of the work, Don realized that a major part of his effort would be to keep the team unified and motivated. Each of the team leads had their own budgets for awards.

Every week there was a small ceremony for the best performers on each team. Even though much of his time was spent with the company's executives ensuring they were completely informed on progress, Don himself personally attended each of the ceremonies and handed out the awards, making certain that each person knew how important his or her individual contribution was. Don's personal interest in each team and in each team member kept the project on schedule and the team was able to successfully deliver on time.

Team Charter

Developing a **team charter** is a nice way to kickoff a project with a little team building. Sometimes coming up with a team mission, name, logo, or motto is a fun way to instill a little camaraderie. The charter is created by the team members to address how they will work together. At a minimum, it should address rules of the road for communications, conflict management, time management, and, if appropriate, team member roles at meetings. A good time to write a team charter is during the project kickoff meeting. Time should be allowed in the agenda for the team to write a team charter for the project.

Communications covers two aspects: interpersonal communications and methodology. The interpersonal aspect deals with how team members treat each other. It establishes certain ground rules, such as treating each other with respect, allowing each person to contribute an opinion without judgment, not allowing one team member to dominate a conversation, making sure everyone is heard, and guidelines on how to call foul if someone breaks these rules.

The other aspect of communication talks about how team members can reach each other. Some people respond to e-mails faster than voicemails. Others want all communication on their cell phone, as they may be traveling and have limited access to e-mail. Some people want you to stop by their office, and others do not like interruptions.

Conflict management is covered in the team charter by the team agreeing to some type of conflict resolution process. This process can be as simple as having a vote, with the project manager having the tiebreaking vote, or a having a vote where each member gets two minutes to voice an opinion beforehand. There may be different processes for different situations, such as in an emergency or in a situation where a subject matter expert should have more influence over decisions than other team members. Whatever the situation, having a system in place before you need it can save a lot of time and bad feelings.

Time management can address guidelines for overtime if needed. For instance, if the team needs to meet during off-hours, the time management part of the team charter will determine whether it is easier to meet before work, during lunch, or after work. It can also establish timeliness thresholds for responses, such as 24 hours for routine business, 4 hours for urgent, and immediately for emergencies. Establishing these standards upfront can make for smoother communications throughout the project.

Team member roles, in this context, does not refer to the responsibility or functional roles of the members. This is more about how the team members take responsibility for the team meetings. Have you ever been in a meeting where one person went on and on, and the goal of the meeting was never accomplished? How about a meeting that got sidetracked on a digression? Or a meeting where someone kept bringing up issues that had already been resolved? These are some of the reasons for inefficient meetings. One way to get around this is to assign meeting responsibilities. Some of the roles can be:

Timekeeper—This person watches the time and makes sure that everything on the agenda is covered by giving time updates and warnings, such as "We have covered three out of our seven agenda items, and we are halfway through our time. We need to move on."

Documentarian—Frequently the project manager is too busy running the meeting to be able to take notes efficiently. The documentarian takes down notes and action items and then forwards them to the project manager to compile after the meeting.

Process police—This person ensures that the processes for time management, conflict resolution, and communication management are being followed. The process police makes sure the team is following the team charter. Making sure that the meeting stays on track is generally the project manager's job, but this person can assist.

Because IT projects rarely have time for team building or team development, taking the 20 to 30 minutes to develop a team charter is a nice way to insert a little team building into the process.

Below is a sample team charter. It can be modified to meet the needs of individual teams.

Team name:	
Team members:	
Team mission	A mission statement for the team that includes the project, but also speaks to how the team will fulfill the project.
Interpersonal communication	Discusses how to keep communication effective by setting out guidelines for respect, time limits, and sharing the floor.
Communication methodology	Addresses how the team members will communicate with each other, which tools they will use, the frequency of communication, and how to address urgent situations.
Conflict management	Defines the process for resolving conflict. May address different styles for different situations.
Time management	Identifies how overtime will be used and the timeliness of communications based on the urgency of the situation.
Team roles:	
Timekeeper	Manages the time at meetings to make sure all items on the agenda are covered.
Documentarian	Takes notes, records action items, and keeps a record of what happens at meetings.
Process police	Ensures that the team is following the agreed-upon process.

Managing Virtual Teams

Having a full-time dedicated team working on a project is not the reality of project management life today for most IT projects. Most IT projects have either a core group of developers who work on daily operations as well as on multiple projects or collections of teams spread around the country or around the world. Teams spread around the country or world rely on technology, which is why we call them **virtual teams.**

> ***What Do You Think?***
>
> Can you recall a time when having a team charter would have made a project easier?

Managing these virtual teams is one of the most difficult management problems that project managers face today. Virtual teams may be composed of full-time or part-time employees. They may be all employees or they may be a mix of employees and contractors. The only thing they have in common is that the team is geographically disadvantaged, to put it politely.

Types of virtual teams include networked teams, parallel teams, product development teams, production teams, service teams, management teams, action teams, and engineering teams. Staffing a virtual team requires specific skill sets for both the project managers and for the team members themselves. New capabilities are required to work successfully within this environment.

Virtual teams offer tremendous opportunities and equally tremendous frustrations. Although many U.S.-based companies are doing development in other countries, some are pulling work back into the U.S. because of the problems they encountered and large unexpected costs. Some companies, such as Nortel, have a reputation for managing geographically diverse teams successfully. Other companies try it and run into such severe problems they cancel the project and vow "never again."

These new teams require a very different set of management skills. The most difficult issues to deal with are in the areas of communications and motivation. Communicating with team members who are 6,000 miles away, speak a different language, have a different culture, and have different concepts of schedule deadlines and priorities is highly challenging. Motivating people whose motivations may be very different from the motivations of the people who surround you is equally challenging. Also, overcoming the lack of trust inherent in virtual teams is one of the biggest issues cited in the literature.

Successfully managing a project that uses a virtual team requires hiring the people who can work within this challenging environment, using the right technology tools to enable close and constant communications, building the processes for communications and coordination, building the trust required to work effectively across large geographic separations, and developing the right motivational approaches for each part of the team.

Project Conflict

We have mentioned that well-functioning teams handle conflict well. They discuss it openly and use it as an opportunity for learning and growth. But where does conflict come from? What types of conflicts are we talking about? How can the project manager ensure that the method of managing conflict is productive? For the balance of this chapter, we will identify common causes of conflict on projects and look at different ways to resolve conflict based on various scenarios.

Common Causes of Project Conflict

As with so many things in project management, project conflict comes back to scope, schedule, and resources—and balancing the priorities among them. As well, many IT professionals are highly educated and have strong opinions. Conflicts over design approaches are common in IT project management.

Scope

Scope-related conflicts can be over what is included and what is excluded, as well as over requirements and technical approaches.

During the initiation and planning process, we may see conflicts arise over the business requirements for the project. This is especially true if we are looking at a system solution as opposed to a project that has only one customer. In cases of multiple customers, there may be conflict around such things as operations believing that the main objective is to have processes as automated as possible, while sales wants to be able to customize as much as possible. Meanwhile, finance is looking to reduce the number of steps in the process. These business requirements translate into very different system requirements, and the project team needs to be able to identify the conflicts and work with the various stakeholders to come to some kind of consensus on the relative importance of each objective.

After the business requirements are nailed down, we might see conflicts on the best approach for the product solution and for the project. One person may want to build a new application that can interface with the existing system and another may want to purchase add-on functionality and customize it.

Throughout the project, stakeholders will want to add or change requirements or functionality. This causes conflict on what is in scope and what is out of scope. A tight change management process can assist in resolving this type of conflict, but it will not be the solution to every situation.

Resources

Resource conflicts center on people, equipment, and budgets. Most frequently, we see people who are overcommitted on too many projects. In these cases, they do not deliver their best work or meet deadlines. Other areas of conflict can occur among project managers as they vie for the same valuable resource. We often see this if there is only one person in the organization who understands how a particular system or area functions. This is indicative of a bigger problem in the organization, as this resource is a bottleneck everywhere.

Sometimes there are conflicts about equipment or locations. For example, if various teams need a testing environment and there is only so much space to go around, or if there is a need for a large meeting room, or a room for training, this can cause conflict as well.

Finally, wherever money is involved there is usually conflict. The budget people want more for less, and the functional people want more resources to get the work done. Many times budget conflicts show up at the beginning of a project when the budget is being negotiated and at the end of the project when the team is running out of budget but still has unfinished deliverables.

Schedule

Schedule conflict emerges in the beginning when the team develops its initial estimates, and then management or the customer says, "That won't do at all—it needs to be done in half that amount of time." This is a common situation if the sales team has made schedule promises to the customer that the IT team cannot deliver. Other schedule conflicts can emerge if certain resources are not available when needed. In addition, like the budget, schedule conflicts will become more intense towards the end of the project when people are working frantically to complete work by the deadline.

Priorities

Most of these situations are compounded by prioritization conflicts. If the timeline is cut, then the budget should be expanded to allow more resources to get the work done in less time. If scope is added, then additional time or money should be added. Prioritization of the project objectives can help the project manager select the best approach. Also, understanding the priority of the project compared to other projects in the organization will assist the project manager and the team in making the best use of limited organizational resources.

Methods for Managing Conflict

Different methods can be used to resolve conflict. All of them require a full understanding of what is causing the conflict. Here are some tips to use to clarify and resolve conflicts:

- Make sure the root cause of the conflict is understood. Sometimes what looks like a schedule conflict will surface, but further questions reveal that the conflict is really about selecting an approach. The conflict over schedule was really just a manifestation of the conflict over approach.
- Define the conflict in a succinct statement, and have all parties agree to the statement.
- Ascertain if you have all the information available to resolve the conflict. Sometimes a conflict is based on lack of information or conflicting information.
- Establish what resolution would look like for each of the parties involved. Weigh this information against the practicality of the suggested resolutions, and make sure that the resolution is smaller or less complex than the problem itself.
- Work towards a consensus solution. From the aspect of both teamwork and results, a collaborative, consensus approach usually yields the best results.

Sometimes the project manager doesn't have time to come up with a collaborative or consensus-based decision, or sometimes it is better to let the conflict resolve itself. For these and other situations, the conflict resolution model most often seen in IT is an offshoot of work done by Ralph Kilmann and Kenneth Thomas in 1974.[2] They developed a tool to help people understand their negotiation styles. Although this work is decades old, it is still a useful way to approach conflict resolution. Using this model helps the project manager assess the situation, the timeliness needed to reach resolution, and the relative power of the parties involved in the conflict. The negotiation styles described by Kilmann and Thomas are described below.

Competing

This is a win/lose style. It is useful when you have most of the power and you need a hard-nosed approach to a situation. It can be useful you have limited time to make a decision and if the decision is important. It is a my-way-or-the-highway approach. The downfall of this style is that it can alienate others.

Accommodating

Accommodating is the opposite of competing. In this situation, you are allowing the other person to win. This style is useful if the other person outranks you or if you feel that maintaining a good relationship is more important than resolving the conflict your way. The negative aspect of this style is that others may see you as weak and not standing up for yourself, and they may try to take advantage of you.

Collaborating

This style usually yields the best results. All parties try to merge their perspectives to come up with a solution that works best for all involved. Not only does this get buy-in from all those concerned, but also you will usually see better and more creative solutions emerge from a group than from any one individual. However, collaborating takes time and cooperation to accomplish.

Compromising

Some people call this a lose/lose scenario; others call it a win/win. In this situation, each party gives up little things to reach a larger agreement. This can be used when both parties have equal power, want to save face, and want to come up with a solution rapidly.

> **What Do You Think?**
>
> Recall a project that you have worked on in the past where there has been conflict. What was the conflict resolution method used by the project manager? Was it effective?

Avoiding

In rare situations, walking away, at least temporarily, may be best. If tempers are hot and a resolution does not appear to be forthcoming, sometimes it is best to leave the issue for the time being. Additionally, if you are in a situation where you cannot win, sometimes avoiding the conflict altogether is best. Avoiding is not usually the best resolution. Many conflicts will only fester and get worse if they are left unresolved. Some conflicts resolve themselves, but these are fewer than the festering kind.

In Practice: Conflict Potential

Harold Kerzner summarizes an article by David Wilemon in *Journal of Management Studies* in 1973 titled "Managing Conflict in Temporary Management Situations." The article identified several reasons why conflicts occur:

- The greater the diversity of disciplinary expertise among the participants of a project team, the greater the potential for conflict to develop among members of the team.
- The lower the project manager's degree of authority and power over rewards and punishment for those individuals and organizational units supporting the project, the greater the potential for conflict to develop.
- The less the specific objectives of a project are understood by the project team members, the more likely conflict is to develop.
- The greater the ambiguity among the participants of a project team, the more likely it is that conflict will develop.
- The greater the agreement on high-level goals by project team participants, the lower the potential for detrimental conflict.
- The lower the need for interdependence among organizational units supporting a project, the greater the potential for conflict.

CHAPTER SUMMARY

- Successful project managers share a set of skills, abilities, and traits. Some of these skills and traits are organized around managing and some are organized around leading. A well-balanced project manager has competence in both management and leadership.
- The project sponsor is the link to the executive offices. The project sponsor provides strategic input to the project manager, monitors the budget and the progress, and assists the project manager with decisions and conflicts that are outside of the project manager's level of authority.

- Team members should have the necessary skills for the project, work well with other team members, understand how their pieces fit in the whole of the project, and communicate proactively.
- Functional managers provide resources for projects. They often assist team members in developing technical solutions. They balance their limited staff resources across multiple projects.
- A team is more effective at getting work done than a group of people. Team building should be undertaken for long-term critical projects. There are some simple ways that project managers can build a team environment for short-term projects.
- Teams go through a development life cycle: forming, storming, norming, and performing.
- Characteristics of effective teams include communication, trust, participation, shared leadership and accountability, and reflection on the team process.
- A team charter helps define how the team will work together and provides opportunity for team development.
- Common causes of project conflict are scope, resources, schedule, and priorities. To manage conflict effectively, the project manager needs to understand the cause of the conflict and work towards a consensus resolution.
- Thomas and Kilmann developed a tool that defines five ways of resolving conflict: competing, accommodating, collaborating, compromising, and avoiding.

Key Terms

Sponsor
Forming
Storming
Norming
Performing
Team Charter
Competing
Virtual teams
Accommodating
Collaborating
Compromising
Avoiding

Key Term Quiz

1. The ________ provides strategic direction for the project manager.

2. The first phase of project team formation is __________.

3. ________ is the stage in team development where there is most likely to be conflict.

4. The most advanced stage in the team development model is ____________.

5. ____________ is a win-lose style of conflict resolution.

6. When you can't win in a conflict situation, you should adopt a(n) ______ style.

7. Putting your heads together with someone else to come up with the best possible resolution to a problem or conflict is called ________.

Chapter Review Questions

1. What are three management skills or abilities that a project manager should demonstrate?

2. What are three leadership skills or abilities that a project manager should demonstrate?

3. What are three leadership traits that a project manager should exhibit?

4. What is the role of the project sponsor in the execution process of the project?

5. When we say team members should have a global perspective, what are we referring to?

6. What are the four stages of team development?

7. What are three of the enemies of team building?

8. List three characteristics of teams.
9. Name three team leadership behaviors.
10. What are three items you might find on a team charter?
11. What is the biggest issue in managing virtual teams?
12. List the five requirements to successfully manage a virtual team.
13. What are the four most common causes of conflict on a project?
14. What are the five methods for dealing with conflict on projects?
15. What style of conflict management usually yields the best results?

END NOTES:

1. Bruce Tuckman, "Development Sequence in Small Groups," *Psychological Bulletin* 63, 1965, 384–399.
2. K.W. Thomas and R.H. Kilmann, *Thomas-Kilmann Conflict MODE Instrument,* XICOM and CPP, Inc., Palo Alto, CA, 1974.

8 Quality Management

After reading this chapter, you will be able to:

- Discuss quality management.
- Describe the differences between product and project quality.
- List the contents of a quality management plan.
- Discuss the components of an IT quality management effort.
- Describe how a testing program fits into the IT quality effort.

A Discussion of Quality Management

If you were to walk up to an IT project manager and ask if he or she is ensuring that the project turns out a high-quality product, you most likely would get a puzzled look and a response like, "Yes, of course I am." However, if you asked to see the quality management plan (QMP), the project manager would likely get an embarrassed look and reply, "We haven't written one."

Everyone agrees quality is important. Saying you're against high quality is like saying you're against motherhood and the national flag. However, many IT projects are unlikely to have a QMP that states the specific quality goals, how they will be achieved, and how they will be measured. Why is this? Because developing and managing quality takes time and resources away from other parts of the project—time and resources that are in short supply. In balancing costs, work, and schedule, quality often does not get the highest priority.

Quality, as it applies to projects, can be broken into two categories: the quality of the product that is being developed and the quality of the project itself. The quality of the product is measured against the quality standards that apply to the product. The quality of the project is measured by how well the project is being managed with respect to the project management standards that are in place in the organization.

In Practice: A Failed ERP

Starting in 2000, a U.S. government agency started a project to implement a financial ERP system in their organization. The implementation went far beyond the scheduled delivery date and was millions of dollars over budget. The system was unable to generate monthly reports (a core requirement of any financial system) for almost a year after the go-live date. The ensuing audit discovered that in an attempt to save money, the IT organization decided to manage the project internally, assigning a project manager with no ERP experience, and hired a contractor that the CIO had worked with before even though the contractor also had no experience in this package. The IT organization also had dispensed with gathering requirements.

The Definition of Quality

What does quality mean to you? Some common answers include:

- The best product possible
- A product that doesn't break down
- A sturdy product
- A product that does what I want
- A product that meets my needs
- The best product I can afford
- A product that's reliable and dependable

Several definitions of **quality** can be used in project management. The *PMBOK® Guide*[1] follows the definition of quality given by the American Society for Quality and defines quality as "the degree to which an inherent set of characteristics fulfills requirements." The ISO 9000 definition of quality is "the totality of features and characteristics of a product or service that bears on its ability to satisfy stated or implied needs." The reference to requirements and needs underscores the importance of gathering, managing, meeting, and testing requirements.

When we manage a project, we need to define quality using **operational definitions.** An operational definition is a definition against which measurements can be made. A quality goal of a 50 percent drop in help desk calls is an operational definition; you can measure whether the product meets it. Another operational definition might be a 75 percent reduction in the amount of downtime in the new system as compared to the existing system. Again, you can measure to see if you're meeting the quality goal. Saying that the end result should be the highest quality possible is not an operational definition, as there is no way to measure whether that criteria is met or not.

In Practice: Quality Standards

Some of the most thorough project management standards and approaches in the government sector can be found on the web site of the New York State Office of Technology (www.oft.state.ny.us/). A downloadable document, *Project Management Guidebook, Release 2,* states:

> "The amazing thing about quality standards is that nobody has them available when the project starts, but everybody knows what they were supposed to be when the product is delivered. Do not accept lack of documentation as an excuse to skimp on your homework. On the contrary, dig down through organizational layers to discover what was used in the past (here's another way your historical data research pays off!) and what will be expected in the future. And if you can't find anything—create it, document it, publicize it, and put it in your Project Status Report and your project repository." (Section 2.2.3, Identify Quality Standards)

Quality Expectations

Who determines quality expectations? Ultimately, it is the customer/user/client. Therefore, quality expectations are set by the marketplace and by competitors who compete for the same customers. Expectations often take the form of expectations of reliability, maintainability, operability, and availability (remember the "ilities" from requirements gathering?). Other expectations are set by the government and by professional societies and regulatory agencies. For example, the IEEE Computer Society sets quality expectations for many of the components used in IT. A product that is inconsistent with the standards is not considered an illegal one, but it will most likely not have a market. These types of standards dictate the expectations for the product.

It is important for the project manager to understand that if he or she does not define quality, the customer/client/user will. It is the customer's expectations of how the system will perform that create the definition of quality for the project effort. Companies typically measure the quality of a product against written specifications. Customers will measure quality against whether the product meets their expectations, its "fitness for use." The closer the product's specifications are to the user's expectations, the more likely the user will be to consider it a quality product.

PROJECT QUALITY AND PRODUCT QUALITY

Distinguishing between project quality and product quality is important. Most quality definitions and approaches apply to product quality, not to project quality. **Product quality** focuses on the product deliverables as they are produced, the pieces of the final product that we are developing. There are many approaches to measuring the quality of those deliverables and of the final product—inspections, measurements, testing, and so on.

Project quality, by contrast, focuses on how well the project itself is managed. It concentrates on whether established project management processes were in place and how well those processes were followed. Project quality is assessed through audits to see how well the project manager and the project team follow the established project management approaches. For example, one of the most common sources of failure in ERP implementations is that the employees will not use the new system. The ERP *products* themselves are capable of working well, but if the implementation of the system was so poorly done that the employees won't use it, it was not a quality *project.*

Unlike some other parts of the project process, there are legal aspects to product quality. A poorly designed or manufactured product can damage systems and hurt people, exposing the company to criminal liability or civil liability. Particular attention must be paid to the project's quality management effort when products have the potential to cause harm.

A **warranty** is a guarantee given to the purchaser by a company stating that a product is reliable and free from known defects and that the seller will, without charge, repair or replace defective parts within a given time limit and under certain conditions. If the product comes with a written warranty, the product must live up to what the warranty states. Even if the product does not come with a written warranty, it must satisfy an implied fitness-for-use assumption by the purchaser. The product must do what the customer buys it for, even if there's not a written warranty.

Two terms that can be confusing in quality management are quality assurance and quality control. **Quality assurance** (QA) is the process of managing the documented quality processes to ensure that the product's quality requirements will be met. **Quality control** (QC) is the more detailed effort of measuring and verifying that the product is being made correctly as the project progresses. QC finds the problems in the system under development; QA ensures that all the right quality specifications are identified and met and that the right processes are followed.

Recent Quality Approaches

Our viewpoint of how we achieve quality has changed over the years. Before World War I, quality was achieved by inspection and by removing defective parts from the production line. In the period from 1920 to about 1950, some quality principles began to emerge, largely as a result of the work of people like Deming, Juran, and Crosby. The field started to develop statistical sampling techniques and process control charts. During the next 20 years, quality began to look upwards into management and quality assurance processes such as Total Quality Control, Reliability Engineering, and Zero Defects were developed.

This growth continued in the 1970s to 1980s with Total Quality Management (TQM) and Six Sigma. It was after the recession in the early 1970s that companies in the United States began to realize that they were losing market share to imported products that were much higher quality than many of the products American companies were producing. In the 1990s, the emphasis on quality moved from primarily inspections into planning quality into a product from the design phase. Strategic quality management principles began to be applied and quality standards became important.

International Standards Organization

The International Standards Organization (ISO) is a consortium of industrialized nations based in Geneva, Switzerland. One set of standards it developed, the ISO 9000 series, relates to quality. Some of the components of the ISO 9000 series include:

- ISO 9000 defines key terms and acts as a road map for the other 9000-series standards.
- ISO 9001 defines the model for a quality system when a contractor shows the capability to design, manufacture, and install products or services.

- ISO 9002 is the quality model for quality assurance in production and installation.
- ISO 9003 is the quality system model for quality assurance in final inspection and testing.
- ISO 9004 develops the quality management guidelines for an organization to develop and implement a quality system.

ISO 10000 also has applicability. ISO 10006 are guidelines to quality in project management. ISO 10006 applies to small companies as well as to large ones.

> **NOTE**
> ISO standards are so prevalent in the European community that companies that are not ISO 9000-compliant will not be able to sell products in the European Union, resulting in a major loss of potential customers.

In Practice: ISO 9000

The 2000 update to ISO 9000 incorporates the following eight principles:

1. Focus on your customers.
   Organizations rely on customers. Therefore:
   - Organizations must understand customer needs.
   - Organizations must meet customer requirements.
   - Organizations must exceed customer expectations.
2. Provide leadership.
   Organizations rely on leaders. Therefore:
   - Leaders must establish a unity of purpose and set the direction the organization should take.
   - Leaders must create an environment that encourages people to achieve the organization's objectives.
3. Involve your people.
   Organizations rely on people. Therefore:
   - Organizations must encourage the involvement of people at all levels.
   - Organizations must help people to develop and use their abilities.
4. Use a process approach.
   Organizations are more efficient and effective when they use a process approach. Therefore:
   - Organizations must use a process approach to manage activities and related resources.

5. Use a systems approach.
   Organizations are more efficient and effective when they use a systems approach. Therefore:
   - Organizations must identify interrelated processes and treat them as a system.
   - Organizations must use a systems approach to manage their interrelated processes.
6. Encourage continual improvement.
   Organizations are more efficient and effective when they continually try to improve. Therefore:
   - Organizations must make a permanent commitment to continually improve their overall performance.
7. Get the facts before you decide.
   Organizations perform better when their decisions are based on facts. Therefore:
   - Organizations must base decisions on the analysis of factual information and data.
8. Work with your suppliers.
   Organizations depend on their suppliers to help them create value. Therefore:
   - Organizations must maintain a mutually beneficial relationship with their suppliers.

Capability Maturity Models

Another approach to improving quality emerged in the development of capability maturity models. The Software Engineering Institute developed the Software Capability Maturity Model (CMM), which implemented processes to improve software development and quality. The original CMM was a hierarchical set of processes an organization could follow with the purpose of gaining better control over its software development process. The original CMM has since been supplanted by CMM-Integrated (CMMI), which incorporates into the software CMM systems engineering, integrated project and process development, and supplier sourcing.

The attempt to improve quality through processes also exists in the project management field. Multiple consulting organizations have created their own internal approaches to rating an organization's project management maturity. In 2003, PMI released the first version of its Organizational Project Management Maturity Model (OPM3), which measures organizational strengths and weaknesses in project management, program management, and portfolio management.[2]

PRINCE2

PRINCE2 (Projects in Controlled Environments, version 2) is a project management methodology that was developed for the British government in 1989 and is used extensively in Britain and in other European countries, primarily on government projects. It puts heavy emphasis on justifying the business case for the project and continually monitoring the progress against the business case. Although it's not as broad based a project management approach as the *PMBOK® Guide* (it says nothing about personnel management, budget control, critical path management, or other aspects of project management), PRINCE2 does provide the following checklist for quality:[3]

- Has the customer specified quality expectations?
- Is there a project quality plan?
- Will the project quality plan achieve the customer's expectations?
- Does the project quality plan point at specific quality procedures?
- Are quality responsibilities defined in the project quality plan?
- Are there stage (phase) quality plans?
- Are individuals and quality methods identified in the stage quality plans?
- Is there a quality log?
- Is the quality log up-to-date?
- Do the teams maintain one central quality log?
- Does the project manger get sufficient feedback to ensure quality is okay?
- Are project assurance personnel sufficiently involved in quality checking?
- Do the quality file and quality log match?
- Is any external quality assurance function happy with its involvement?

Six Sigma

No discussion of modern quality initiatives can be complete without mentioning the Six Sigma approach. Six Sigma is a quality effort first undertaken by Motorola in the 1980s to reduce defective products. The goal of Six Sigma is to reduce defects to 3.4 per million opportunities through the five-phase improvement process of **define, measure, analyze, improve, and control (DMAIC).** The goal of 3.4 defects per million opportunities was not chosen arbitrarily. In a normal Gaussian distribution, this is the point that is six standard deviations (that is, six sigma) out from the central point of the curve (called the mean). The Six Sigma approach reduces defects by reducing the statistical process variations that exist in all processes.

What does **defects per million opportunities (DPMO)** mean? Assume a company is trying to reduce the error rate on its payroll process. There could be several errors on a typical paycheck, due to erroneous social security numbers, incorrect addresses, misspelled names, errors in the tax status or insurance deductions, and so on. There might be 50 opportunities on a single paycheck for errors to occur. Instead of measuring the number of defects per paycheck, Six Sigma measures the number of defects based on the number of opportunities.

The typical company operates its processes in the range of 3 to 4 sigma, or 3 to 4 standard deviations, away from the center of the curve. Companies in this range have somewhere between 6,210 and 66,800 DPMO, a very high error rate in comparison to 3.4 DPMO. For companies that operate at the 3 to 4 sigma level, i.e. most companies, quality problems consume 25 to 40 percent of potential revenues. In order to implement Six Sigma processes, companies must be totally dedicated to incorporating the process into the culture, from top management down to the lowest level of employee.

Cost of Quality

Developing and managing a quality plan takes time, effort, and money. How much quality management is enough? If you have no quality management at all, then anything is an improvement. In general, you have enough quality management when the cost of increased quality is higher than the cost associated with obtaining it.

Instituting or improving your quality program will generally increase your costs in the short-term as people are hired, tools purchased, and new processes implemented. However, in the long-term significant savings can be achieved from fewer product failures and less rework. (See Figure 8-1.)

Quality costs can be broken down into two areas: the cost of conformance and the cost of nonconformance. The **cost of conformance** is how much it will cost to attain a given level of quality. "If we institute a quality program on this project, how much will it cost?" This will include the cost of the personnel involved in the quality effort, the cost of each part of the quality effort, such as inspections, analysis, testing, etc., and the cost of the quality documents

Figure 8-1. Changes in Costs Due to Quality Programs

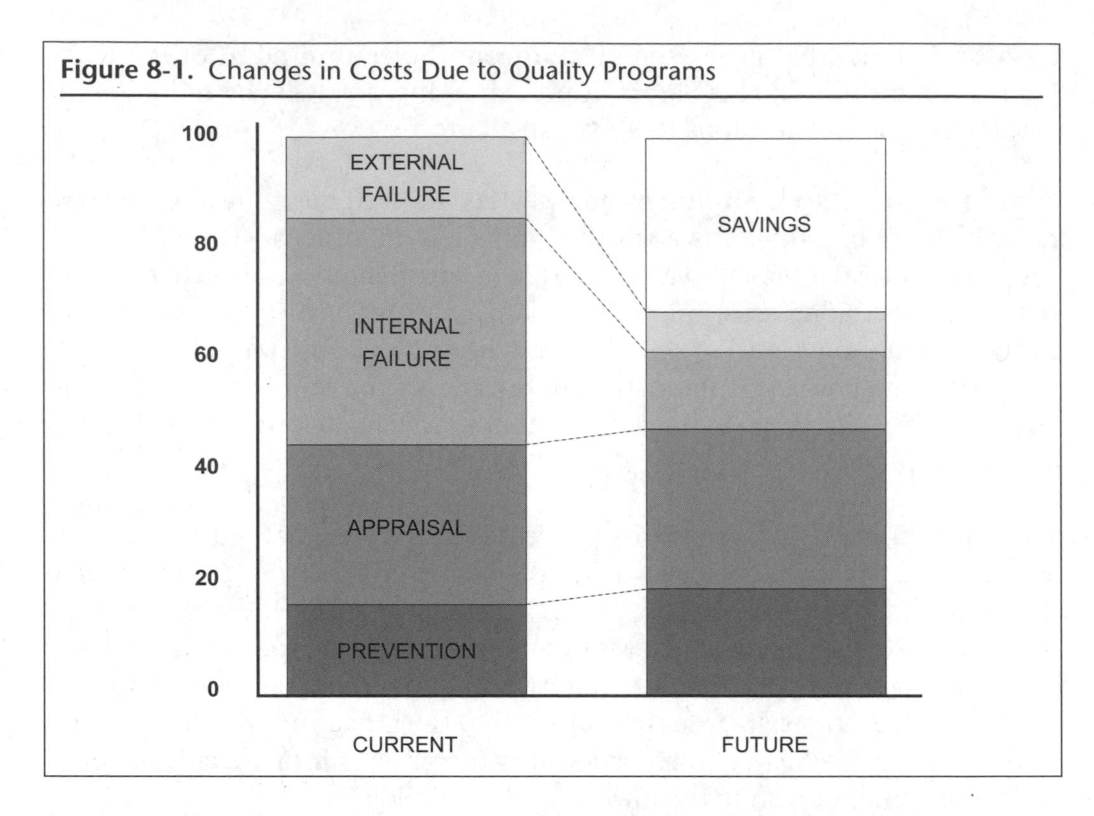

produced. If organizations outside of the project are used, such as company quality assurance departments, your company policies will dictate whether those costs are included in your project costs.

The **costs of nonconformance** are more difficult to determine. These are the costs of low quality—having bugs in the software or having a new system fail. If a product is released to the rest of the company, the costs increase greatly due to the amount of lost productivity and errors by the users of the product. Too many such problems will create a poor reputation for the IT department, as others in the company will have to struggle with products that do not meet their needs.

If the product is released to the external market, the costs grow exponentially. Not just because the product has to be fixed and those fixes applied to each purchaser, but also because of the poor reputation the company will earn, which will lead to lost sales and reduced income. These costs may be difficult to quantify, but they are very real. In 2003, Dell Computer purchased a large quantity of capacitors to be installed on the motherboards of its laptops. Unknown to Dell, the company it purchased the capacitors from had stolen the design from another company in a case of intellectual property theft. The company did not steal the entire design, only a part of it, and manufactured vast quantities of defective capacitors. Dell ended up taking a $300 million dollar write-off from income in order to fix the problem.[4]

How much quality should the project pay for? Although the costs of conformance are readily identifiable, the costs of nonconformance are approximations. However, the project manager can identify a range of how much quality is enough. Look at the graph in Figure 8-2, which shows how the cost of conformance grows as the defect rate goes down.

Figure 8-2. Cost of Conformance

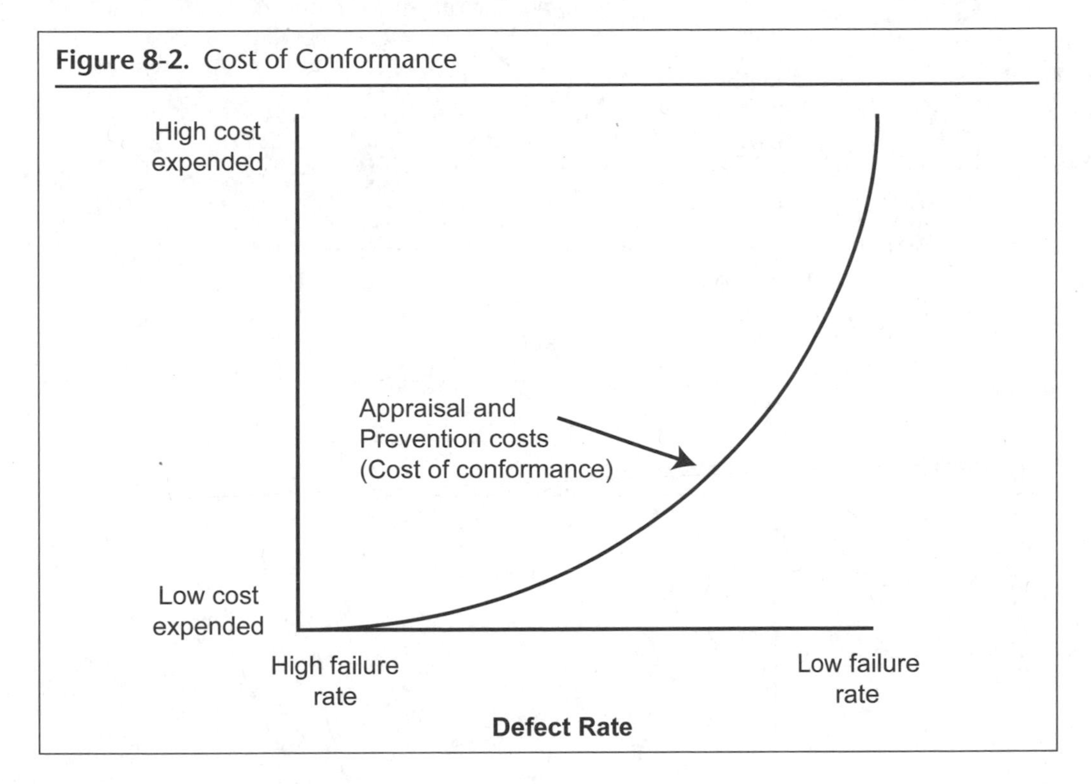

A similar chart, shown in Figure 8-3, illustrates that the cost of nonconformance increases along with a higher failure rate—the more failures due to quality problems, the higher the costs associated with them.

To assess where to get the best return for quality investment, overlap the two graphs as shown in Figure 8-4.

At the best cost point, increasing the quality efforts will not provide as much benefit as the money expended, although decreasing quality efforts will lead to increased costs due to higher failure rates. At this optimal point, the project is getting the greatest payback for the quality dollars.

Figure 8-3. Cost of Nonconformance

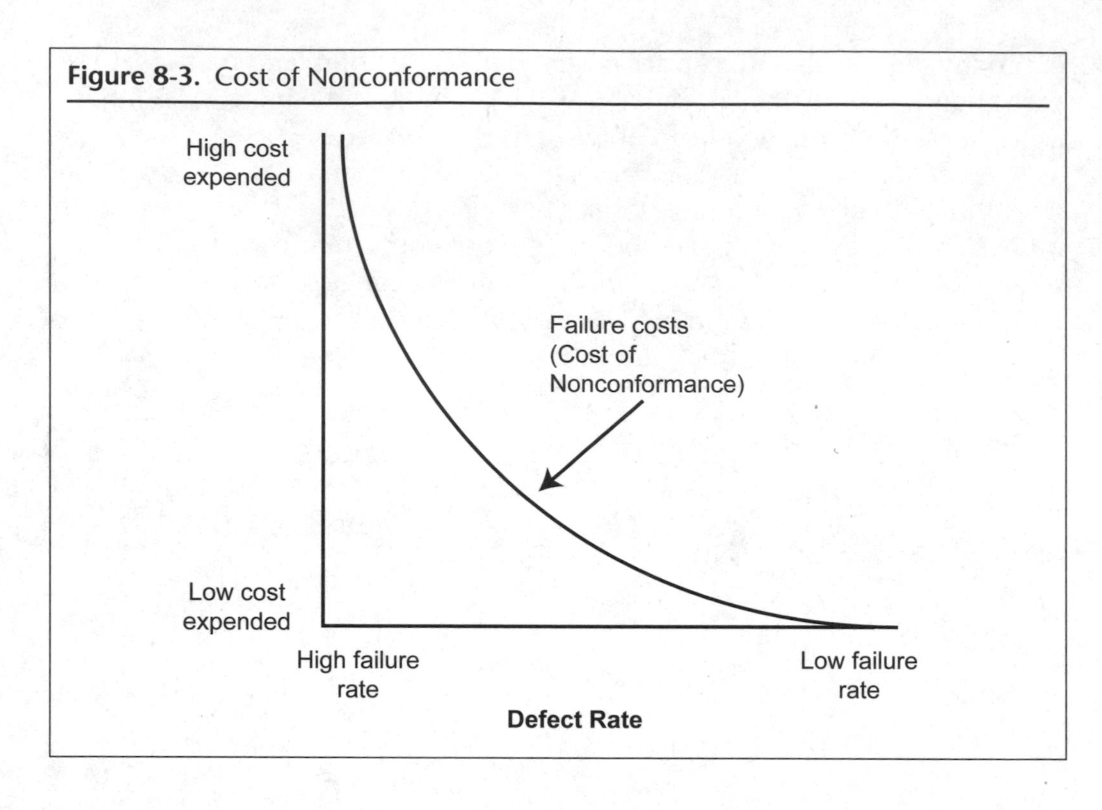

Figure 8-4. Optimal Quality/Cost Point

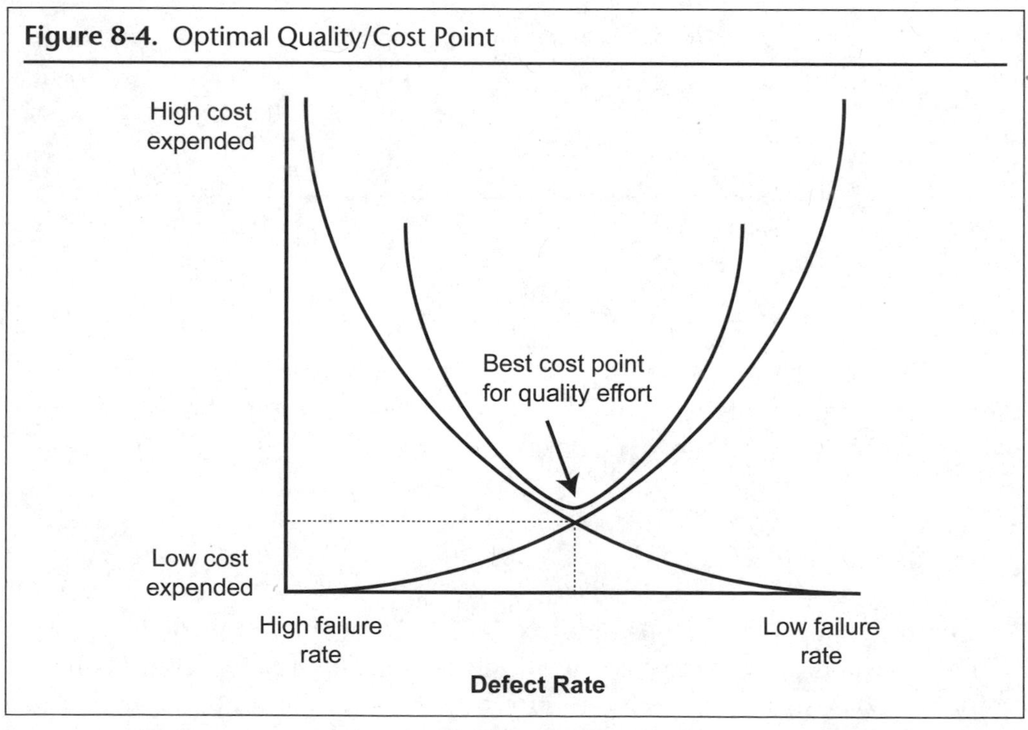

PM in Action

Go on the web and research project management quality. Write a one to three page paper on one of the methodologies you find online.

The Quality Management Plan

After all this discussion about quality, you're probably wondering what IT project managers really need to do.

Step one is to assign someone to be in charge of quality for the product. Since most IT projects are short-staffed, this assignment may be shared with other work or shared among several people. The lead developer may be put in charge of product quality, whereas the lead tester may be put in charge of quality assurance. Very clear roles and responsibilities must be defined so that everyone involved understands their assignment, including the customer/user representative (who is often the business analyst for internal projects). Ultimately, the project manager is responsible for delivering a quality product; the details of the quality management work should be assigned to someone else.

Once a person has been assigned to be in charge of quality, he or she takes the lead in writing the **quality management plan (QMP).** The QMP defines the organizational structure, responsibilities, procedures, processes, and resources needed to implement quality management. The details of the QMP depend on the company and whether it has an existing quality organization or all quality work must be done within the project. A typical table of contents for a QMP is in Figure 8-5, which shows the document used by the state of North Carolina for its software quality assurance efforts.

Part of the quality process is identifying the standards that are applicable to the product. The standards may be professional standards (such as the IEEE standards), government-mandated standards, or internal company standards. All of the appropriate standards must be identified, documented in the QMP, and incorporated into the project's quality effort.

Quality Management Tools

There are many tools and techniques for managing both product quality and project quality. Because the typical IT project is not large enough or does

Figure 8-5. Sample Quality Management Plan

North Carolina
Software Quality Assurance Plan
Table of Contents

Figure 8-5. Sample Quality Management Plan (continued)

9.3 Methodologies
9.4 Code Control
9.5 Media Control
9.6 Security
9.7 Disaster Recovery
9.8 Supplier Controls
9.9 Records Collection, Maintenance, and Retention

10. TRAINING
10.1 User Training
10.2 Development Team Training
10.3 Transition to State Team Training

11. RISK MANAGEMENT
11.1 Project Self Assessment
11.2 Project Risk Assessment and Management Plan
11.3 Risk Review and Management Process
11.4 Tools

12. Lessons Learned

13. Document Approvals

APPENDIX A—GLOSSARY

APPENDIX B—STANDARDS

APPENDIX C—SUPPORTING DOCUMENTATION

not last long enough to perform statistical quality analysis or have detailed control charts, we will limit our discussion of quality tools to those that are applicable to relatively short-term projects that have small-to-medium size teams (with team members who might be working on multiple projects) and limited funding.

One of the most basic things a project manager can do to assess project quality is to define a good set of metrics that tell him or her how well things are going. For example, the project manager could measure not only the number of change requests, but also the number of change requests against requirements. Too many changes requested against the approved requirements is an indication that the project is not going to deliver a quality product, because the real needs have not been captured.

Another set of solid metrics can be taken from the **discrepancy reports (DRs)** written by the testers. The DRs should be analyzed to determine whether there are any particular problem areas. For example, if the performance testing shows severe slowdowns in the system performance during normal loaded conditions, this tells the project manager that the system will not perform well in normal usage. As another example, if too many deficiency reports are written against one particular software module, that module will continue to cause problems even after the system goes into production. The module should be looked at carefully and perhaps redesigned. The right metrics can identify potential quality problems for the product.

One set of core tools relates to problem solving on the project. Once a problem has been identified, how does the team get to the root—the ultimate cause—of the problem? One basic tool is a cause-and-effect diagram, also called an **Ishikawa diagram** or a fishbone diagram. (See Figure 8-6.)

Figure 8-6. Ishikawa Diagram

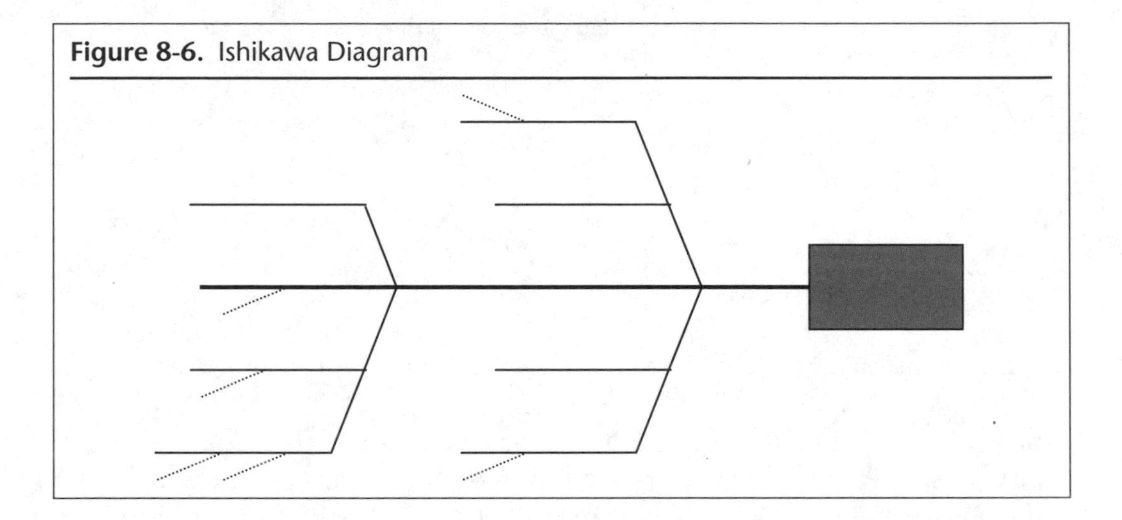

Kaoru Ishikawa wrote a book in 1972 titled *Guide to Quality Control.*[5] He developed the use of fishbone diagrams in the quality arena and showed how to use them to trace complaints about quality back to the root cause of the problem. The box on the right side of the diagram is a statement of the problem, the main branches are system pieces that may be causing the problem, and the smaller branches are specific potential causes.

As an example, let's assume Jim has just installed a new LAN into the building where the company's financial offices are located, and the finance people cannot get into their financial software. This is a two-tier LAN with the applications stored on the servers. Inability to log in is a huge problem. Jim can use a cause-and-effect diagram to identify possible causes, as shown in Figure 8-7.

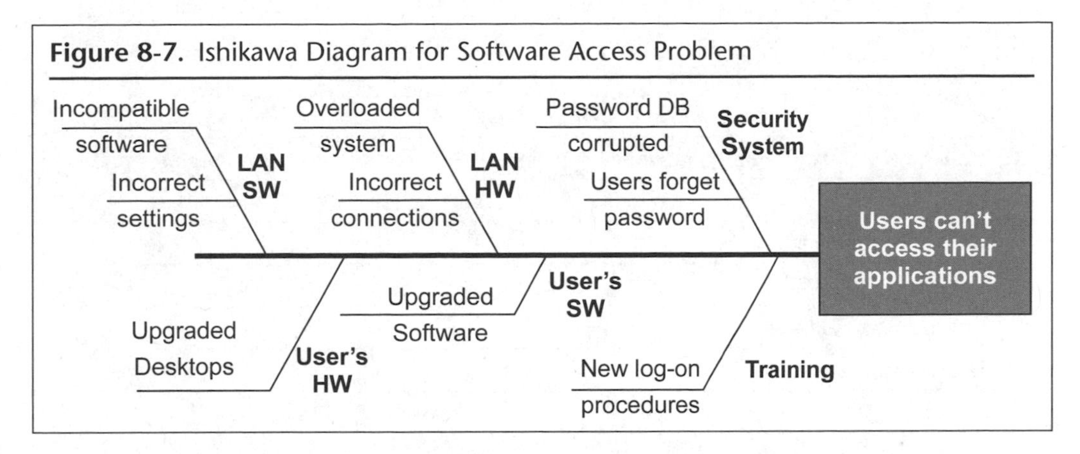

Figure 8-7. Ishikawa Diagram for Software Access Problem

Now that he has identified potential causes, Jim can investigate each potential cause to see which ones might be creating or contributing to the problem.

Another quality analysis tool is called a Pareto analysis. A Pareto analysis helps not only identify the contributors to quality problems, but also ranks and quantifies them. The majority of problems are caused by only a small set of causes. After identifying that small set, most problems can be resolved by focusing on those causes. This realization led to the 80:20 rule, which states that 80 percent of the problems are caused by 20 percent of the causes.

A Pareto analysis often results in a histogram called a **Pareto diagram.** In a Pareto diagram, the columns depict the causes of a particular problem and the scale on the left shows the number of times that cause occurs. The graph is the cumulative percentage of all the occurrences. Recall the problem that the financial people have logging into their system after the new LAN has been installed. The data Jim collected is in the table. The resulting Pareto diagram, shown in Figure 8-8, charts this data.

The Pareto diagram tells Jim which of the causes to focus on and how much benefit he will obtain by tackling and resolving each root cause.

Although it's not normally listed in the quality analysis tool set, peer reviews are another valuable tool. The purpose of peer reviews is to get project team members to look at and comment on each other's requirements, design, and code. Peer reviews can be a very valuable source of potential problem identification. Some team members have expertise and knowledge that others do not, so getting team members to look at each other's work will help identify

Figure 8-8. Pareto Diagram for LAN Access Problem

Analysis of Log-in Inability by Finance			
Cause	**Frequency**	**Percent Failure**	**Cumulative Percent**
Incompatible SW	60	40	40
Overloaded system	38	25	65
Upgraded user SW	30	20	85
Incorrect LAN settings	15	10	95
Users forget password	8	5	100

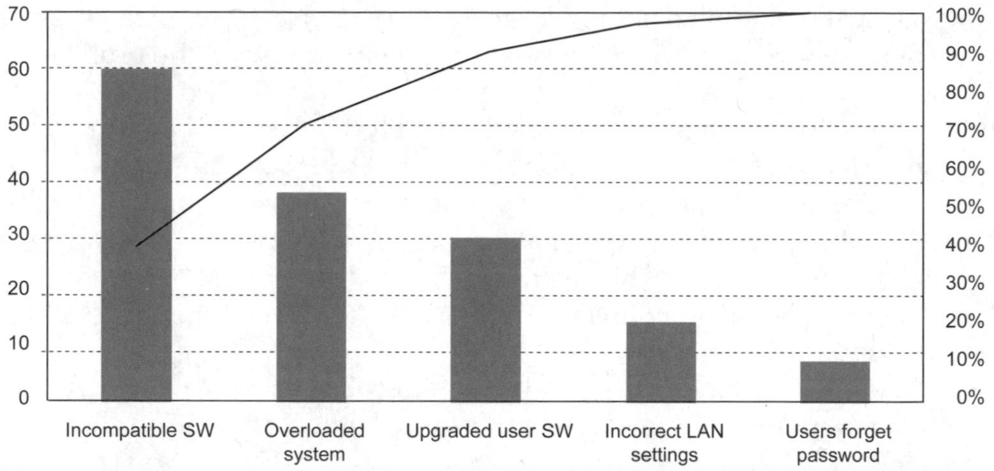

possible problems and improve the quality of the product. Peer reviews are mandated in the Software Engineering Institute CMM at level 2 and above for just this reason.

Of course, the ultimate quality tool in the IT project manager's toolbox is testing and integration.

TESTING

Testing often forms the core of an IT project's quality assurance effort. The project manager's primary responsibility is to ensure that the delivered product meets the user's needs and is acceptable. Testing is an integral part of that effort.

No one would ever suggest canceling a testing program in order to save schedule, yet, in the real world, testing is often cut back when the project runs into time or money difficulties. Thorough testing is expensive, and nobody can predict exactly what problems testing will catch, only that it will catch them. A spectacular example of failure due to a cancelled test occurred in the development of the Hubble space telescope. The primary mirror was ground incorrectly due to an operational error. The $10 million test that would have caught the error was cancelled by NASA because of budget cutbacks. The fix required a separate space shuttle flight at a minimum cost of $250 million. Ask yourself: How much money was saved by canceling the test? Cutting testing can save money and schedule in the short-term, but the price is always an increased risk of failure of the product after it is delivered. Although not all failures from cancelled tests are so spectacular, inadequate testing is a common problem in the IT world. In June 2004, the Royal Bank of Canada suffered a major failure in its IT system when a software upgrade caused problems in the accounts of thousands of Canadians. In September 2003, Westpac customers had millions of dollars incorrectly removed from their accounts during the weekend because of a computer glitch. Both of these problems could have been caught by adequate testing.

The Testing Program

Multiple types of testing can be performed during an IT development effort. Typical tests include:

- Unit tests
- System and subsystem tests
- Interface tests
- Integration tests
- Regression tests
- User acceptance tests (UAT)
- Compatibility tests
- Alpha and beta tests (for new software)
- Disaster recovery and business continuity tests
- Data conversion tests

- Security tests
- Capacity and load tests
- Stress tests

Not all of these tests need to be done on every project. It is up to the test lead to select the right tests. When selecting the types of tests to be done, remember two key guidelines:

- Testing can only determine the presence of defects, not their absence.
- Quality can't be tested into the product. It has to be designed in from the start.

Like every other aspect of projects, the testing philosophy must balance thoroughness with cost and schedule constraints. Testing every possible aspect of a typical IT product is impossible, and compromises must be made in order to test the highest priority portions. Modern operating systems have tens of millions of lines of code. Even everyday applications are huge. For example, in MS Word for Windows, there are:

- More than 850 command functions (bold and italic are the same command function).
- More than 1,600 distinct commands (bold and italic are distinct commands).

At any given time, roughly 50 percent of these commands are enabled (a conservative estimate). With just three steps, the possible combinations of code execution paths exceeds 500 million.

This is an impossible number of permutations to test, and so testing priorities must be established.

A basic tenet of testing is that the majority of the testing should always be done against the requirements, not against the detailed design. Why is that? Because if you test against the design, the design will almost always pass the test. However, it is more important that the user needs—the requirements—are met. By testing against the requirements, the project manager can determine whether the product will meet its promised objectives. Since we'll be testing against the requirements, we need to do a thorough job of gathering the requirements in the first place. As we stated in Chapter 5, requirements should be written in a way that makes them testable. By doing so, the team can verify that the requirement was actually satisfied by testing against it.

A second basic tenet of testing is that a dedicated group outside of the developers should do the tests. Developers should perform their own unit-level testing, but any testing outside of a single module should be done by someone who is not involved in the development of that module. This is called **independent validation and verification (IV&V).** It ensures that the testing will be done by people who have their own interpretation of the requirements and who will not just test against the developer's view of the requirements.

There is a hierarchy to the tests we listed, starting from the lowest-level, unit-level, testing and increasing the amount of integration testing as more components of the product are added. Once the entire system has been tested to ensure it operates as a single unit, thorough testing of the required functionality and performance testing should be started to show how the system will operate under fully loaded conditions. (See Figure 8-9.)

Testing activities, their durations, and their dependencies should be a major area within the project WBS. By properly incorporating test activities, the WBS will allow accurate schedule and resource determination.

Testing In-House Developed Systems

If an entire system is being developed in-house, the testing program should reflect a thorough understanding of both the business requirements and the design for the system. This will lead to detailed testing of as many interfaces and pathways as can be done within cost and schedule constraints. This is sometimes called **white box testing**—testing in which the tester has knowledge of the inner workings of the final product.

The testing philosophy here should be to follow the testing hierarchy shown in Figure 8-9 and to test to the requirements as thoroughly as possible in a production-like environment.

Figure 8-9. Hierarchy of Testing

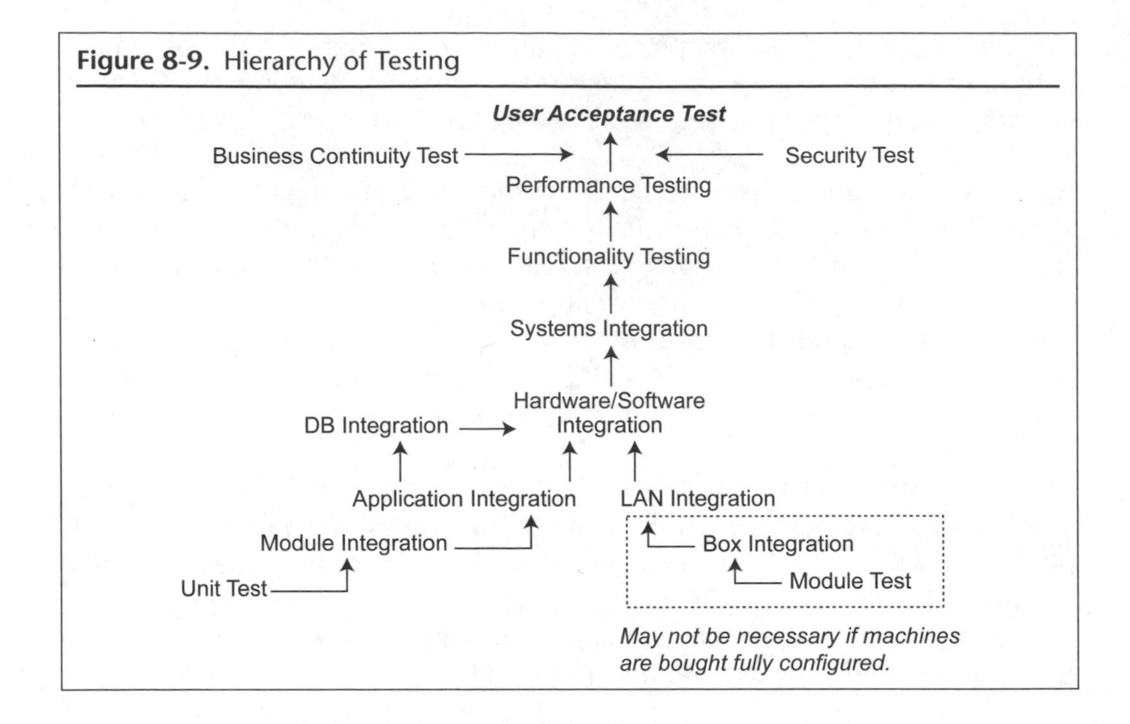

In Practice: New Software Ownership

Toyota USA's IT department has built a very practical approach into its software development processes. When a new piece of software is developed and put into production, the maintenance team does not accept ownership of it until it has been in the production environment for two months. At this point the majority of the bugs have been worked out and the number of beeper pages received at 2 A.M. to fix a problem has been strongly reduced. Who owns it until then? The developers do. Knowing that they'll get paged in the middle of the night to fix problems with their software is a good incentive for them to release software as bug free as possible!

Testing Commercial, Off-the-Shelf (COTS) Products

If the system being developed utilizes COTS packages—for example, if it's an ERP system or an OS upgrade—the testers will not have detailed knowledge of the inner workings of the product. This is called **black box testing.** The COTS product is considered to be a "black box" and is tested as a unit. The inputs to the product are carefully defined, and the outputs of the product should satisfy the test success criteria.

It is not safe to assume that just because something comes from an outside vendor it is free of defects. Even operating systems contain defects. Linux has an estimated 30 million lines of code; Microsoft XP has an estimated 40 million lines of code. A full implementation of the ERP system SAP contains an estimated 100 million lines of code. If there were only 10 bugs per 1,000 lines of code, there would be significant bugs.

The emphasis of COTS testing is to ensure that the product meets the user needs and that it is compatible with the environment in which it will be installed. A new software package or upgrade that breaks existing packages is not acceptable to the business. Of particular importance with COTS products is security testing, which ensures that the product introduces no new security problems. For example, consider Microsoft's ActiveX software component. Although the product is highly useful, it allows easy access and control of a desktop machine from outside the system and can be considered a serious security risk.

If the COTS product will be deployed at different facilities with different environments, then the product should be tested for operational compatibility in each environment.

Test Documentation

IEEE has developed Standard 829 to ensure a thorough software test program. This standard includes eight types of documents:

- Comprehensive test plan
- Design specification
- Case specification
- Procedure specification
- Transmittal report
- Log
- Incident report
- Summary report

In Practice: IEEE Standards

In the early phases of the project, the specific quality standards that will apply to the project should be identified. The following is a list of relevant IEEE standards that may be applicable to common software projects:

- 729: Glossary of Software Engineering Terminology
- 730.1: Standard for Software Quality Assurance Plans
- 730.2: Guide for Software Quality Assurance Plans
- 828: Standard for Software Configuration Management Plans
- 829: Standard for Software Testing Documentation
- 830: Guide for Software Test Documentation
- 1008: Standard for Software Unit Testing
- 1012: Standard for Software Verification and Validation Plans
- 1028: Standard for Software Review and Audit
- 1042: Guide to Software Configuration Management
- 1044: Standard Classification for Software Anomalies
- 1058.1: Standard for Software Project Management Plans
- 1059: Guide for Software Verification and Validation Plans
- 1061: Standard for a Software Quality Metrics Methodology
- 1063: Standard for Software User Documentation
- 1219: Standard for Software Maintenance

The comprehensive test plan is the start of the testing effort. The test plan is a written document that describes the testing philosophy and the overall approach to testing. Within the test plan, the approach should be described in sufficient detail to permit identification of the major testing tasks and estimation of the time required to do each task. The test lead should identify the types of testing to be performed along with the methods and criteria to be used in performing test activities. Specific methods and procedures for each type of testing and detailed criteria for evaluating the test results should be defined in the test plan as well.

The test plan's table of contents should include the following elements:

- Introduction, including the objectives of the testing program, testing strategy, scope of the test plan, and any reference materials, definitions, and acronyms.
- Test items.
- Features to be tested.
- Features that will not be tested.
- Approach.
- Pass/fail criteria. (Specify the criteria to be used to determine whether each item has passed or failed testing.)
- Suspension criteria/resumption requirements. (Specify the criteria used to suspend all or a portion of the testing activity on test items associated with the plan. Specify the conditions that need to be met to resume testing activities after suspension. Specify the test items that must be repeated when testing is resumed.)
- Testing process:
  - Deliverables
  - The specific testing tasks
  - Responsibilities
  - Resources
  - Staffing and training needs
  - Schedule
- Environmental requirements:
  - Hardware
  - Software
  - Security
  - Tools
  - Risks, assumptions, and dependencies
  - Contingencies
- Change management procedures
- Plan approvals

After the comprehensive test plan is written and approved, the more detailed test documentation should be developed, as listed in the IEEE 829. The test lead should develop the documentation with support from the test group. The project manager's responsibility is to ensure that the test cases are documented, test data is defined, pass/fail criteria for each test is established, test logs are kept, a discrepancy reporting process is available, and the approval process for successful tests is adequate.

All of these efforts take time and require advanced planning. Although the testing activities themselves may not occur until the end of the project, after the major development effort is substantially completed, there is a significant amount of time required to properly prepare for testing. Test personnel need to begin work as early in the project as the design phase so that the test environment can be developed, user IDs created, test data prepared, test scripts written and checked, and all the other test-related activities can be accomplished. In the project's detailed schedule, much of the testing work will go on in parallel with the prime development effort.

PM in Action!

Write a test plan for a project you are working on. If you're not currently working on a project, create a project of the type you are most likely to work on, give a brief description of it, and then write a test plan.

User Involvement

Although some users might declare that they don't need to be involved in testing, the more actively they are involved the better the end result is likely to be. The testing phase of the project is when the product is really integrated for the first time and the users can see how it all works. When end users get involved in the final stages of testing, light bulbs go on and they often have an "aha, now I see" moment.

If users don't have time to get involved in IT testing, representatives should be designated to support this part of the project. Typically, these are business analysts (BAs). BAs should actively collaborate on the comprehensive test plan and in defining the tests that need to be done. There should be a specific RAM written for the testing effort. An example of such a RAM is given in Figure 8-10.

Figure 8-10. Sample Testing Responsibility Assignment Matrix (RAM)[1]

Test Type	Developer (may be contractor or staff)	Testers (usually staff, but may be contractor)	Project Configuration Mgr	Project Test Mgr	Project QA Mgr	Project Deliverable Mgr/Librarian	Sponsor	User	IV&V
Unit	– Primary responsibility for conducting tests	– Audit/observe testing or review test materials and results	– Review Prime's CM logs and test results or – Track version and code units where the verification takes place	– Review test mgmt activities and test documentation for completeness and correct process	– Review test activities and documentation for adherence to processes and standards	– Coordinate review of test materials – Store test deliverables and supporting documentation in project library	No involvement	No involvement	– Review test activities and documentation for adherence to processes and standards and for appropriate rigor, if appropriate
Unit Level Vertification of Non-Testable Requirements	– Participate as needed	– Primary responsibility for verification	– Track version and code units where the verification takes place	– Coordinate verification of non-testable requirements	– Review test activities and documentation for adherence to processes and standards – Ensure verification methods are correctly applied and documented	– Store copies of test information	– Receive report on results and methods for verification of requirements – Sometimes report is delayed until system testing	No involvement	– Review test activities and documents for adherence to processes and standards – Ensure selected verification method is correct and appropriate for the type of requirement being verified
Component or Module or Functional	– Primary responsibility for conducting tests	– Observe or review test mateirals and results	– Review CM logs and test results or – Track versions and code units	– Review test mgmt and test documents for completeness and correct process	– Review test activities and documentation for adherence to processes and standards	– Coordinate review of test materials – Store test deliverables and docu-ments in project library	No involvement	No involvement	– Review test activities and documentation for adherence to processes and standards and for appropriate rigor

Figure 8-10. Sample Testing Responsibility Assignment Matrix (RAM)

Test Type	Developer (may be contractor or staff)	Testers (usually staff, but may be contractor)	Project Configuration Mgr	Project Test Mgr	Project QA Mgr	Project Deliverable Mgr/Librarian	Sponsor	User	IV&V
Integration	– Participate or support test execution[2]	– Participate, observe or review test materials and results – Participate in checkpoint decision	– Review Prime's CM logs and test results or – Track versions and code units – Participate in checkpoint decision	– Review test mgmt activities and test documents for completeness and correct process – Coordinate with PM Checkpoint Decision	– Review test activities and documentation for adherence to processes and standards – Participate in Checkpoint Decision	– Coordinate review of test materials – Store test deliverables and supporting documentation in project library	No involvement	No involvement	– Review test activities and documentation for adherence to processes and standards and for appropriate rigor – Participate in checkpoint decision
System	– Participate or support test execution	– Participate, observe or review test materials and results	– Review Prime's CM logs and test results or – Track versions and code units	– Review test mgmt activities and test documents for completeness and correct process – Coordinate with Project Mgr Go/No-Go Decisions	– Review test activities and documents for adherence to processes and standards – Review or perform requirements traceability analysis to ensure all requirements have been tested	– Coordinate review of test materials – Store test deliverables and supporting documentation in project library	No involvement	No involvement	– Review test activities and documentation for adherence to processes and standards and for appropriate rigor – Review or perform requirements traceability analysis to ensure all requirements have been tested

Figure 8-10. Sample Testing Responsibility Assignment Matrix (RAM)

Test Type	Developer (may be contractor or staff)	Testers (usually staff, but may be contractor)	Project Configuration Mgr	Project Test Mgr	Project QA Mgr	Project Deliverable Mgr/Librarian	Sponsor	User	IV&V
Performance/ Stress	– Participate or support test execution	– Prepare or assist with preparation of test plans and scripts – Participate, observe or review test materials and results	– Review Prime's CM logs and test results or – Track versions and code units	– Review test mgmt activities and test documentation for completeness and correct process	– Review test activities and documentation for adherence to processes and standards – Review test results to ensure performance requirements have been met	– Store test deliverables and supporting documentation in project library	No involvement	No involvement	– Review test activities and documentation for adherence to processes and standards and for appropriate rigor – Make recommendation about system scaleability, growth and throughput
Regression	– Participate or support test execution	– Participate, observe or review test materials and results	– Review Prime's CM logs and test results or – Track versions and code units	– Review test mgmt activities and test documents for completeness and correct process – Coordinate Go/No-Go Decisionto enter UAT	– Review test activities and documentation for adherence to processes and standards – Review test results to ensure sufficient testing has been performed	– Store test deliverables and supporting documentation in project library – Store results and supporting materials about Go/No-Go Decision	No involvement	No involvement	– Review test activities and documentation for adherence to processes and standards and for appropriate rigor
Decision to enter UAT		– Make recommendation about readiness for UAT	– Make recommendation about readiness for UAT	– Prepare and distribure preparatory materials regarding UAT conduct to all, especially Sponsor and User	– Make recommendation about readiness for UAT	– Store test deliverables and supporting documentation in project library			– Make recommendation about readiness for UAT

Figure 8-10. Sample Testing Responsibility Assignment Matrix (RAM)

Test Type	Developer (may be contractor or staff)	Testers (usually staff, but may be contractor)	Project Configuration Mgr	Project Test Mgr	Project QA Mgr	Project Deliverable Mgr/Librarian	Sponsor	User	IV&V
User Acceptance	– Participate, as needed – Respond to test incidents – Participate in testing meetings	– Participate or observe testing – Assist with analysis of test incidents, as needed – Participate in testing meetings – Review test materials and results	– Track UAT configuration and any changes due to fixes – Participate in testing meetings – Make recommendation for Acceptance Decision	– Coordinate testing efforts and report to stakeholders on status – Lead test meetings – Track test incident status and disposition – Coordinate Acceptance Decision	– Review test activities and documentation for adherence to processes and standards – Make recommendation for Acceptance Decision	– Store test deliverables and supporting documentation in project library	– Execute tests and business workflows, as appropriate – Participate in test status meetings – Participate in Acceptance Decision	– Prepare test use cases[3] – Executive tests and business workflows – Make recommendation for Acceptance Decision	– Review test activities and documentation for adherence to processes and standards and for appropriate rigor – Make recommendation for Acceptance Decision and on readiness for system rollout
Pilot	– Participate, as needed – Respond to test incidents – Participate in testing meetings	– Participate or observe testing – Assist with analysis of test incidents, as needed – Participate in testing meetings – Review test materials and results	– Monitor pilot configuration and any changes due to fixes – Participate in testing meetings	– Coordinate testing efforts and report to stakeholders on status – Lead test meetings – Track test incident status and disposition – Coordinate Pilot Decision, if appropriate	– Review test activities and documentation for adherence to processes and standards	– Store test deliverables and supporting documentation in project library	– Execute tests and business workflows, as appropriate – Participate in test status meetings – Participate in Pilot Decision, as appropriate	– Execute tests and business workflows – Make recommendation for Pilot Decision, as appropriate	– Review test activities and documentation for adherence to processes and standards and for appropriate rigor – Make recommendation for Pilot Decision, as appropriate

[1]Source: Adapted from North Carolina Information Resources Management Commission document.

[2]For integration, system, performance, and regression testing, the primary resonsibility for test execution varies depending on the type of project and contract. Either the developers or testers may have the primary responsibility or it may be a joint effort.

[3]It is HIGHLY recommended that the users prepare or actively assist with preparation of the test use cases and scenarios, to ensure that the system is tested using actual business cases. Project staff should supplement the user's use cases with additional test scenarios as necessary to ensure critical requirements are verified and the outcomes are reviewed by the user and sponsor.

The final test before putting the new system into production is the user acceptance test (UAT). This is a full-up functionality and performance test. It shows the users what will be delivered. Although the user community is required to participate in the UAT, users' participation should be highly encouraged in all parts of the testing program. The system cannot be said to be ready for deployment or operations until the UAT is approved and signed off by a representative of the user community, the client, or the project sponsor.

LESSONS LEARNED FOR TESTING

Testing is a critical piece of project success. The following list of lessons learned can help make it less painful and more productive.

1. Don't underestimate testing time—and DON'T cut it.

2. Ensure all business functional requirements are verified and validated.

3. Remember that retesting is required to verify that bugs have been corrected. Build retesting into the schedule.

4. Configuration management is not optional.

5. Never, never, never test in the production environment—never.

6. Test disaster recovery and/or business continuity plans.

7. Involve stakeholders in testing. Remember, the primary stakeholder has to sign off on the UAT before the project is completed.

8. Use the testing process to ensure knowledge is transferred.

9. Develop a frequently asked questions (FAQ) document during testing.

10. Use automated testing tools when possible.

11. Ensure conversion and/or interface testing is built into the project plan for historical data/legacy systems. It often takes multiple passes to convert all the data, so start early.

12. A phased rollout approach for IT systems is good but may require even more testing on a cumulative basis.

13. Make sure you have the right resources during testing. For example, have a security administrator available to identify and correct access problems during testing.

14. Establish toll-free numbers, vendor support onsite, documentation/manuals, security officer assistance, and other support as necessary.

15. For COTS products, evaluate the components for acceptable performance, appropriate design, expected quality, and conformance to enterprise architecture.

    Do this BEFORE you buy any commercial product. Too many IT departments have been surprised when a business manager tells IT that he just bought a wonderful new product, but it only works on a Windows LAN and the company is on a Novell LAN.

16. Preparing for testing takes a lot of time.

17. Start the test effort early in the project.

18. Develop the test data, and then test the test data and test procedures. Know what the correct results of a test should be before you start testing the system being developed. For example, when you test security during the UAT, do not test with a superuser ID. Test with normal IDs.

19. Did we mention that you should never test in the production environment?

PM in Action!

For more resources and information on testing, you can check out these web sites.

- http://www.sei.cmu.edu/plp/frame_report/testing.htm
- http://www.gao.gov/policy/itguide/info_src.htm
- http://www.oft.state.ny.us

Chapter Summary

- Developing a quality approach and plan is critical when starting off a project. Too many project managers and teams start off developing the product without clearly defining what the quality goals for the product are.
- When defining quality on a project, use an operational definition—one you can actually measure to see if you've achieved.
- Understand that the ultimate definition is provided by the client, customer, or user. They are the ones who will tell you if the product meets their expectations.
- There is a difference between product quality and project quality. Product quality focuses on the product itself as it's being developed. Project quality focuses on how well the project is being managed with respect to the project management standards established in the organization.
- The approach to quality has changed over the years. It is no longer just inspecting a product to identify and remove defects. The current approach to quality is to design quality into the product from the very beginning, not to just do some testing at the end. Management has a significant role in developing the quality approach used by the organization.
- There are international standards that must be complied with in developing products to be used outside the company. The most common of these is the ISO 9000 series of quality standards.
- Quality has two costs associated with it: the cost of implementing a quality program and the losses incurred if products are of inferior quality. The costs of conformance include testing, inspection, the salaries of the personnel involved, documentation, etc. The cost of nonconformance is the cost associated with defective products, waste, lost time, and rework.
- The quality management plan is a document written during the planning phase of the project. It describes the overall quality approach to be used during the project.
- In IT projects, testing often forms the core of the quality assurance approach. The testing program must be started early in order to allow enough time to develop the testing approach, write the test documentation, prepare the test scripts and test data, and ensure that the testing program will do a thorough job in testing the product.

- Testing is hierarchical. It begins with each developer testing his or her pieces of software, and continues by testing increasingly large and complex pieces of the product. The final test is the user acceptance test (UAT), which should be witnessed by the user or client and verifies that the product works as expected.
- Never test in the production environment.

Key Terms

Quality
Product quality
Warranty
Quality control
DMAIC
Cost of conformance
DRs
Pareto diagram
Ishikawa diagram
White box testing
Test plan
Operational definition
Project quality
Quality assurance
Six Sigma
DPMO
Cost of nonconformance
QMP
Fitness for use
IV&V
Black box testing
UAT

Key Term Quiz

1. A _______ is a guarantee given to the purchaser by a company stating that a product is reliable and free from known defects and that the seller will, without charge, repair or replace defective parts within a given time limit and under certain conditions.

2. _______________ is the process of managing the documented quality processes to ensure that the product's quality requirements will be met.

3. Customers measure quality against whether the product meets their expectations or not, in other words, it's _____________.

4. _______________ focuses on the product deliverables as they are produced, the pieces of the final product that are being developed.

5. The ______ defines the organizational structure, responsibilities, procedures, processes, and resources needed to implement quality management.

6. __________ is the quality effort with a goal of reducing defects to 3.4 per million.

7. The __________________ is how much money it will take to achieve a given level of quality.

8. ________________ is the detailed effort of measuring and verifying that the product is being made correctly as the project progresses.

9. The results of a ________________ tell us what percentage of the problems result from what percentage of the causes.

10. The _____ is the final test, signed off by the sponsor or customer, to ensure that all requirements have been met.

Chapter Review Questions

1. Why is writing a quality management plan at the beginning of the project important?

2. What is an operational definition?

3. Who determines the level of quality you need to achieve with the product you're developing on the project?

4. What is the difference between product quality and project quality?

5. What is the goal of Six Sigma?

6. What are the five phases in the Six Sigma approach?

7. In measuring the cost of quality, what are the differences between the cost of conformance and the cost of nonconformance?

8. List some metrics that can be used to measure the project quality.
9. An Ishikawa diagram helps you to identify what?
10. The 80:20 rule was created from the results of what type of analysis?
11. What program forms the core of most IT projects' quality efforts?
12. In what phase of the project should the testing effort be started?
13. True or False: It is permissible to test against the design rather than the requirements because the design accurately reflects the requirements.
14. True or False: It is permissible to test the new product on the production system as long as care is taken to not impact production processes.
15. When testing COTS software, what are two areas of testing emphasis?
16. True or False: Users should never get involved in the testing because it is too complex for them to understand.

END NOTES:

1. Project Management Institute (PMI®), *A Guide to the Project Management Body of Knowledge (PMBOK® Guide)*, 3d ed., page 180, Project Management Institute, Newtown Square, PA, 2004.
2. Project Management Institute (PMI®), *Organizational Project Management Maturity Model (OPM3)*, Project Management Institute, Newtown Square, PA, 2003, www.pmi.org/info/PP_OPM3.asp.
3. *Managing Successful Projects with PRINCE2*, 9th ed., published by the Office of Government Commerce under license from the Controller of Her Majesty's Stationary Office, Norwich, England, 2004.
4. Louise Lee, "It's Bad to Worse at Dell," *Business Week*, November 1, 2005.
5. Kaoru Ishikawa, *Guide to Quality Control*, Asian Productivity Association, 1972.

9 Project Communications

After reading this chapter, you will be able to:

- Identify the communications needs for a project.
- Define content and format for project communications.
- Describe effective project communication.
- Develop a communication plan.

Planning Project Communications

We have stated that a major part of a project manager's job is to communicate—regarding status, progress, issues and problems, forecasts of budget, schedule completion, and so forth. Much of this communication will be informal, such as hallway conversations or responding to e-mails. The most visible part will be formal communications, such as status reports, meeting minutes, presentations, and management documents. Because of the central role communication plays in project management, one of the most important aspects of project planning is to plan communications: who needs to be communicated with, what they need to know, how often they should be communicated with and in what format.

Identifying Project Stakeholders

The first part of planning for project communications is to identify your project stakeholders, both internal and external. **Internal stakeholders** include the project sponsor, the team members, the functional manager, internal clients, and the final user (for internal IT projects). If multiple departments are involved, such as on an ERP project, the list of internal stakeholders can be extensive.

External stakeholders can include vendors, the general public (such as when the project is a web site), regulatory agencies, clients, and so forth. It is important to identify these stakeholders and include them in communications early and often. Sometimes stakeholders can derail a project at the last moment because they weren't involved in the early planning phases. This is particularly true if the project is in the public sector, as in a government IT project.

Project managers often believe that every stakeholder has an interest in making their project successful. This is a common belief, but it's naive. In reality, many stakeholders are completely indifferent. Further, there may be stakeholders who do not want the project to be successful. A major risk in many process improvement projects is that the employees themselves will not support the project because it will change how they work, something most people don't want.

Every project manager should be aware that there might be subversive stakeholders who will try to harm the project and cause it to fail. Project managers, like most employees in an organization, prefer to ignore issues like this and pretend they're not there. However, a project manager who ignores anything that may cause the project to fail is shirking his or her responsibility to make the project successful. If you even suspect that there might be people who are negatively affected by the project, the project communications effort must take them into account and ensure that special attention is paid to these detractors or subversive stakeholders.[1]

The best approach is to create a simple stakeholder spreadsheet with the following information:

1. Their name or job title

2. What the impact to them might be if the project is successful (positive or negative impact)

3. How strongly they are affected

4. How much influence or power they have in the organization

5. How they might respond to the project

6. What the project needs from them

7. How to gain their support, or at least get them to be neutral

Items 3 and 4 might be charted on a simple 1 to 10 scale. This spreadsheet will help to prioritize communications efforts and to preplan responses.

> ***PM in Action!***
>
> Consider the following types of projects and make a list of internal and external stakeholders for each:
>
> 1. An operating system upgrade
> 2. An internally developed sales contact management system
> 3. Implementing a new call center phone system
> 4. Becoming Sarbanes-Oxley compliant

Factors that Affect Communications Planning

When planning for project communications, there are a number of factors to keep in mind. As in all things in the project world, when it comes to communications no two projects are the same. Communications is affected by the complexity of the project, the urgency of the project, and the availability of the communications technology.

Project Complexity

Two types of complexity affect project communications—technical complexity and organizational complexity.

If the project is technically very complex (e.g., developing new computer chip technology), communication needs will be very complex. Communication will involve sharing information among scientists, engineers, the customer, maybe outside consultants, perhaps research institutes or universities, and others. Much of the information for these stakeholders will be related to the product, the risk, and quality specifications. Additionally, the project manager needs to report product status and project status to the sponsor, customer, team members, and functional managers. All of these people will want differing levels of detail in their communications, and some of them may want it in specific formats.

If the project or its product influences multiple parts of the organization, then the project has organizational complexity. For example, implementing a new ERP system within the company affects virtually all divisions and groups. Each one of these will need to be communicated with on project status and issues, as will the executive branch. A project that has a great deal of organizational complexity should identify a person other than the project manager to be in charge of communications, because communications will become a major, time-consuming effort. Having a formal group dedicated to organizational change management (OCM) is a common approach to identifying the organizational issues and communicating with all of the stakeholders involved.

Contrast these projects that have complex communication needs with a project that simply upgrades a LAN server. The server may hold business-critical information, and it may be the latest and greatest, but the number of stakeholders and the amount of communication that needs to take place is very different.

> **NOTE**
>
> As more people are added to the communication chain, the number of communication channels increases exponentially. A mathematical equation describes this principle: [N (N – 1)] / 2, where N is the number of people involved in the communications. Thus, a group of 4 people has 6 communication channels and a group of 10 people has 45 communication channels. Not only does that mean a lot of time and effort is spent on communicating, but there are also 45 different ways for the information to be misunderstood, as the following graphic shows.

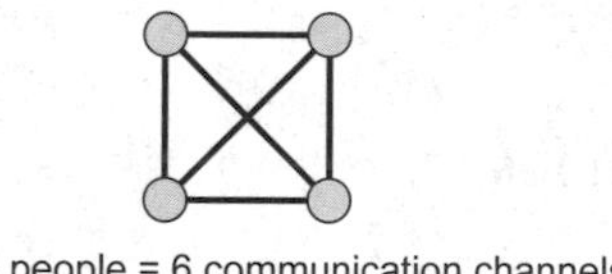

4 people = 6 communication channels

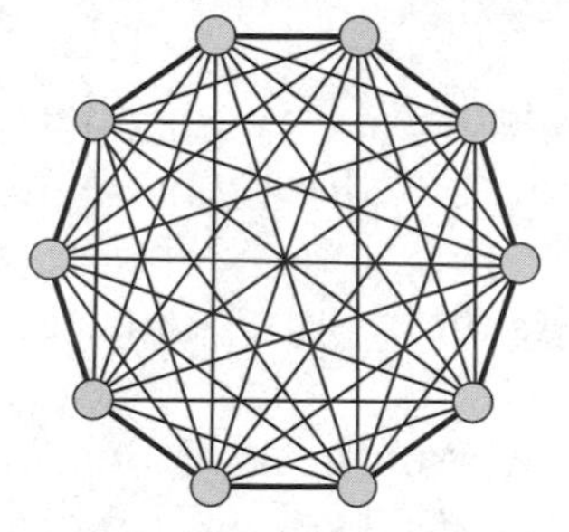

10 people = 45 communication channels

Communications Urgency

One of the factors that influences communications planning on the project is the urgency of the communications. Consider a project for replacing a faulty piece of equipment on the outside of the space station. Not only is the complexity high, but the communications—particularly while the equipment is being replaced—are critical. The communication planning for this type of project would include ensuring the best communications equipment is available, real-time communications is in place, viable backup procedures are in place, and so forth.

The urgency of the communications often depends on how critical the project is to the particular stakeholder. To the IT department, upgrading an application is usually not a critical project; to the department that relies on that application, it is. If different stakeholders have a different sense of urgency or criticality, the project manager should prioritize communications with that stakeholder according to the stakeholder's priority.

Communications Technology

Technological advances have made many parts of project management communications much easier. Rather than trying to hold a weekly status meeting when only part of the team is local, teams can now hold a videoconference or webinar. Rather than writing up a weekly status report, printing it, making copies, and distributing it to stakeholders, project managers can now simply update a project's web site with current information and send an e-mail to the stakeholders telling them where to find it. PMOs can create document templates for deliverables, perform configuration management on them, and keep everything on a LAN where team members can access the most current versions of the documents. When used correctly, technology can make the communications job easier.

There are other instances where the technology itself can be a hindrance. Consider a consulting firm that uses a different software or OS than its client. This can be problematic when sending information back and forth over the Internet. Even having different versions of the same software can be a problem. As a project manager, you may run into instances where you send out a project schedule in MS Project and a key stakeholder does not have that program. In this case, you need to find a way to get the information to the person in a format he or she can use. There is another danger in being heavily dependent on technology—if it breaks (or *when* it breaks), you still need to get information out but are without your normal method of doing so. For example, when there's an outage at the host site for your project web page, communications can be severely affected.

COMMUNICATION CONTENT AND FORMAT

After you have identified the key stakeholders for your project, you should work with them to identify the information they will need, how it can best be delivered, and the format it should be delivered in. This is not to say that you are going to customize the communications for every stakeholder, but you should be able to create categories of stakeholders that require separate communications channels, formats, and timing.

Content

Different audiences have different needs for information about the project. The project sponsor and other executives want to know what has been accomplished since the last report, and they are primarily interested in whether the project will finish on time and on budget. They may also want to know the current status and what is planned for the next report. This information should be presented at a high level without many details. For example, on a six-month project with 400 tasks, they only want to hear about eight to ten high-level milestones, major risks, and progress-to-date.

If a risk or an issue might affect the delivery date or budget, the project sponsor and executives will definitely want information on that. They will want to know what occurred, and why, and what you are planning to do about it. If the solution requires significant resources, they also want to know the amount.

Performance variances are another area that is of concern to executives. Variance outside the acceptable range should be brought to their attention, along with the root cause for the variance and plans to address the variance.

> **NOTE**
> A *progress report* talks about what has been accomplished since the last reporting period. A *status report* talks about the current state of the project. A *forecast report* talks about what is planned for the next reporting period or further in the future.

Functional managers want to know information that affects their functional area and the resources they are lending to the project, particularly if changes to their resources are expected. If resources are going to be released sooner or needed longer than normal, the functional manager wants to know.

Other managers have other needs. For instance, the quality assurance and testing manager wants to know how many bugs were identified, how many have been fixed, how many hours his or her people have put in since the last report, the cumulative hours by person, and how many hours are expected over the next reporting period.

Team members want to be apprised of how their tasks are going, when a predecessor task is about to finish, and if there are any changes to the plans. Generally, team members get the most detailed information, and they get it in a more informal presentation than the sponsors or functional managers. Sometimes e-mail is sufficient to alert team members that a task is about to be completed and that they should get ready to do their part in the next task.

When communicating with external stakeholders, care needs to be taken about communicating proprietary information. This applies to stakeholders outside the project as well as stakeholders who are outside the organization.

PM in Action!

Make a list of the information you think should be sent to executives, functional managers, other managers, and team members. Start by identifying the stakeholder, then create a list of the documents the stakeholder should receive. Next, define the detailed elements that would be part of one of the documents and create a sample template.

Format

Format of the communication material refers to three aspects: formal versus informal, written versus verbal, and push versus pull. Let's address push versus pull first. When information is pushed out, it means that the project manager sends it, or gives it, or delivers it to someone. The manager is proactive in getting information distributed. Examples of pushed information include progress reports that are e-mailed monthly or weekly steering committee meetings where a formal presentation is delivered.

When information is pulled, it means that the recipient has to take the initiative to receive the information. For example, there may be a project web site posting all the up-to-date information. If someone wants to know the status of the project, he or she can go to the web site and download the latest progress report, training plan, or whatever else is available.

In discussing the other two aspects (formal versus informal, written versus oral), it is easier to consider them in a matrix presentation as shown in Figure 9-1. This shows what types of communications would be considered formal-written, informal-written, formal-oral, and informal-oral.

Figure 9-1. Information Formats

	Written	**Verbal**
Formal	• White papers • Business cases • Progress, status, or forecast reports • Project plan components • Meeting minutes • Project audits	• Presentations • Team meetings • Change review board meetings • Advisory board meetings
Informal	• Memos • Notes • E-mails	• Most one-on-one meetings • Hallway conversations • Most phone calls • Ad hoc meetings

E-mails are traditionally considered to be informal written communications. However, there is a body of case law that is being built up that shows that in a lawsuit or a criminal investigation, e-mails may be subpoenaed and entered as evidence. This puts them more into the category of formal communications. If you are in doubt as to whether an e-mail you're sending may be formal or informal, be safe and treat it as a formal communication.

THE COMMUNICATION PLAN

After defining the project stakeholders, their information needs, and the format and the timing of the communications, the project manager is ready to build a communication plan that integrates all this information. This plan documents who needs what information, when they need it, how it will be given to them, and, sometimes, how to communicate under special circumstances, such as during emergencies.

The communications plan does not have to be a detailed deliverable. The easiest way to build it is to create a table in a word-processing application or to create a spreadsheet. List the stakeholders across the top and the type of information down the left side. Where the squares intersect, you can include a description of the information and the timing of the distribution. Examples are shown in Figures 9-2 and 9-3.

Figure 9-2. Sample Communication Plan 1

	Client	Sr. Management	Sponsor	Team Members	Sub-contractors	Suppliers	Gov. Agencies	Community
Status Reports	Scope and Schedule progress reports. Bi-weekly. Use client reporting template.	Scope, Schedule and Budget status reports. Bi-weekly. Use template.	Scope, Schedule and Budget status reports. Bi-weekly. Use reporting template.	Schedule updates. At team meetings.	Schedule updates for defined work. At team meetings.			
Forecasts	Schedule forecast at the milestone level, and if changes.	Budget forcast monthly. Changes to scope, schedule or cost.	Budget forecast bi-weekly. Changes to scope, schedule or cost.	Schedule updates. At team meetings.				
Informational Articles	Copies only	Copies only	Sign off prior to release	Copies only				Quarterly. Sanitized.
Schedule information	Milestone progress	Milestone progress	Detailed baseline requires sign off. Updates bi-weekly.	Keep on web site for team member access.	Milestones and detailed budget as needed.	As needed.		
Risk information	Specific risks as appropriate.	Any high risks	Review risk management plan monthly. Any high risks or unexpected risks above threshold.	Risk register updated monthly on web site for team access.	As appropriate	As appropriate	As appropriate	
Changes	Changes to scope or schedule baseline.	Changes to any baseline	Changes to any baseline	Changes to scope or schedule baseline	Changes to baseline that impact subcontractor	Changes to baseline that impact supplier		
Regulatory Forms							Quarterly Form QX-741. Others as required.	
Public Relations Information								At kick-off and completion. Quarterly progress.
Other						Purchase orders. 2 weeks prior to need.		

Figure 9-3. Sample Communication Plan 2

Project Name:				
Project Manager:				
Key Stakeholders	**Key Messages**	**Format**	**Frequency**	**Other**
Client				
Senior Management				
Sponsor				
Project team members				
Employees				
Subcontractors				
Suppliers				
Government Agencies				
Community				
Other				

An empty box indicates that most projects will not need to worry about communications on that particular issue to that organization or group.

It is a good idea for the project manager to define the team communications guidelines in the communication plan. For example, the project manager may want to mandate that team members respond to project e-mails or voice-mails within 24 hours. For urgent situations, this could be changed to 4 hours. (The communication plan should include a clear definition of what qualifies as an urgent situation.) These guidelines are particularly important if part of the team is located somewhere other than the main project site—especially when part of the team is located overseas. The document should specify the time zone to be used for measuring against (e.g., U.S. Pacific Standard time or Universal Standard time), as well as the expectations for the timeliness of the response.

Part of the communication plan includes defining communications protocols, such as the example about defining standard time in the paragraph above. A protocol should also be defined for e-mails. Many people are swamped daily with e-mails. Defining protocols for e-mail subject lines can make e-mail more effective. For example, if a team member wants to inform the project manager of something, but does not need the project manager to take action, the team member can preface the subject line with "FYI." If the team member needs the project manager to take action, the subject line can contain "action required." Most popular e-mail programs allow the setting of mail priority. Usage for those priority settings can be defined in the communications plan.

COMMUNICATING EFFECTIVELY

Effective communication is the responsibility of the person delivering the communication. If you want to get your message across, you have to assume full responsibility for doing so. It doesn't matter how clear you think you are if the person receiving the information does not understand it the way you want. You need to keep working on it and cannot blame the other person for not seeing things your way.

Communication Myths

Most people think they communicate clearly. In fact, with some people they do. However, many times when people think they are being clear, the person receiving the information has a totally different interpretation of it than was intended. Here are some common communication myths:

Myth: I said what I meant; it's their problem if they don't understand it.

Truth: As the sender of a communication, you are 100 percent responsible for the communication. You can choose whether you want to be right about how you communicated or whether you want the result you are after.

Myth: Words have the same meaning for everybody.

Truth: Meanings are contextual. Words can mean different things in different situations and to different people. If you looked up the 500 most frequently used words in the English language, you would find they have over 14,000 meanings.

Myth: I only communicate what I choose to communicate.

Truth: You are never not communicating. What you don't say is as important as what you do say. Your body language speaks more than your words.

Myth: Everyone will hear my presentation the same way.

> ***What Do You Think?***
>
> What are some other communication myths that you know of?

Truth: Everybody has different listening styles. Some people want to hear your bottom-line first and then understand how you arrived at it. Some people want to see all the analysis first and then see your recommendation. Understand your audience's listening style.

Myth: I only have to say something once in my presentation for people to remember it.

Truth: Research has shown that within one hour after we hear something we have lost 56 percent of what we heard, after one day we have lost 66 percent, and after one month, 80 percent of it is gone.

In his book *Silent Messages*, Dr. Albert Mehrabian states that the believability of what we communicate is influenced 7 percent by words, 38 percent by tone of voice, and 55 percent by body language.[3]

> * **NOTE**
>
> There is a well-known communication model called the sender-receiver model. It is quite simple. The sender is responsible for sending a clear and complete message. The receiver is responsible for receiving the message in its entirety and indicating what he or she heard. The sender then confirms that the message was received and understood. A conversation might sound like this:
>
> Sender: We need the following items delivered to the Jonesville office by Monday the 22nd: 4 laptops, 15 desktops, and a server.
>
> Receiver: Okay, I will get you 4 laptops, 15 desktops and a server for the Jonesville office by Monday the 22nd.
>
> Sender: You got it. Thank you.

Barriers to Communication

Communicating should be easy. You merely open your mouth and speak, right? Obviously, this is not the case. Anyone who has ever raised a teenager understands that no matter how clearly you think you are communicating, there are barriers in the communications process. Many things can create communication, and the message, the sender, the receiver, and the environment can each present obstacles. Let's look at each of these in turn. The tables that follow have lists of what to do and what not to do.

The Message

What to Do

- Have a clear and concise message.
- Clarify assumptions.
- Include enough background information to set a context.
- Be organized.
- Frontload the most important information.

What Not to Do

- Use jargon and slang.
- Use ambiguous words.
- Add superfluous information.
- Go into too much detail.

The Sender

What to Do

- Prepare, prepare, prepare.
- State the objective of the communication.
- Use simple language and check for understanding.
- Allow questions and participation.
- Respond to verbal and nonverbal feedback.
- Summarize decisions and next steps.
- Be vivid, descriptive, and passionate (as appropriate).

What Not to Do

- Withhold relevant information.
- Send mixed messages.
- Add emotions, attitudes, and self-interest.
- Speak too quickly, speak too softly, mumble.
- Give too much information at one time.
- Speak in a monotone or ramble.
- Engage in power games.

The Receiver

What to Do

- Listen.
- Provide feedback.

What Not to Do

- Stereotype.
- Have preconceived notions.
- Selectively listen.
- Engage in power games.

The Environment

What to Do

- Use face-to-face communication whenever possible.
- Make sure the location is appropriate for the method.

What Not to Do

- Leave messages on the answering machine.
- Allow background noise and other distractions.

Project Documentation

Project documentation consists of everything written by the project manager, by the team, or by other project stakeholders. It includes the most minor project-related e-mails as well as the major project deliverables: the project management plans, design documents, requirements documents, test results, published status reports, and all other formal documents.

Project documentation needs must be planned out: the documents that will be needed, whether templates are available (and if so, where), who will write the documents, who will review them, how they will be kept current, where the documents will be stored, and how the documents relate to each other. Each document requires resources; time is required to produce, review, and approve it. Effort is also required to manage and distribute the document. All this needs to be thought-out ahead of time.

One critical aspect of managing the project documentation is the document-configuration management process. Everybody on the project needs to be working off the most current version of the documents. This configuration management process may be no more than a spreadsheet or a low-end database to log who has a copy of the document and which version they have. When changes are made to a document, this process allows the project manager to identify who needs to get the updated version quickly. Any time a document is changed, the document version changes and all appropriate stakeholders are notified of the change.

What Do You Think?

What barriers to communication do you most often see in your work environment? What about in your personal relationships?

Many horror stories happen because the design team is designing the system from old versions of documents that the architecture team has updated, or the test team is designing its tests from an old document that the programmers updated months ago. In September 2005, a major part of the city of Los Angeles lost power when workers upgrading a power substation created a massive outage. What was the cause? It happened (at least partially) because the documentation the workers were using was outdated and inaccurate.[4]

It may help to create a document tree as shown in Figure 9-5. This is a hierarchical list of the project's documents, showing how they relate to one another. (See Figure 9-4.)

Figure 9-4. Document Tree

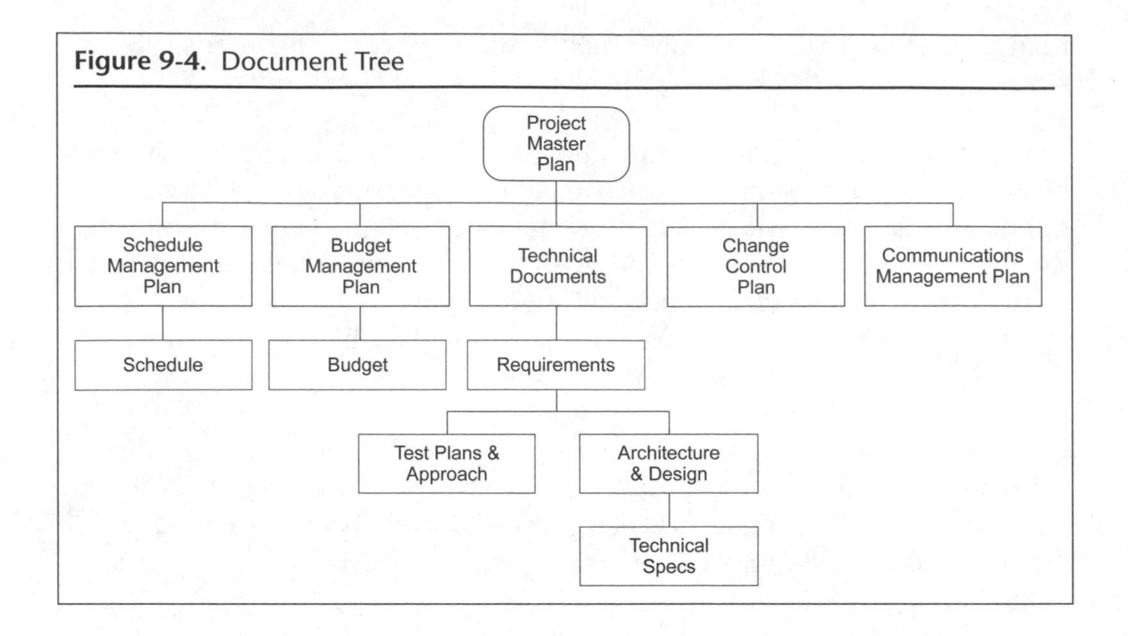

TIP

Rather than printing out an updated version each time a change is made to a document, keep the most current version of the document on the LAN or on an intranet and send an e-mail describing what changes were made and where to get the current version. This approach allows stakeholders to download the documents that are important to them and to ignore any that are not important to them.

In Practice: What to Avoid

This is a sample of what not to do:

MENUAL
QX-1004
VER 3.2A

Thank you for your order 4CH PCI SOUND CARD (QX-1004). It's easy to install to your PC system as follow step:

1. Turn off your PC system power (disconnect the power cable)
2. Open the PC case (please be careful the screw, we need to use it assembly again), and find out the PCI slot.
3. Remove the PCI slot pannel cover (nomatter it with screw or not,if with screw please keep the screw if not with screw plaese check the system parts box and find out the screw),and plug the QX-1004 on PCi slot with right position,please check the QX-1004 PCI bus(gold finger) is all plug into the PCI slot,put the screw to fix the card on the case.

4. Close the case withthe screw you just disassembly the case,and plug the power cable.
5. Plug the speaker(up to 4pcs),microphone,aux in,MIDI/game connect.
6. Turn on the PC system power and bootnig just same as before, find the CD driver (come with QX-1004) put into computer CD ROM DRIVER,and install again,the software will install itself.
7. If anything not correct plaese install again with very carefully.

Thank again to purchase our QX-1004,please fell free to give us advise how to improve our product.

Status Reports

The most common form of written communication on a project is the regular status report, both from the project team to the project manager and from the project manager to upper management and other stakeholders. At a minimum, these status reports should include the work that was accomplished in the past reporting period (weekly, biweekly, or monthly), the work that is scheduled during the upcoming reporting period, and any issues and concerns that the team has. What are the stakeholders interested in? Typically, they have an interest in the current status of the project; forecasting future status, particularly as to whether the project will meet its schedule and budget commitments; and the areas of scope, quality, risks, and issues.

Written and Verbal Communications

Project communications come in two forms: written and verbal. This section presents the basics to keep in mind for both written and verbal communication.

Written Communication

The essence of written project communication is clarity. It's not about writing the great American novel. It's about attempting to communicate business or technical concepts. Good written communication is at the level the readers will understand. This applies whether the communication is a monthly status report to the executive steering committee or a comment on someone's code.

Very few things can get a person in as much trouble as inappropriate written communication. Think about the person who meant to send a link to an X-rated web site to a friend, but mistakenly sent it to the senior management list (we saw this happen, and it wasn't pretty!).

TIP

Few things send red flags like misspelled words, misused words, or poor phrasing. Think of your own experiences in reading something where the writer irritated you with his or her style or poor spelling. If your writing skills are not great, ask someone to proofread and edit important written communications before you send them out.

There is a large body of literature on business writing. A search on the web generates thousands of sites. Here are few key points to keep you from committing an unintentional faux pas:

- Avoid the use of slang or technical vernacular.
- Do not use many abbreviations (and spell them out the first time they show up in the document).
- Avoid clichés or, at the very least, use with caution.
- Take great care to spell the names of people and companies correctly.
- Place quotation marks around any directly quoted speech or text.
- Keep sentences short.
- Make sure the document is clear and concise.
- Check for information that can be misinterpreted. If in doubt, get a second opinion.
- Validate that it makes the point you need to get across.
- Proofread (have someone else proofread as well if the document is important).
- Stay in the same tense and use the same perspective (first person, second person, etc.) throughout.
- Avoid the passive tense where possible.
- Try to cut down on the number of words used.

Make sure that what you write is organized and that it flows logically from one point to the next. It should be easy to read and have all the information necessary to achieve the objective, with no extraneous information. In e-mails and memos, close with a call to action, such as "Please call me next week" or "Please advise if you approve this approach." Make sure you include your contact information, preferably a phone number and e-mail address, in the communication.

> ***PM in Action!***
>
> If you want to assess your communication skills, try Queendom.com. It is a large online testing center. It has over a hundred professionally developed and validated psychological tests, over a hundred just-for-fun tests, and numerous mind games and quizzes.

Verbal Communication

The first thing to understand when you are communicating is that people will listen more effectively if you first explain the benefit to them. Everyone listens to radio station WIIFM, "What's In It For Me."

There are some deceptively simple keys for speaking effectively. The first thing you want to keep in mind is **who** your audience members are. Are they internal or external stakeholders? Executive level? Manager level? Team members? This will assist you in defining the content as well as the formality of your presentation.

The next step is deciding **what** you want out of the communication, and **why** you are doing it. Do you want sign off? Do you want to deliver information? Are you looking for a decision?

How you communicate is very important. Not just the words you choose, but the tone in which you deliver them and the nonverbal actions in your presentation. Also, consider if you will have a visual presentation as a backup or if you are relying only on your knowledge of the material. Will you be asking the audience to participate in brainstorming? Exercises? Or will you just ask them to listen?

The **where** also plays a role. If you are in a meeting room, you will have different options than if you are meeting in someone's office. If you are doing a formal presentation in a meeting room or classroom, try to visit it ahead of time so you can arrange it to meet your needs.

You can communicate more effectively if you understand the knowledge level of the audience members. Are they hearing this material for the first time? Do they understand the background of what you are discussing? Do they understand the acronyms you are using? How much background material, if any, do you need to include?

Nonverbal Aspects of Verbal Communication

Verbal communication is easy to recognize—someone is talking. Nonverbal communication can also be easy to recognize, and it has a big impact on how successfully you communicate. **Nonverbal communication** includes tonality and body language. By tonality, we mean how you say what you say. Are you talking slowly or quickly, excitedly or calmly, authoritatively or in a way that invites collaboration, loudly or softly? All these are your tonality.

Nonverbal communication includes gestures, facial expressions, posture, eye contact, and sighs. Nonverbal cues are very powerful, which makes it crucial that you pay attention to your actions and the nonverbal cues of those around you. If, during your meeting, participants begin to doodle or chat amongst themselves, they are no longer paying attention to you: your message has become boring or your delivery is no longer engaging.

PRESENTATIONS

Presentations are a high impact form of formal communication. To give an effective formal presentation, you should follow the same guidelines we talked about in the section on verbal communication. You should define **who, what, why,** and **where.** For presentations, you should especially focus on **how.**

You should first determine how much time you have to present; this will give you an idea of how long your presentation can be. If you are presenting using an overhead projector, a good rule of thumb is to cover one slide every two to three minutes. If you have an hour, anticipate five minutes before and after the presentation for meeting logistics and five to ten minutes for questions and answers. This leaves 40 to 45 minutes of presentation time, which means you need 15 to 25 slides for an hour-long presentation, depending on the level of detail and complexity.

The next thing to do is to plan your opening, your closing, and the three to four main points you want to get across. Take those points and decide how much time each should be allocated. Then you can build your presentation around this outline using subpoints, charts, and graphs.

Each one of us is a more effective listener when the speaker is interesting and keeps our attention. Your job as a speaker is to keep people's attention during the presentation. Remember, your audience members are judging you by your nonverbal communication just as you are judging their level of interest. If you have confidence in both your material and your ability to communicate, you will be an effective presenter.

In Practice: Communication Failure

In a report published by the National Aeronautics and Space Administration (NASA), the committee investigating the explosion of the Columbia shuttle placed part of the blame on the confusing information, including nested bullet points and massive amounts of statistics, presented during a PowerPoint presentation. The report stated: "It is easy to understand how a senior manager might read this PowerPoint slide and not realize that it addresses a life-threatening situation."[5]

TIP

- Avoid putting too many statistics and too much confusing information in your presentation. Instead, put this information in a handout for participants to refer to later.
- Make sure you do not cram too much information onto any single visual. A good rule of thumb to follow is to keep each visual to six lines or less. Make sure the text and graphics are large enough for the audience to see clearly from all seats. Make sure the colors used are easy on the eyes, and take into account the lighting.
- Use the KISS principle: Keep It Simple, Stupid.
- Additionally, use the "tell them three times" principle: tell them what you're going to tell them, tell them, and then tell them what you have just told them. That is, prepare your audience for what you are going to present, present the information, and summarize it at the end.

The following checklist should assist you in delivering effective presentations. It does not cover everything, but it is a good general place from which to start.

Pre-Presentation

- Make sure your objectives are clearly stated in the beginning.
- Have something to grab their attention in the first four slides.
- Use graphics to the extent possible. People can understand information more easily when it's in a graphic than when it's in words.
- Make certain your text is large enough to read from the back of the room after being projected.
- Put your points in a logical sequence.
- Summarize your presentation at the end.
- Have a clear call to action, as appropriate.

Delivery

- Have your notes in order.
- Make sure your equipment functions.
- Make sure your appearance and grooming are appropriate to the situation.
- Don't read from your slides. Your audience is literate and can read from your slides themselves. Use your slides as summary points and expand on the material.
- Check that your presentation can be seen from all seats in the room.
- Sound confident. If you hesitate, mumble, or slur your words, your message will get lost in the poor presentation.

PROJECT MEETINGS

Planning and managing a meeting can be challenging. But a meeting that is poorly planned and managed can be a very frustrating experience for everyone.

An effective meeting requires three phases: the premeeting work, the actual meeting, and the post-meeting follow-through.

- The premeeting requires identifying the agenda, who should be there, and how the meeting will be run.
- The meeting itself requires good facilitation skills and clear objectives.
- The post-meeting work requires follow-up from action items and other aspects from the meeting.

Premeeting

About a week to ten days before the meeting, send out a preliminary agenda and a call for agenda items. For a kickoff meeting, you may not get any agenda item suggestions from the team, but for most meetings you should give team members the opportunity to get issues they are working with onto the agenda. Several days before the meeting, you should send out the finalized agenda, with each agenda item given a time. Additionally, if there is any prereading you want the team members to do, give them a couple of days to do so. For the kickoff meeting you may send out a draft of the charter or scope statement to give the team members time to digest the information and identify any questions or issues they may have.

You will also want to identify the equipment you need for the meeting. You may need a projector for a presentation, flip charts, markers, sticky notes, and so forth. Start to compile any handouts as well. As part of your preparation, you will want to make sure you have someone taking notes during the meeting.

The Meeting

Get to the meeting room early and set up whatever equipment and handouts you may have. Start on time. (We know vice presidents who charge latecomers a dollar for every minute they are late.) It only takes about two or three meetings structured like this to cure the five to ten minute delay that ensues because people are not on time. If this is the first meeting, begin with introductions. If there is no team charter, lay out the rules of the road for how you will run the meeting. Address such issues as sidebar conversations, cell phones, PDAs, pagers, and off-line conversations. The other item you will want to handle in the first several minutes is the intended outcome of the meeting.

Once you are into the agenda, you should start to open the conversation to interaction and feedback, unless it is a strictly informational briefing. Even then, be open to questions and requests for clarifications. Ask whether anything is unclear or people have questions, comments, or suggestions on items that you have covered. If you think someone has an unasked question, address him or her specifically and ask for perspective or input. Sometimes you will have simultaneous feedback from multiple people. In that case, it is useful to acknowledge all the people who want to contribute, and let them know the order in which they will be addressed. For example, "Okay, first will be Savannah, then Josh, then Barbara, and then Patrick." This way people know they will be heard and can settle down to listening to other people.

If you are getting conflicting views and opinions, acknowledge all input neutrally and gather input from others. If the issue can't be resolved in the meeting, or if it is taking up too much time, put it in a "parking lot" as something that will be addressed after the meeting or captured as an action item for someone to take care of. If appropriate, you may want to take a vote on an approach to an issue. However, sometimes it is appropriate for the SME to make the final call, or it may be appropriate for you, as the project manager, to make the final call. You may want to consult with the customer or sponsor before finalizing any critical issues.

TIP

Getting 100 percent agreement before making a decision is not necessary. You can establish three positions for people:

1) I agree and support this decision.

2) I don't agree, but will not oppose this decision.

3) I oppose this decision, and will not support it.

If you can get all or the majority of the people into groups 1 and 2, move on. It's a victory. Some people even use different color flashcards for voting: green for support, yellow for do not oppose, red for oppose.

It is often useful to give people a visual representation when working through an issue or coming up with a solution. Perhaps you are working through the WBS or figuring out the order of precedence in a series of tasks. Use the flip chart and start drawing the connectivity, or categories, or whatever else is needed. People become more involved if they can visualize something or help in its creation. In some meetings, such as early WBS planning or risk planning meetings, it is appropriate to give team members sticky notes and have them do the work of identifying deliverables or risks.

As the meeting wraps up, you will want to review what was accomplished against the intended outcomes. You will also want to summarize key decisions and action items. Let people know the next steps and thank them for participating and making the meeting a success.

After the Meeting

After the meeting, make sure you send out the meeting notes or meeting minutes. Follow up on any outstanding items, off-line conversations, and action items. If you think it would be useful, get some feedback from meeting participants on what went well and what could be improved next time.

Chapter Summary

- Projects have internal stakeholders, who may be team members, the sponsor, functional managers, senior managers, and other employees. Projects also have external stakeholders, who may be the client, vendors, subcontractors, unions, government agencies, and the public.
- Three factors affect communication planning: project complexity, project urgency, and communications technology.
- When planning for communications, the content of the message and the format of the message are things to keep in mind. The various project stakeholders will have different communication needs. For example, sponsors want high-level information, whereas team members need detailed information. The format can be written or verbal, formal or informal, pushed or pulled.
- The communication plan documents the audience, the type of message, and the timing of project communications. It also defines response times to various types of communications.

- Communication is the crux of project management. There are numerous barriers to effective communication. These barriers can be grouped by the message, the sender, the receiver, and the environment.
- Poorly written communication can reflect negatively on you. Spend time using some of the basic tips to increase your writing skills.
- To be more effective in your verbal communication, understand what you want to say, why you are saying it, how you are going to communicate, and where the communication will take place.
- Presentations are a formal type of communication. You can improve your presentations by preparing and following a checklist for your presentation and your delivery.
- To run an effective meeting requires upfront work as well as work during and after the meeting. The premeeting work requires identifying what will be covered, who should be there, and how the meeting will be run. Good facilitation skills and clear objectives are required to run the meeting itself. The post-meeting requires follow-up from action items and other issues identified at the meeting.

Key Terms

internal stakeholders

external stakeholders

nonverbal communication

communication plan

Key Term Quiz

1. The ________________ documents who should receive what information, when they will get it, and how it will be delivered.

2. Vendors, regulatory agencies, and the general public are examples of __________________.

3. Shrugging, facial expressions, and doodling are examples of _________.

4. The project sponsor, the team members, and the project manager are all ___________.

Chapter Review Questions

1. What are the two types of stakeholders?
2. What are the three factors that impact project communication planning?
3. If you have five-person project team, how many communication channels do you have? What if you have a ten-person team?
4. What kind of information might your senior management want to know about a project?
5. What is the difference between pushing information and pulling information?
6. What is the purpose of a communication plan?
7. So as not to create barriers to communication, what are three things to avoid when creating your message?
8. As the sender of information, what are three things you can do to avoid creating barriers to communication?
9. As someone receiving information, what are three things you should avoid so as not to create barriers to communication?
10. What are three examples of nonverbal communication?
11. To make your presentation as effective as possible, what are four things you should keep in mind about your presentation itself?
12. To make your presentation as effective as possible, what are four things you should keep in mind about the delivery of your presentation?
13. What are steps the project manager should take after the meeting?
14. To make your written communication clear, what are four things you should avoid?

END NOTES:

1. Lauren Gibbons Paul, "It's Your Move," *PM Network,* April 2005, page 34.
2. Project Management Institute (PMI®), *The PMI Compendium of Project Management Practices,* Project Management Institute, Newtown Square, PA, 2003.
3. Albert Mehrabian, *Silent Messages,* Wadsworth Publishing, Belmont, CA, 1981, page 7.
4. Hector Becerra and Susannah Rosenblatt, "The Power Goes Out," *Los Angeles Times,* Sept. 13, 2005, page A22.
5. Clive Thompson, "PowerPoint Makes You Dumb," *New York Times Magazine,* Dec. 14, 2003, available at http://www.nytimes.com/2003/12/14/magazine/14POWER.htm.

10 Project Risk

After reading this chapter, you will be able to:

- Identify sources of project risks.
- Use tools to identify project risks.
- Analyze project risks.
- Develop responses for project risks.

Understanding Project Risk

What is project risk? Does risk entail only the things that can go wrong with your project? Does it also include things that can go right? How do you identify all the risks lurking out there, just waiting to scuttle your project? If you do not have enough team members, is that a schedule risk? How do you know which risks you should respond to and which ones you should monitor? How can you develop effective responses to risks? These are the critical questions that risk management tries to answer.

We begin by defining specifically what we mean by a **risk.** According to the *PMBOK® Guide,*[1] a risk is an uncertain event that, if it occurs, has a positive or negative effect on at least one project objective, such as time, cost, scope, or quality. It is interesting to note that in this definition, a risk can have a positive outcome. Most times, we think of risk as only having negative impacts. IT project managers barely have enough time to worry about things that can harm our project, let alone things that can benefit it. If we look at positive risks as opportunities, we are more likely to look for things that can make our project more successful—the things that we call positive risks.

In the above paragraph, we said that we were concerned with the outcome if the risk event actually happens. The risk event itself is not what we are concerned about; it is the outcome—the impact to the project—that we care about. The impact is the result or possible result that occurs because of the risk event. Impacts can be felt in the project scope, schedule, budget, and stakeholder satisfaction. How serious is the impact if the risk happens? How badly will the schedule or budget be hurt?

In addition to seriousness of the impact, the other aspect to watch in risk management is the probability of a risk event actually happening—the likelihood that something will occur.

Risks and issues are sometimes confused. A risk is a potential future event. An **issue** is something that is occurring right now and has to be dealt with now. For example, a risk might be a 50 percent chance that our delivery will be late, causing a one-week delay in the schedule. This is something that could happen in the future, but since it has been identified, we can plan for it. An issue would be if the delivery truck with critical testing equipment had an accident on the way to the office and the equipment was destroyed. Now there is a crisis, and the team has to decide how to work around the problem.

By their nature, projects are more susceptible to risk than are normal operations. Projects are unique one-time activities and are not ongoing or repetitive. The team tries to mitigate the risk inherent in projects by developing defined and proven techniques to implement projects. One of those techniques is methodical risk management. The process of risk management is a very distinct one that continues throughout the project.

This chapter deals with all the steps necessary to effectively plan for risk. The steps are most effective when done in a particular order. The first step is identifying risks, the next is analyzing them, and the third is developing a response. In the chapter on project monitoring and control, we will look at how to monitor risks.

We are only discussing qualitative risk analysis in this book. There are many quantitative techniques, such as Monte Carlo simulations, decision trees, and statistical computations. We will leave these to the people who analyze risk on large, complex projects. You can find many books on quantitative techniques for risk analysis if you are interested in learning more.

SOURCES OF PROJECT RISK

Risks occur at multiple levels of the project. Ask team members to identify risks they see and they are most likely to identify technical risks. Ask the project sponsor and the sponsor is most likely to identify organizational risks.

The project manager is able to identify risks regarding the skill sets and experience of the project team. Everyone involved in the project has a different view of what is risky.

One of the more challenging aspects of risk management is training the team to address risk in a consistent manner. Another challenge is taking the time to do risk management methodically and not jump from identifying a risk to solving it by saying something like, "Oh, don't worry, I will talk to so-and-so and make sure that doesn't happen." It is human nature, and especially a project manager's nature, to try to solve a challenge or a risk once it is identified. How many times have you heard some version of the following conversation?

> Albert: "I think we are at risk for not meeting our deadline on this deliverable."
>
> Betty: "Oh, we will just work overtime, or we can bring in another person to help us out."

What Albert did was identify a risk, and rather than note it as a risk, Betty went right into solution mode. However, the risk was never documented or analyzed. Maybe the deliverable was not on the critical path and there was nothing to worry about. Maybe they assumed a resource would be available when, in fact, that resource was already overcommitted. Perhaps other team members are out there doing the same thing, but none of this is documented so that it can be managed in a coordinated fashion. It is important to keep the risk identification process separate from the analysis and response development process.

Where to begin identifying risks? One way is to develop risk categories. Some of the common categories in risk management are team members, technology, project management, the organization, and external factors.

Team Members

Since team members do the projects, they can be the biggest source of risk. Some of that risk is centered on the skills of the team members, specifically technical skills and people skills, and some of it is centered on their availability.

Skills

On a simple, routine project that uses team members who have already done that type of work, there is a minimal amount of risk that the team members will not have the appropriate technical skills for the project. However, not all projects are simple. In fact, some are highly complex and require advanced and specialized skills.

Suppose the project is to install a new, fully automated logistics and inventory tracking system for an organization that has over 10,000 products, 200 stores, 10 warehouses, and a fleet of trucks. Moreover, suppose that the project includes replacing all the existing hardware, moving to handheld tracking devices, developing the software for entry, stocking, transfer, and sales, and training 200 people on the new equipment, processes, maintenance, and use. This project needs people who are skilled in the system design and capabilities, process development, hardware setup and functionality, software interfaces and performance, and training and documentation. These needs provide some juicy resource risks that must be addressed. Because the company has never done this project, it is highly unlikely that all those skills are in-house. The project manager will have to hire consultants, bring in new employees, and train existing staff. There are risks inherent in each of those activities.

In addition to technical skills, the project manager also needs to be aware of a team member's ability to work well *on* a team and *as* a team member. In project management, this is referred to as playing well with others. In Chapter 7, we said that it would be preferable to have a team member with average technical skills and good people skills rather than someone with outstanding technical skills but poor people skills.

A team member who always sees the negative side of things, is demeaning, always misses deadlines, or does not treat others with respect is a risk to the project team. These people lower morale, influence the effectiveness of the team, and may cause other team members to want to leave the project. By identifying this risk early, the project manager has the opportunity to correct the situation or at least be prepared for some of the fallout that may occur.

Availability

With the proliferation of projects in organizations and the ongoing demand to do more with less, it is not uncommon to have a resource be pulled onto another project or have a resource's availability on any particular project be reduced. In a weak matrix organization, there is a very strong risk of having a project resource pulled off the project by a functional manager, often without the project manager even being told that the resource is being removed.

Project managers need to pay particular attention to team members who have skills that are unique in the organization or are in demand for numerous projects. A team member who developed a homegrown application for the organization and is the only person who really knows how it works is always going to be in demand. Frequently this person will be a bottleneck on a number of projects. Identifying this resource constraint and risk early in the project will assist the project manager in planning how to respond to the risk of the person not being available.

Technical

Technical risks are present in all projects these days. However, they are most prevalent in IT projects, due to the rapid changes in technology and the fact that IT touches virtually everyone else in the organization. This creates both technical and organizational risks.

The larger and more complex the project, the more time and places it has to fail. Many organizations have learned this lesson the hard way through failed implementations of ERP systems, CRM systems, and supply chain management systems, and they have begun phasing large projects to limit the probability and impact of failure. After each phase, they reanalyze the needs and the output of the project and do a lessons-learned exercise to see how to improve performance in the next phase.

There are four aspects to technical risks: technology, testing, technical requirements, and contractor/vendor relationships.

IT Technology Risks

Specific risks are common across most IT projects, regardless of the industry. For starters, the technology itself is not simple, and when multiple types of technology from multiple vendors are combined into one system, the end result can require a lot of testing and integration to ensure that it works properly under all conditions.

For example, in a typical three-tier LAN (Figure 10-1), multiple client machines and peripherals connect to the middle tier, which interfaces with the data server(s) and the outside world. Each of the different machines might come from different vendors, creating multiple sources of potential incompatibility. Even individual areas, such as the servers, might come from

Figure 10-1. Three Tier LAN

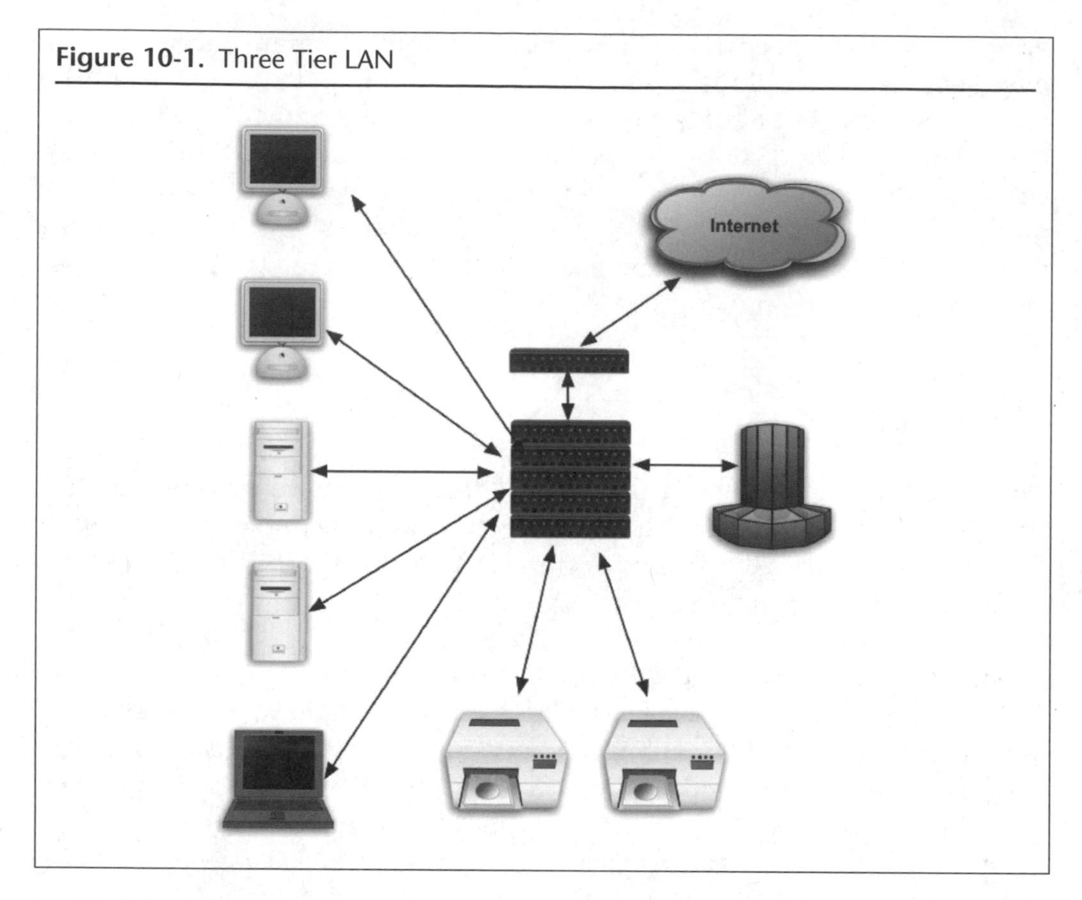

multiple vendors, like Hewlett Packard, SUN, CISCO, and IBM. An enterprise-wide system might include databases such as IBM's DB2, Oracle, MySQL, MS SQL Server, and Teradata. The network architecture itself, such as Novell or Microsoft, interacts with virtually all parts of the system. Even more complex are the systems common at large corporations, where mainframe systems may be mixed in with the client/server systems.

In Practice: Technical Project Risks

Technical risks can have large impacts, as the following two examples show:

A large U.S. insurance company planned on going live with a systems update at one of its subsidiaries on July 1. On June 30th it deactivated the old system. Seven weeks went by before it could mail out premium notices, write commission checks, or even issue policies. Almost 70 percent of the sales force quit during this period.

A U.S. federal government agency implemented PeopleSoft financials and did such a poor job of it that the agency went 10 months without being able to generate a financial report.

Requirements-Related IT Risks

The primary risks for requirements center around not identifying the correct requirements, not identifying the complete requirements, or not making the requirements clear and unambiguous. Recall from the Standish Company's *CHAOS Report* that the vast majority of projects fail because of problems with the requirements.

Function and performance requirements are generally considered as risks associated with scope; therefore, project managers normally depend on the project sponsor or customer to give them the basic requirements of the system. However, there are technical areas where customers are unable to articulate or even fathom requirements, for example, data security, data privacy and access, and the increasing level of spam and phishing on the Internet. These areas are where technical experts must depend on their knowledge to develop requirements that will go into the final product. These requirements are often complex and difficult to manage. Because these areas are transparent to the customer (if they are done correctly) special effort must be taken to bring them to the customer's attention and ensure they are understood. Security must automatically just work, despite the technical complexities of ensuring that it does.

! WARNING

If you are going to put in a new system that changes how people work, you will usually have some adoption issues. Twenty percent of the people will never support it. They do not see a reason to change, they have always done it this way, and they have years of experience invested in the current system. Twenty percent of the people will be on your side because they do not like how the current system works or they're so new they have no investment in the current system. The remaining 60 percent will go either way with the new system. If you can show them how it benefits them, they will be supportive. If they feel threatened by it, they will turn against it. Your communications effort should be devoted to capturing the hearts and minds of that middle 60 percent.

Testing

The complexity of IT systems leads to a particular risk area in managing IT projects—the danger of cutting testing when the schedule is running tight. During a normal project, testing and integration are at the far right of the project schedule. They are often the next-to-last efforts to be completed.

When the project starts running behind schedule, the only activities left to compress or cut are those remaining on the schedule, such as testing.

A thorough testing program, as shown earlier, is a strong risk-mitigation tool. The more testing the team does, the more likely the team is to find problems before implementing the system. Cutting testing, although it may save the schedule, always increases the risk of releasing a system with undiscovered problems.

Think about what normally happens on an IT project. During the testing and integration phase, it is normal to find problems that could not be found earlier. The tester writes a problem report, and the piece of software goes back to the developer for rework. However, almost nobody plans rework into the project schedule during the initial planning phase of the project, so this perfectly normal testing activity has now created schedule risks by adding unplanned work!

If the test environment is not architecturally similar to the production environment, there may be integration problems when the product is moved into production. If there is no time allocated to validate the testing process and test scripts, the testing team will spend a lot of time trying to determine if a failed test is due to a true failure of the product or if it's a false negative because of the testing process itself.

TIP

A good practice is to have a test group that is separate from your development team. This test group should work on a test platform that is as close to the production platform as possible. Developers will always test to their own design. The proper way to test is against the requirements, not against the design. An independent test group will provide additional viewpoints of the requirements that the developers may not have considered, and ensure that the final product will meet the requirements the user specified.

Vendor-Related IT Risks

IT projects rarely develop their basic components from scratch. They usually purchase existing vendor products and integrate them into a final system. There are several risks associated with this. The first is giving the vendor's marketing literature or sales personnel too much credence. The vendor's goal is to sell the product. The project's goal is to buy something that is cost-efficient and that satisfies the requirements. Often these are not compatible goals. Many IT project managers have purchased a vendor product based on assurances by the vendor's sales staff that the product will do everything the buyer needs, only to discover too late that the promised features don't work, or don't work in the buyer's environment, or the feature is a planned future upgrade.

If a system is provided by multiple vendors, there are problems inherent in upgrading. If Microsoft upgrades its Windows OS, should the organization:

a. Buy the latest upgrade and install it on each desktop immediately?

b. Wait and read the discussion forums to see problems other people are having with it?

c. Buy it and install it on a test system to check for compatibility with the organization's existing applications?

These are all things that the project manager needs to keep in mind. History shows that once a decision is made to buy a particular vendor's system, the IT department is locked into that system for a long time and is forced to deal with that vendor for many years, because there are significant costs associated with changing core systems.

In Practice: Vendor Risks

In 1999, Nike, the market leader in athletic shoes, began a project to integrate its supply chain by implementing supply chain management software by i2. The $300 million project was not, to put it kindly, a complete success and cost Nike $100 million in lost sales. An issue of CIO magazine had an article analyzing the project. "Nike's supply chain project is supposed to drive the manufacturing cycle for a sneaker down from nine months to six. Cutting out that three months would match Nike's manufacturing cycle to its retailers' ordering schedule—they order 90 percent of their sneakers six months in advance of delivery. This means Nike could begin manufacturing its sneakers to order rather than three months in advance and then hoping they can sell them. Converting the supply chain from make-to-sell to make-to-order is the dream of any company desirous of gaining competitive advantage through its supply chain. Dell has done it, famously, with PCs; Nike wants to do it just as famously with sneakers.

> "Wolfram [Nike's VP of Global Operations and Technology] called the i2 problem—a software glitch that cost Nike more than $100 million in lost sales, depressed its stock price by 20 percent, triggered a flurry of class-action lawsuits, and caused its chairman, president and CEO, Phil Knight, to lament famously, 'This is what you get for $400 million, huh?'—a 'speed bump.'"[2]

Another vendor-related risk occurs when part of the project is developed offshore in order to save on personnel costs during development. Although cheaper programmer salaries are available by offshoring, the cost savings are often offset by the increased amount of effort required to develop the business and technical requirements, the more thorough testing required to ensure the delivered product will actually work in the technical environment, and rework due to communications problems. It is hard enough to develop clear understanding in a culture with a common language. Communications problems are exacerbated when working cross culturally and any misunderstanding of the requirements has the potential to increase project risk significantly.

Project Management-Related Risks

Risk related to project management has four sub-categories: scope, schedule, cost, and project management itself.

Scope

Poor requirements gathering, unclear requirements, or changing requirements significantly increase risk and are the main reasons that projects fail. One area where project managers often do a poor job is in identifying the user's performance expectations for the new system. The project team can install the most up-to-date hardware and software available, but if users have to wait five minutes for applications to open, they will be very unhappy. If an SQL query to report on last week's sales takes 24 hours to run, the sales managers are going to stop using the system. Performance expectations must be identified as part of the requirements process so they can be designed into the system. These performance requirements can have major impacts on the design of the system and may lead to major redesign if the user is not happy. Failure to educate stakeholders on how to describe their needs and wants can lead to multiple scope risks.

Perhaps saying that change is inevitable on projects is an overstatement, but change is certainly the norm. There are risks involved in locking down the design too early, and there are risks involved in keeping the design open too long. Not having a formalized change management program is a sure way to put the scope and schedule at risk. What good is a baseline if there are no teeth to keep it in place? Having a change management program that is just a series of forms to complete before accepting the change is almost as bad. A good change management program screens out unnecessary changes and allows the beneficial ones, ensuring that the scope, schedule, and budget baselines are updated in the process. Chapter 13 covers this in more detail, but for now, suffice to say that change involves risk.

In Practice: Requirements Risks in IT Projects

Experience shows that up to 70 percent of IT project failures result from poor requirements gathering, analysis, and management. Even in the '80s, we knew that more than 50 percent of all software defects could be traced to requirements errors. These figures on the risks of not having strong requirements have held up consistently in research.

Schedule

Most schedule risks are a result of overly optimistic estimates. Sometimes the estimates come from team members who think that everything will go as planned and assume they will not be sidetracked or need to rework anything. Other times the estimates come from senior management defining a hard end date or looking at a schedule and then arbitrarily reducing it by some amount and calling it a "challenge." Project managers should review the estimates for each task, the critical and near critical paths, and the project as a whole to see if the estimates are realistic or if some estimates need a reality check.

Another type of schedule risk is called merge bias. On the network diagram, when two (or more) activities are predecessors to a later activity, a delay in any one of the predecessors can delay the successor activity. The additional schedule risk at this merge point is called merge bias. Let's say that unit testing, system testing, and load testing need to be complete before integration testing can begin. Testing is difficult to predict duration estimates for. Therefore, assume that for each of these tests there is about a 75 percent certainty that the testing will be complete on or before the date on the schedule. Does this mean that there's a 75 percent chance that integration testing will start on its estimated start date? The answer is no, because if each task has only a 75 percent likelihood of ending on its scheduled date, then the likelihood of the whole path having an on-time completion is .75 × .75 × .75, or .42. There is a less than 50 percent chance integration testing will start on schedule based on the above information. That is a significant schedule risk.

We will talk about finalizing the schedule in the next chapter. For now, we will just touch on two ways of compressing the schedule: crashing and fast-tracking. Crashing is the process of reducing the duration of tasks on the critical path to get the project done faster. Fast-tracking is doing tasks in parallel that would normally be done sequentially. Both of these, although shortening the schedule, introduce risk, because you are performing tasks in a way that is not optimal. In addition, if you are crashing by adding people, you are adding complexity in the communication structure and increasing the probability that there will be a miscommunication leading to rework, a delay, or worse.

Another schedule risk can occur when team members are rushed to get a project done quickly, either because there is another project they are expected to start working on or because they are working on multiple projects and trying to get through them as fast as possible.

Budget

Common project budget risks include predefined budgets, poor cost estimates, and overly optimistic cost estimates. Predefined budgets are far too common in IT. They occur when the project manager is given the project and the budget at the same time (often with a pre-defined schedule as well). The budget was determined by management using no analysis (it is usually someone's best guess at what the project should cost) and now you have to live with it.

Poor cost estimates are those that are developed without the proper research. We talked about different types of estimates in Chapter 6: analogous, parametric, and bottom-up. Anything other than a recently developed bottom-up budget carries a risk that it may not be met. We also talked about levels of accuracy—ROM, approximate, and budget-level estimates. A ROM and an approximate estimate are risky because they have a good chance of being inaccurate. Poor cost estimates often derive from poor schedule estimates. Underestimating the duration of the project is almost guaranteed to lead to an underestimate of the costs, as resources are kept on longer than planned.

Overly optimistic cost estimates are similar to overly optimistic schedule estimates. The risk can lie with the team members who gave the estimate, with a project manager who believes he or she is making management happy with a low budget number, or with management that is looking for cost to be reduced without scope being reduced.

Project Management

Project management risks include poor project manager skills and insufficient experience as well as inadequate project management infrastructure, processes, templates, and methodologies.

An inexperienced project manager, or one who is new to the company or the technology, is a risk. There are many opportunities for that project manager to make a wrong decision. A common problem in IT project management is promoting a strong technical person into a project management role without proper training or guidance. The skills and knowledge required to manage a project are very different from those required to be a good architect or programmer.

Having a solid project management methodology with well-established processes, approaches, and templates can reduce some of the variability of project management results. It can make things easier for project managers, as they do not have to reinvent the wheel for every project. The methodology gives them a path to follow. They know what steps to take, where to coordinate, where to find document templates, how to communicate, what the metrics are, and so on. Much of the guesswork is taken out of managing projects. However, a methodology that is too prescriptive, that is wrong for this type of project, or that is not adaptable to project size and complexity may be worse than no methodology at all. Additionally, if the methodology is too clunky or too bureaucratic, then project managers will see it as a hindrance and not really use it. Remember, each project is unique. Established methodology should be a guideline, not a railroad track.

Organization

The organization in which the project is being performed carries with it its own set of risks. Take, for instance, the organizational structure. If it is a functional organization, there is the risk that the project's needs will be put on the back burner and that the project manager will not have the influence or authority to get the project done well. A matrix environment has risks with conflict over resources and unclear performance or reporting priorities.

Another aspect of organizational structure to keep in mind is the different categories of team members and their various backgrounds. Some team members may be exempt and be strictly salaried. Others may be contractors from outside the organization. In large organizations, with large projects, there may be unionized team members who are paid hourly. In this case, there is the risk of going over budget if the need arises to pay overtime for hourly workers; even worse, there is the risk of losing some workers if a strike occurs.

Another set of risks revolves around the culture in the organization. Some organizations are so risk averse they suffer from analysis paralysis. They're afraid of making the wrong decision, so they want to think everything through again, and again, and again. Others have an entrepreneurial, shoot-from-the-hip culture. Some organizations believe that all decisions should be made collaboratively, and some have a very dictatorial decision-making process. Each of these cultures presents different risks to the project.

An organizational risk that is quite common is changing priorities. Sometimes this is called *project du jour,* or project of the day. Sometimes it seems that resources are moved from project to project on a monthly basis. What was important in June is yesterday's news in July, and the resources are pulled from the has-been projects one-by-one, until yesterday's projects slowly suffocate or produce a shadow of their original scope.

! WARNING

Take care how you identify organizational risks. Some organizations recognize their weaknesses and can even laugh at them. But in some organizations and some cultures, just mentioning risk is taboo. In these cultures, if you state that you have risk on the project, you're labeled a bad project manager. There is risk in every project; you just have to be sensitive to how you phrase it. There's an old adage: "It's not what you say, it's how you say it."

External

External risks are risks that are outside the project and maybe outside the organization; these are often out of our control. Risks external to the project include those that have been mentioned in previous sections: competition for resources, shifting or competing priorities, budget cuts, etc.

Risks that are external to the organization include new regulations, weather, changes to the price of a required material or resource, changes with an external client organization, labor strikes, and so on. The project manager will need to do some of the proverbial outside the box thinking to identify these types of risks.

Risk Identification Tools

From reading the previous section, it should be clear that risks are, in fact, everywhere. Right about now you may be thinking, "How can I possibly identify all the possible risks?" Well, fear not—this section has some tools that will help you.

Project Documents

One of the easiest places to look for risks is the project plan. The project charter will have assumptions, constraints, and any high-level risks in it. The assumption log is also a very good place to start looking for risks. Anything that is an assumption is a risk, because the project team members don't *know* for certain it is true, but they are planning as if it were. What if this is not the case?

Also, are the assumptions consistent throughout your project documents? Let's say that the assumption log shows that the project has a certain resource 50 percent of the time, but the schedule shows the person allocated 100 percent of the time. This is inconsistent, and one of the documents is inaccurate.

Identified constraints should also be reviewed. For instance, with a mandated due date, a pre-defined budget, or a level of performance, risk exists because the constraint may not be feasible and failure to meet the constraint could cause the project to fail. A project manager who receives the project's delivery date and budget at the same time he or she learns about the project will automatically have schedule risks and cost risks because the numbers for schedule and cost were determined without detailed analysis.

Technical documentation is a good source for identifying technical risks. The project manager will find requirements, details on specific technology, detailed design documents, and more in the technical documents. These documents are fertile ground for identifying aspects of the project that could cause a negative impact.

One of the best sources for risk identification in the project scope is the WBS. The WBS allows the project manager to see all the activities and deliverables in the project at a glance. The project manager can see risks at the deliverable level or at the higher levels, so the project manager gets a holistic view of the project and can spot any systemic risks.

Performing a schedule review can help identify risks to the project's schedule—risks to milestones and the promised delivery date. It can also help identify inaccurate duration estimates, missing dependencies, and other schedule problems. In addition, the schedule usually shows assigned resources. The project manager should look at the resource view of the schedule and identify any resources that are over allocated. Any directed dates are possible risks. A directed date is a date in the schedule that was not derived from the logic of the schedule. Other schedule risk items are having too many activities flow into a single successor or having one activity with too many successors. If a critical path activity is dependent on ten direct predecessors, there is likely a schedule risk, because the probability of that many predecessors staying exactly on schedule is very slight.

Similarly, the project budget will help to identify cost estimates that may be inaccurate, or times when cash flow is likely to be steeper than originally estimated. Comparing the budget to the schedule, the resource list, assumptions, and constraints may enable the project manager to find some inconsistencies that present a risk to the project.

Finally, look at any contracts for the project. There may be penalty clauses, constraints, or other verbiage that indicates a challenge in meeting project objectives.

Interviews

Usually the people who know the most about project risks are the people who are working on the project—the team members. The project manager can take time to interview them one-on-one or have a team meeting dedicated to identifying project risks. During the interview process, the project manager should use some of the tools described above, such as reviewing the technical documentation with the technical team lead or resource allocation with functional managers.

> **TIP**
> When interviewing project stakeholders to identify risks, two of the best questions you can ask are "What would you be worried about if you were managing this project?" and "What should I be concerned about that I have not yet identified?"

Risk Breakdown Structure

One of the modern risk gurus, Dr. David Hillson, has developed a tool called a **risk breakdown structure (RBS).** He describes an RBS as "A source-oriented grouping of project risks that organizes and defines the total risk exposure of the project. Each descending level represents an increasingly detailed definition of sources of risk to the project."[3] It is similar to the tree format of a WBS in that it is a hierarchical structure, but it is concerned with areas of potential risk sources rather than deliverables.

A key benefit of using an RBS in the risk identification process is that it allows the team to brainstorm project specific risks in a structured way. This facilitates a thorough and organized depiction of risk for the project.

Dr. Hillson produced a generic RBS based on a joint research project undertaken by the PMI® Risk Specific Interest Group and the International Council on Systems Engineering (INCOSE). This RBS is presented in Figure 10-2.

Figure 10-2. Generic Risk Breakdown Structure

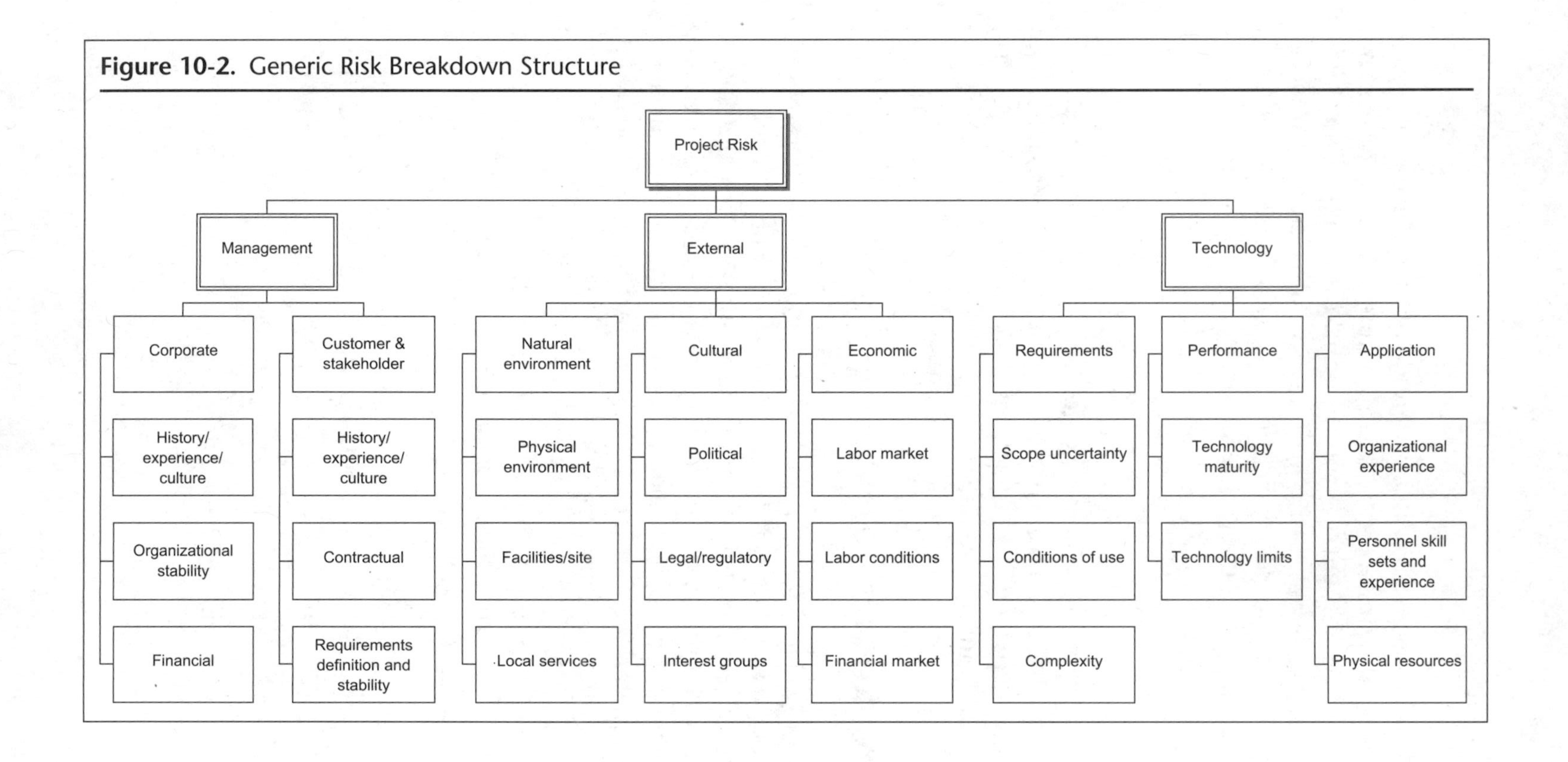

In Practice

Dr. Hillson created the following project RBS for defense software development. It was first published in the June 2003 issue of *Journal of Facilities Management.* More information on risk can be found in Dr. Hillson's book *Effective Opportunity Management for Projects: Exploiting Positive Risk.* There are also many interesting articles on his web site: www.risk-doctor.com.

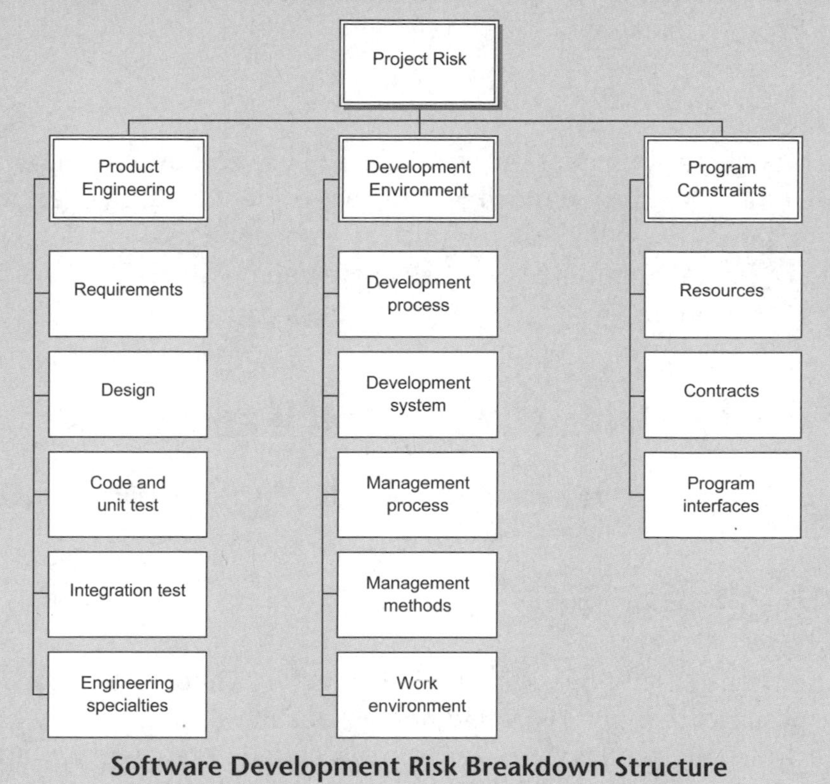

Software Development Risk Breakdown Structure

PM in Action!

Create a generic risk breakdown structure for your organization and for the types of projects you usually work on.

Brainstorming

Brainstorming is probably the most common way to identify risks. The project manager gathers the project team, technical experts, the client, the project sponsor, and anyone else who can provide input, and the team starts generating ideas on possible project risks. The project manager or facilitator can use a "blue sky" approach to begin, where people blurt out any risk they can think of without regard for how reasonable or critical it is. That evaluation is done as a separate step. If it helps the process, the project manager can create a RBS to use as a guide.

Once there is a comprehensive list of risks, the team starts to identify how probable they are and what the impact might be. This process is covered in the section on risk analysis.

TIP

If your organization does the same types of projects on a regular basis, it would be worthwhile to develop a risk identification checklist or template that will guide the project manager and the risk manager in identifying the typical risks associated with IT projects in the organization.

DOCUMENTING PROJECT RISKS

Risk statements and the risk register are used to document project risks.

The Risk Statement

Risk statements should be as specific as possible. There is no way to identify a response to a vague risk statement like "milestone XYZ may be late." The milestone being late is the effect; the risk statement doesn't say anything about the cause of the risk. Therefore, there is no viable action to take to respond to the risk. Another example of a vague risk statement is "technical specifications may be at risk." Now, what does that mean? What about the technical specifications? Which ones? What are they going to do—swallow the project whole? You get the idea. Risk statements should be phrased in such a way that they give clear and useful information about the risk event and the possible impact.

When writing a risk statement, start by describing the event as specifically as possible, then explain the impact and state the cause of the risk. For example, "The shipment of monitors could be late due to a backlog at the vendor's warehouse, *causing* a delay in opening the office." At the beginning of a project, you are looking for anything that could negatively affect the project. As you enter the execution portion of the project, your risks may become more detailed, which is why it is important that risk processes be conducted throughout the project, not just once or twice at the beginning. Do not try to include in the risk statement the possible response to the risk or any ideas on how to mitigate it. Those are written separately. At this point, you may not know the likelihood that the monitors will be late, and you may not know how late they may be. This information can be elaborated as you analyze the identified risks. For now, it is enough to identify risks to the project.

The Risk Register

The output deliverable from the risk identification process is the **risk register.** At this point, it is where the team lists the risks it has identified along with their priorities, potential responses to them, and the root causes of the risks. The risk register is usually created in an MS Excel spreadsheet or an MS Word table and is sometimes referred to as the **risk log.** Some enterprising individuals create a risk database so they can slice and dice the risk information.

The first items to go into the risk register are the list of risks, their probabilities, and their potential impacts. This is where the risk register starts during the project planning phase. As the risk management process continues, the risk register expands to include the personnel identified to respond to that risk if it occurs. It also expands to include the response strategies, actions, symptoms, and warning signs that tell us the risk is occurring (called trigger events), the contingency reserves that have been set aside, the secondary and residual risks, and other information the project manager feels is appropriate to manage the project risks. Figure 10-3 shows a sample format of a risk register.

The risk register is the tool that pulls everything together. The identified risks are entered into the register in the beginning of the process. After the analysis process, the probability and impact are added. During the response phase, an action is entered and a responsible party assigned. The best person to assign to a risk is the person who has the most influence over the event.

Analyzing Project Risks

At this point, you have identified a whole pile of risks. In fact, you may have so many risks that you're thinking, "What are we, nuts? This project will never turn out!" Don't worry. Remember that these are only things that *could* hap-

Figure 10-3. Project Risk Register Template

Project Risk Register

Project Information								Last Updated:	
Project Name							Project ID #		
Project Manager									

Risks	Directions – Enter the data in the fields below. See the Project Risk Worksheet instructions for details on the field content. This risk log is a summary sheet of the risks and is not intended to capture as much detail as the Risk Worksheets.

Legend:	Response – the action taken to reduce the risk
PO = Probability of Occurrence. Use a score from 1-5, with 5 being high	Response Owner – the person in charge of performing the mitigation
PI = Project Impact. Use a score from 1-5, with 5 being high	Contingency – the actions that will be taken if the risk event occurs

				Response		Contingency		
Risk #	**Description**	**PO**	**PI**	**Action**	**Owner**	**Trigger**	**Owner**	**Action**

pen. The good news is that you have identified the risks. Consider this: if you don't manage risks, you remain at their mercy.

Now you are going to analyze and rank your risks. This is a relatively easy process compared with trying to capture the risks. You are now going to take each risk that you entered into your risk register and define the probability of the risk occurring and the impact if it does occur. Before we review the steps involved in risk analysis, let's look at some of the finer points of assessing probability and impact.

Assessing Probability

For our purposes, we are going to keep the analysis relatively simple and assume that the probability of something occurring is high, medium, or low. This rough estimation works well for most IT projects (the exceptions are when you're doing something as complex as an ERP or SCM implementation). In order to ensure that everyone involved in the risk process ranks risk in approximately the same manner, it is useful to create some guidelines for the project that establish what is meant by high, medium, and low. For example, guidelines could set high probability at a 60 percent or more likelihood, medium probability at 20 to 60 percent, and low probability at less than 20 percent. A more conservative organization may set high probability at 40 percent and set low probability at 10 percent or less.

WARNING

Stakeholders have different levels of risk tolerance. Your sponsor may be a risk-taking cowboy kind of person. However, your customer may be somewhat risk averse. Your job is to figure out how to balance these perspectives and come up with the right level of risk tolerance. Remember, we never said this would be easy!

The probability assessment may be somewhat subjective, a gut feel of what's risky based on experience. This is an acceptable approach on small, noncritical projects. On larger, complex, and critical projects, the project manager will need to take a more objective approach. He or she may interview experts to get an opinion on the probability. He or she may run simulations or establish some statistical measurements to assess the likelihood of a risk occurring. These are all necessary approaches for large projects; however, they are beyond the scope of this book.

What Do You Think?

Think of some of the projects you have worked on and the various stakeholders' attitudes towards risk. Can you identify any situations where different risk attitudes created conflict?

Assessing Impact

As in probability, the project manager can assess impact as being high, medium, or low. When assessing the impact of a risk, defining impact in different areas is useful to keep the risk register organized and precise. Consider using the areas of schedule risk, scope/performance/quality (SPQ) risk, budget risk, and stakeholder satisfaction risk as impact categories in the register. Most risks will affect many or all of these areas, but the primary impact will be in one area.

Schedule Risk

In most IT projects, schedule risk is created by one of three things: the schedule was dictated by management or by the client without regard to the amount of work involved; the productivity of the resources was underestimated so the work will progress slower than planned; or critical-path tasks were underestimated. All of these create risk to the schedule.

When assessing the severity of the impact for the schedule, consider anything that will affect the critical path as a high risk. The merging of several paths onto the critical path, a resource that is in short supply and is assigned to tasks that are on the critical path, or any other number of circumstances could affect the critical path. A medium risk could be something that minimally affects a near critical path or something that would use up a significant amount of float on a noncritical path. A low risk would be something that has a negligible affect on a noncritical path.

Scope/Performance/Quality Risk

Scope/performance/quality (SQP) risks are associated with product requirements, scope, product performance to specifications, and deliverables. Unclear, unstable, or incomplete requirements, components that are not going to meet the performance requirements, and untried or unstable technology create high SPQ risk. Technology that has been proven in the market but that your company doesn't have a great deal of experience with creates medium risk. Proven technology used in a new way might create low risk.

Budget Risk

Budget risks are typically created by the same factors that create schedule risk: the budget was dictated without regard to the amount of work to be done, the schedule was underestimated and the project will require more work and more money than planned, or the cost of materials was underestimated.

When there is potential for budget impacts due to risks, there are two basic approaches to plan for it. The first is to set aside a fixed dollar amount to compensate for the risk, such as having a $50,000 contingency fund. The second is to take some percentage of the project budget and set it aside for risk response. For example, a high-risk project might require a contingency fund of 50% or more of the entire project budget, whereas a lower risk project might only require 10% of the budget be set aside for risk contingency.

Stakeholder Satisfaction

Stakeholder satisfaction is concerned with the customer, end-user, sponsor, team members, and any other significant stakeholders on the project. Remember, it is not okay to meet all of the project specifications if the client is unhappy at the end of the project.

The real question is how to identify stakeholder satisfaction as a risk item and identify the impact on the project. Unhappy or unmotivated team members can cause schedule and budget problems. A difficult client who expresses dissatisfaction with the product being developed can halt the entire project. The end-users may not use the new application. A project sponsor who is not happy with progress can demand additional communications and reporting, putting more work on the project manager and on the team members. All of these are potential risk areas for the project and can be identified during risk analysis efforts.

In Practice: Typical Impacts of Risks on IT Projects

Experience has shown that the most common impacts for IT projects are:

- Cost and schedule overruns
- Technical performance that does not meet expectations
- Incompatibility of the new system with the existing infrastructure
- Process changes that were not taken into account in the organization
- Users who are unable or unwilling to use the new system
- Failure to obtain all or many of the expected benefits because of implementation problems

A Risk Analysis Process

When performing a risk analysis there are some simple guidelines to follow:

1. Keep the risks in the categories established for risk identification. Whether an RBS or another categorization technique is used, analyzing by category is a good idea.

2. Assess the probability of each event occurring using high, medium, and low rankings. For a medium or large project, it may be appropriate to be more

sophisticated and establish risk rankings of 1 to 5 or 1 to 10. In either case, guidelines should be established that define what the ranking means.

3. Assess the impact of the event occurring. Use the following categories for impact: schedule impact, cost impact, scope/performance impact, and stakeholder satisfaction impact. On a medium or large project, establish guidelines that indicate what each ranking means against these categories.

4. Sort the list by RBS (or whatever categorization scheme you have established) then by severity. Start with the high probability and high impact at the top of each category, then medium probability and high impact, then high probability and medium impact, and so forth until you arrive at the bottom where there are events with low probability and impact. The result is a prioritized set of risks against which you develop responses.

PM In Action!

Grid computing is being used more and more for high performance computing. When using many smaller computers to do what mainframes have done in the past, some risks are reduced and others are introduced. Go onto the Internet and learn more about grid computing (if you need to). Assume you have a project to move a 400-bed medical school hospital from a mainframe environment to a grid environment. Create a risk breakdown structure to at least four levels. Identify 15–25 risks that you identified using the risk breakdown structure.

Risk Analysis Tools

A number of tools, both manual and automated, can assist you in analyzing risks. The specific tools you can use are highly dependent on the type of project and the extent of the risks you anticipate. Three of the most commonly used tools are a preliminary risk analysis, a probability-impact matrix, and a project risk profile.

A Preliminary Risk Analysis

In the book *Corporate Information Systems Management,* Cash, McFarlan, and McKenney determined that during the early stages of a project, such as during the project selection process, there are three primary risk control factors: [4]

- Experience with the technology

- Project size
- Project structure

Using this risk framework, a project manager can characterize IT projects according to their level or risk based on size, technology, and structure.

		Low Structure	***High Structure***
Low Technology	Large project	Low risk	Low risk
	Small project	Very low risk	very low risk
High Technology	Large project	Very high risk	Medium risk
	Small project	High risk	Medium-low risk

While the specific determination of each of these terms will be dependent on the company and on the project, Cash, McFarlan, and McKenney describe the terms as follows:

- **Low technology:** The technology is familiar to the company and does not represent a drastic change from the way things are now. It is evolutionary technology.
- **High technology:** The technology of the project is unfamiliar to the company and to the project team. A substantial learning curve could exist. This is revolutionary technology.
- **Low structure:** The project is poorly organized, with a high likelihood of changes that will change the requirements or possibly the entire focus of the project. Often the goals are not clear at the beginning of the project and continually evolve throughout the project.
- **High structure:** The project is well-organized with clearly defined outputs. Management is unlikely to request changes during the project.

Using the structure vs. technology matrix above, we can define four high-level categories of projects:

Low Structure-Low Technology

- These projects are low risk when good project management processes are used.

- Gaining high-level support is important.
- The project manager must periodically evaluate the project to ensure it still satisfies the business goals.
- Continual communication is critical to ensure management is aware of project status and issues.
- Staying within cost and schedule constraints is important.
- Because of the low structure, change requests will be common on the project.
- Project leadership must come from the business side instead of the technical side to compensate for the low structure.

Low Structure-High Technology

- Because of the low structure, the project deliverables and goals are not clear in the early phases.
- The combination of high technical complexity and low structure makes this a very high risk project.
- The project manager and team leads require technical experience in the technology and in working on high risk projects.
- Early management commitment to the requirements, design, and specifications is critical.
- Because of the low structure, the project can expect many change requests.
- Automated project management tools are of limited utility, since their usefulness depends on strong project management processes in order to be effective.
- The project manager must evaluate the project regularly to ensure it meets management's expectations. If needed, the project may be broken into multiple subprojects or a phased set of upgrades to deliver full functionality.

High Structure-Low Technology

- The strong project structure makes these the easiest to manage with the lowest risk.

- The project is likely to adhere to deadlines and schedule.
- Goals and activities are well-defined and rarely change through the project.
- The low level of technology means that there is not a steep learning curve to becoming productive.
- The project manager does not need a high level of experience with the technology.

High Structure-High Technology

- The strong project structure means that tasks and activities are well-defined.
- Interaction with end-users will be very important due to the new technology being introduced.
- Change occurs more often than in low-technology projects, but the strong project structure will have a strong change management process built into it.
- The project manager and the team leads need strong technical backgrounds in addition to experience in managing complex projects.
- Teamwork becomes critical on these projects.

Probability-Impact Matrix

A **probability-impact matrix** is a good way to get a visual representation of the project risks. After identifying the risks, the project manager assesses the probability and impact of each risk and then plots it on the matrix. Doing so can give the project manager an overall view of the project. A probability-impact matrix is also a useful tool to use in a project team meeting when doing a group risk analysis. (See Figure 10-4.)

Project Risk Profile Form

Figure 10-5 shows a project risk profile form for IT projects. It has categories, scores, weights, and definitions of overall project risk. This is a good start for both risk identification and risk analysis. Use Figure 10-5 as a template; you can customize it for your organization and your project. This form can be used in the project selection process as well.

Figure 10-4. Probability-Impact Matrix

Low Impact High Probability	Medium Impact High Probability	High Impact High Probability
Low Impact Medium Probability	Medium Impact Medium Probability	High Impact Medium Probability
Low Impact Low Probability	Medium Impact Low Probability	High Impact Low Probability

Figure 10-5. New Project Risk Profile—Technical Risk

Project Name: ______________________ **Project #:** ______________

Project Manager: ______________________ **Date:** ______________

Client: ______________________

Project Total Risk Score*: **0**

Risk Area	Risk Weight	Risk Score	Area Score
Technology			
1. Non-standard hardware required			
a. None		0	
b. Servers		High - 3	
c. Peripherals	5	High - 3	
d. Clients		High - 3	
e. Routers		High - 3	
f. Unknown		High - 3	
2. Team has little experience with the software			
a. Not Applicable		0	
b. Programming language		High - 3	
c. Data base	5	High - 3	
d. Data Communications		High - 3	
e. Other - specify (Unknown)		High - 3	
3. The system will use state of the art components			
a. Yes	3	High - 3	
b. No		Low - 1	

Figure 10-5. New Project Risk Profile—Technical Risk (continued)

Risk Area	Risk Weight	Risk Score	Area Score
Technology			
4. The user/client has experience in the new system			
a. No experience, brand new to them		High - 3	
b. Some limited knowledge or experience	5	Med - 2	
c. Familiar with the technology		Low - 1	
5. Number of vendors that are involved in the new system			
a. One		Low - 1	
b. Two		Med - 2	
c. Three or more	2	High - 3	
d. Unknown		High - 3	
Project Size			
6. Total development man-hours for the System			
a. 100 to 1,00	5	Low - 1	
b. 1,000 to 5,000		Med - 2	
c. 5,000 to 50,000		Med - 3	
d. Over 50,000		High - 4	
7. Total system development duration			
a. 12 months or less	4	Low - 1	
b. 13 months to 24 months		Med - 2	
c. Over 24 months		High - 3	
8. The work will be performed by:			
a. Mostly by on-site personnel	2	Low - 1	
b. Significant portions by on-site personnel		Med - 2	
c. Mostly by off-site personnel		High - 3	
d. Mostly by offshore personnel		High - 4	
e. A combination of on-site and off-side personnel		High - 4	
9. Number of departments (other than IT) involved with the system:			
a. One	4	Low - 1	
b. Two		Med - 2	
c. Three or more		High - 3	
10. Approximate number of end users			
a. Up to 25	1	Low - 1	
b. 25–50		Med - 2	
c. Over 50		High - 3	
11. Number of geographic locations in which the system will operate			
a. One	2	Low - 1	
b. Two or three		Med - 2	
c. More than three		High - 3	
12. Number of existing IT systems the new system will interface with			
a. None	3	Low - 1	
b. One		Low - 1	
c. Two		Med - 2	
d. More than two		High - 3	

Figure 10-5. New Project Risk Profile—Technical Risk (continued)

Risk Area	Risk Weight	Risk Score	Area Score
System			
13. The new system			
a. Totally new system		High - 3	
b. Replacement of an existing manual system	1	Med - 2	
c. Replacement of an existing automated system		Low - 1	
14. If a replacement system, the percent of existing functions that will be replaced on a one-to-one basis			
a. 0–24		High - 3	
b. 25–50	5	Med - 2	
c. 50–100		Low - 1	
d. Unknown		High - 3	
15. The severity of process changes needed for the new system			
a. Low - 1		Low - 1	
b. Medium - 2	5	Med - 2	
c. High - 3		High - 3	
d. Unknown		High - 3	
16. User organization changes needed to utilize the new system			
a. None		0	
b. Minimal		Low - 1	
c. Somewhat	5	Med - 2	
d. Major		High - 3	
e. Unknown		High - 3	
17. Comfort level of the users/client			
a. Poor - resents the change		High - 3	
b. Fair - some reluctance	5	Med - 2	
c. Good - looks forward to the change		0	
18. Upper-level user management commitment to the system			
a. Somewhat reluctant, there are internal politices		High - 3	
b. Adequate	5	Med - 2	
c. Extremely enthusiastic		0	
19. Client/user is actively represented on the project team			
a. None		High - 3	
b. Part-time user representative appointed	5	Med - 2	
c. Full-time user representative appointed		Low - 1	
20. The new system implementation will be			
a. A phased implementation	4	Low - 1	
b. Done all at once		High - 4	
21. There is a backup system available (even a manual one)			
a. Yes	3	Low - 1	
b. No		Med - 2	
22. The project team includes members with experience in the relevant business processes			
a. Yes	4	Low - 1	
b. No		High - 4	

*In order to obtain the final score, multiply the Risk Weight with the Risk Score for each question. Add these totals. High Risk is greater than 166; Medium Risk is between 140 and 166; Low Risk is less than 140.

Planning for Risk Response

Identifying and analyzing risk is only part of the process. The next step is figuring out how to respond to the risk. For positive risks (opportunities), the possible responses are to exploit the opportunity and use it, share the opportunity with someone who can take advantage of it better than you can, enhance the opportunity and increase the probability of it happening and the impact if it does happen, or simply accept it.

For negative risk, the possible responses are to avoid the risk, mitigate the risk, transfer the risk, or accept the risk.

Negative Risks

The following sections provide information on avoiding, mitigating, transferring, and accepting risk—your four choices when it comes to managing negative risk.

Avoiding Risk

Avoiding risk involves making a change to the project or to the product that gets rid of the risk. Let's say that for your project you plan to use a new suite of software test tools to help run test scenarios for a new application you are developing. Your lead tester has identified this as a risk and has written the following risk statement: "There is a risk that the testing phase will not complete on time because the testing staff is unfamiliar with the new testing suite." One option you have is to test using the prior tool, which **avoids** the risk altogether because the testing staff is familiar with the process.

Whenever possible, you should avoid risks that have high impact and high or medium probability.

Mitigating Risk

Mitigating a risk means reducing the probability that the risk will occur, reducing the impact that it will cause if it does occur, or both of these. If we return to our example of the new software test suite, you can find ways to mitigate the situation. For instance, you can send some staff to training on the new software or you can run parallel tests with the old system and the new system. Another option is to build in more time for the testing process. This is called adding schedule reserve, and we will discuss it in more detail shortly.

You should mitigate risks down to an acceptable level in your project. For instance, if you originally decided that this risk had a medium impact and a high probability, perhaps sending people to training and running the two testing plans in parallel will bring this down to a low probability and a medium impact.

TIP

When developing risk responses, look for root causes to a series of risks. Sometimes you can find one event that can potentially cause a myriad of risks. If you can address one root cause and thereby eliminate or reduce a series of risks, that is wise risk management!

Transferring Risk

By **transferring** risk, you are transferring the responsibility for managing the event. For example, in the testing scenario, perhaps you can bring in a consultant who is familiar with the new software to manage the process. This transfers, via a contract, the risk of meeting the timeline to the consultant. However, the interesting thing about transferring risk is that you are still left with some impact if it occurs. In other words, if the consultant delivers late, you still have a late project. However, by transferring it, you reduce the probability of the risk happening and the impact if it does happen.

Contracts and insurance are the most common methods of transferring risk. If you choose to transfer risk, make sure you are transferring it to someone who has the ability to reduce the probability and, if possible, the impact. Know that you will have secondary risks that arise out of transferring the risk.

Accepting Risk

You may decide to **accept** a risk if it is a low impact and a low probability risk. Mitigating the risk may be more trouble than just dealing with it if it arises, or you may mitigate a risk as much as you can and accept the residual risk. You will want to track the risk so you don't lose it or forget about it in the rush of managing the project, but it may be so small that you don't want to deal with it.

TIP

Use your risk analysis worksheet, your project risk profile, or your RBS to identify general areas that are more risk prone than others. Focus your risk response efforts on these areas first.

Positive Risks

Lately, the concept of managing risk by managing opportunities as well as threats has begun to make headway in the project risk management world. The third edition of the *PMBOK® Guide* has an enhanced section on positive risks. The 2004 edition of the U.K. Association for Project Management's *Project Risk Analysis & Management (PRAM) Guide* defines a risk event as "an event or set of circumstances which, should it occur, will have an effect on achievement of one or more objectives."[5] The *PRAM Guide* goes on to state that "A key principle in the definition of risk event used in this guide is the recognition that uncertainty can affect achievement of project objectives either positively or negatively. The term risk event is therefore used to cover both uncertainties that could hinder the project (threats) or help the project (opportunities)." This opens up the risk management process and lets it minimize threats and maximize opportunities, thereby increasing the likelihood of meeting project objectives.

Returning to Dr. David Hillson and his book, we find that there is a mirror process for managing opportunities, which can be integrated with a threat-focused risk process or can be implemented separately.[6]

- Risk identification: Brainstorm for opportunities; conduct a SWOT analysis to identify opportunities as well as threats. Create a combined risk register or create a threat register and a separate opportunity register
- Risk analysis: Create a mirror format combined matrix with opportunities on one side and threats on the other or create an opportunity matrix for opportunity management and a risk matrix for risk management.
- Risk response: Select appropriate strategies for each opportunity, choosing from exploit, share, enhance, or accept.

Proactively dealing with opportunities can stack the deck in your favor for meeting or exceeding project objectives. In addition, wouldn't it be great to go to your sponsor with good news on how you improved project performance?

Additional Risk Items

There are still a few items we need to cover, some of which were mentioned previously. We are going to look at contingency plans, risk triggers, secondary and residual risks, risk reserves, and fallback plans.

Contingency Plans

A **contingency plan** is a plan you put in place to deal with the risk, should it occur. The plan may include bringing in extra resources, working overtime, trying a different approach, or anything else that will help deal with the risk once it becomes an issue.

Let's assume that you are working on a project to open a new office, and one of the risks is that the build out will not be done in time. If in fact the office is not open on the date promised, but you still need to be open for business, your contingency plan is to set up a secondary location temporarily until the office can be completed.

Risk Triggers

In the above example, would you wait until the night before to realize that you weren't going to make the deadline? Of course not. You would set up a deadline by which to make the call on whether to find a backup location. You might say something like, "If the build out is not complete two weeks prior to the live date, we will use a secondary location." This build out date two weeks before the live date is a **risk trigger.** It identifies that a risk has occurred or is about to occur.

Secondary and Residual Risks

A **secondary** risk is a risk that occurs because of a selected risk response. For example, in our software testing scenario, let's say that you decide to transfer the risk to an outside consultant. You now have contractual risks that you did not have before. You may also have risks because the consultant is not familiar with your policies, procedures, forms, personnel, etc. All these could cause stakeholder dissatisfaction and/or schedule delays. Secondary risks need to go through the risk planning process as well.

Residual risks are risks that are leftover after you have applied your risk response strategy. Let's say you decide to send people to training for the new software. There may still be some residual risk that the testing will be late. Even though the people are trained, they still haven't used the new software before. However, the risk is much lower. You accept this residual risk.

Reserve

One risk management tool is **reserve.** You can set aside schedule reserve and budget reserve. You would have to be naïve to think that everything is going to go according to plan. On a project, it is certain that something will go wrong; it's just a matter of what will go wrong, when it will go wrong, and how bad it will be. Therefore, a wise project manager sets up reserves. Some companies have set reserve amounts. For instance, on a simple project, there may be a 10 percent schedule and/or cost reserve. For projects that are of medium complexity, a 25 percent reserve may be more appropriate. For highly complex projects, upwards of 50 percent is not unheard of.

How does the project manager use reserve? Cautiously. In the example of the software testing, the project manager may want to insert two weeks of contingency into the testing process. This does not mean that the testing process should take two weeks longer and that the team leader should not work to meet the original date. It means that in recognizing the risk, the project manager has inserted a two-week schedule reserve to be used if the mitigation strategies do not work as planned.

In another example, with regard to the new office build out there is no room for schedule reserve and the scope is locked down. The project manager may need budgetary reserves to pay for an offsite location on a temporary basis, or he or she may use the reserve to pay overtime for the people doing the build out.

Schedule reserve usually is at the discretion of the project manager. On small and medium projects, budget reserve is usually held by the project sponsor. On a larger project with an experienced project manager, there may be a certain amount of budget reserve at the project manager's disposal. Again, this will depend on the policies and maturity of the organization. The goal is to not use the reserve, but the reserve is there if you need it, kind of like a savings account.

Fallback Plans

A **fallback plan** is an "if all else fails" plan. If the project manager decides that he or she is going to use the new software for the project and send people for training, but that doesn't work, then as a fallback plan the project manager will test using the existing system and work overtime to catch up as much as possible.

Fallback plans are particularly important when implementing software or a new LAN configuration. In the case where the new system doesn't work, the project manager wants to be able to restore the previous capability as quickly as possible so that the company's daily operations are not affected. There are numerous horror stories in the IT literature where a software upgrade was put into production without proper testing and it brought the entire production system down. In the cases where this has happened to financial institutions, the impacts can be measured in many millions of dollars. Always have a backup plan if the implementation does not go as expected.

In Practice: Continuous Risk Management

The Software Engineering Institute (SEI), along with the Project Management Institute and many risk organizations, recommends that risks be identified and assessed continually throughout a project. SEI has a developed a process titled Continuous Risk Management in which the steps of identify, analyze, plan, track, control, and communicate are performed throughout the life of the project. Each risk nominally goes through these functions sequentially, but the activity occurs continuously, concurrently (e.g., risks are tracked in parallel while new risks are identified and analyzed), and iteratively (e.g., the mitigation plan for one risk may yield another risk) throughout the project life cycle.

Function	Description
Identify	Search for and locate risks before they become problems.
Analyze	Transform risk data into decision-making information. Evaluate impact, probability, and timeframe, classify risks, and prioritize risks.
Plan	Translate risk information into decisions and actions (both present and future) and implement those actions.
Track	Monitor risk indicators and mitigation actions.
Control	Correct for deviations from the risk mitigation plans.
Communicate	Provide information and feedback internal and external to the project on the risk activities, current risks, and emerging risks.

CHAPTER SUMMARY

- A risk is an uncertain event that could have an impact on your project. The two components of a risk are the probability that it will occur and the impact if it does occur.
- IT projects have five overall sources of risk: team members, technology, project management, the organization, and external factors. Team member risks

include skills and availability. Technical risks are comprised of technology, approach, and the technical environment. Project management risks include scope, schedule, budget, and the project management aspects of the project. Organizational risks are made up of the structure and culture of the organization. External risks are those risks that are outside of the control of the project manager, including risks external to the project and the organization.

- To identify risks, the project manager should review project documentation, conduct interviews, use checklists, and/or create a risk breakdown structure (RBS). An RBS is a source-oriented grouping of project risks that organizes and defines the total risk exposure of the project. It allows the team to identify risks in a structured fashion.
- To complete the process of risk identification, the project manager should create risk statements and enter them into a risk register.
- Analyzing project risks entails estimating the probability that a risk will occur and the impact if it does occur. A matrix of high, medium, and low probability and impact is used to analyze risks. A risk event can impact on the scope/performance/quality, the schedule, the budget, and stakeholder satisfaction.
- Tools for risk analysis include a preliminary risk analysis that considers the size, technology, and project management structure; a probability-impact matrix; and a project risk-profile form.
- Risk responses include avoiding the risk, mitigating the risk, transferring the risk, and accepting the risk.
- Contingency plans are put in place to deal with the risk if it occurs. Risk triggers alert the project manager that a risk has occurred or is about to occur. Secondary risks are risks that are the result of a risk response strategy. Residual risks are those risks that are left after the risk response is developed. Sometimes schedule or budget reserve can be used to reduce risk to the project. A fallback plan is used if the risk response does not work and the risk occurs.

Key Terms

Risk
Risk breakdown structure
Risk log
Probability-impact matrix
Issue
Risk register
Risk statement
Avoid

Mitigate
Accept
Risk triggers
Residual risks
Fallback plan
Transfer
Contingency plans
Secondary risks
Reserve

Key Term Quiz

1. Another word for a risk log is a ______________.
2. A risk has two components to it, probability and __________.
3. A risk that remains after you have developed a risk response is ____________.
4. A _____________ is put in place to deal with a risk should it occur.
5. A ___________ indicates that a risk has occurred or is about to occur.
6. A source-oriented grouping of project risks that organizes and defines the total risk exposure of the project is called a ____________________.
7. By assigning the risk to another entity, the project manager is ____________ the risk.
8. Finding a way to reduce the probability of a risk occurring is an example of ____________ a risk.
9. A description of an event with an explanation of the impact is a ____________.
10. A risk that is the result of a risk response is a _______________.

Chapter Review Questions

1. What is the difference between a risk and an issue?
2. What are the three risk planning processes?

3. What are the risk categories you can use to identify risks?

4. There are four aspects of technical risk on a project. What are they?

5. When you install a new system, you can count on what percentage of people to resist using the new technology?

6. What are the three aspects of risk involved in the actions of managing the project?

7. What are three of the risk identification tools we talked about?

8. What is a risk register used for?

9. What are three risk analysis tools?

10. Using a preliminary risk analysis form, what type of project has very low risk? What type of project has very high risk?

11. What are the four risk responses?

12. What is a positive outcome to a risk?

13. What are the four opportunity responses?

14. What type of risk might you want to accept?

15. What is a method of mitigating risk by putting in extra time or money?

END NOTES:

1. Project Management Institute (PMI®), *A Guide to the Project Management Body of Knowledge (PMBOK® Guide),* 3d ed., page 238, Project Management Institute, Newtown Square, PA, 2004.
2. Christopher Koch, "Nike Rebounds," *CIO Magazine,* June 15, 2004.
3. David Hillson, "Use a Risk Breakdown Structure (RBS) to Understand Your Risks," PMI Annual Seminar & Symposium, October 2002, San Antonio, TX.
4. James I Cash, F. Warren McFarlan, James L. McKenney, and Lynda Applegate, *Corporate Information Systems Management,* 3rd ed., Irwin Professional Publications, Homewood, IL, 1992.
5. The Association for Project Management, *Project Risk Analysis and Management Guide,* 2nd ed., APM Publishing, UK, 2000.
6. David Hillson, *Effective Opportunity Management for Projects: Exploiting Positive Risk,* Taylor & Francis CRC Press, London, 2003.

Finalizing the Schedule and Budget

After reading this chapter, you will be able to:

- Finalize project resources.
- Optimize your schedule.
- Manage your schedule with multiple projects.
- Create a budget baseline.

In Chapter 6, we created a preliminary schedule and some preliminary cost estimates. Since then, we have refined our project plan by defining the quality plan, developing the team, defining communication needs, and planning for risk. Now we can finalize our schedule to create a schedule baseline and finalize our budget to create a cost baseline. These baselines will be approved by the project sponsor or by the client, and the project manager will manage the project and monitor progress against them.

Finalizing Project Resources

In the early phases of planning, the project manager defines the equipment, skills, supplies, facilities, and other resources needed to complete the project. He or she also derives estimates for activity durations and cost estimates. As the planning phase of the project moves to a close, the project manager will need to verify that the resources for which he or she planned will actually be assigned to the project. Most project managers want the most experienced people on their project. Frequently these team members are committed to other projects and are not available full time, if they're available at all. In some instances, the necessary skill set is not available in the organization, and outside resources have to be contracted to meet the needs of the project. As part of finalizing the schedule, the project manager starts to apply more precision in scheduling the resources.

Loading Resources

Recall the example from Chapter 6 about a project to upgrade 300 systems with the newest version of MS Project. At that time, the project manager defined generic resources to do the work: junior trainer, senior trainer, SME, and so on. The resource requirements were based on what the project manager and the functional manager knew the tasks required. Figure 11-1 has a sample assumption log based on the information we had been given up to that point.

In order to finalize the schedule, the project manager will need to define those resources in more detail. This is called **resource loading,** and entails loading specific resources and their availability into the schedule. For example, the assumption log states that the junior and senior trainers are available 50 percent of the time. However, that has not been noted in the project schedule as a constraint. In addition, the preliminary schedule did not take into account the nature of the tasks that they are doing. Recall that some tasks, such as creating the first draft of the training content, are effort driven—a certain amount of effort is required to create content, and the task duration is based on the effort involved. Other tasks, such as validating questions with SMEs, have a duration that is fixed rather than effort based. The SMEs have a certain amount of time to review and get their feedback to the trainers. The effort is not the driver; the duration of two days is the driver. (See the tip in Chapter 6 on the differences between these types of tasks.)

Not everyone uses MS Project. However, it is a pretty pervasive piece of software in the project management world, and therefore we'll walk through the process here with instructions that are specific to MS Project. Other project management tools have equivalent steps. During the PM in Action exercise you will have an opportunity to go through these steps on your own.

Take our practice project where we have a constraint on the amount of time our junior and senior trainers can work. To enter this constraint into MS Project, go to the View tab and click on the Resource Sheet view. Under the column Max Units, enter 50% for the trainers.

To define the task type, return to the Gantt View and double click on a task to get the task information box. Then go to the Advanced tab and look at the Task Type. You can choose between fixed units, fixed duration, and fixed work. Then click Okay. Check whether this has changed the schedule. You

Figure 11-1. Assumption Log, version one

#	Assumption	Validated by	Date	Comments
1	Pine Grove, Palm View, Whispering Springs and 25 remote users will have their MS Project application upgraded.			
2	Pine Grove has 150 users, Palm View has 75 users and Whispering Springs has 50 users.			
3	Pine Grove and Palm View can be upgraded via the server.			
4	Whispering Springs will need to have the application loaded manually.			
5	The 25 remote users will have to bring their laptops to a location to receive the upgrade manually.			
6	Training will include 3 hours of best practices and 1 hour of training on the new functionality.			
7	The project will begin on March 1, and complete by April 30, including training.			
8	The 5 help desk staff will arrange for the server installation and the manual loading for the Whispering Springs and remote users.			
9	There are two people that are available 50% of the time from the training department; a Jr. Trainer and a Sr. Trainer. They will develop and deliver the training.			
10	Training will be held at all 3 locations.			
11	15 people at a time can be trained, and there are sufficient machines at all sites to accommodate the training.			
12	Remote users can have their laptops upgraded while they are in training.			
13	Users will have to pass an on-line test after the class.			
14	SMEs will work with the training department on content, testing and mentoring.			
15	The Sr. Trainer will deliver training at Pine Grove. The Jr. Trainer will deliver training at Palm View and Whispering Springs.			
16	The Jr. Trainer will interview all SMEs and develop Draft 1 of the training.			
17	The Sr. Trainer will approve training and create testing materials.			
18	The Jr. Trainer will develop the presentation.			
19	The Sr. Trainer will identify people who do not pass and must do the remedial training.			
20	The Jr. Trainer will deliver the remedial training.			

may have to make adjustments after loading resources. We will explain ways to do so shortly.

Let's take a look at the Activity List and analyze the tasks to define which are effort driven and which are not. After doing that, we can define if the task is a fixed unit, fixed duration, or fixed work. We will start with the Activity List that we left off with in Chapter 6, expand our work to include the installation and project management, and add some additional assumptions on our assumptions log. (See Figure 11-2.)

Note that, in addition, we have added in some duration estimates based on meetings with our team members, and that we have added two activities: loading test questions into the databank and testing the databank. So, to start with, our project schedule looks like Figure 11-3.

Using the information from the schedule and the assumption log, we can start to load resource availability into the schedule.

To set the start date of a project, go to the Project menu, select Project Information, and enter the project start date. In this case it is March 1. Also in Project Information is an option to schedule from the project start date or from the project finish date. Make certain this option is set to schedule from the project start date.

When you have a resource that is not available 100% of the time, you have to manually enter in the percentage of time the resource is available for each task. Go to the Task Information box, click on the Resource tab, and enter in the percentage of time the resource is available. Note that this change only affects the resource usage for that task, not for the resource on other tasks. This is different from setting up the resource's availability in the resource sheet, which affects that resource's usage on all tasks. Where do you get the availability information? From the resource itself or from the resource's manager. One basic practice is to identify any days where you know the resource is not available (vacations, planned training, and other days) and build individual calendars for those resources.

Figure 11-2. Assumption Log, version two

#	Assumption	Validated by	Date	Comments
1	Pine Grove, Palm View, Whispering Springs and 25 remote users will have their MS Project application upgraded.	Sponsor		This project was approved by the Project Steering Committee to support the objective of having users on one version of software.
2	Pine Grove has 150 users, Palm View has 75 users and Whispering Springs has 50 users.	HR		
3	Pine Grove and Palm View can be upgraded via the server.	IT Director		
4	Whispering Springs will need to have the application loaded manually.	IT Director		Connectivity between Whispering Springs and the main server is not configured optimally to support this function.
5	The 25 remote users will have to bring their laptops to a location to receive the upgrade manually.	IT Director		
6	Training will include 3 hours of best practices and 1 hour of training on the new functionality.	Sponsor		The Sponsor wants to use this opportunity to improve the user skills and have a baseline set of competencies on the software.
7	The project will begin on March 1, and complete by April 30, including training.	Sponsor		The duration is based on the need for resources on other projects as directed by the Project Steering Committee.
8	The 5 help desk staff will arrange for the server installation and the manual loading for the Whispering Springs and remote users.	IT Director		
9	There are two people that are available 50% of the time from the training department; a Jr. Trainer and a Sr. Trainer. They will develop and deliver the training.	Sr. Trainer		

Figure 11-2. Assumption Log, version two (continued)

#	Assumption	Validated by	Date	Comments
10	Training will be held at all 3 locations.	Sr. Trainer		
11	15 people at a time can be trained, and there are sufficient machines at all sites to accommodate the training.	Sr. Trainer		
12	Remote users can have their laptops upgraded while they are in training.	IT Director		
13	Users will have to pass an on-line test after the class with a score of 80% or better.	Sponsor		
14	SMEs will work with the training department on content, testing and mentoring.	Sponsor		
15	The Sr. Trainer will deliver training at Pine Grove. The Jr. Trainer will deliver training at Palm View and Whispering Springs.	Sr. Trainer		Palm View will be held first, followed by Whispering Springs.
16	The Jr. Trainer will interview all SMEs and develop Draft 1 of the training.	Sr. Trainer		
17	The Sr. Trainer will approve training and create testing materials.	Sr. Trainer		
18	The Jr. Trainer will develop the presentation.	Sr. Trainer		
19	The Sr. Trainer will identify people who do not pass and must do the remedial training.	Sr. Trainer		Remedial training will take place one week after the candidates are identified.
20	The Jr. Trainer will deliver the remedial training.	Sr. Trainer		Delivery will take place in the morning with the testing in the afternoon.
21	Students will be able to download the new application once they have passed the class.	IT Director		
22	Manual installations will be available on the first day of training at Whispering Springs, or by appointment at Pine Grove.	IT Director		
23	The test will be comprised of 20 multiple choice questions and 5 scenarios where students need to create a schedule based on given assumptions.	Sr. Trainer		

Figure 11-2. Assumption Log, version two (continued)

#	Assumption	Validated by	Date	Comments
24	SMEs can be identified prior to executing the project (start on 2/22). We expect 4 SMEs for this project.	Sponsor		Sponsor will work with functional managers to identify resources and insure they have time to work with trainers the week of 3/1.
25	It takes 3 hours of development for every hour of training delivery.	Sr. Trainer		12 hours of development effort.
26	The presentation should be 75 slides with each slide taking approximately 10 minutes to develop, thus 12.5 hours development time.	Sr. Trainer		
27	Test questions and scenarios will be developed in tandem and will take 16 hours combined to complete.	Sr. Trainer		Allocate 8 hours each on schedule.
28	Classes will be held 8A–noon M–F.	Sr. Trainer		This is JUST enough to get everyone through, consider adding some make up classes.
29	An IT resource will be available 25% of the time to load questions and scenarios into the test databank and to test and finalize the databank.	IT Director		
30	PM will begin planning 1 week prior to the project start date of 3/1 and will spend 25% of their time on planning this project.	PM		
32	PM will spend 15% of their time in project execution and control once the project starts, until closure.	PM		
33	PM will spend 50% of their time in the closure process, which is expected to take 2 days.	PM		

Figure 11-3. MS Project Installation Activities

Figure 3: MS Project Installation Activities

ID	WBS	Task Name	Resource Names	Predecessors
1	**1**	**Install MS Office Project on 300 work stations**		
2	**1.1**	**Project management**		
3	1.1.1	Planning		
4	1.1.2	Executing and control		
5	1.1.3	Close out		
6	**1.2**	**Installation**		
7	1.2.1	Pine Grove		
8	1.2.2	Palm View		
9	1.2.3	Whispering Springs		
10	**1.3**	**Training**		
11	**1.3.1**	**Define user training requirements**		
12	1.3.1.1	Identify subject matter experts (SMEs) to interview	Sponsor	
13	1.3.1.2	Interview SMEs for content needs	Jr. trainer	12
14	**1.3.2**	**Develop training**		
15	1.3.2.1	First draft of training content	Jr. trainer	13
16	1.3.2.2	Validate content with SMEs	SMEs	15
17	1.3.2.3	Finalize content	Sr. Trainer	16
18	1.3.2.4	Put content into workbooks	Jr. trainer	17
19	1.3.2.5	Develop presentation	Jr. trainer	17SS
20	**1.3.3**	**Develop testing**		
21	1.3.3.1	Create test questions	Sr. Trainer	17
22	1.3.3.2	Create test case scenarios	Sr. Trainer	21FF
23	1.3.3.3	Validate questions with SMEs	Sr. Trainer	22
24	1.3.3.4	Validate scenarios with SMEs	Sr. Trainer	22
25	1.3.3.5	Finalize test questions	Sr. Trainer	23
26	1.3.3.6	Finalize scenarios	Sr. Trainer	25SS
27	1.3.3.7	Load questions and scenarios into test databank	IT Resource	26
28	1.3.3.8	Test and finalize test databank	IT Resource	27
29	**1.3.4**	**Deliver training**		
30	1.3.4.1	Pine Grove	Sr. Trainer	28
31	1.3.4.2	Palm View	Jr. trainer	26
32	1.3.4.3	Whispering Springs	Jr. trainer	31
33	**1.3.5**	**Remedial train and test**		
34	1.3.5.1	Identify users who did not meet 80% on exam and scenarios	Sr. Trainer	30,31,32
35	1.3.5.2	Conduct remedial training	Jr. trainer	34
36	1.3.5.3	Retest	Jr. trainer	35

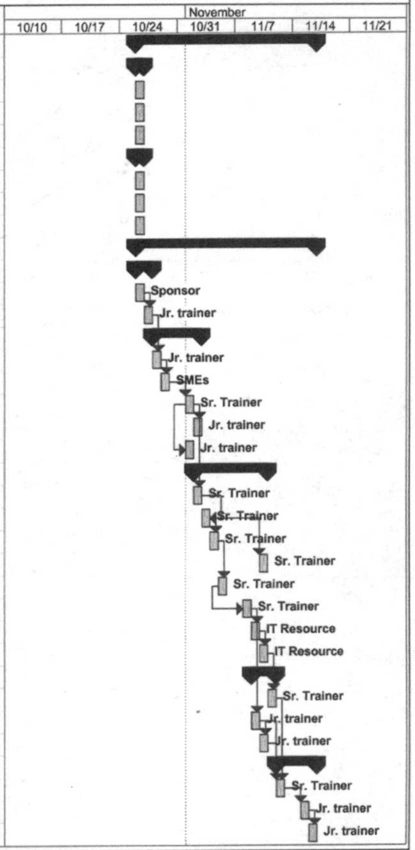

Page 1

PM in Action!

Use the information in Figures 10-2 and 10-3, plus the information below, to create an updated schedule for the MS Project installation.

Effort Driven	Fixed Units	Fixed Duration	Fixed Work
No		All installations	
No		Define user training requirements	
Yes	First draft of training		
No		Validate content with SMEs	
No		Finalize content	
Yes	Put content into notebooks		
Yes	Develop presentation		
Yes	Create test questions and scenarios		
No		Validate questions and scenarios with SMEs	
Yes	Finalize test questions and scenarios		
Yes	Load questions into test databank		
Yes	Finalize test databank		
No		Deliver training	
No		Remedial train and test	
No		Project management	

Your schedule should look like this at the end:

MS Project Installation Resource Loaded

ID	Task Name	Duration	Start	Finish	Predecessors
1	**Install MS Office Project on 300 work stations**	**49 days**	**Tue 2/22/05**	**Fri 4/29/05**	
2	**Project management**	**49 days**	**Tue 2/22/05**	**Fri 4/29/05**	
3	Planning	1 wk	Tue 2/22/05	Mon 2/28/05	
4	Executing and Control	7 wks	Tue 3/1/05	Mon 4/18/05	
5	Close out	2 days	Thu 4/28/05	Fri 4/29/05	36
6	**Installation**	**15 days**	**Mon 4/4/05**	**Fri 4/22/05**	
7	Pine Grove	2 wks	Mon 4/11/05	Fri 4/22/05	30
8	Palm View	1 wk	Mon 4/4/05	Fri 4/8/05	31
9	Whispering Springs	1 wk	Mon 4/11/05	Fri 4/15/05	32
10	**Training**	**35.75 days**	**Tue 2/22/05**	**Tue 4/12/05**	
11	**Define user training requirements**	**9 days**	**Tue 2/22/05**	**Fri 3/4/05**	
12	Identify subject matter experts (SMEs) to int	1 wk	Tue 2/22/05	Mon 2/28/05	
13	Interview SMEs for content needs	4 days	Tue 3/1/05	Fri 3/4/05	12
14	**Develop training**	**8.13 days**	**Mon 3/7/05**	**Thu 3/17/05**	
15	First draft of training content	24 hrs	Mon 3/7/05	Wed 3/9/05	13
16	Validate content with SMEs	2 days	Thu 3/10/05	Fri 3/11/05	15
17	Finalize content	2 days	Mon 3/14/05	Tue 3/15/05	16
18	Put content into workbooks	8 hrs	Wed 3/16/05	Wed 3/16/05	17
19	Develop presentation	25 hrs	Mon 3/14/05	Thu 3/17/05	17SS
20	**Develop testing**	**8 days**	**Wed 3/16/05**	**Fri 3/25/05**	
21	Create test questions	16 hrs	Wed 3/16/05	Thu 3/17/05	17
22	Create test case scenarios	16 hrs	Wed 3/16/05	Thu 3/17/05	21FF
23	Validate questions with SMEs	2 days	Fri 3/18/05	Mon 3/21/05	22
24	Validate scenarios with SMEs	2 days	Fri 3/18/05	Mon 3/21/05	22
25	Finalize test questions	8 hrs	Tue 3/22/05	Tue 3/22/05	23
26	Finalize scenarios	8 hrs	Tue 3/22/05	Tue 3/22/05	25SS
27	Load questions and scenarios into test data	8 hrs	Wed 3/23/05	Wed 3/23/05	26
28	Test and finalize test databank	16 hrs	Thu 3/24/05	Fri 3/25/05	27
29	**Deliver training**	**10 days**	**Mon 3/28/05**	**Fri 4/8/05**	
30	Pine Grove	2 wks	Mon 3/28/05	Fri 4/8/05	28
31	Palm View	1 wk	Mon 3/28/05	Fri 4/1/05	28
32	Whispering Springs	1 wk	Mon 4/4/05	Fri 4/8/05	31
33	**Remedial train and test**	**1.75 days**	**Mon 4/11/05**	**Tue 4/12/05**	
34	Identify users who did not meet 80% on exa	1 day	Mon 4/11/05	Mon 4/11/05	30,31,32
35	Conduct remedial training	4 hrs	Tue 4/12/05	Tue 4/12/05	34
36	Retest	2 hrs	Tue 4/12/05	Tue 4/12/05	35

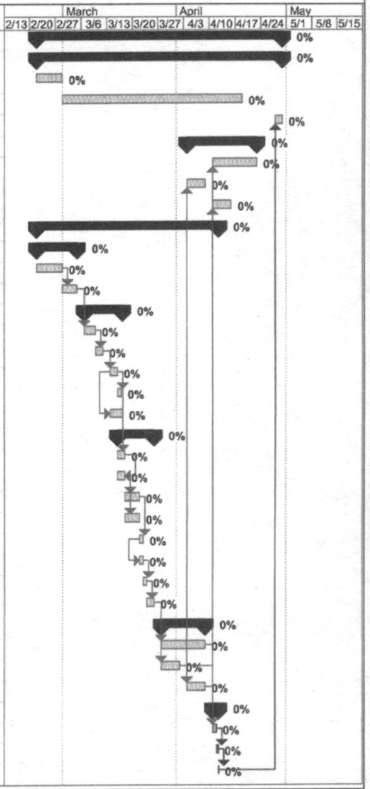

Page 1

Notice that wherever you changed the resource allocation from 100% to 50% on an activity that was effort driven, the length of time doubled for the task. This is why it is important to understand the type of task. It would create significant schedule risk if you assumed that eight hours of effort would be completed in eight hours of time if you only had a resource 50% of the time for tasks that were effort driven.

Leveling Resources

After you have loaded your resources, you may find that you have some resources who would have to be cloned in order to do all the work that they need to do. This usually happens when you have too few resources or you have one resource who has such a wide range of responsibilities that he or she is needed on multiple areas of the project. These people usually become bottlenecks in projects, and they should be identified as risk areas. The question is, who is over allocated, by how much, and what can you do about it? The answer is **resource leveling.**

The easiest way to ascertain who is over allocated is to look at the resource views in your software tool. In MS Project, click on Views and go to Resource Graph. Here you can get a bar chart view of the usage by resource. If you scroll through the column on the left, it will show you different resources. If you scroll through the column on the right, it will show you different time spans. Over allocated resources show up in red. In this case, you will see that the junior trainer is over allocated on April 21st. That is because he or she is leading the remedial training session for four hours and conducting the retest for two hours. With the 50% work constraint, the junior trainer is only supposed to work four hours per day. However, we can assume that this will be fine for this one day. We may need to validate this with the person's manager, but other than this one occurrence, we have not used the resource more than the 50% allotted.

In our example there is another instance of over allocation with the senior trainer. He or she is creating the test questions and test scenarios at the same time. Each of these takes four days. The senior trainer is allocated at 50%; for these four days, he or she shows 100% allocation. There are a couple of ways to handle this. You can change the allocation for those tasks to 25%, or combine the tasks, or note that you show an overage and ignore it, since you know that the resource will be working on these tasks in tandem for a total of four hours per day.

TIP

If a resource appears to be over allocated, that's not automatically a bad thing. It depends on the circumstances. Sometimes the over allocation is caused by our planning processes or the limitations of the tool we are using.

When you assess an over allocation, do so with a full understanding of the limits of scheduling. If you use the default task duration of days for MS Project, how do you handle over scheduling when a resource has six tasks to do in one day? This is a common occurrence in IT projects.

You can use fractions of days to schedule each task, but that's a lot of administrative work with the scheduling software. Or you can create a more generic comprehensive task to capture all of them, and just schedule one day for it. You can also schedule each for one full day, and accept the fact that the software will show this person to be 500 percent over allocated. This over allocation is not a real problem; it's an artifact of the scheduling software. The goal should be to have team members working as close to 100 percent of their availability as possible, with nobody truly scheduled for 150 percent or for 50 percent. When you build the schedule, do so intelligently.

TIP

In some larger, very dynamic IT organizations, identifying a resource by name may not make sense. What works well in this environment is to name the team lead for the type of work to be done (such as mainframe programming), and depend on him or her to identify a specific resource by name when the task is actually ready to be worked on. This allows you to schedule the project accurately, but still gives some flexibility on allocating resources.

We are going to show you one more little trick that MS Project can do with your over allocated resources: it can even out the excess hours. Resource leveling means that anytime someone is over allocated, MS Project will split tasks or push completion dates out to keep the resources within the usage constraints you assign. Follow along in the PM in Action! exercise.

PM in Action!

If you haven't already, go into your schedule, go to the View tab, and select Resource Sheet. Set the Max Units for the junior and senior trainers for 50% and the IT resource for 25%.

Next, go to the Tools tab and select Level Resources. In the box, make sure Manual is selected, leave all the defaults as they are, and click on Level Now.

Notice what this does to the task "Create test case scenarios."

Notice what this does to the end date of the project.

Your project schedule should now look like this:

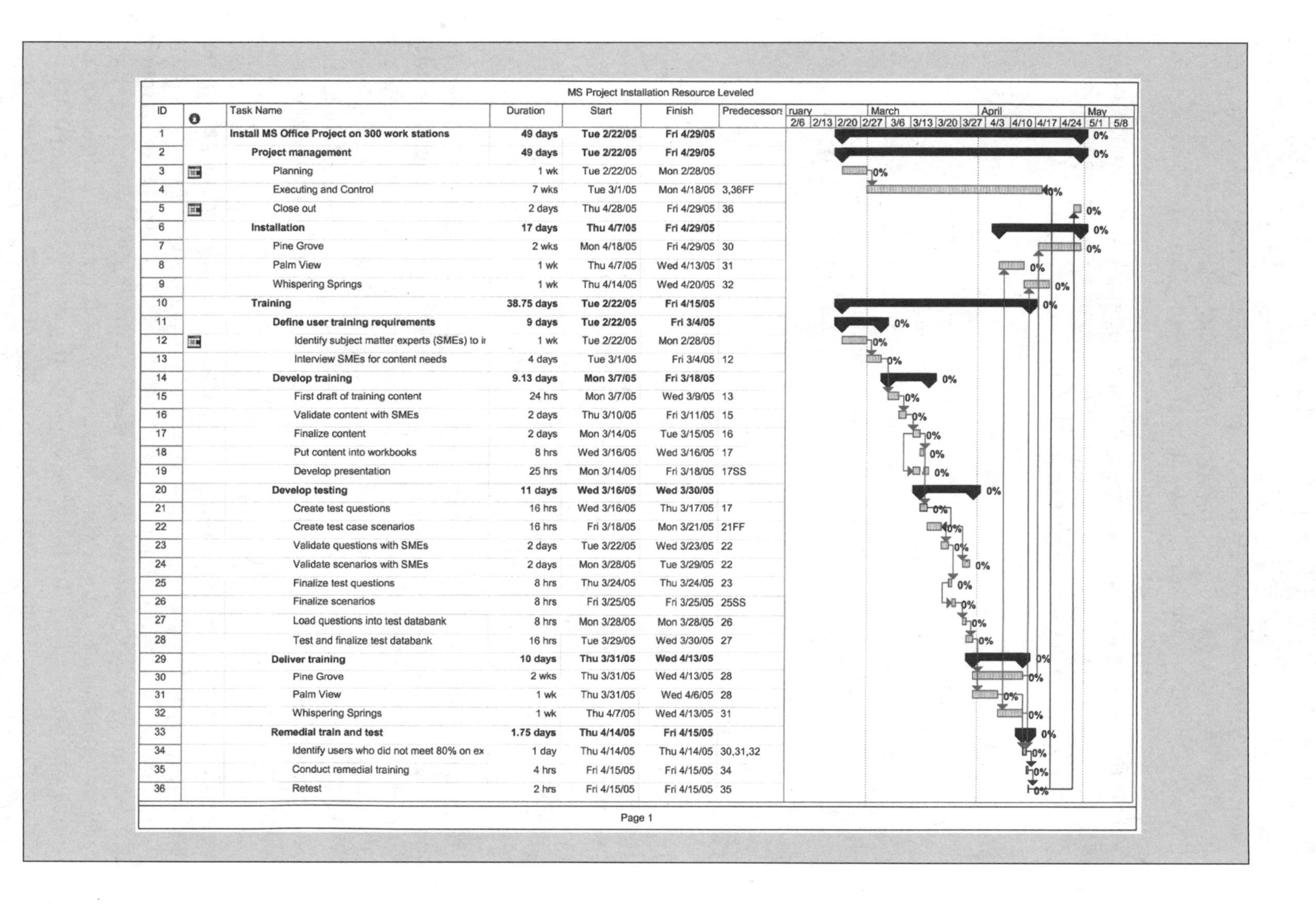

MS Project Installation Resource Leveled

ID	Task Name	Duration	Start	Finish	Predecessors
1	**Install MS Office Project on 300 work stations**	**49 days**	**Tue 2/22/05**	**Fri 4/29/05**	
2	**Project management**	**49 days**	**Tue 2/22/05**	**Fri 4/29/05**	
3	Planning	1 wk	Tue 2/22/05	Mon 2/28/05	
4	Executing and Control	7 wks	Tue 3/1/05	Mon 4/18/05	3,36FF
5	Close out	2 days	Thu 4/28/05	Fri 4/29/05	36
6	**Installation**	**17 days**	**Thu 4/7/05**	**Fri 4/29/05**	
7	Pine Grove	2 wks	Mon 4/18/05	Fri 4/29/05	30
8	Palm View	1 wk	Thu 4/7/05	Wed 4/13/05	31
9	Whispering Springs	1 wk	Thu 4/14/05	Wed 4/20/05	32
10	**Training**	**38.75 days**	**Tue 2/22/05**	**Fri 4/15/05**	
11	**Define user training requirements**	**9 days**	**Tue 2/22/05**	**Fri 3/4/05**	
12	Identify subject matter experts (SMEs) to ii	1 wk	Tue 2/22/05	Mon 2/28/05	
13	Interview SMEs for content needs	4 days	Tue 3/1/05	Fri 3/4/05	12
14	**Develop training**	**9.13 days**	**Mon 3/7/05**	**Fri 3/18/05**	
15	First draft of training content	24 hrs	Mon 3/7/05	Wed 3/9/05	13
16	Validate content with SMEs	2 days	Thu 3/10/05	Fri 3/11/05	15
17	Finalize content	2 days	Mon 3/14/05	Tue 3/15/05	16
18	Put content into workbooks	8 hrs	Wed 3/16/05	Wed 3/16/05	17
19	Develop presentation	25 hrs	Mon 3/14/05	Fri 3/18/05	17SS
20	**Develop testing**	**11 days**	**Wed 3/16/05**	**Wed 3/30/05**	
21	Create test questions	16 hrs	Wed 3/16/05	Thu 3/17/05	17
22	Create test case scenarios	16 hrs	Fri 3/18/05	Mon 3/21/05	21FF
23	Validate questions with SMEs	2 days	Tue 3/22/05	Wed 3/23/05	22
24	Validate scenarios with SMEs	2 days	Mon 3/28/05	Tue 3/29/05	22
25	Finalize test questions	8 hrs	Thu 3/24/05	Thu 3/24/05	23
26	Finalize scenarios	8 hrs	Fri 3/25/05	Fri 3/25/05	25SS
27	Load questions into test databank	8 hrs	Mon 3/28/05	Mon 3/28/05	26
28	Test and finalize test databank	16 hrs	Tue 3/29/05	Wed 3/30/05	27
29	**Deliver training**	**10 days**	**Thu 3/31/05**	**Wed 4/13/05**	
30	Pine Grove	2 wks	Thu 3/31/05	Wed 4/13/05	28
31	Palm View	1 wk	Thu 3/31/05	Wed 4/6/05	28
32	Whispering Springs	1 wk	Thu 4/7/05	Wed 4/13/05	31
33	**Remedial train and test**	**1.75 days**	**Thu 4/14/05**	**Fri 4/15/05**	
34	Identify users who did not meet 80% on ex	1 day	Thu 4/14/05	Thu 4/14/05	30,31,32
35	Conduct remedial training	4 hrs	Fri 4/15/05	Fri 4/15/05	34
36	Retest	2 hrs	Fri 4/15/05	Fri 4/15/05	35

Page 1

Resource leveling using MS Project can do some pretty scary things to your schedule. We recommend copying your project schedule before playing with this tool. Of course, you can always clear the leveling, but you may want to think twice before turning the brains of the schedule over to a machine. Especially with a project that has hundreds of tasks, you may not see all the ramifications until it is too late. In general, we don't recommend using a software tool to do resource leveling. Very few of the tools do it very well.

WARNING

The resource loading and leveling examples underscore the importance of remembering that project software tools are just tools, nothing more. Do not spend ridiculous amounts of time trying to make your tool fit reality. Use it to organize your work, alert you to any risks or issues, and track your progress. Don't be a slave to your software!

Task Linkages

The importance of ensuring that the tasks and activities are linked together and that the precedence relationships are all accurate cannot be emphasized too heavily. The entire project schedule depends as much on those linkages as it does on the duration of each task. If a critical precedence relationship is missing, the project may well be under scheduled. If a relationship is built into the schedule that doesn't exist in reality, the project may be overscheduled.

The best tool for understanding the precedence relationships in the project is the network diagram. Recall from Chapter 6 that the network diagram is the schematic display of the logic of the tasks in the project. It shows the relationships you have established among the tasks and activities. For example, in your exercise, the task "Create test questions" has a precedence relationship established for it. If you remove that relationship, the entire schedule collapses by several weeks.

These linkages can sometimes be used to remove resource conflicts on the schedule. A task dependency created by resources is called a discretionary dependency (covered in Chapter 6). The nature of the work doesn't require the dependency; the dependency is caused by something else. Usually, that something else is a resource who is working on both tasks. If a different resource were assigned to the task, the dependency would be removed. When you go through the project and find out who is over allocated, you can examine the task to see if someone else can do it. If so, you will schedule another resource and remove any resource-driven dependencies.

WARNING

Scheduling abuses you need to know about:

- Assuming unlimited resources during the scheduling process
- Excessive use of fixed dates, such as a fixed end date
- Missing relationships, identifiable by having activities with 300 weeks of float
- Excessive number of predecessor or successor links for any one task
- Having no good basis for duration-estimating assumptions

Using Scheduling Tools for Other Types of Resources

You can use your scheduling tool to track resources other than your team members. Let's say that you need a training room. Enter the training room as a resource. Perhaps you need to use a specific piece of test equipment; you can enter it into the resource sheet. If your resource has a cost associated with it, you can enter the cost in the resource sheet as well. You may choose to track this information using a different method, such as a spreadsheet, but virtually all project-planning software has the capacity to add non-personnel resources.

Optimizing Your Project Schedule

You may have noticed that after the resources were loaded and leveled in the example, the project comes in later, In fact, with the resources loaded, the completion date is April 25, and that doesn't even account for any risks on the project! Let's look at a few risks for our project and ways to account for those risks in our schedule.

Accounting for Risk

Remember how, in Chapter 10, you spent all that time identifying, analyzing, and planning responses to risks? Now you have to adjust the schedule based on those responses. Let's look at a couple of risks to see how they would alter the schedule. Use this abbreviated version of a risk register as an example; it merely identifies the risk and the response rather than going through the risk analysis process. We are merely trying to demonstrate the process of schedule baselining, not the process of risk management.

ID	Risk	Response	Comment
1	Unexpected results in testing could cause training to be delayed.	Add two days of reserve to the schedule for testing.	This will show up as a lag on the schedule.
2	There are only enough slots to train everyone if every class is full. This could cause some classes to be overbooked, or else prevent everyone from being trained.	Add two make-up days of training in Pine Grove and one each in Palm View and Whispering Springs.	Add a task called make-up training for each location.
3	The project schedule shows that the finish date is April 25, which leaves only five days of float should anything go wrong.	Considering finding a way to compress the schedule. Negotiate with managers for more time with the trainers.	*See the section in this chapter on schedule compression for options.*

By adding two days of lag time between testing and training, you can reduce the probability and impact of the risk that unexpected results in testing would cause the training to be delayed. Moreover, by adding a make-up class you have reduced the probability that people will not be able to attend a training class or that the classes will be overbooked. These responses have reduced the risk for certain tasks, but they have increased the duration of the project. What do we do about the third risk in the risk register? The next section will talk about reasons for compressing the schedule and ways to do so. But first, a discussion about the critical path.

The Critical Path

The **critical path** is the longest series of tasks through the project. The critical path determines the duration of the project. Any task on the critical path that is late will make the project late. For every day you can shorten the critical path, you can shorten the project. In some situations, there can be more than one critical path if many tasks are being done simultaneously.

A schedule with a fixed end date may have float. **Float** is the amount of time a task on a path can slip without affecting the final date of the project. For example, if Monica is managing a project with a predetermined end date of November 15 and the schedule shows she will be done by November 10, there are five days of float. If on the other hand the schedule shows she will be done on November 25, then she has ten days of negative float. In other words, if she doesn't do something, the project will come in 10 days later than the predetermined end date. In a situation like that, Monica will need to look for ways to compress the schedule. By definition, the critical path is the path through the network with the least amount of float. Usually there is zero float, and the critical path determines the end date. However, with a fixed end date, there may be positive or negative float.

TIP

You can view the critical path in MS Project by going to the View menu and selecting Tracking Gantt. The path in red is the critical path. The path in blue has float; the more red that appears in the schedule, the higher the risk of being late.

Compressing the Schedule

It seems like everyone wants things done faster. No matter how much you try to get things done in a timely manner, people always want it sooner. Is this arbitrary? Are people just impatient? That's probably part of it, but let's look at some of the other reasons people have for wanting to compress schedules.

Sometimes, like in the MS Project installation example, the schedule must be shortened because of a fixed deadline dictated by forces outside the project. Sometimes schedules have to be shortened because resources are promised somewhere else, or maybe a contractual constraint requires the project be completed by a certain date. Sometimes the schedule must be shortened because the marketing department has already promised that the product will be introduced by a certain date. Sometimes with projects done under contract there are bonuses tied to early delivery or penalties associated with late delivery.

Other reasons for accelerating work may have to do with project issues. For example, an earlier deliverable may have fallen behind and now you have to compress part of the project to try to make up for lost time. Or perhaps a resource was pulled from the project and the project has fallen behind because of the need to bring in someone new and get him or her up to speed on the project.

Whatever the reason for reducing the schedule, you incur additional risk, additional cost, or both.

There are various ways to shorten the schedule. Some of them involve spending money and some of them do not.

Whether schedule-compression techniques require spending additional funds depends on the resources you have available. If you are paying contractors by the hour, any approaches requiring additional work will cost additional money. If your resources are salaried personnel, then reducing the schedule by increasing work hours may not cost anything. You may have an issue with team morale, but no additional cost is involved.

Shortening without Spending Money

One of the most prevalent ways to shorten the schedule is to **fast-track** some of the tasks. This means doing activities in parallel that would normally be done in sequence. Recall that before you leveled the project schedule, you had "create test questions" and "create test scenarios" happening simultaneously. When the software leveled them, because of a resource constraint, it pushed "create test scenarios" to start after "create test questions" was complete. You could fast-track by rescheduling them to be performed at the same time.

The downside to fast-tracking is that it usually increases risk on an IT project. Whether the risk is acceptable or not depends on the tasks being overlapped. It is never recommended to parallel requirements-gathering tasks with development tasks. Starting development before the requirements are substantially completed is asking for trouble.

Another way to shorten the schedule is to divide the work into smaller segments. For example, assume that Jennifer is on a project with three components that need to be planned, developed, tested, and rolled out. Each of these tasks takes two weeks per component. If each phase of the project has all three components, and each phase has to be complete before the next phase begins, the project will take 24 weeks. (See Figure 11-4.)

Figure 11-4. Regular Schedule

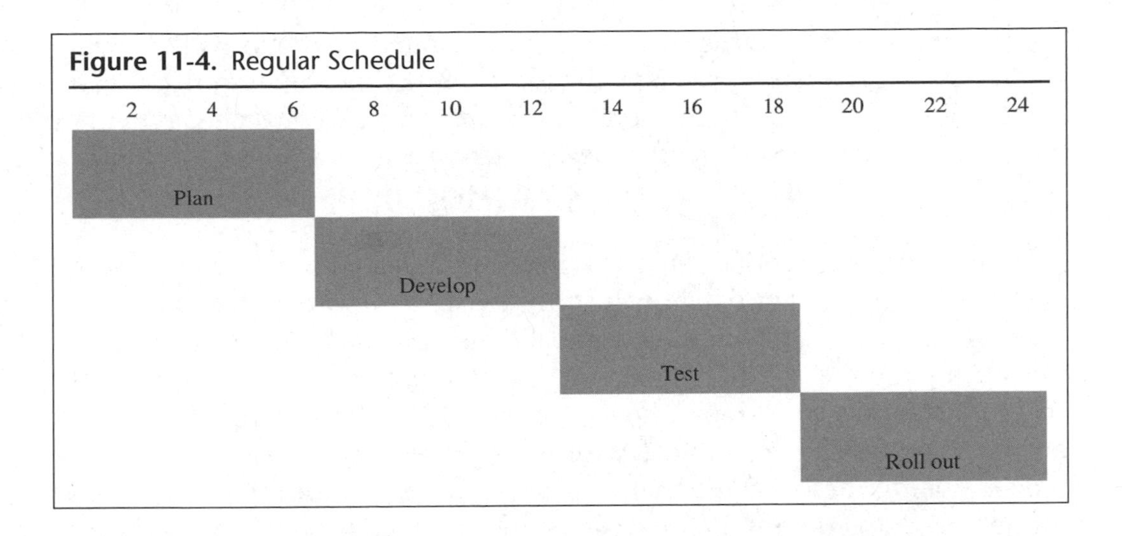

However, Jennifer needed it before then, so she set up the project so that as soon as the first component was planned it went right into development, and as soon as it was developed it could go right into test. By chunking the work in this manner, she can cut the project time in half. If she had to add another task to integrate and system test, that would be fine as it probably would not take all of the 12 weeks she saved. Figure 11-5 shows the chunked version of this scenario.

Figure 11-5. Chunked Schedule

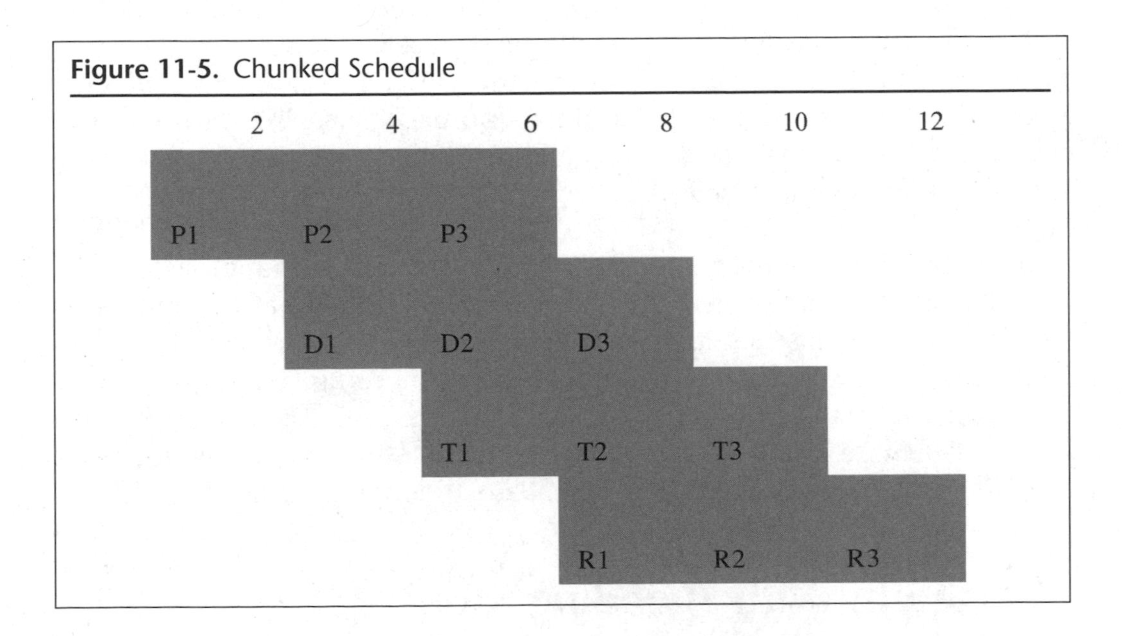

Another way to shorten the schedule without spending money is by moving resources that are not on critical path tasks to work that is on the critical path. Of course, this assumes that resources are exchangeable, which is often not the case. Doing this may create a new critical path. However, if the circumstances justify it, and resources are exchangeable, this is an option.

A final option is descoping or rephasing the project. You may be able to go back to the customer and define the critical aspects of the project, those that are nice to have, and those that are really just a wish list (if you did not do this during the requirements-gathering portion of the project). At this point, you can take out the wish list altogether (which is called descoping), or maybe create phases for the project, with phase 1 being the essential elements, phase 2 being the elements that are nice to have, and (if there is time and money) perhaps putting in the wish list in phase 3. This approach, which is called rephasing, also allows the team to learn from one phase to the next so that each later phase is smoother.

Descoping and rephasing should be used with caution. Reducing functionality to save schedule may give the impression that the project was badly planned or scoped from the beginning. The approach may be justifiable if the schedule was dictated by management or by the customer without any understanding of the true amount of work to be done. Although this may save money and time on the project in work, by the time the originally promised full functionality has been delivered in later phases, the whole project will have taken much longer and cost more than originally planned. Reducing scope should be considered a last-ditch approach to saving schedule. The project sponsor or the client won't be happy if you can't deliver everything that was originally promised.

Some companies are using a rapid software development approach called extreme programming where they are not documenting their requirements or code; they are just getting it out as fast as possible and reworking it as required. In these scenarios, schedule is more important than quality and maintainability. We do not recommend this as an ongoing approach because of the inefficiencies and risks inherent in the process. Significant amounts of rework are common in this approach and documentation is nonexistent.

Shortening with Spending Money

Another approach to reducing the project's calendar duration is to crash the schedule. **Crashing** entails looking at the longest activities on the critical path and reducing them by adding resources. Resources aren't always money, but they usually involve money either directly or indirectly. You may add staff, equipment, vendors, overtime, pay bonuses, or some other variant of resources. All of these options consume resources in one way or another.

Does crashing the schedule cost money? Often it does, but not always. If you reduce the duration of critical path tasks by adding additional resources to those tasks, those additional resources will cost money. If you reduce the duration by asking salaried employees to work overtime, that does not cost any additional money (but you may reduce their morale if you do this too often!).

When crashing a schedule, the key point is to crash only those activities that are on the critical path. Why is that so? Because crashing a non-critical task does not save any time.

The best approach is to crash those activities on the critical path where you can save the most amount of time for the least amount of money. The mathematicians tell us we should look for the **time/cost slope** for each task and choose the option with the least amount of slope. That sounds complex. Actually, it isn't all that bad.

Assume you have five tasks on the critical path, and each task has a duration and a cost associated with it. Some of the tasks can be shortened. To shorten tasks costs money, so what you want to do is create a chart that shows the regular time and the crash time, and the regular cost and the crash cost. If you can shorten a task in increments, show a crash cost per unit of time (day, week, or month, whatever makes sense). Then, by looking at the chart, you can determine how to get the most time for the least amount of money. If you only need to make up one week of time, then find the cheapest week. We should note that sometimes you need to do a full crash; in other words, sometimes you have to spend whatever it takes to reduce the schedule as much as possible.

Unfortunately, while crashing sounds reasonable, it may be the wrong approach. The new resources coming onto the project don't have the project knowledge of existing team members, so they need to be brought up to speed. This takes time away from the current team members and reduces their productivity. The loss of productivity often overcomes the apparent advantage of adding more people. It is much better to have staffed the project properly at the start. In addition, crashing a schedule invariably increases risk. If the team member said a particular task is going to take ten days, and you now want the same work done in seven days, you have increased the risk of not meeting the date.

Another way to improve the schedule might be to create a subproject that you subcontract to someone else (this is often also a way to reduce risk). For example, imagine your IT project is to create and install a new data mart or a data warehouse and to transfer all of your company's existing data into it. The process of extracting, transforming, and loading the data (referred to as ETL) from the old formats and fields to the new ones is a highly specialized and risky effort. If not done correctly, the data will be worthless. Yet, this is not something for which you need a full time employee, because it is a temporary effort until the data is loaded in the new database. You might create a separate project for this effort, and subcontract it to a company that does this type of thing frequently. The company you subcontract with can typically save you time and money and reduce risk because of its knowledge and experience.

PM in Action!

Given the following information, fill in the chart.

Task A costs $1,000. Task E costs $1,500. Task B is three times as expensive as task A. Task C costs $2,400. Task D is twice as much as Task A. To crash A will cost 50% more to save one day. It cannot be crashed more than one day. To crash B will cost $300 more per day, and it can be crashed up to two days. Task C can be crashed by one day for a cost of $600. Neither D nor E can be crashed.

Task	Regular Cost	Crash Cost	Regular Time	Crash Time	Crash Cost Per Day
A					
B					
C					
D					
E					

Another way of showing the time/cost trade off is by creating a graph that shows the time/cost slope of each task. Put the costs on the y-axis and the time on the x-axis. Figure 11-6 shows this.

NOTE

Not every task can be crashed. If you have a three-day critical design review planned where the customer will review and approve the final design, there may not be any way to crash that task.

Figure 11-6. Time/Cost Slope

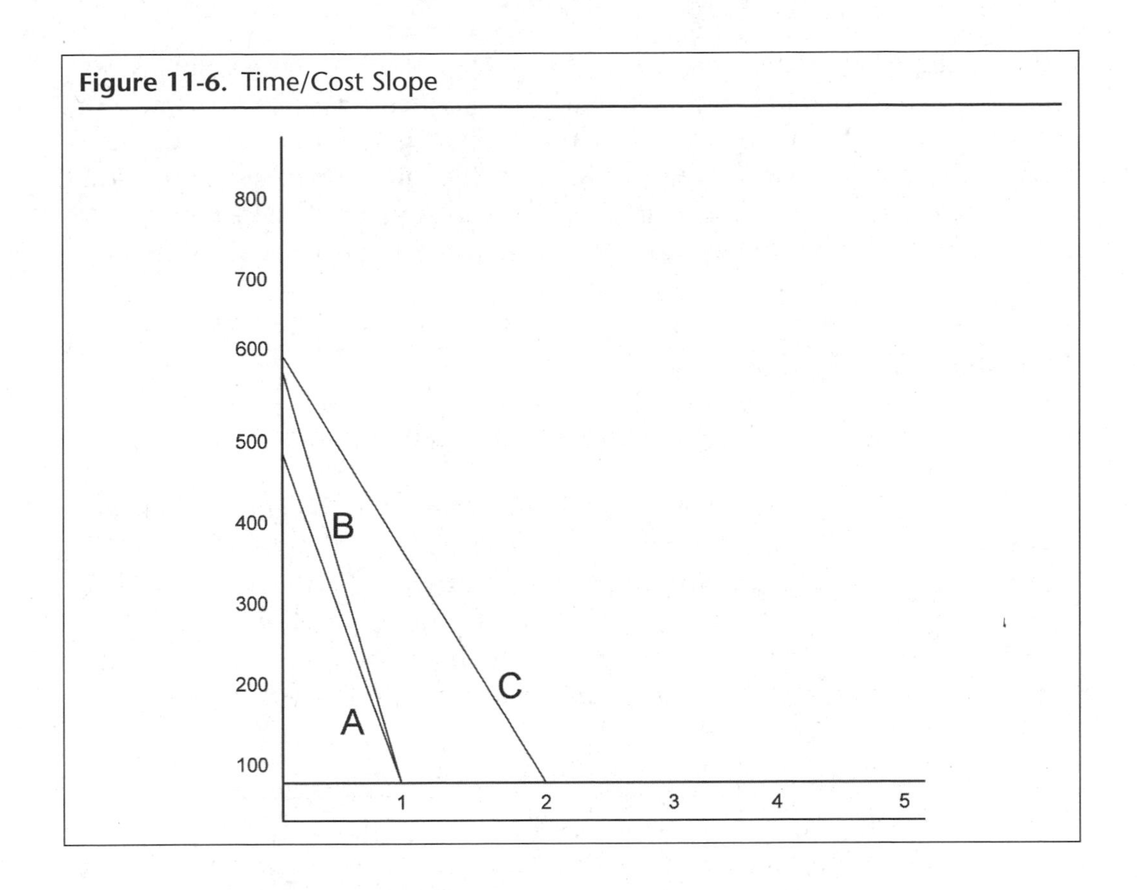

NOTE

For those of you who like math, the crashing equations are:

Cost per unit saved = (crash cost – normal cost)/(normal time – crash time)

Slope = (crash cost – normal cost)/(crash time – normal time)

Types of Schedule Constraints

The two things that are going to drive the schedule are time and people. In some cases, time is the most important factor and the bottom line is "Get it done as fast as possible." If this is the case, use whatever resources you have available to get the work done.

In other instances, you are going to be **resource constrained.** In other words, you have limited resources to get the work done, and the schedule gets pushed out to accommodate the lack of resources. For example, if your organization only has three people who can sign off on a QA check for the testing process, and two of them are on projects that are more critical and one is on vacation, you have a resource constraint. Your project isn't going forward until one of those three resources can review your QA activities and sign off on them. Limited resources are just a fact of life in IT project management. There never seems to be enough resources available to do all the work that needs to be done.

Schedule Myths

This is a good time to point out some common scheduling myths:

- *Eight hours of planned effort will take eight hours.* This is not true. People are about 75 to 80 percent productive. The rest of the time is spent on e-mail, phone calls, breaks, interruptions, and so on. Uninterrupted work for eight hours straight almost never happens. One way to get around this is to build it into your schedule by defining the workweek as 32 hours rather than scheduling a 40-hour workweek. You will end up with a much more realistic schedule.
- *If we work enough overtime, we will get the job done.* People lose productivity at increasing rates the more hours they work and the longer they've had to work overtime. Having to work overtime for two days won't make that big an impact. But two months of continual overtime significantly reduces productivity. The quality of the work also suffers.
- *Adding people to a project that is running behind will bring it in on time.* Not necessarily, because often adding people to a late project makes it later. As mentioned earlier, this is because people who know what they are doing have to stop and educate the new people, plus you have more channels of communication, new team dynamics, and more confusion. Sometimes throwing more resources on a late project is like throwing gasoline on a fire.
- *Giving people a challenging deadline makes them work harder.* Maybe to a point. A ridiculous deadline demoralizes people, and constantly having to work overtime to make deadlines leads to burnout.
- *A person can be just as effective working on three smaller projects as he or she can be on one large project.* Human beings are not computers. Our brains need time between projects to release whatever we were doing on project A, put it away, and clean up. Then we need time to bring out project B, remember where we left off, and get into the groove of all the issues, risks, and activities happening in project B. The setup and breakdown alone take time, plus it can get downright confusing remembering where you are on

each project, which project has a schedule risk, which is resource starved, and so on. Having to switch from project to project has been proven to reduce productivity.

- *I can get it all done by multitasking.* Your brain does not do two things at once. It does one thing, then another, then another, then another. Sometimes it does them really fast, but it is still bouncing between tasks. Usually this results in silly mistakes and rework. Sometimes it results in doing something wrong that has significant ramifications. Multitasking creates the same problems as those stated in the preceding bullet, only they occur faster.
- *It's okay to put constraints such as "must start on" dates or "must end on" dates onto tasks.* In real life, you should not add these constraints if you can avoid doing so. Constraints such as these will prevent the software from accurately determining the end date of the project.

  If you must put constraints in because of contractor deliverables, supplier shipments, or for other reasons, put them into the schedule *after* you've determined where the project will end without them. After you've completed the schedule, run the software to determine the normal end date. Then put in the constraints and rerun the software to see the impact of the dates. You will most likely have to adjust the schedule afterwards.

The bottom line is you can only do what you can do. Every so often, it is appropriate for you and your team members to go beyond the call of duty or to pull out all the stops. However, this should not be the modus operandi. To get consistent quality performance, set up your schedule to allow people enough time to get work done. Add in contingency time where appropriate, based on your risk response plan. If you need to compress your schedule, look for ways to do things in parallel, and if you are going to add resources, only add them where you can compress the maximum time for the least amount of money and have a plan to bring new team members up to speed efficiently.

What Do You Think?

1. Which option do you most often use to shorten duration on your projects?
2. Which option do you not use very often that you think would be beneficial?

Scheduling Multiple Projects

Many IT project managers work on several projects at once. Much of the time, they have team members who are also working on several projects. This can lead to some interesting situations when it comes to scheduling. For instance, let's say you are the project manager on project A, and you have Manny as a system engineer on your project. You load him into your schedule on the dates that you need him, and everything is fine. He is not over allocated on project A. In fact, he isn't even fully utilized on project A, and so life is good.

Now, let's say you are also the project manager on project B, and Manny is also scheduled to do the system design on project B. You load him into the schedule and he is not in there full time, and there is no over allocation for project B, and life is good. Maybe he's even scheduled during different time slots on project A and project B. Okay, so far, so good.

However, what if he is also scheduled on project C, which is being managed by Joe? In addition, let's say that project C is running late, and you cannot get Manny on time for project A, and then his work time runs into the time that he is allotted for project B. Now, project A is behind and because Manny is working on A, which is late, he is not available for project B, causing it to also be late. Now this is getting ugly. You can complain to your boss and your customer that it's Joe's fault both your projects are late, but do they really care? No. Your project is late, Manny is over allocated, and nobody was coordinating the schedule for multiple projects.

If you have ever been in this situation, you know it is an uncomfortable predicament. You have a couple things happening. First, you have a resource bottleneck. You have a resource that is being used on multiple projects, and if you add up the time on all the projects, the resource is most likely over allocated. In addition, you have cascading schedule impacts. A delay in one project causes a delay in other projects.

This can get even more treacherous if you have project managers who have had this happen to them repeatedly. Sometimes in an effort to avoid the situation, project managers will pad the time they really need the resource, knowing that the resource is a bottleneck. In other words, they will book Manny for longer than they need him, assuming that something like the above situation will happen because it has happened in the past. Now you have a resource booked for 60 hours when he is only needed for 40 hours. This is called **suboptimization.** You have created a schedule that is utilizing resources less than optimally. You are protecting your schedule, but the organization as a whole is not served by this kind of compensation, even though the culture of the organization is what propagates it.

So, how do you get around these situations? Well, pain is often the best teacher. Often it takes repeatedly running into this type of situation before somebody has the idea of keeping a **project master schedule (PMS)** that includes all projects using the same resources. At the very least, you will want to create a PMS for all your own projects. There may or may not be dependencies among your projects, but if there are, you can note them on your PMS. If there aren't, you will at least see whether the schedules on your combined projects are creating any schedule conflicts. This is effectively what a portfolio management system does—it puts all projects and resources into one system so that conflicts such as these can be identified.

It is the job of the PMO, the manager of project managers, or the portfolio management team to add in all the resources for all the projects. At the very least, if you know that you have a resource that is on multiple projects, you can identify this as a risk and make accommodations for it in your schedule and by proactively working to coordinate with the resource, his or her manager, and other project managers.

In Practice: Critical Chain Project Management

We have been describing the traditional approach to creating and managing project schedules—critical path management. But this is not the only approach used by project managers. One approach, called critical chain project management (CCPM), takes into account the resource constraints we have just talked about and builds these constraints into the schedule. When a project schedule is created using a critical chain approach, not only are the task durations and dependencies taken into account, but the resource constraints are also taken into account. The project schedule that results is one that has no resource constraints. If you want to find out more about critical chain project management, there are many articles on the web.

Creating a Budget Baseline

Cost and schedule are intimately related. The more activities in your project and the longer their duration, the greater the project cost.

Recall in Chapter 6 we talked about creating estimates and developing a ROM budget. Now that the scope has been well-defined, our resources are allocated and loaded in the schedule, and we have performed our risk planning, we can develop a more detailed, bottom-up budget. After approval by the project sponsor or by the client, this will serve as the cost baseline for the project.

Task-Related Costs

In many, if not most, IT projects, the primary costs are the salaries of the people working on the project. The next highest category of costs is either going to be from purchasing or licensing software or from hardware purchases.

Software and hardware costs are easy to identify and to build into the project budget. For personnel costs, there are two possible approaches and you need to understand which one your company uses.

The simplest approach is to use the hourly salary of the employees or the hourly rates of any contractors. This is straightforward and the figures can be obtained from the resource's manager or from the human resources department. In some companies, the specific hourly salary of each employee is not released; in that case, the average hourly wage for employees at that salary grade can be used as an approximation.

The other approach is to use the hourly salaries of the employees, but add in overhead costs to the project's cost baseline. This overhead cost can be a simple percentage that management will provide or it can be the fully burdened cost of the employee. A fully burdened cost is one that includes not only the salary, but also everything else the company has to pay in order for that employee to work there. This includes vacation time, medical benefits, a proportion of the facilities used, insurance costs, and more. It is not uncommon for the fully burdened cost of employees to be twice their base salary. Management will give you the approach you must use in costing your project. Here are a few simple steps to move from your approximate budget to your definitive budget. If you are using scheduling software, you can produce budgets by giving the program the cost data.

1. Start with the cost estimates you developed by category and phase (see Chapter 6, Figure 6-8, to refresh your memory if necessary).

2. Review these cost estimates and your assumptions log to see if there have been any changes or updates to the original estimates. If there have been, update your estimates.

3. Create a spreadsheet with the months across the top and the major categories of tasks with their detailed components down the side.

4. Use your schedule to enter the cost estimates for each task in the appropriate monthly column. For your resources, this will be the salaries to be paid for planned work. For equipment, take into consideration that for some you will need to pay a deposit upfront, and then a balance at delivery. Also note that for contracts and vendors, you may not be billed until 30 days after the work is completed.

5. Review your risk response plan and enter any indicated amounts into the budget to account for risk management activities, contingency plans, and budgetary reserve.

6. Total across by category and total by month. Create a cumulative total at the end by month as well. Using the chart capability in your spreadsheet, create a cost curve that shows the amounts needed by month and the cumulative cost by month.

7. Get sign off and approval by your sponsor or customer as appropriate.

This is your cost baseline. You will use this to track actual expenses against planned expenses. Any deviation from the budget will need an explanation and approval. We will talk about tracking budget performance in the chapter on monitoring and control. Figure 11-7 has a sample of a cost baseline.

In Practice: Materials Costs

It would be a mistake to assume that you can easily estimate the cost of purchased materials needed for your project. Estimating material costs can be the most complicated part of the early project work. Anyone whose project has required ordering RAM within the past five years can readily testify to the severe fluctuations in prices that are possible.

Here are some common reasons why estimates will vary from the actual costs of purchased materials:

- Vendors and prices change regularly.
- Specifications change.
- Specified parts may be unavailable and substitutions made.
- Vendors may change parts and not notify customers.
- Perishable parts may have a shelf-lifetime.
- Quality may not be as desired.

Figure 11-7. Cost Baseline

Category/Months	January	February	March	April	May	Total
Cost of Desk tops						
O/S cost each			40000			40000
Application suite each			15000			15000
Machines and Monitors		52000				52000
Printers				14000		14000
LAN costs						
Data storage units	25000					25000
Print servers	15000					15000
Application servers	35000					35000
Routers	5000					5000
Internet access				1500	1500	3000
Cabling costs				500		500
Labor						
Cost/desktop			2000			2000
Cost/cable drop				2000		2000
Cost/server				1500	3000	4500
Risk Management	4000	2600	2850	975	225	10650
Total by Month	84000	54600	59850	20475	4725	223650
Cumulative Total	84000	138600	198450	218925	223650	

Assumptions:

O/S costs $400 each—we need 100

Application Suite costs $150 each—we need 100

Machines and monitors cost $520 each—we need 100

Printers cost $700 each—we need 1 for every 5 machines

Data Storage Units cost $25000 each

Print servers cost $7500 each—we need 2

Application Servers cost $35000 each

Routers will run $5000 total

Internet access is $15 per user per month—we need it for all machines. Project will absorb through May

Cabling is $500 total

Labor per desktop hook up is $20

Labor for cable is 2000 total

Labor per server is $1500

Data Storage and all servers will be purchased and paid for in January

Machines and monitors will be bought and paid for in February

Software will be bought, paid for and installed in March

Printers, network access and cabling and routers will be bought, installed and paid for in April

Labor for servers will be incurred for the applications in April and the printers in May

Risk Management costs of 5% per month are assumed for this project

> ## *In Practice: The Northridge Earthquake*
>
> In 1994 the Northridge earthquake caused the collapse of several bridges on the Santa Monica freeway, one of the busiest freeways in the world. The government, the California Department of Transportation (Caltrans), the prime contractor (C.C. Myers, Inc.), multiple subcontractors, and a veritable army of workers worked together to get traffic rolling again in record time. Rather than going through the usual contracting process, Caltrans was able to award the contract within days. Less than a day after that, work had commenced. It was estimated that the job would take 140 days; in fact, it came in at 66 days, 74 days ahead of schedule.
>
> Everything on the project was crashed. No expense was spared. Crews worked around the clock, bonuses were paid liberally, inspectors were onsite at all times so there were no delays waiting for inspections. All the quality objectives were met and there was almost a perfect safety record on the job sites. Because the bridge was impassible after the earthquake, all traffic on the freeway had to be routed onto side streets and back onto the freeway a mile later. The people who drove the freeway every day were the happiest of everyone involved when the bridge was reopened.

Non-Task-Related Costs

It is easy to forget that some of the costs associated with project work are not tied to any one task. These include the costs associated with the project management, developing and publishing management documents, configuration management, change management, and other non-task-specific activities. These are real costs that must be accounted for.

For the project management–related activities, the easiest way to avoid missing them is to put them into your WBS. All those management plans, significant meetings, and other management activities are part of your defined project activities and are scheduled and costed along with everything else.

If you utilize a centralized change control system, document management system, configuration management system, or any other administrative system that the company follows for all projects, whether the costs count against your budget needs to be established during the early budgeting activity, so they can be incorporated in the overall project budget.

CHAPTER SUMMARY

- To finalize the schedule, you enter specific resources into the schedule and the amount of time they are available to work on your project. You also define whether tasks are effort driven, and select the type of task: fixed units, fixed duration, or fixed work.
- The longest series of tasks through the project is called the critical path. If there is a difference between the end date of the critical path and a directed end date, that is float.
- You can level your resources to smooth out resource peaks and valleys and instances of resource over allocation.
- Once your resources are loaded, you should add in estimated durations to account for risk responses.
- You can compress your schedule in a number of ways. Some ways require additional funds, such as adding resources, and some do not, such as chunking work or fast-tracking. Shortening the schedule creates risk.
- Challenges in finalizing resources on one project are difficult enough, but finalizing resources across multiple projects can be daunting. A project master schedule can help.
- Once the schedule is finalized, you can create a cost baseline. You will need to allocate costs across the schedule and add in any necessary funds for risk management.

Key Terms

Resource loading

Resource leveling

Critical path

Float

Fast-track

Crashing

Time/cost slope

Resource constrained

Sub-optimization

Project master schedule

Key Term Quiz

1. A schedule that has a team member who is over allocated and causing a bottleneck is said to be ______________.

2. Extending the length of time that a resource is on the project schedule to ensure he or she is available when you need the resource is an example of ______________.

3. Adding more people to get an activity done quicker is called _________.

4. Doing activities in parallel that would normally be done sequentially is called ____________.

5. Removing the over allocation of resources by extending the due date, using float, and splitting tasks is known as ____________.

6. $400 to shorten a task by a week is an example of ______________.

7. To manage multiple projects and avoid resource over allocation, you should create a __________________.

8. Entering the availability of a resource into the schedule is called ______________.

9. The __________________ determines how soon the project can finish.

10. ________________ is the amount of a time an activity can be late and not impact the end date of the project.

Chapter Review Questions

1. What is the difference between resource loading and resource leveling?

2. What are the three options you have to classify a task in MS Project?

3. If you mark a task as effort driven, what will happen if you reduce the amount of time a resource is available on that task?

4. What are the two ways that MS Project levels resources on a project?
5. What does it mean to optimize a schedule?
6. What are four reasons for compressing the schedule?
7. What are some ways to crash the schedule?
8. When you are crashing the schedule, should you crash the task with the steepest or shallowest slope?
9. True or False: You should crash the schedule wherever you can save time without spending an inordinate amount of money.
10. What is the equation for calculating the slope of an activity?
11. When people are 100% allocated to your project, what percent of the time are they actually working?
12. Explain why adding people to a project that is behind will not necessarily bring it in on time.
13. True or False: People are just as effective working on three projects as they are working on one.
14. How can you get around resources being over allocated because they are working on multiple projects?
15. How do you use the risk response plan when creating cost and schedule baselines?

12 Project Execution

After reading this chapter, you will be able to:

- Describe the steps necessary to execute the management of a project.
- Discuss the components of communication needed to manage a project.
- Define the tools and process of change management.

After all the planning and preparation, it's finally time to start carrying out the project activities. This phase of the project is all about accomplishing the project objectives. Sometimes becoming stuck in planning or in the technical aspects of the project is easy, but remember that the goal is to meet the objectives. The schedule and the technology are just a means to an end. So, what's involved in meeting the objectives? For starters, let's talk about managing the project and the project team.

Managing the Project

The project plan, with all its components, is the baseline for executing the project. (The project plan is also known as the project management plan, as described in Chapter 4.) Project managers will reference this tool in their daily management activities. A number of documents comprise the project plan. The specific components of each project plan are different because each project is different, but in general the project plan consists of most or all of the following:

- Project charter
- Project scope statement
- Requirements
- WBS
- Milestone dates

- Network diagram
- Schedule baseline
- Resource requirements
- Cost estimates
- Cost baseline
- Quality plan
- Communication plan
- Risk register
- Technical architecture or designs

A significant part of managing a project involves managing the stakeholders as well as negotiating for resources, changes, approvals, and other things to keep the project running smoothly.

Stakeholder Management

Stakeholder management can be a very challenging part of managing a project. Hidden stakeholders can appear out of nowhere. You may have had buy-in and input from everybody you could possibly imagine. However, if you missed someone, you can bet that he will show up in the middle of your project, want to be brought up to speed on everything, second-guess all your decisions, and decide that he needs to have inputs to your project. At worst, he can derail everything.

The main tool for managing stakeholders is communication. Much of the communication is documented in the communication management plan that was discussed in Chapter 9. However, a lot of the day-to-day management occurs in formal and informal face-to-face meetings with sponsors, customers, team members, vendors, and other stakeholders. Sometimes a phone call or e-mail is a better way to communicate, as long as the situation at hand is not a critical issue for the project. The more critical the issue, the more important it is to have face-to-face communication. Follow up face-to-face communication with written verification of what was discussed.

Another tool is the **issue log.** The issue log may look similar to an assumption log. Figure 12-1 is an example of an issue log. This is used to document and

Figure 12-1. Issue Log

Issues Log

Project Information

Updated (MM/DD/YY):

Project:

Project ID#:

Project Manager:

Project Sponsor:

Issues Recorded

KEY ST = Status Use the following codes within the *ST* field to indicate the status of an issue: O = Open; C = Close; I — In work; D = Deleted

Issue #	Originator Name	Issue Description and Impact	ST**	Issue Owner	Resolution Comments	Date Opened (MM/DD/YY)	Due Date (MM/DD/YY)	Date Closed (MM/DD/YY)

monitor the resolution of issues. Some issues are risks that have occurred and need to be acted upon; some issues are the result of a conflict among stakeholders, challenges that have arisen, or situations that require a formal process for resolution.

Negotiation

Negotiation is a skill that every project manager uses constantly, yet it's not commonly covered in the project management literature. Negotiation is an integral part of project management, but often the project manager does not even realize that he or she is negotiating. Project managers negotiate for additional resources, for enough money, for keeping the resources they already have, the project priorities, and so on. Negotiation is a key part of stakeholder management, team management, and vendor management. A project manager who is a poor negotiator has an increased chance of having a failed project or having a project with a longer schedule or higher costs than could have been achieved.

One key rule to remember in negotiating is that everybody has a stake in a successful conclusion. Negotiations begin when someone wants to change something. A negotiation where both parties get what's important to them but give up what is not is called a win/win situation. It is to nobody's benefit to win a conflict at the total expense of the other person—this type of win is always short-term and will cause problems in the long-term.

Most of the time project managers negotiate informally as part of daily communication. However, there are times that they need to adopt a more formal strategy.

Let's assume you are the project lead for a consulting firm that has bid on a large project. You have gotten to the final round of negotiations before the winner will be selected. Here are a few pointers for winning the contract.

Develop a Negotiating Strategy

The first thing to do is clearly define the issues that are going to be negotiated. Understand each of the areas that can be negotiated. Don't define the needed outcomes yet, just the issues. Next, define the strategic goals and objectives for the negotiations. What is your overarching or strategic desire, and what goals go along with that strategic desire? Then prioritize the goals. Define the most important goal, the second most important goal, and so on, continuing down the line. For each of the areas that are under discussion, define the minimum acceptable result.

Once all these items are identified, analyze strengths and weaknesses for both sides of the negotiation. Then start brainstorming some win/win situations. It's a good idea to identify possible win/lose and lose/win situations in order to be prepared for them should they arise. This upfront work can be time-consuming, but for an important negotiation it is necessary.

The Negotiation

Negotiations are more successful when they are approached looking for ways that both parties can have their needs met. Spend time trying to understand the goals of the other party. Both sides want to get what is important to them, but nobody wants to be the bad guy. Understanding both sides will enable the parties to find a win/win scenario.

During the negotiation, discuss the issues at hand, including deadlines, criteria for acceptance, payment, and any other issues. Make sure the conversation stays on track and that the strategic goals are being addressed. Watch the body language of the people in the negotiation. A good rule of thumb is to be hard on the issues but soft on the people. It is okay to take a strong position; it is not a good idea to be belligerent about it. Remember that the strategic goals are more important than the position. Another important factor is to separate the people from the conflict. The negotiation is about a favorable outcome, not the people involved in the negotiation.

At the close of the negotiation, document the status of open items and closed items. Confirm acceptance by all parties. Define the next steps and when the steps will occur.

> * ***NOTE***
>
> During the execution phase of your project, you will be using your conflict management skills and tools. We discussed the types of conflicts and methods of handling conflict in Chapter 7. Much of what we discussed in that chapter will be utilized here.

The Project Kickoff Meeting

What should be one of the first things you do after you've thought through the project? Hold a project kickoff meeting.

Project kickoff meetings are critically important. There's an old saying among experienced project managers that a good start is 90 percent of project success. The kickoff meeting is the first opportunity the project manager has to formally lead the team members and other stakeholders in the right direction to make the project successful. The kickoff meeting is where the project manager sets expectations for the project, the team members, and the culture for the rest of the project. It is also where the project team members establish their expectations about the project manager.

The primary goal of the kickoff meeting is to present an overview of the project: schedules, budget, performance expectations, roles and responsibilities of the participants, and how the project manager will manage the project. When done right, the kickoff meeting builds a sense of team and shows that everyone is working on the project together. This is where the project manager can foster trust in the team and perform the relationship building that will support the project in the future.

Including everyone in the kickoff meeting helps obtain buy-in to the project goals and constraints, and everyone walks away with a full understanding of what needs to be done and how their piece fits into the project. By the time the kickoff meeting is over, everyone should have a clear understanding of what will happen on the project and their role in the project. The people attending come in as part of a group. They leave the meeting as part of a team. There is no better way to start the project.

TIP

For a complex IT project—one that spans multiple departments and has multiple teams—plan on spending at least a day for the kickoff meeting. Using a facilitator leaves the project manager free to do team building and not get bogged down with the administrative details of running the meeting.

Managing Scope, Schedule, and Resources

At this point, the project manager has met with the customer, team members, and the other stakeholders to define the management approach the project manager is going to take. Now is when the project manager follows that approach. The project is out of the planning phase and into the execution phase, so the project manager will start to manage the progress of the activities that team members are carrying out on a daily basis according to the schedule. The project manager will also start to track hours and costs incurred in creating the deliverables.

The project manager's responsibilities during project execution are not just to track and control project work, but also to ensure that project work happens successfully. This means making sure project team members have all the resources they need. Do they have the right equipment? Are the facilities adequate?

In today's corporate environment, the IT project team members are most likely working on multiple projects. Because of this, the project manager spends part of his or her time working with functional managers or other project managers to ensure that the team members the project manager has planned to use are not running into other conflicts. Another project may run late, affecting the planned use of a particular resource. A functional manager may have started an initiative that requires a team member who the project manager had scheduled during the same period.

Some companies manage their projects as a portfolio, with all the projects and all the resources in a database that allows conflicts to be identified. Some companies have regular coordination meetings among the project managers to identify resource conflicts. However it is done, ensuring that the resources the project manager had planned to use are available when needed is part of the project manager's responsibilities.

A good practice is for project managers to keep their attention on what should be happening two reporting periods out. If status is reported every two weeks, the project manager should be looking at what will need to happen between now and four weeks from now. What supplies, people, and tools will be utilized between now and then? Are they ready to go? Do all the appropriate people know that you will be utilizing those resources in the coming weeks? Are there any situations that could arise that would delay the resources? Finding a potential delay a few weeks beforehand rather than the day before gives the manager a better chance to rectify something that could potentially throw the project off track.

The other thing he or she will be doing is a lot of walking around to check and validate the progress on deliverables. This includes ensuring that the deliverables are consistent with the documented plan and making sure that progress is occurring as planned. This is not to say that the project manager should hover over the team members and get in the way of their work being done. Micromanagement is one of the most effective ways to slow progress. However, the manager can informally check every couple of days. He or she should ask team members how it's going, if there's anything they need, or if anything is a concern. In the early days of Hewlett Packard, the management style was MBWA—"management by wandering around." The project manager can learn a lot by talking regularly to team members and showing them that he or she cares about their work.

When the project manager does hear about a concern, he or she should act on it as soon as possible. There are few things more frustrating for team members than telling the project manager about a problem they are having and then not getting any help in the resolution. No one likes to deal with problems, but avoidance is not an option. To build the team member's trust and respect, help them get their jobs done and assist in resolving their problems.

> **! WARNING**
> One of the easiest ways to tell a new project manager from an experienced project manager is that the new project manager spends more time doing the technical work than managing the project. It does not matter if you can do the job better, faster, and cheaper than a team member, your job is to MANAGE the project, not do it!

Quality Assurance

One area that often is overlooked in the commotion of managing a project is quality assurance (QA). Quality for the product is often integrated into the project work, but the project quality, discussed in Chapter 8, is addressed during project execution. Is the team following the steps agreed upon in the quality plan? Is the quality of the project management process itself adequate? Is the project manager following methodical and structured project management processes or running around aimlessly? Is the project being managed to the right level of detail? Too much detail and the project manager will lose sight of the project goals, too little detail and things will get away from him or her. Finding the right amount of project management is always a balancing act.

Risk Management

A lot of risk management takes place during project execution. It is here that the project manager follows the risk response plan. He or she will be monitoring risks to see if they occur, if he or she needs to implement the planned responses, if those planned responses handle the risk the way they were intended to, or if a fallback plan is needed. The team will also identify new risks and send them through the analysis and response processes identified in Chapter 10. As we stated earlier, too many project managers, even if they write a good risk management plan, tend to put it on the shelf and never look at it once they get involved in the day-to-day management of the project. That is not a good practice!

Part of risk management is implementing preventive and corrective actions, which is something that occurs on a small basis every day. A team member may mention that he or she is concerned that a piece of equipment needed for the deliverable is not in yet and will be needed in the next few days. The project manager should track down the equipment and ensure that it is delivered on time. That is **preventive action.** He or she is preventing a concern from becoming a risk or an issue.

Taking **corrective action** is also part of life as a project manager. Let's say a deliverable is completed on time, but does not meet the specifications. Now the team member needs to rectify the deliverable and get the schedule back on track. That is corrective action. Chapter 10 defined the difference between a risk, which is a possible future event, and an issue, which is a problem that is occurring right now. Undertaking corrective and preventive action is a big part of the project manager's job. Some corrective and preventive actions are formal, such as implementing a risk response, and some are informal, such as calling a vendor to expedite shipping.

Leading the Project Team

During the execution phase of the project, you will start to add significant staff hours and costs. Figure 12-2 shows the curve of cost and staffing levels as the project progresses.

Figure 12-2. Cost and Staffing Levels

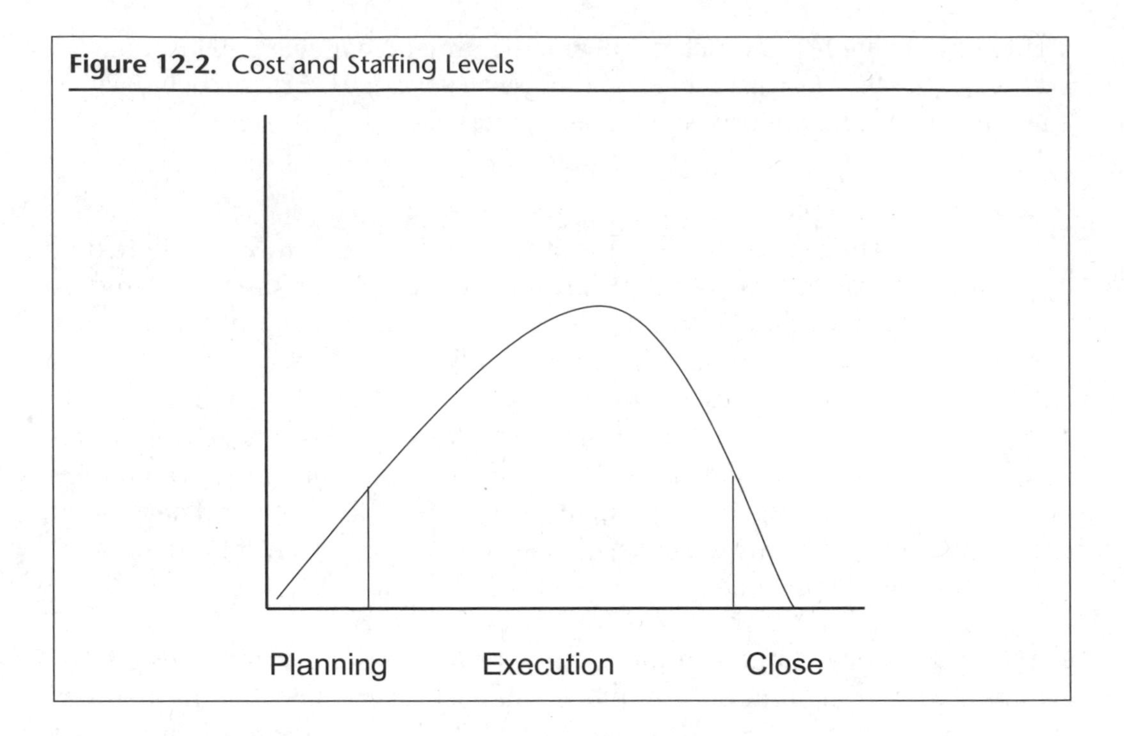

The project manager follows the staffing plan developed in the planning phase of the project. This tells how to bring staff onto the project. During the execution phase, the project manager develops the individuals and the team as a whole, motivating them and managing them. Recall from Chapter 7 that some of the challenges and frustrations involved with leading teams include:

- Uncommitted, uninvolved, and apathetic team members
- Conflicts, power struggles, and challenges to authority
- Inability to reach team consensus
- The team's unwillingness to confront significant issues
- Multitasking
- Inability to influence team members

Most likely, during the planning phase the team has moved through the forming and storming stages of team development. Now it is starting to reach the norming and performing stages. What a relief! The project manager can nurture this development during team meetings by starting to release some of the control to the team itself. If the team is starting to resolve issues on its own, team members can lead the parts of the meeting that relate to work they are performing. The project manager can spend time at the meeting making sure that it stays on track, that there is balanced participation, and that the overall needs of the project and organization are being met. Of course, while the project manager can start to share leadership, he or she does not abdicate leadership. The project manager still organizes meetings, collects status information, resolves conflicts, and follows up on items from the meeting.

IT projects, more than many other types of projects, tend to have a lot of ambiguity in them. Even well-managed technical projects have a lot of ambiguity in them. The client's requirements are not as well-defined as they need to be. The technology is not static but changes as the project progresses. Even if the team has built 10 data warehouses, the 11th one will be different because the requirements are different, the team members have not worked together before, the network environment is radically different, the database has had a significant upgrade since the last implementation, and the schedule is different. The phrase "flying an airplane while learning how to fly" is often used. Most IT people wish, once they have completed a project, that they could do it over again because this time they would do it better.

To a technical person, ambiguity is very unsettling. Technicians tend to like things well-defined and rational. They enjoy challenges, but they enjoy technical challenges, not people challenges or undefined requirements. Part of the project manager's job is to be able to manage that ambiguity and to guide the team(s) in managing it.

Why is motivating people so important? According to an article in the February 2004 edition of *Training and Development* magazine, employees who have an above average attitude toward their work have 22 percent higher productivity. This is a significant contribution towards meeting a schedule.[1]

This part of the project emphasizes a personal skill that has not been needed before—leadership. No matter how good someone is at planning and identifying costs and risks, those skills alone are not enough during execution. The primary job during the execution phase is to motivate and lead. To do this effectively, the project manager needs to understand the team's personal needs, desires, and issues. The manager has to motivate the team members to do the work even if there are problems on the project. The success of the project depends on the project manager's abilities to ensure that it is the team, not the project manager, who completes the project. A good project manager will likely spend many hours every week just talking with the team members.

Doing so is very important to team members, even if the project manager feels it's detracting from other work. The best project managers have strong project leadership skills as well as strong project management skills.

> **PM in Action!**
>
> Create a checklist template that has all the things you might need to do on a daily basis as part of leading and managing the project. Make it generic enough so that it can be adapted and specialized based on the needs of individual projects.

MANAGING PROJECT COMMUNICATION

Recall that in the prior section we talked about how a large part of your job is preventive and corrective action. The other big part of your job is communication. You will be communicating up and down the organization, across departments, and internal and external to the project. You will communicate in writing and verbally, formally and informally.

In Chapter 9, we talked about the audiences you will communicate with and some techniques for effective communication. Here we want to look at establishing your communication infrastructure and collecting project information.

Communication Channel Management

Project communications go much more smoothly when the project manager spends the time establishing communication channels early. The information that was documented in the communication plan, such as the information that will collected from team members and the information that will be reported to the project sponsor, is carried out during the execution phase.

It is a good practice to ensure team members have a structured way to communicate with each other. It would seem evident that the system designer would need to collaborate with the QA team lead or the testing team lead, but it is surprising that a number of projects fall behind because no one takes the initiative to cross those departmental boundaries and proactively establish communication channels.

Another set of communication channels that the project manager should keep a close eye on are those that relate to people outside the company. This includes vendors, contractors, and external customers. For the project manager to be the liaison to external communication works well. In order to sell more business, external consultants and vendors could "pollute" the team with ideas that are inconsistent with the objectives of the project or the methodology that the organization follows. Few things are more frustrating than trying to fix a solution that an outside consultant has suggested to the project team members.

The project manager should be the only communications interface with external customers. It can be pretty ugly if the customer asks a team member how things are going and that team member relates the daily personal challenges and frustrations encountered. Managing all client interaction is not micromanagement; it is insuring that a consistent and accurate message about the project is delivered to the customer.

In Practice: Project Communication

While most project communications take place within the project and from the project manager to other stakeholders, sometimes project communication can reach far outside the project itself. During the Year 2000 mitigation projects (often referred to as Y2K), many companies set up formal communications efforts through the media and through their web sites, advertising the work they were doing to become Y2K compliant. A major utility in California, for example, put a liaison from the company's communications office on the Y2K corporate project team. This person was responsible for ensuring that a consistent message regarding the company's Y2K efforts was being released to the public, from press releases, television and radio advertising, filings with the Public Utilities Commission, the monthly inserts in the utility bills, and even the telephone answering messages on the project's public telephone number. All communications were a joint effort of the communications office and the company's legal department, and the project manager had to authorize any communications about the project.

Collecting Information

The communication plan defines the type of reporting information that will be collected. Specifically, it addresses the necessary information on schedule status, technical progress, budget performance, and resource utilization.

Scope and Performance Information

Scope and performance information should reflect how the deliverables are progressing against the plan. This information should also relate projected progress and any performance issues and risks. Information on progress should start with the deliverables, specifically the deliverables that have been completed since the last report. Performance information should also include data on what is currently in progress and what is supposed to start during the upcoming reporting period. Additional information on technical challenges, performance of the deliverables, and quality concerns are also a part of scope and performance reporting.

Schedule Information

Schedule information should include any significant milestones that have been achieved since the last reporting period. Then information on the progress that has been made towards milestones, such as percent complete on activities in progress, should be noted. Information on activities that have started and those that have completed should be included. For those activities that are in progress, an estimate on when they will be complete should be included as well.

For schedule information, the project manager should get detailed information from the project team members and summarize it for management. For example, he or she can track the progress of activities, then roll these up to track the progress of the milestone, then roll this up to track the progress of the project overall.

Cost and Resource Information

Sometimes tracking cost can be a challenge because you're trying to track costs that tie to deliverables, and frequently the costs and the deliverables are out of sync because billing cycles and reporting cycles have their own separate timelines. One way to work within these constraints is to note what costs have been authorized, what costs have been incurred based on the work done during the last reporting period, and what costs have actually showed up on the financial reports.

Cost information includes information on resources and any other items that are charged to the project. This can include the number of people who were working on particular tasks, equipment that was ordered and has arrived, supplies that have been utilized, and so forth.

In Practice: Collecting Project Costs

One popular manufacturer of laptop computers has set up a project costing system in which only contractors are charged against the project, employees are not. The result is a strong competition, and often conflict, among the project managers to get as many employees on their project as possible to keep their costs low. This is certainly not an accurate way to account for costs.

One government entity installed an ERP system in its headquarters in 2003 and 2004. While it hired contractors for implementation and for testing and integration, it also used internal employees for some of the work. It laid out a high-level project budget, but the project manager was not required to track against the budget. During an audit, it was discovered that the time spent by internal employees was not charged against the project unless the employees were *officially authorized* to spend more than 50% of their time on the project. The majority of the employees working on the project were spending significant amounts of time on it, but they were not officially authorized to spend over 50% of their time on the project and so none of their work was charged against the project budget.

In neither of these two examples is there an accurate knowledge of the project costs. Determining how much similar projects in the future will cost is virtually impossible, because there is no accurate baseline from which to judge.

Other Project Information

On some projects, collecting and reporting on the risk status is important: You might collect information on risk events that have passed, those that have occurred, and the status of risk responses that have been implemented. Other projects may require you to track information on contracts.

One of the more useful pieces of information that frequently does not get collected, documented, or utilized is information on lessons learned. When a risk occurs that the team did not identify, or if estimates were significantly over or under, the root cause should be ferreted out and the corresponding lesson should be documented. This should happen while the event is fresh in the team's mind. Don't wait until the end, as the details and the significance will be lost. A **lessons learned** log that is continually updated throughout the project can be a very useful tool. During project closure, the project manager can compile and categorize the information to tie it up in a report. During the project, the log collects the information as it occurs.

MANAGING CHANGE

Imagine that you are happily managing your project, it has been well planned, your team is performing nicely, the customer is content, and the sponsor is staying out of your hair. You decide to take a stroll over to Seymour, your reporting team lead, to see how things are going. While blithely chatting, Seymour happens to mention that the customer called and said he would really appreciate it if Seymour could ensure that the reports include information on run times and tabulate that information on a monthly basis. You look at Seymour with a puzzled expression on your face as you ask him how he replied to this request. Seymour looks back at you with a bland expression as he replies, "Well of course I said okay, he is the customer, after all."

You have just been the victim of scope creep. Your scope has increased without your knowledge and without an assessment of the impact of the change. Do you suppose that Seymour assessed the impact of this change on schedule, cost, quality, testing, documentation, or team member resources? Probably not. He just assumed that since the customer asked for it, he had to do it. Thus, we have a case for managing change.

Defining Change

Change is anything that expands or reduces project scope, product scope, schedule, processes, plans, requirements, development approach, or resources. The first step in managing change is to define, very clearly and upfront, what constitutes a change for all of these aspects of the project. If the project includes any internal or external contracts, define what constitutes a change in contracts as well if this is not handled by the contracting, purchasing, or legal department.

For example, here's a possible definition of schedule change: A schedule change is anything that affects a milestone, a critical path, a near critical path, or reduces float on a non-critical path to less than two weeks. A schedule change also includes any modification of the sequence or duration of activities. A revision to the schedule that modifies the duration of a task within its float is not considered a change, unless that modification falls into the categories mentioned above.

You can see that this example clearly defines what is considered a schedule change and what is not. This definition is very clear and there is no wiggle room in the definition. The same type of definition should be developed for scope, technical approach, cost/resources, quality, requirements, approach, and processes. As a project manager, you will have requests for changes on a daily basis. Not all of them will require a formal change management approach. You will have to decide what goes through the change management process and what does not based on criteria you establish during the planning phase.

> ***PM in Action!***
>
> Using the information above as a guideline, create definitions for scope change, budget change, and requirements change.

Comparing Product and Project Scope Change

Sometimes product scope and project scope can be hard to separate. Consider that a change to the product scope usually changes the deliverable(s). Examples include:

- Added features or functions—tighter tolerances, higher performance requirements, a new report, a new data format
- Changes to environmental requirements—tolerance to temperature, moisture, shock, and vibration
- Changes to physical characteristics—weight, size, color

Changes to project scope include a shortened schedule, exchanging a team member, adding more testing, and reducing the budget.

Uncontrolled **scope creep** is one of the most frequent causes of project failure. Most often, scope creep occurs because of poorly defined objectives. Not applying a rigorous change control process runs a close second in causes of project failure. The impact of scope creep includes schedule delay, rising costs, and stakeholder dissatisfaction. The cure—just say no. Many times the project manager is afraid of annoying someone, causing a conflict, or looking bad in front of the boss or the team. Sticking to the original baseline has a lot of benefits, most notably the success of the project. Rather than accepting scope creep, the project manager should use his or her negotiation and communication skills to point out the long-term impact of scope creep and then find a polite but firm way to reject changes that are not really necessary.

In Practice: Not Saying No

We have seen one instance where an internal project grew 3000% over its original scope. The project sponsor was a director-level with a strong personality and the project manager was a young contractor hired to manage this one project. She never felt she could say no to the sponsor. The project was eventually cancelled and she was let go. As a contractor, you may not be comfortable saying no to a request for a change, but you can always say "Yes, and here's the impact of the change. Do you still want to do it?"

Sources of Change

Where do changes come from? Normally they come from five places:

- Errors in defining the product—Frequently, as the team begins to execute the project and carry out the project plan, it encounters things for which it did not plan. These things cause the team to expand, reduce, or modify the product. When the project team learns more about the project they often find a need to change the product, to make it better suit the client's objectives.
- Errors in defining the project— The team may have done an acceptable job in defining the product, but it may have underestimated or overestimated the work involved in creating the product.
- Value-added change—This is a pleasant surprise. A value added change usually comes from a team member who finds a way to do something faster, better, or cheaper. These are good changes, but they still have to be managed.
- A customer-directed change—These are changes that the project manager gets from customers. The customer might call and begin with something like, "You know I was thinking that it would be really great if. . . ."
- An external change—These are changes outside the control of the project team. They include changes that are a result of the economy, competition, politics, or anything else outside the organization or the project.

What Do You Think?

Look at some of the projects you have managed and assess where most of your changes came from. Were they errors in defining the product? External changes? Customer driven?

Cost of Change

Change is almost never free. Most often, it increases the cost of the project, although very rarely it will reduce the project's cost or schedule. The further along in the project, the more impact the requested change has on the project budget. Figure 12-3 is a guideline for the cost of change over time.

Figure 12-3. Cost of Change Over Time

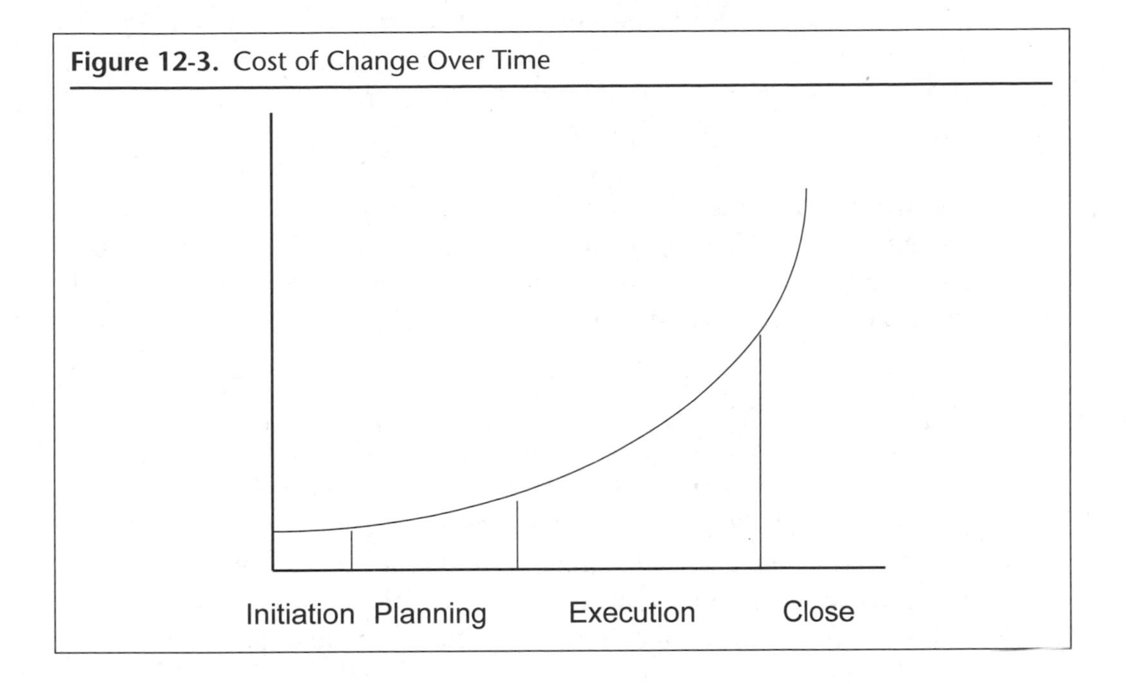

However, there is more to the cost of change than this chart shows, and that is the cost of assessing the impact of the change. Let's say you work for a company that has been hired to create an application to support nine call centers around the country with the capacity to collect data from 2,200 phone lines. Let's say you are 8 months into this 14-month project and you are called into the office of the director of the customer care center. She is the customer for the project. She informs you that her organization has decided to outsource all its West Coast customer care to an offshore location. Therefore, your project will now include three East Coast sites, two Midwest sites, and headquarters, in addition to the offshore location in Thailand. She realizes that this will affect the scope, schedule, and cost of the project and would like to know how bad the impact will be.

Before you even *think* about concocting numbers, stop. The appropriate place to begin this type of conversation is to point out that the analysis necessary to give her an updated schedule, budget, and scope will take several weeks and that you will get back to her within a week with an estimate on the amount of time and cost involved in getting her that estimate. That's right. The effort involved in estimating that kind of change is significant. Therefore, you will need to define the scope, schedule, and cost just to develop the impact of such a change on the project. You're probably looking at two weeks, at least, to determine the impact of the change, and that isn't time that your firm plans to donate to the customer because it decided that outsourcing would be a nice idea. Those two weeks are also time you did not plan for in the project schedule. Anything that takes this long, for whatever reason, will have an impact.

In addition to the impact of the change itself, it is important to take into consideration the time and cost of assessing the impact of the change. Sometimes this additional time and cost, in and of itself, is enough to have people reconsider their change request.

> **NOTE**
> One of the best ways to reduce the number of frivolous change requests is to have a rigorous change control system. People are happy to suggest change when someone else has to do the work. However, if they have to assess the impact of the change, document the impact to the schedule and budget, and justify the reason for the change, the number of change requests will drop sharply.

Change Control Infrastructure

As with all things in project management, you will set up a structure that suits the needs of the project. For small projects, you do not need a complex change-management system. However, for a project like the call center mentioned above, you will definitely need an infrastructure set up to manage change. All change requires integration. A change to the product scope will most likely affect the quality, schedule, cost, and risks on a project. A change to project resources could affect the cost, schedule, and risks. All aspects of the project are interconnected and need to be managed that way. When you assess the impact of any change, don't forget the documentation changes needed to formalize the change to the product. Any new or changed requirement, for example, must be documented in the requirements document, the design document, the testing document, and so on. This means re-releasing updated documents to everyone who has a copy of the old document or is affected by the change (so you will also need infrastructure to manage the configuration of your project documentation).

Change management on a large project requires rigorous documentation. We spoke earlier about configuration management. On large projects, change management is just a part of configuration management. The *PMBOK® Guide* defines configuration management as

> A collection of formal documented procedures used to apply technical and administrative direction and surveillance to: identify and document the functional and physical characteristics of a product, result, service, or component; control any changes to such characteristics; record and report each change and its implementation status; and support the audit of the products, results, or components to verify conformance to requirements. It includes the documentations, tracking systems, and defined approval levels necessary for authorizing and controlling changes.[2]

Thus, managing the changes to the product, results, or components is just one piece of a rigorous configuration management system.

In order to manage change, you begin with the baselines. For scope, this means the scope statement and WBS. For schedule, it means the baselined schedule. For cost, it means the budget. Finally, for requirements it means the baseline requirements document. Any non-administrative variance to these documents constitutes a change. The process that is followed will be set up during the planning phase of the project and should be commensurate with the size and complexity of the project. For a simple project of a month or less, it is usually enough for the project manager to talk with the technical lead, and perhaps the customer and sponsor, depending on the change. If it is agreed that the change should be approved and implemented, the project manager will update the project documents, advise the team, and implement the change.

On larger, more complex projects, a more formal **change control system** is needed. A change control system is comprised of the forms, policies, procedures, and processes needed to carry out change management. One such form is a change request form. The person requesting the change fills out the form and sends it to the designated person. There should be a **change control board (CCB)** that meets periodically to review change requests. The CCB is generally comprised of the project manager, sponsor, technical leads, and ad hoc members as deemed appropriate. The CCB will review all change requests and approve or deny them or request further information before making a decision. The CCB should understand the impacts of any requested change on a project before making a decision. On a fast-paced project, the CCB should meet no less frequently than weekly in order to avoid holding up the project.

If a change is approved, the project manager updates the appropriate project documents, including configuration management documents as needed, communicates the change, and integrates it into the management of the project. If the change is denied, the project manager or the designated person on the CCB communicates the decision to the person requesting the change. If further information is requested, someone on the project team is identified to lead the effort to gather and provide the information.

Figure 12-4 shows an example of a change request form and Figure 12-5 has an example of a change request log. These are samples that you can use as a template to create something that will work on your project.

As in most things in project management, you should only have as much structure as necessary to manage the project effectively. Too much is overkill, and too little will lead to confusion.

Figure 12-4. Project Change Request Form

Project Name ____________________ PCR # ____________

Change Request Title ____________________

Requested by ____________ Requested Priority* [1] [2] [3] [4]

Telephone # ____________ Date Requested ____________

Assigned to ____________ Date Resolution Needed ____________

Description of Proposed Change:

Project Area Impacted:

Requirements/Scope	[ ]	Architecture/Design	[ ]
Budget	[ ]	Testing	[ ]
Schedule	[ ]	Documentation Only	[ ]

Other (describe) ____________

Impact not not making this change:

Other projects or efforts impacted by this change: ____________

Resolution

Labor Impacts (in hours):

Project Phase	Change Request Effort				
	IT	Testing	PM	Config	Others
Planning					
Analysis					
Design					
Development					
Test & Integration					
Implementation					
Totals					

Scheduled for CCB on MM/DD/YY

Approved/Rejected [A] [R]

* Priority:
1 Within 24 hours
2 Within 1 week
3 Within 1 month
4 When resources available

Signed:

Requestor ____________ CCB Chair ____________

Project Manager ____________ Technical Lead ____________

Project Sponsor ____________

Figure 12-5. Project Change Request Log

Project: ______________________ **Project #** ______________

Project Manager: ______________ **Last Updated:** ______________

#	Change Request Title	Priority	Date Submitted	Requested By	Assigned To	Due Date	Status	CCB Date	Closed Date

Fields:

Priority 1 - The change must be incorporated into the project within 24 hours
2 - The changes must be incorporated into the project within 1 week
3 - The changes must be incorporated into the project within 1 month
4 - The changes must be incorporated at some convenient time

Requested by: The person requesting the change
Assigned to: The person doing the analysis
Status O = Open
W = In work
C = Complete
X = Canceled

Chapter Summary

- The project plan, with all its components, is the baseline for managing the project.
- Daily activities include: managing activities, tracking hours, costs, and resources, and checking in with team members to validate progress and to make sure they have all they need to accomplish their work.
- Managing project stakeholders requires ongoing communication.
- Negotiation is a skill that project managers need throughout the project, particularly when negotiating a contract. A formal negotiation necessitates setting a negotiation strategy, selecting and preparing a negotiating team, and holding the negotiation.
- The project manager should ensure that the product and project quality objectives are being met and make sure that the risk management plan is performing as expected.
- A good start is 90 percent of project success, and an effective kickoff meeting is a good start.
- The majority of the project manager's time managing a project is spent on corrective action, preventive action, and communication.
- During project execution there is a heavy emphasis on leadership, motivation, and conflict management skills.
- As part of project execution, the project manager will collect information on project status in the areas of scope, performance, schedule, cost, resources, risks, contract performance, and lessons learned.
- Change is anything that expands or reduces project scope, schedule, processes, plans, requirements, approach, or resources.
- Change can come from five sources: errors in defining the product, errors in defining the project, value-added change, customer-directed change, and external change.
- Change usually incurs capital expense, as does assessing the impact of requested changes. It is more costly to make a change later in the project.
- The change control system should be commensurate with the size and complexity of the project. For complex projects, you may need a CCB and a rigorous configuration management system.

Key Terms

Issue Log

Corrective action

Scope creep

Change control system

Preventive action

Lessons learned

Change

Change control board

Key Term Quiz

1. Documenting a risk that occurred that was not identified or determining which estimates were significantly off is an example of collecting ________________.

2. Adding requirements or product features without adding schedule or cost is called _____________.

3. _____________ is something that expands or reduces project scope.

4. Taking action to bring project performance into line with the project plan is _____________.

5. _________________ is taking action to reduce the probability of the project not performing to plan.

6. A group of people that reviews change requests to approve or deny change requests is a _______________.

7. A set of policies, procedures, and forms to manage change is called ________________.

8. An ____________________ is used to document and monitor the resolution of issues.

Chapter Review Questions

1. If you report progress every week, how far in the future should you be looking?

2. During project execution, much of your job is to perform two kinds of action. What are they?

3. By the time project execution begins, what development stage should the team be in?

4. As team development progresses, the project manager can start to share leadership in some of the team meetings. However, in certain areas the project manager should not abdicate his or her responsibilities. What are these?

5. Give two examples of managing communication channels.

6. Why is it important to collect lessons learned information throughout the project?

7. What is the first step to managing change on a project?

8. Change can impact what aspects of the project?

9. List the five sources of change.

10. Give an example of an externally caused change.

11. Give an example of a value added change.

12. In addition to developing a cost and schedule impact for a change request, what else should the project manager develop an estimate for?

13. On a large and complex project, change management is part of what?

14. To assess the degree of change, the project manager should measure against what?

15. A Change Control Board will likely be comprised of who?

END NOTES:

1. *Training and Development Magazine,* February 2005, page 62.
2. Project Management Institute (PMI®), *A Guide to the Project Management Body of Knowledge (PMBOK® Guide),* 3d ed., page 238, Project Management Institute, Newtown Square, PA, 2004.

13 *Project Monitoring and Control*

After reading this chapter, you will be able to:

- Define project monitoring and control.
- Discuss methods to analyze performance information.
- Describe appropriate responses to performance variances.
- Describe how the execution and control process work together.

Defining Project Monitoring and Control

In Chapter 12, we discussed the first part of project execution: collecting information on the status of the project. A primary role of the project manager during the execution phase is monitoring and controlling the project.

Monitoring includes measuring and analyzing the information collected. Monitoring entails:

- Comparing actual performance to planned performance
- Assessing trends in the performance data
- Developing forecasts of future cost and schedule performance

Controlling goes hand in hand with monitoring and includes:

- Analyzing variances in performance
- Evaluating alternative actions to bring performance in line with the plan
- Recommending preventive or corrective action as appropriate, and managing the preventive or corrective actions to ensure they have the desired effect

In this chapter, we present activities in the order the project manager would see them. However, monitoring and controlling are not one-time events. They are ongoing throughout the project. They occur equally in the planning, execution, and closing phases. We discuss them separately because they require specific actions, but they take place throughout the project. Figure 13-1 is a depiction of formal monitoring and control based on periodic progress reports. However, the project manager is always collecting information informally and analyzing it to keep things on track. Remember, most of the project manager's job is preventive and corrective action, which is what control is. Sometimes control is formalized, such as the change control process, and sometimes it is more informal, such as a suggestion to a team member.

When we monitor the project we continually compare the actual performance to the planned performance—the baseline. A **baseline** is the approved plan that has been signed off on by management and/or by the customer, plus or minus any approved changes. Recall that the baseline for scope is the scope statement and the Work Breakdown Structure, the baseline for time is the schedule, and the baseline for cost is the budget. The baseline does not change to match actual progress. It only changes based on an approved change request, if events dictate the schedule be expedited or delayed, or if the existing baseline is so far off that measuring against it has become an exercise in futility.

During the entire execution phase of the project, the project manager will be measuring actual progress against what he or she planned at the beginning of the project when he or she knew the least about it. If the project is behind schedule or over budget, it may indicate a significant problem on the project or it may indicate that the original estimates were flawed. Upper management will generally assume that there's a problem on the project when the actual status does not meet what the plan says. This is a very strong incentive for the project manager to plan as thoroughly as possible.

Determining What to Report

It's easy to fall into the trap of reporting information that is convenient and simple to collect. However, the information that is easy to obtain is not always the most relevant. For example, the project manager may have determined that the IT technician will have 100 workstations wired and functioning by the end of the week. This assumes that the technician does 20 workstations

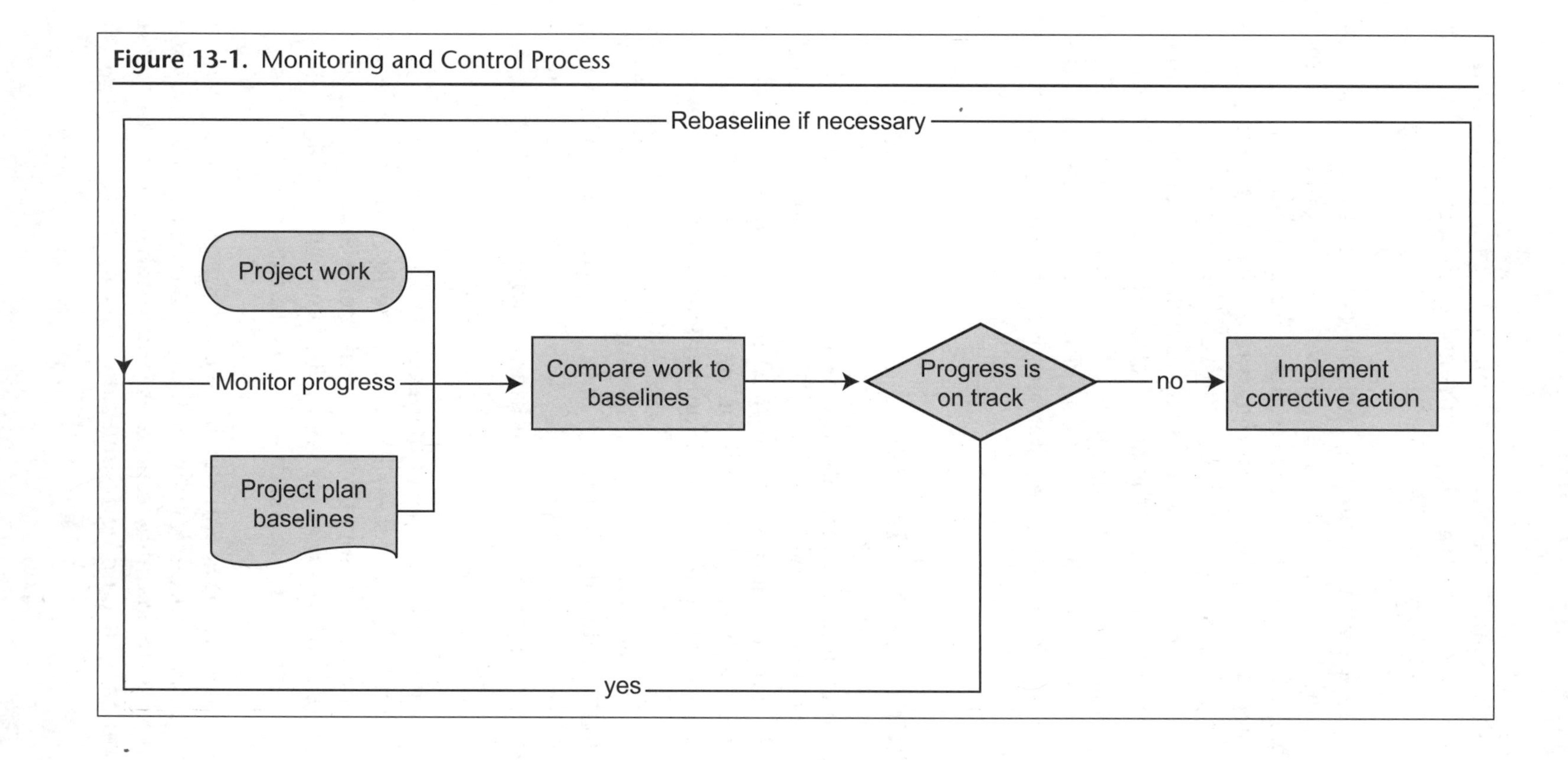

Figure 13-1. Monitoring and Control Process

per eight-hour day. The easy thing is to collect information on how many workstations are up and running by the end of the day—and, in fact, this is a logical piece of information to collect.

However, knowing if the work was actually done in the confines of an eight-hour day would also be useful. Did it take more time? Less time? Were there any problems? Knowing the answers to these questions will assist the project manager in making better estimates next time. In addition, if the project manager is paying installers by the hour, the answers will have an impact on the budget. In-house projects use salaried people, so project managers often don't really pay attention to the actual effort it takes to perform tasks. Management assumes that salaried people will stay late, come in early, or come in over the weekend in order to get the work done. It is better to update original estimates with more accurate estimates rather than perpetuate inaccurate assumptions.

Planning for Monitoring

To collect meaningful information, it is useful to develop project plans in a way that is consistent with the way information will be collected and analyzed. For example, suppose you're the IT lead on a project to open three new offices. Assume that as the IT lead you are responsible for defining the equipment requirements, the software requirements, the peripheral requirements, and the LAN and WAN requirements, but not the telecom requirements. There are a few ways you could set up your WBS to manage this, but it might be useful to consult with the project manager to determine how progress will be tracked before you arrange your WBS. After you check with the project manager, you can plan and accomplish your work in a way that is consistent with the measurement.

We will assume that the project manager is going to be tracking each office separately, and that he or she will also be monitoring the cost for the equipment as a separate category from everything else, since equipment is a major cost driver. You decide that for your WBS you will combine a life cycle approach with a location approach and you come up with Figure 13-2.

For measuring purposes, you will be asked to report on your progress gathering the various requirements by location. The cost of the equipment will be tracked against the baseline estimates. The installation will be tracked by the project manager according to milestones set by location. However, for the

Figure 13-2. New Office Openings WBS

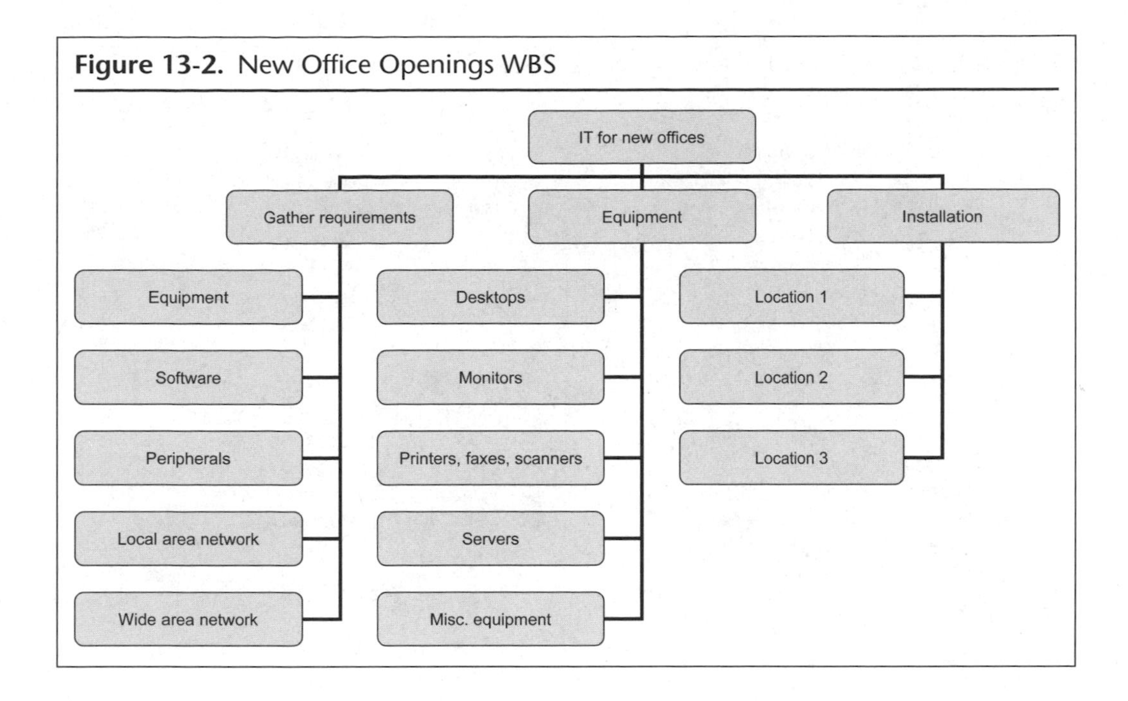

equipment you will not want to track by location. That would be meaningless. You will want to track the equipment order date, delivery date to the home office, and delivery date to the new satellite office. The installation milestones are desktops installed and connected, software installed, peripherals in place and connected, LAN functional, and WAN functional. Based on this information, you can set up the schedule so that it is easy to report progress in the way it will be monitored. Your activity list may look something like Figure 13-3.

Measuring Progress

If you ask most project managers how they measure progress on their projects, they would probably answer, "By percent complete, of course." While the percent complete of the task may be a very common way of measuring progress, there are alternatives that are more accurate. Any project manager who has been managing projects for a while has come across the team member who says, "Oh, I'm 40 percent complete with this task." How does the team member know? And more importantly how do you know? Is that a subjective 40 percent complete? How do you measure percent complete in a software project? Lines of code? Unless you have ten units and four are complete, or you have agreed upfront what 40 percent complete means, then you are at the mercy of your team member's estimate and you are operating

Figure 13-3. WBS Activities

ID	WBS	Task Name
1	**1**	**Gather Requirements**
2	**1.1**	**Equipment**
3	1.1.1	Location 1
4	1.1.2	Location 2
5	1.1.3	Location 3
6	**1.2**	**Software**
7	1.2.1	Location 1
8	1.2.2	Location 2
9	1.2.3	Location 3
10	**1.3**	**Peripherals**
11	1.3.1	Location 1
12	1.3.2	Location 2
13	1.3.3	Location 3
14	**1.4**	**Local Area Network**
15	1.4.1	Location 1
16	1.4.2	Location 2
17	1.4.3	Location 3
18	**1.5**	**Wide Area Network**
19	1.5.1	Location 1
20	1.5.2	Location 2
21	1.5.3	Location 3
22	**2**	**Equipment**
23	**2.1**	**Desktops**
24	2.1.1	Order
25	2.1.2	Deliver home office
26	2.1.3	Deliver on site
27	**2.2**	**Monitors**
28	2.2.1	Order
29	2.2.2	Deliver home office
30	2.2.3	Deliver on site
31	**2.3**	**Printers, Faxes and scanners**
32	2.3.1	Order
33	2.3.2	Deliver home office
34	2.3.3	Deliver on site
35	**2.4**	**Servers**
36	2.4.1	Order
37	2.4.2	Deliver home office
38	2.4.3	Deliver on site
39	**2.5**	**Misc. Equipment**
40	2.5.1	Order
41	2.5.2	Deliver home office
42	2.5.3	Deliver on site
43	**3**	**Installation**
44	**3.1**	**Location 1**
45	3.1.1	Desktops wired
46	3.1.2	Software installed
47	3.1.3	Peripherals in place
48	3.1.4	LAN functional
49	3.1.5	WAN functional
50	**3.2**	**Location 2**
51	3.2.1	Desktops wired
52	3.2.2	Software installed
53	3.2.3	Peripherals in place
54	3.2.4	LAN functional
55	3.2.5	WAN functional
56	**3.3**	**Location 3**
57	3.3.1	Desktops wired
58	3.3.2	Software installed
59	3.3.3	Peripherals in place
60	3.3.4	LAN functional
61	3.3.5	WAN functional

on faith, which is not a good way to control a project. An old saying in project management is that tasks quickly achieve 90 percent completion and then stay 90 percent completed forever.

In order to circumvent this situation, it is useful to lay down some guidelines on how you will measure progress on the tasks upfront. Let's return to the example of the three new offices. For requirements gathering, having most of the requirements done is not really useful. You really need all of them done in order to have something to work with, so assume that for all the activities in the requirements gathering section, something is either 100 percent done or it gets no credit. This is a example of **fixed formula reporting.** You can also establish fixed formulas with other values, such as 25 percent when you meet with the stakeholder and the remaining 75 percent once you have developed the requirements document and received sign-off by all parties.

For the equipment, the project manager is only collecting costs, but you want to track various tasks along the way. You might set up a monitoring schedule that would give you 20 percent completion when the equipment is ordered, 40 percent additional when it arrives at the home office, and the final 40 percent when it is delivered to the satellite location. This is an example of **weighted milestone reporting.**

The project manager is very interested in the installation and wants to track it closely. You agree that each location is worth 100 percent, and that each of the interim milestones are weighted as 20 percent each. The installation of the machines is worth 20 percent of the milestone. There are 100 workstations. 100 x .20 = 5, so five installed workstations account for one percent complete for the location. Five workstations is 5 percent of the 100, but only 1 percent of the entire milestone. Same with the software installation. Different scenarios will have to be worked out for the peripherals and LAN and WAN, but you get the idea.

By setting up the plan this way and agreeing ahead of time what the measurements are, you ensure there are no surprises. Everyone is clear how progress will be measured, which makes collecting status information much easier. Once dates are added, detecting variances from plan is quite simple. In more advanced project management approaches, such as earned value project management, these different ways of measuring progress are clearly defined ahead of time for each part of the project.

Types of Measurements

All kinds of things can be measured on a project. It is important to define the information that will provide meaningful information versus the information that just provides data. Too often project managers fall into the trap of measuring something just because they *can* measure it. Before measuring anything, the project manager needs to determine what information he or she needs to effectively manage the project. Then the project manager can figure out how to collect the data and how to process the data so that it becomes meaningful information.

What types of information should be collected? Certainly schedule and cost information, to answer the questions "Is the project on schedule?" and "Is the project within budget?" This is **status** information and looks at what has been accomplished as of the date the information was collected.

Another type of information relates to the progress that has been made. This looks at what the team has accomplished in the past—what deliverables have been completed or what milestones have been met, for example. Figure 13-4 has an example of a **progress report.**

While information on progress is important, it not sufficient. The client, the project sponsor, and upper management are often more interested in where the project is going than in where it has been. They want to know if the project is going to complete on schedule and budget. This type of information is a **forecast.**

Forecasting is usually done by conducting a trend analysis on past behavior and extending it into the future. Sophisticated mathematical formulas can be applied to predict future outcomes based on scenarios or assumptions about what might happen, but for the most part these are a bit above and beyond what's required for IT projects. Forecasting requires some analysis. Using information from the past and projecting progress into the future, the project manager usually assumes that the performance in the past will continue into the future. Forecasts are updated and reissued based on work performance information provided as the project is executed.

The status, progress, and forecast information is used to monitor the overall health of the project. If there are no red flags, then all is well and the project team continues executing the project. If there are variances, the project manager analyzes them to assess the degree of variance and determine whether any corrective action should be taken and what that action should be.

Figure 13-4. Sample Progress Report

<Project Name>

<Project Manager>

Project Phase: **Reporting Date:**

Project Status Summary

Project Progress		Planned Start	Planned Finish	Actual Start	Actual Finish	New Date
By Phase	Date Approved					
	Proposal Phase					
	Design/Analysis Phase					
	Development Phase					
	Test & Integration Ph.					
	Implementation Phase					

Milestones – (Last 2 weeks)	Planned Date	Actual Date	New Date	**Upcoming Milestones**	Planned Date

Deliverables	**Status**	**Items for Management Attention**
Project Overall Status		
Project Charter Approved		
Budget Baselined		
Schedule Baselined		
Requirements Documents Approved		
etc.		

Information Analysis

Now that we have collected relevant information, we analyze it to assess how well the project is doing against the plan. There will almost always be variances, but variances are not necessarily bad. The project manager needs to judge whether the variance is something to merely keep an eye on or whether it requires corrective action. In order to determine the appropriate actions, it is useful to preestablish some thresholds and acceptable variance limits for performance, quality, schedule, and budget.

Thresholds and Variances

A **threshold** is a parameter that sets the limit for taking action. If performance is above or below a certain threshold, then the project manager should employ corrective action to get back on track.

A **variance** is a quantifiable deviation from the baseline. A variance can be within the threshold value or outside of it. Some variances are small and may not require any action. Variances that are large enough to cross the threshold value will require action to bring the variance back into compliance with the plan.

Variance and threshold limits should be established for performance, schedule, and budget during the planning process. Doing so ensures that the limits will be objective and that decisions won't be subjective or open to interpretation. Setting strict limits in the beginning and then relaxing them as the project progresses is a better approach than tightening limits after the project is out of control.

Schedule thresholds may be different depending on whether an activity is on the critical path or not, or they may be expressed as a function of the path and not the activity. Examples:

- Any negative variance on the critical path or near-critical path requires corrective action.
- Any negative variance of more than 10 percent on a non-critical path requires additional analysis.
- Performance that uses more than 25 percent of the available float requires additional analysis.

Cost thresholds generally focus on overruns, but the project manager should also pay attention to underruns, as these could signal trouble with late deliveries or substandard parts. Examples:

- Five percent over budget for any project over $100,000, 10 percent over for any project over $50,000, and 15 percent over for all projects smaller then $50,000.
- Any purchase that exceeds the planned value by more than 10 percent.

- Paid labor that exceeds the planned value by more than 5 percent.
- Material usage that exceeds planned usage by more than 10 percent.

Product performance may have thresholds as well. Some examples are:

- Performance should fall in the range of 100 +/– 5 percent.
- Service levels that are more than 5 percent under the planned value require immediate investigation and appropriate action.

Establishing these values prior to the start of project execution will alleviate much discussion during the project. It is best to get agreement on these levels with the sponsor and the team members.

> ***NOTE***
> Many project management tools can be configured to deliver variance reports. For example, one web-based tool, PlanView, can be set up so that any variance over 10 percent (either plus or minus) will identify the task or the project as being in trouble.

Analyzing Information

Information analysis may be very informal on a small project. The project manager may simply walk over to the team member, have a conversation, and ask about any late tasks and why they are late. The project manager may look at a cost variance and make a phone call to establish the reason for the variance, note if the variance falls within the threshold amount, and call it a day. However, on large projects, the project manager has to do a bit more than that, maybe quite a bit more. For large projects, the project manager needs to conduct the analysis using more rigorous and analytical techniques. Variances in product scope and performance are specific to each project and we will not look at the analysis here. Before taking a look at some tools to analyze schedule and cost variance, we begin with a brief description of the types of metrics used to analyze information.

Metrics

A metric is simply a quantifiable measure of progress—for example, the project is 15 percent over budget. Some categories of metrics are:

- **Variance metrics**—These metrics tell the project manager if scope, schedule, and cost are performing to plan, and if not, they calculate the degree of variance. They are project specific, in that a two-week delay on a one-month project is significant, but on a two-year project the same delay is not nearly as significant.
- **Performance efficiency metrics**—Performance metrics tell the project manager how efficiently the project is performing. They give a percentage, so the size of the project is normalized and projects from across an organization can be compared.
- **Forecasting metrics**—A forecasting metric indicates how the schedule or budget is likely to end up if the current performance continues.

Metrics must be understood and agreed-on by the project's major stakeholders, such as the project sponsor, the team members and the client. One commonly used and visually appealing approach to reporting project status is to show the project as green (everything is good), yellow (things are pretty good, but there are some issues), or red (we've got problems). Even this simple level of reporting needs clear definition of what the terms mean. For example:

Project Objective	*Green*	*Yellow*	*Red*
Cost	< 5% cost increase	5–10% cost increase	> 10% cost increase
Schedule	Schedule slippage < 5%	Overall 5–10% schedule slippage	> 10% schedule slippage
Requirements	Minor increase in requirements	More than 20% increase in requirements	More than 33% increase in requirements
Quality	Only very demanding parts are affected	Quality reduction requires client approval	Quality reduction unacceptable to client

Common Metrics

Some commonly used metrics include:

Progress metrics: Metrics designed to capture how well each project is doing compared to the baselined cost and schedule as well as to identify trends:

- Percentage of deliverables completed
- Percentage of tasks behind schedule
- Percentage of effort left to complete
- Percentage of budget expended
- Budget trend

Project risk metrics: Metrics designed to identify risky projects for additional attention:

- Number of high-risk items
- Number of project change requests (PCRs) opened
- Scope change
  - Number of PCRs opened against requirements
- Percentage of PCRs open divided by total number of PCRs written
- Percentage of tasks completed that finished late
- Number of tasks behind schedule
- Resource change
  - Number of resources on project divided by number planned

Product quality metrics: Designed to measure areas that would indicate a poor quality product is being developed:

- Number of bug reports written
- Percentage of requirements met
- Percentage of tests failed the first time

Analyzing Schedule Variances

Let's go back to the sample project of bringing up three offices. We established what to measure in the planning phase. Now let's fast forward in time, show some progress, and look at some ways of analyzing that progress. Refer to Figure 13-5 for the baseline schedule.

To refresh your memory, we decided that requirements would be measured as 0/100%. We would not take credit until all the requirements for a certain element were complete. We said that equipment would be broken into a 20/40/40 progress plan with 20% credited when equipment is ordered, 40% more when it is delivered to the home office, and the final 40% when the equipment reaches the satellite office. The installation is broken out by location, and each of the interim milestones is worth 20%. Look at the schedule as of June 1, Figure 13-6, and check the status.

If you look, you will see there are some variances. By adding a column called Finish Variance, you can see which tasks have positive variances and which ones have negative variances. We don't recommend using the variance information as anything other than a flag to notify you to look at the details. Don't assume that the actual days are reflective of the actual variance, but look at a start or finish variance as a simple way to find the tasks that require your attention. In this case, we can see that our servers were late coming in from the vendor, and so they will be late reaching the satellite offices. There was some float there, so we may be okay, but we should probably take some corrective action by expediting shipping to the satellite offices.

WARNING

MS Project shows a task that finishes early with a negative (–) sign in front of it. Therefore, a variance that shows –3 days indicates a task that finished three days early, not three days late. This is a bit counterintuitive and can cause confusion if you are not aware of it.

The installation at Location 3 is what we should be concerned about. This installation started late and is taking longer than estimated. This is something that we want to spend a bit more time analyzing.

The first step in analyzing the variance in Location 3 is to do a variance analysis. You can see a variance in the start and finish dates, so check to see if there is a variance in the task duration. This does not have to be a sophisticated analysis. You can use some simple formulas to get useful quantifiable data. For the task "desktops wired," there is a one-week duration (five days). Remember that there are 100 desktops to be wired. You can count to see that 80 are wired, so therefore you are 80% complete. With 100 to be wired in five

Figure 13-5. Baseline Schedule

Figure 3: Chapter 12 Baseline Schedule

ID	Task Name	Duration	Plan Start	Plan Finish	Predecessors	Gantt bar label
1	**Gather Requirements**	**10 days**	**Mon 4/4/05**	**Fri 4/15/05**		
2	**Equipment**	**5 days**	**Mon 4/4/05**	**Fri 4/8/05**		
3	Location 1	1 wk	Mon 4/4/05	Fri 4/8/05		Business Analyst
4	Location 2	1 wk	Mon 4/4/05	Fri 4/8/05		Business Analyst
5	Location 3	1 wk	Mon 4/4/05	Fri 4/8/05		Business Analyst
6	**Software**	**5 days**	**Mon 4/4/05**	**Fri 4/8/05**		
7	Location 1	1 wk	Mon 4/4/05	Fri 4/8/05		Business Analyst
8	Location 2	1 wk	Mon 4/4/05	Fri 4/8/05		Business Analyst
9	Location 3	1 wk	Mon 4/4/05	Fri 4/8/05		Business Analyst
10	**Peripherals**	**5 days**	**Mon 4/4/05**	**Fri 4/8/05**		
11	Location 1	1 wk	Mon 4/4/05	Fri 4/8/05		Business Analyst
12	Location 2	1 wk	Mon 4/4/05	Fri 4/8/05		Business Analyst
13	Location 3	1 wk	Mon 4/4/05	Fri 4/8/05		Business Analyst
14	**Local Area Network**	**5 days**	**Mon 4/11/05**	**Fri 4/15/05**	**2,6,10**	
15	Location 1	1 wk	Mon 4/11/05	Fri 4/15/05		Business Analyst
16	Location 2	1 wk	Mon 4/11/05	Fri 4/15/05		Business Analyst
17	Location 3	1 wk	Mon 4/11/05	Fri 4/15/05		Business Analyst
18	**Wide Area Network**	**5 days**	**Mon 4/11/05**	**Fri 4/15/05**	**2,6,10**	
19	Location 1	1 wk	Mon 4/11/05	Fri 4/15/05		Business Analyst
20	Location 2	1 wk	Mon 4/11/05	Fri 4/15/05		Business Analyst
21	Location 3	1 wk	Mon 4/11/05	Fri 4/15/05		Business Analyst
22	**Equipment**	**34 days**	**Mon 4/11/05**	**Thu 5/26/05**		
23	**Desktops**	**28 days**	**Mon 4/11/05**	**Wed 5/18/05**		
24	Order	1 day	Mon 4/11/05	Mon 4/11/05	2	Tech Lead
25	Deliver home office	1 day	Tue 5/10/05	Tue 5/10/05	24FS+4 wks	Vendor
26	Deliver on site	1 day	Wed 5/18/05	Wed 5/18/05	25FS+1 wk	Admin
27	**Monitors**	**28 days**	**Mon 4/11/05**	**Wed 5/18/05**		
28	Order	1 day	Mon 4/11/05	Mon 4/11/05	2	Tech Lead
29	Deliver home office	1 day	Tue 5/10/05	Tue 5/10/05	24FS+4 wks	Vendor
30	Deliver on site	1 day	Wed 5/18/05	Wed 5/18/05	25FS+1 wk	Admin
31	**Printers, Faxes and scanners**	**28 days**	**Mon 4/11/05**	**Wed 5/18/05**		
32	Order	1 day	Mon 4/11/05	Mon 4/11/05	10	Tech Lead
33	Deliver home office	1 day	Tue 5/10/05	Tue 5/10/05	32FS+4 wks	Vendor
34	Deliver on site	1 day	Wed 5/18/05	Wed 5/18/05	33FS+1 wk	Admin

Timeline: April (3/27, 4/3, 4/10, 4/17, 4/24), May (5/1, 5/8, 5/15, 5/22), June (5/29, 6/5, 6/12, 6/19)

Mon 8/14/06 Page 1

Figure 13-5. Baseline Schedule (continued)

Figure 3: Chapter 12 Baseline Schedule

ID	Task Name	Duration	Plan Start	Plan Finish	Predecessors
35	**Servers**	**28 days**	**Mon 4/18/05**	**Wed 5/25/05**	
36	Order	1 day	Mon 4/18/05	Mon 4/18/05	14,18
37	Deliver home office	1 day	Tue 5/17/05	Tue 5/17/05	36FS+4 wks
38	Deliver on site	1 day	Wed 5/25/05	Wed 5/25/05	37FS+1 wk
39	**Misc. Equipment**	**28 days**	**Tue 4/19/05**	**Thu 5/26/05**	
40	Order	1 day	Tue 4/19/05	Tue 4/19/05	36
41	Deliver home office	1 day	Wed 5/18/05	Wed 5/18/05	40FS+4 wks
42	Deliver on site	1 day	Thu 5/26/05	Thu 5/26/05	41FS+1 wk
43	**Installation**	**14 days**	**Thu 5/19/05**	**Tue 6/7/05**	
44	**Location 1**	**14 days**	**Thu 5/19/05**	**Tue 6/7/05**	
45	Desktops wired	1 wk	Thu 5/19/05	Wed 5/25/05	26
46	Software installed	1 wk	Thu 5/26/05	Wed 6/1/05	45,6
47	Peripherals in place	1 wk	Thu 5/26/05	Wed 6/1/05	34,45
48	LAN functional	2 days	Thu 6/2/05	Fri 6/3/05	38,42,47
49	WAN functional	2 days	Mon 6/6/05	Tue 6/7/05	38,42,48
50	**Location 2**	**14 days**	**Thu 5/19/05**	**Tue 6/7/05**	
51	Desktops wired	1 wk	Thu 5/19/05	Wed 5/25/05	26
52	Software installed	1 wk	Thu 5/26/05	Wed 6/1/05	51
53	Peripherals in place	1 wk	Thu 5/26/05	Wed 6/1/05	51
54	LAN functional	2 days	Thu 6/2/05	Fri 6/3/05	53
55	WAN functional	2 days	Mon 6/6/05	Tue 6/7/05	54
56	**Location 3**	**14 days**	**Thu 5/19/05**	**Tue 6/7/05**	
57	Desktops wired	1 wk	Thu 5/19/05	Wed 5/25/05	26
58	Software installed	1 wk	Thu 5/26/05	Wed 6/1/05	57
59	Peripherals in place	1 wk	Thu 5/26/05	Wed 6/1/05	57
60	LAN functional	2 days	Thu 6/2/05	Fri 6/3/05	59
61	WAN functional	2 days	Mon 6/6/05	Tue 6/7/05	60

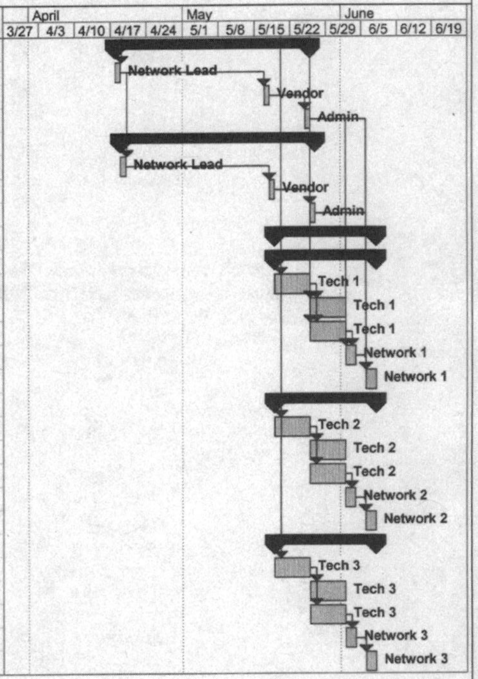

Mon 8/14/06 Page 2

Figure 13-6. Schedule on June 1

ID	❶	Task Name	Duration	% Complete	Baseline Start	Actual Start	Baseline Finish	Actual Finish	Finish Variance
1	✓	Gather Requirements	11 days	100%	Mon 4/4/05	Mon 4/4/05	Fri 4/15/05	Mon 4/18/05	1 day
2	✓	Equipment	5 days	100%	Mon 4/4/05	Mon 4/4/05	Fri 4/8/05	Fri 4/8/05	0 days
3	✓	Location 1	1 wk	100%	Mon 4/4/05	Mon 4/4/05	Fri 4/8/05	Fri 4/8/05	0 days
4	✓	Location 2	1 wk	100%	Mon 4/4/05	Mon 4/4/05	Fri 4/8/05	Fri 4/8/05	0 days
5	✓	Location 3	1 wk	100%	Mon 4/4/05	Mon 4/4/05	Fri 4/8/05	Fri 4/8/05	0 days
6	✓	Software	5 days	100%	Mon 4/4/05	Mon 4/4/05	Fri 4/8/05	Fri 4/8/05	0 days
7	✓	Location 1	1 wk	100%	Mon 4/4/05	Mon 4/4/05	Fri 4/8/05	Fri 4/8/05	0 days
8	✓	Location 2	1 wk	100%	Mon 4/4/05	Mon 4/4/05	Fri 4/8/05	Fri 4/8/05	0 days
9	✓	Location 3	1 wk	100%	Mon 4/4/05	Mon 4/4/05	Fri 4/8/05	Fri 4/8/05	0 days
10	✓	Peripherals	5 days	100%	Mon 4/4/05	Mon 4/4/05	Fri 4/8/05	Fri 4/8/05	0 days
11	✓	Location 1	1 wk	100%	Mon 4/4/05	Mon 4/4/05	Fri 4/8/05	Fri 4/8/05	0 days
12	✓	Location 2	1 wk	100%	Mon 4/4/05	Mon 4/4/05	Fri 4/8/05	Fri 4/8/05	0 days
13	✓	Location 3	1 wk	100%	Mon 4/4/05	Mon 4/4/05	Fri 4/8/05	Fri 4/8/05	0 days
14	✓	Local Area Network	5 days	100%	Mon 4/11/05	Tue 4/12/05	Fri 4/15/05	Mon 4/18/05	1 day
15	✓	Location 1	1 wk	100%	Mon 4/11/05	Tue 4/12/05	Fri 4/15/05	Mon 4/18/05	1 day
16	✓	Location 2	1 wk	100%	Mon 4/11/05	Tue 4/12/05	Fri 4/15/05	Mon 4/18/05	1 day
17	✓	Location 3	1 wk	100%	Mon 4/11/05	Tue 4/12/05	Fri 4/15/05	Mon 4/18/05	1 day
18	✓	Wide Area Network	5 days	100%	Mon 4/11/05	Tue 4/12/05	Fri 4/15/05	Mon 4/18/05	1 day
19	✓	Location 1	1 wk	100%	Mon 4/11/05	Tue 4/12/05	Fri 4/15/05	Mon 4/18/05	1 day
20	✓	Location 2	1 wk	100%	Mon 4/11/05	Tue 4/12/05	Fri 4/15/05	Mon 4/18/05	1 day
21	✓	Location 3	1 wk	100%	Mon 4/11/05	Tue 4/12/05	Fri 4/15/05	Mon 4/18/05	1 day
22		Equipment	42 days	97%	Mon 4/11/05	Mon 4/11/05	Thu 5/26/05	NA	8 days
23	✓	Desktops	21 days	100%	Mon 4/11/05	Mon 4/11/05	Wed 5/18/05	Mon 5/9/05	-7 days
24	✓	Order	1 day	100%	Mon 4/11/05	Mon 4/11/05	Mon 4/11/05	Mon 4/11/05	0 days
25	✓	Deliver home office	1 day	100%	Tue 5/10/05	Thu 4/28/05	Tue 5/10/05	Fri 4/29/05	-7 days
26	✓	Deliver on site	1 day	100%	Wed 5/18/05	Mon 5/9/05	Wed 5/18/05	Mon 5/9/05	-7 days
27	✓	Monitors	21 days	100%	Mon 4/11/05	Mon 4/11/05	Wed 5/18/05	Mon 5/9/05	-7 days
28	✓	Order	1 day	100%	Mon 4/11/05	Mon 4/11/05	Mon 4/11/05	Mon 4/11/05	0 days
29	✓	Deliver home office	1 day	100%	Tue 5/10/05	Mon 5/2/05	Tue 5/10/05	Mon 5/2/05	-6 days
30	✓	Deliver on site	1 day	100%	Wed 5/18/05	Mon 5/9/05	Wed 5/18/05	Mon 5/9/05	-7 days
31	✓	Printers, Faxes and scanners	33 days	100%	Mon 4/11/05	Mon 4/11/05	Wed 5/18/05	Wed 5/25/05	5 days
32	✓	Order	1 day	100%	Mon 4/11/05	Mon 4/11/05	Mon 4/11/05	Mon 4/11/05	0 days

Project: Chapter 12 Status 2
Date: Mon 8/14/06

Task | Milestone | External Tasks
Split | Summary | External Milestone
Progress | Project Summary | Deadline

Page 1

Figure 13-6. Schedule on June 1 (continued)

ID	Indicators	Task Name	Duration	% Complete	Baseline Start	Actual Start	Baseline Finish	Actual Finish	Finish Variance
33	✓	Deliver home office	10 days	100%	Tue 5/10/05	Sun 5/1/05	Tue 5/10/05	Fri 5/13/05	3 days
34	✓	Deliver on site	4 days	100%	Wed 5/18/05	Fri 5/20/05	Wed 5/18/05	Wed 5/25/05	5 days
35		**Servers**	**37 days**	**67%**	**Mon 4/18/05**	**Mon 4/18/05**	**Wed 5/25/05**	**NA**	**9 days**
36	✓	Order	1 day	100%	Mon 4/18/05	Mon 4/18/05	Mon 4/18/05	Mon 4/18/05	0 days
37	✓	Deliver home office	1 day	100%	Tue 5/17/05	Mon 5/30/05	Tue 5/17/05	Mon 5/30/05	9 days
38		Deliver on site	1 day	0%	Wed 5/25/05	NA	Wed 5/25/05	NA	9 days
39	✓	**Misc. Equipment**	**26 days**	**100%**	**Mon 4/18/05**	**Mon 4/18/05**	**Thu 5/26/05**	**Mon 5/23/05**	**-3 days**
40	✓	Order	1 day	100%	Mon 4/18/05	Mon 4/18/05	Mon 4/18/05	Mon 4/18/05	0 days
41	✓	Deliver home office	10 days	100%	Wed 5/18/05	Sun 5/1/05	Wed 5/18/05	Sun 5/15/05	-3 days
42	✓	Deliver on site	1 day	100%	Thu 5/26/05	Mon 5/23/05	Thu 5/26/05	Mon 5/23/05	-3 days
43		**Installation**	**18 days**	**57%**	**Thu 5/19/05**	**Thu 5/19/05**	**Tue 6/7/05**	**NA**	**4 days**
44		**Location 1**	**18 days**	**66%**	**Thu 5/19/05**	**Thu 5/19/05**	**Tue 6/7/05**	**NA**	**4 days**
45	✓	Desktops wired	1 wk	100%	Thu 5/19/05	Thu 5/19/05	Wed 5/25/05	Wed 5/25/05	0 days
46	✓	Software installed	1 wk	100%	Thu 5/26/05	Thu 5/26/05	Wed 6/1/05	Wed 6/1/05	0 days
47		Peripherals in place	1 wk	50%	Thu 5/26/05	Thu 5/26/05	Wed 6/1/05	NA	0 days
48		LAN functional	2 days	0%	Thu 6/2/05	NA	Fri 6/3/05	NA	4 days
49		WAN functional	2 days	0%	Mon 6/6/05	NA	Tue 6/7/05	NA	4 days
50		**Location 2**	**14 days**	**74%**	**Thu 5/19/05**	**Thu 5/19/05**	**Tue 6/7/05**	**NA**	**0 days**
51	✓	Desktops wired	1 wk	100%	Thu 5/19/05	Thu 5/19/05	Wed 5/25/05	Wed 5/25/05	0 days
52	✓	Software installed	1 wk	100%	Thu 5/26/05	Thu 5/26/05	Wed 6/1/05	Wed 6/1/05	0 days
53		Peripherals in place	1 wk	80%	Thu 5/26/05	Thu 5/26/05	Wed 6/1/05	NA	0 days
54		LAN functional	2 days	0%	Thu 6/2/05	NA	Fri 6/3/05	NA	0 days
55		WAN functional	2 days	0%	Mon 6/6/05	NA	Tue 6/7/05	NA	0 days
56		**Location 3**	**14 days**	**32%**	**Thu 5/19/05**	**Tue 5/24/05**	**Tue 6/7/05**	**NA**	**3 days**
57		Desktops wired	1 wk	80%	Thu 5/19/05	Tue 5/24/05	Wed 5/25/05	NA	3 days
58		Software installed	1 wk	40%	Thu 5/26/05	Mon 5/30/05	Wed 6/1/05	NA	2 days
59		Peripherals in place	1 wk	0%	Thu 5/26/05	NA	Wed 6/1/05	NA	3 days
60		LAN functional	2 days	0%	Thu 6/2/05	NA	Fri 6/3/05	NA	3 days
61		WAN functional	2 days	0%	Mon 6/6/05	NA	Tue 6/7/05	NA	3 days

Project: Chapter 12 Status 2
Date: Mon 8/14/06

Task | Milestone | External Tasks
Split | Summary | External Milestone
Progress | Project Summary | Deadline

Page 2

Figure 13-6. Schedule on June 1 (continued)

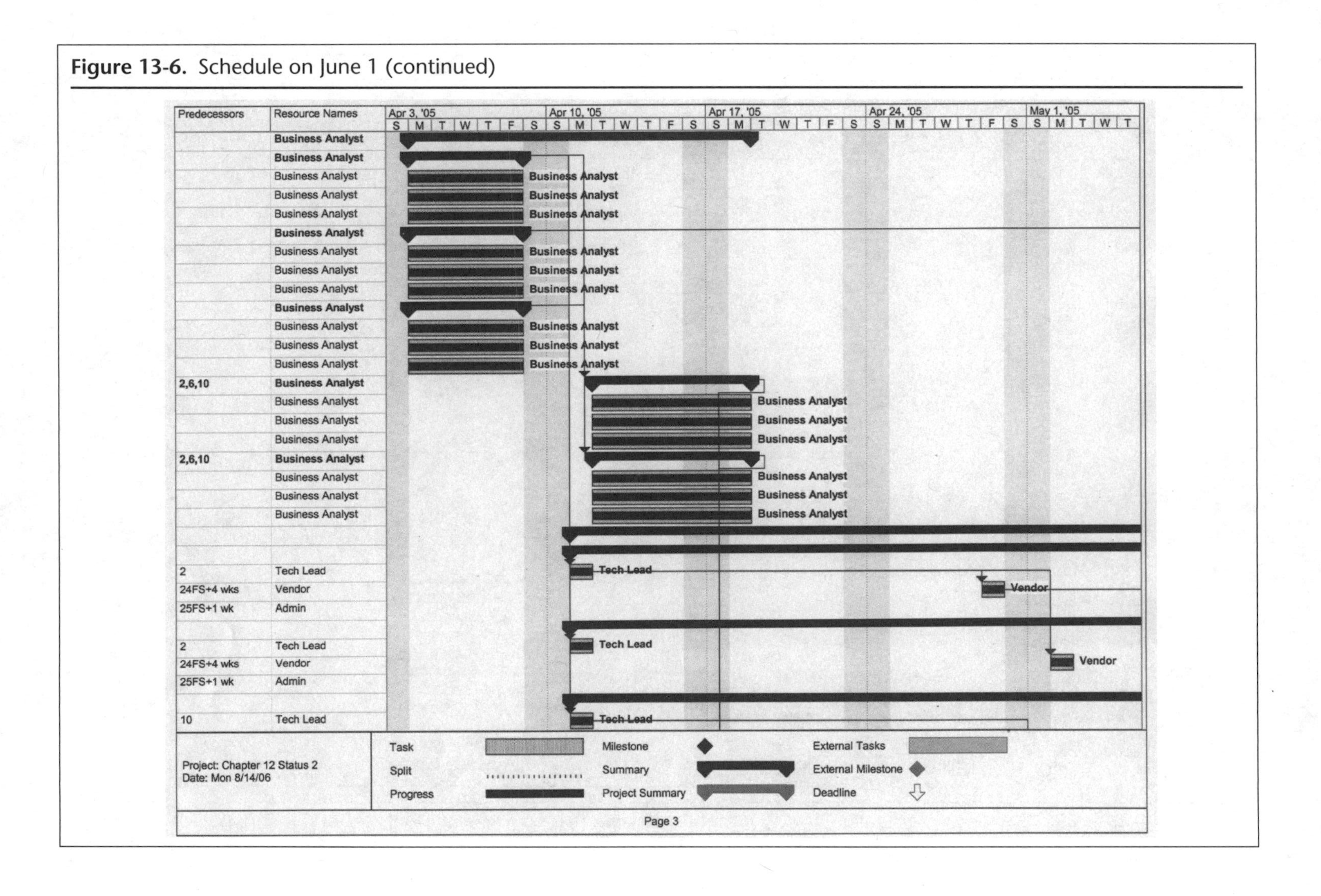

Figure 13-6. Schedule on June 1 (continued)

Predecessors	Resource Names
32FS+4 wks	Vendor
33FS+1 wk	Admin
14,18	Network Lead
36FS+4 wks	Vendor
37FS+1 wk	Admin
14,18	Network Lead
40FS+4 wks	Vendor
41FS+1 wk	Admin
26	Tech 1
6,45	Tech 1
34,45	Tech 1
38,42,47	Network 1
38,42,48	Network 1
26	Tech 2
51	Tech 2
51	Tech 2
53	Network 2
54	Network 2
26	Tech 3
57	Tech 3
57	Tech 3
59	Network 3
60	Network 3

Apr 3, '05 S M T W T F S
Apr 10, '05 S M T W T F S
Apr 17, '05 S M T W T F S
Apr 24, '05 S M T W T F S
May 1, '05 S M T W T

Network Lead
Network Lead

Project: Chapter 12 Status 2
Date: Mon 8/14/06

Task
Split
Progress
Milestone
Summary
Project Summary
External Tasks
External Milestone
Deadline

Page 4

Figure 13-6. Schedule on June 1 (continued)

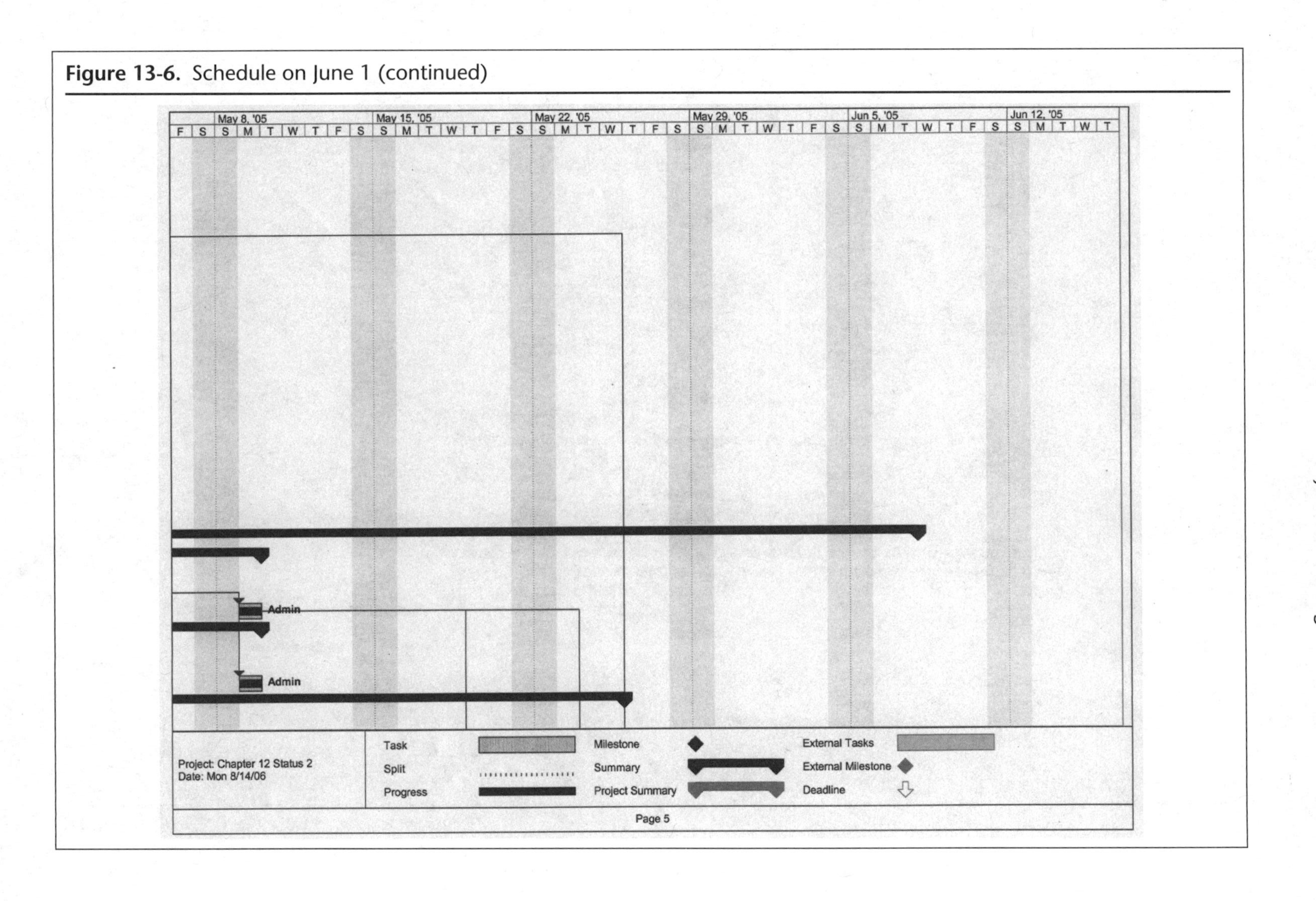

Figure 13-6. Schedule on June 1 (continued)

Project: Chapter 12 Status 2
Date: Mon 8/14/06

Task
Split
Progress
Milestone
Summary
Project Summary
External Tasks
External Milestone
Deadline

Page 6

days, that comes to 20 per day. You have 80 wired, and therefore you have earned four days worth of work. But how long has it taken to earn those four days of work? You started on 5/24, it is now 6/1, and you are measuring what was completed by the end of the day on 5/31. There was a weekend in that period, so it has taken six working days to accomplish four days' worth of progress. You have only earned four days' worth of value for the six days you have spent on this task.

One question you will want to answer is, given this rate of work, when do you think you will be done? By dividing the six days it has taken by the 80% that is complete, you come up with seven and a half days. So, you should finish sometime on June 2nd. The planned duration was five days, the estimated duration is seven and a half days, so you can see your duration variance is two and a half days, or 50% of your planned five days. Not good.

PM in Action!

Using the information below, and the calendar provided, figure out the estimated finish date and the duration variance for the software installation for the 100 machines.

Sun	Mon	Tues	Wed	Thurs	Fri	Sat
5/22	5/23	5/24	5/25	5/26	5/27	5/28
5/29	5/30	5/31	6/1	6/2	6/3	6/4
6/5	6/6	6/7	6/8	6/9	6/10	6/11
6/12	6/13	6/14	6/15	6/16	6/17	6/18

It might help to fill out the following table:

Task	Planned start	Actual start	Start var.	Planned finish	Est. finish	Planned duration	Est. duration	Duration Variance
Software	5/26	5/30		6/1		5d		

One other measurement that can be useful is a performance efficiency metric for duration. This metric helps you see how efficient you are based on your duration estimates. Looking at the desktop installation, dividing the estimated duration by the planned duration gives you 1.5. This means it is taking 50% longer to do the work than the original estimate. With the software installation and peripheral set up, it is taking the same amount of time you planned, but you started late. These are useful pieces of information to have when you are looking at developing corrective action and documenting lessons learned.

The above scenarios were looking at a task-by-task analysis, but recall in the beginning you established the metrics that the project manager would track. The project manager was to track the installation of each office, and each of the five tasks per office is worth 20%. Based on this, you can roll up the progress for each office and get a summary view of the information. By the end of the day on June 1, each office should be complete with the tasks of wiring the desktops, installing software, and setting up the peripherals. This equates to 60% completion based on the measurements established in the planning phase. For ease of calculation, let's assume these percentage complete measurements were taken at the end of the day on 6/1. You can calculate the following:

Site	*Planned % Complete*	*Actual % Complete*
Location 1	60%	50%
Location 2	60%	56%
Location 3	60%	24%

We get the rolled-up percent complete by multiplying the task percent complete by 20%, which is the amount that each task is worth as part of the whole.

The table above is a very persuasive view of how the installation is going. It can be used to verify the need for corrective action, additional resources, or overtime. It also points to the fact that if something isn't done immediately, Location 3 will not be complete on time.

Analyzing Cost Variances

Cost variances can be analyzed in a similar fashion as schedule variances. You start with the value you have earned and compare it to the actual cost. However, don't forget to consider that while you may have spent what you planned to spend, perhaps you did not get the value you planned to achieve for that expense. Let's look at an example to help explain this concept. Figure 13-7 has a budget for the IT costs of opening the three offices.

Now let's take a look at the actual costs at the end of the day on June 1st, shown in Figure 13-8.

Figure 13-7. Baseline Budget

	Price	Quantity	Total
Equipment			
Machines	$ 500.00	300	$ 150,000.00
Software licenses	$ 1,400.00	300	$ 420,000.00
Monitors	$ 125.00	300	$ 37,500.00
Printers	$ 750.00	30	$ 22,500.00
Fax/scanner	$ 240.00	15	$ 3,600.00
Copier	$ 8,000.00	3	$ 24,000.00
Servers	$ 25,000.00	3	$ 75,000.00
Misc.	$ 10,000.00	1	$ 10,000.00
Equipment Total			**$ 742,600.00**
Installation			
Tech labor	$45	240	$ 10,800.00
Network labor	$75	96	$ 7,200.00
Labor Total			**$ 18,000.00**
Total Office IT Cost			**$ 760,600.00**

From this information, you can see that you have a favorable variance on the software licenses and the copiers. On all other equipment you have an unfavorable variance. However, the favorable variance outweighs the unfavorable

Figure 13-8. Actual Costs

	Price	Quantity	Total	Actual Cost	Variance
Equipment					
Machines	$ 500.00	300	$ 150,000.00	$ 156,000.00	$ (6,000.00)
Software licenses	$ 1,400.00	300	$ 420,000.00	$ 392,000.00	$ 28,000.00
Monitors	$ 125.00	300	$ 37,500.00	$ 37,500.00	$ -
Printers	$ 750.00	30	$ 22,500.00	$ 24,000.00	$ (1,500.00)
Fax/scanner	$ 240.00	15	$ 3,600.00	$ 3,600.00	$ -
Copier	$ 8,000.00	3	$ 24,000.00	$ 16,000.00	$ 8,000.00
Servers	$ 25,000.00	3	$ 75,000.00	$ 82,000.00	$ (7,000.00)
Misc.	$ 10,000.00	1	$ 10,000.00	$ 11,875.00	$ (1,875.00)
Equipment Total			**$ 742,600.00**	**$ 722,975.00**	$ 19,625.00
					$ -
Installation					$ -
Tech labor	$45	240	$ 10,800.00	$ 11,160.00	$ (360.00)
Network labor	$75	96	$ 7,200.00	$ -	
Labor Total			**$ 18,000.00**	**$ 11,160.00**	
					$ -
Total Office IT Cost			**$ 760,600.00**		

variance, and it *appears* that you are doing well, from an overall perspective. On labor, you have a slight overrun, but without more information it doesn't look like anything to worry about. Ah, but you do have other information that you don't see when just looking at the dollars.

This report may look reasonable on the surface, but you know from the schedule analysis that there is a schedule problem. Labor costs and schedule are tightly linked—the longer you need people, the more money they will cost. For the sample project, you know that the labor costs are going to continue to rise. Remember that you have information from the schedule that shows that you have a duration variance on installing the machines at Location 3. It will take 12 hours longer than expected. Therefore, that negative labor budget variance is going to increase. In addition, if schedule is the driver and you have a hard end date, you are going to end up paying overtime or adding more resources, either of which will only increase the negative budget variance.

From your weekly status meetings, you learned that the issue lies with the technical labor, so see if you can isolate that and look a bit closer. Go back to what you have earned and compare that to what you have spent. Doing so will give you a true variance. Then you can look at how well you are performing efficiency-wise and forecast the end costs for the project.

First, take look at the installation of the software and setting up the peripheral equipment, both of which are scheduled to take place at the same time. Note that one person is doing both of them. The breakout in hours is 30 hours for software and 10 hours for peripheral equipment. Therefore, the plan indicates that you should spend 40 hours for computer installation at $45 per hour, for a total of $1,800. You should take 30 hours for software installation for a total of $1,350, and 10 hours for peripherals for a total of $450. Therefore, the technical costs for each office set up should total $3,600. This breaks out to $360 per day. Using the schedule, you can see how much time (duration) you have actually spent and paid for and you can also see how much you have accomplished or earned. Then, using that information, you can determine a cost variance by task and location and for the installation as a whole. Figure 13-9 shows the cost variance by subtracting what you actually spent from what you earned.

Figure 13-9. Cost Variance

	Earned value	Actual cost	Cost variance
Location 1			
Machines	1800	1800	0
Software	1350	1350	0
Peripherals	225	450	-225
Location 2			
Machines	1800	1800	0
Software	1350	1350	0
Peripherals	360	450	-90
Location 3			
Machines	1440	7 days = 2520	-1080
Software	540	3 days = 1080	-540
Peripherals	0	0	0

We can further analyze this information by location:

Location 1 cost variance = –$225

Location 2 cost variance = –$90

Location 3 cost variance = –$1,620

Another way to view the information is to create an index of the performance. You can do so by dividing how much you have really accomplished—that is, how much value you have actually earned—by the actual cost. If you do this as a summary by location you come up with the following for Location 1:

Earned value = $3,375

Actual cost = $3,600

Cost performance = 3375/3600 = .9375

The **cost performance** can be rounded up to .94. What this information tells you is that for every dollar you spend on the installation labor, you are getting 94 cents worth of value. That is useful information to have when you are comparing the performance of multiple projects. And guess what—you've just done the type of calculation that characterizes earned value project management (EVM)! EVM is such a sophisticated project management tool that it is mandated by the federal government for all federal agencies and is used on the largest aerospace and defense contracts.

> ! **WARNING**
> Remember to compare what you spent to how much you've actually accomplished. This gives you the true variance or performance figure. If you compare what you spent to what you planned to spend, this only gives you information on cash flow.

PM in Action!

Using the information in Figure 13-9, find the cost performance of Locations 2 and 3.

> ! **WARNING**
> When you aggregate information at too high a level, you may miss trouble signs. For instance, you may have a cost variance of –$3,500 on one task and a cost variance of +$4,000 on another. Overall, the variance is +$500, not too much to worry about. But in reality, you have two large variances that need your attention!

> ! **WARNING**
> Corporate accounting and project accounting are two very different beasts. For a project, ideally you want to book costs as they are used. However, this is not how it happens. Let's say you've ordered a big, new, state-of-the-art server for $55,000. You order it in February and pay half down ($27,500). You get it and set it up in April, which is when you claim the value for it. The balance is invoiced in May and paid in July. For months, your financials will be off. You will be carrying $27,500 for something you receive no value for, and then you will be getting $55,000 worth of value that you will only have paid $27,500 for. This is an example of why, when we plan our monitoring in the beginning, we keep our large purchases separate. You may also run into this issue with labor, especially if labor bills on a project basis. You will have to notate your project budget with these anomalies so that your reports don't give skewed information.

If you want to estimate what your final costs will be based on current performance, all you have to do is take your total budget, sometimes called the budget at completion, and divide it by your cost performance factor. For instance, if you have a project with a budget of $100,000, and it currently is performing at 94% efficiency, if the performance remains the same, you should end up spending $106,383 for the project.

Displaying Information

The old adage that a picture is worth a thousand words is particularly true in reporting. Compare the following:

Description: We have some negative cost variances that are putting us over budget. If we continue this way we will have a significant overage.

Equation:

Location 1 cost variance = –$225

Location 2 cost variance = –$90

Location 3 cost variance = –$1,620

Total Cost Performance Index = .82

Graph:

The equations mean something to you, but the charts (Figures 13-10, 13-11, and 13-12) are far more powerful when you are talking with stakeholders and want to get a point across about the project's performance.

DEVELOPING RESPONSES

Notice that you have calculated the variances and the performance efficiency, but you haven't found out what caused the variances and a way to correct them. Especially on a large project, monitoring and control need to be on an exception basis. In other words, pay attention to what is not performing the way you expect it to.

> ***What Do You Think?***
>
> What other information do you think would be useful to collect and analyze to monitor and control the budget?

Figure 13-10. Cost Variance by Location

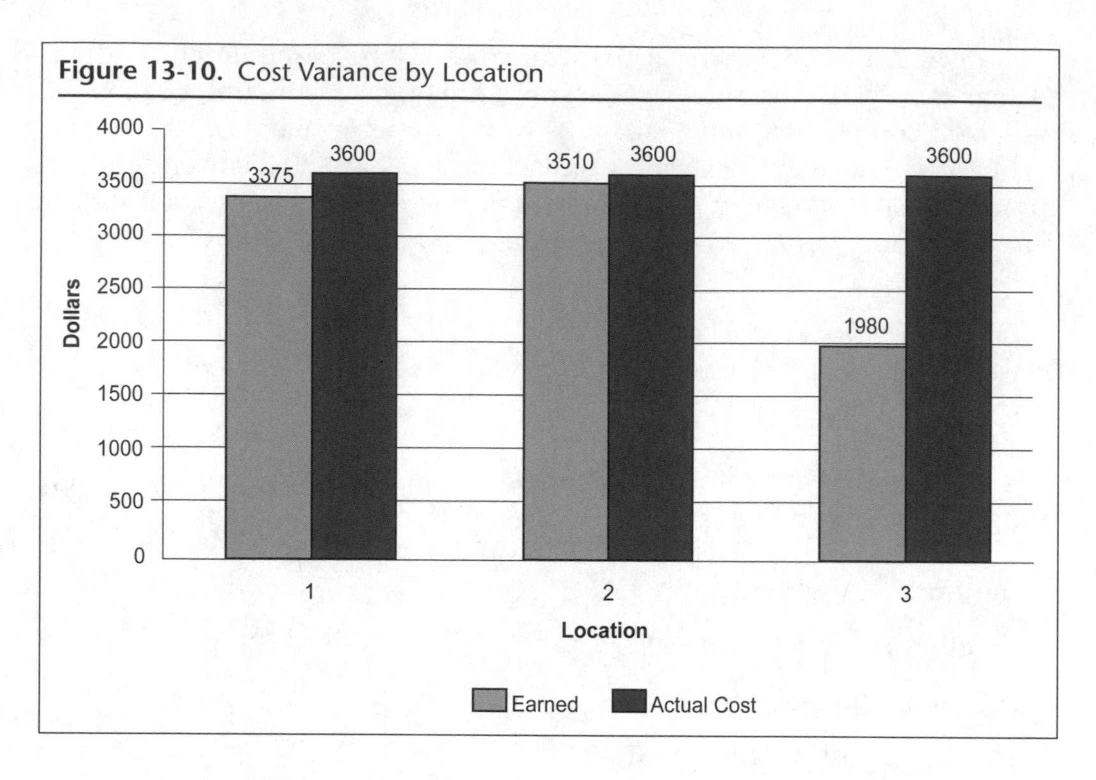

Figure 13-11. Cost Performance by Location

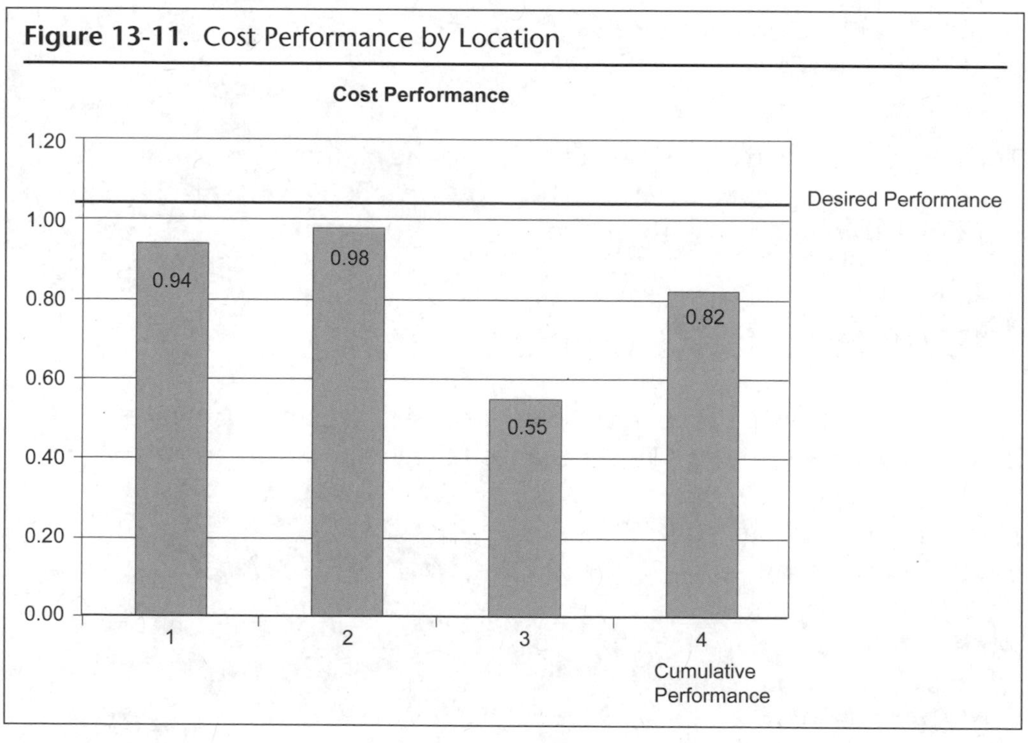

Figure 13-12. Forecast Cost at Completion

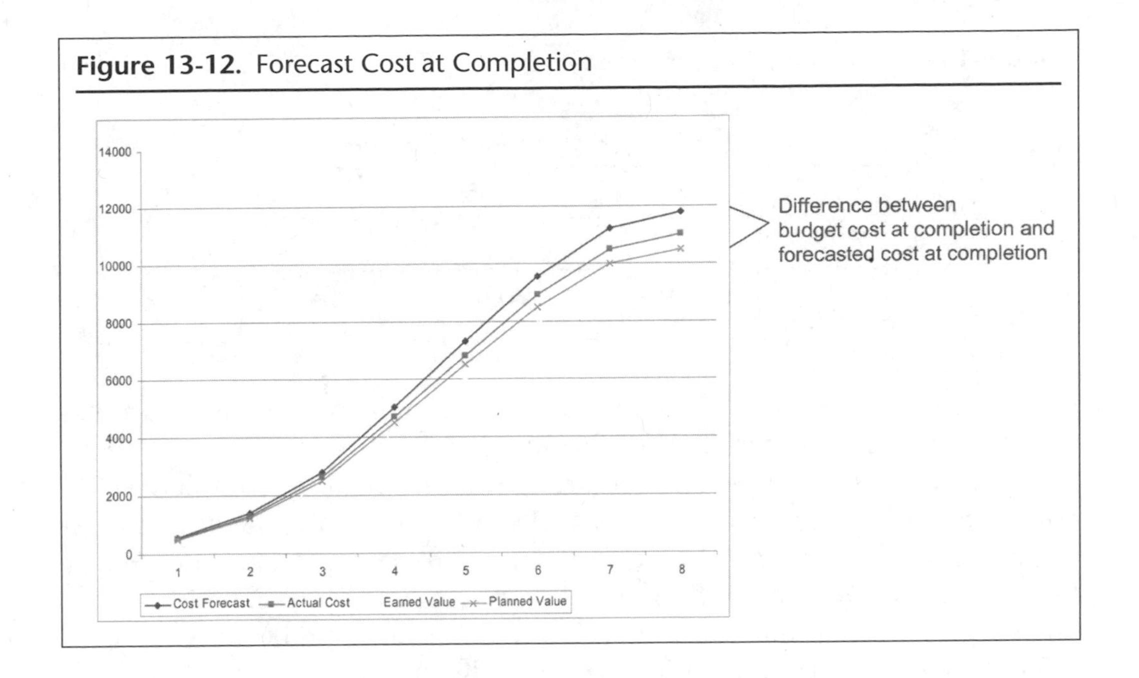

Root Cause Analysis

Start with conducting a root cause analysis. Find out why variances occurred and if they are expected to continue. The following paragraph presents a simple issue of whether the cost of the materials was more than planned or whether more materials were used than planned.

Two similar projects are going in separate locations. Project A reports that the budgeted expense for creating a module of code is $22,500 and that it has completed the code at a cost of $26,250. Project B reports that the budget for creating a module of code is $22,500 and that it has completed the code at a cost of $26,400. On the surface, we might assume that both projects ran into some unexpected problems, but beneath the surface we find that they both assumed using a programmer for 300 hours at a rate of $75 per hour. In Project A, the programmer actually took 350 hours at the rate of $75 per hour. On Project B, the programmer took 300 hours, as predicted, but charged $88 per hour. So one project had a price difference and one had a usage difference. Figure 13-13 show a table with this information.

When you are looking at schedule variances, it is useful to determine whether one task is behind or a whole series of tasks is causing a problem. Determining this will help you treat the problem appropriately. Find out whether

Figure 13-13. Price versus Usage Comparison

	Plan	Project A	Project B
Hours	300	350	300
Rate	75	75	88
Total	22500	26250	26400

your team members are spending more or less effort on the task than was planned. Or perhaps there was a delay in getting some component or piece of information that they needed before they could begin or complete work. Sometimes a resource is substituted that has less skill than the one that estimated the work involved. In most organizations, you cannot obtain salary information for individuals from the HR department and so you have to use an average salary for that job grade. If the person you get on your team has a salary higher or lower than the average, this will impact your calculations and your cost variances.

For schedule control, like cost control, you will focus on the exceptions. However, unlike cost control, if there are minor exceptions and they aren't on a critical or near critical path, you don't have to worry too much. Checking in is a good idea, but don't exert a lot of effort on getting a task with a lot of float back on track. Spend your energy elsewhere.

Every so often you find that the original estimates that you were working with are so far off that to continue monitoring against them is a waste of time. In this case, you want to develop new estimates, using what you have learned so far, and rebaseline. But don't rebaseline just so your numbers look good. Rebaselining should only be done in extreme circumstances, or if you are adding scope to the project. Remember that the project sponsor and/or the client must approve any changes to the baseline, so you had better have a really strong argument for rebaselining or they won't approve it.

Another time to rebaseline is when there is a significant change to the project, such as when a customer requests new features that were not planned. In this case, a formal change request should be written and assessed. If approved, the schedule or cost may be so different that the project needs to be rebaselined to accommodate the change.

Some Corrective Action Options

Once you have identified what is causing the variance in the project performance, you can start to do something about it. Here are some generic suggestions for getting your project back on track. You will have to adapt these suggestions to your project and project environment.

Schedule

In Chapter 11, we talked about two ways to shorten your schedule: fast-tracking and crashing. Fast tracking includes replanning activities that are on the critical path so that they occur either at the same time or overlap in places. You can also crash your schedule by adding resources (which almost always costs money), extending the work day, adding weekend shifts, and so forth. Another option is to break your work into smaller chunks to accomplish multiple tasks simultaneously.

Sometimes it works to find either the easiest tasks or the longest tasks and go back to the team member who gave you the estimates to see if you can shorten those durations. However, don't spend time trying to shorten tasks that are not on the critical path unless by doing so you can free up those resources to work on tasks that are on the critical path.

WARNING

The most dangerous way to reduce schedule, and one that is tried too often in IT, is to reduce the amount of testing. Assuming the testing program was well thought out to start with, reducing testing can only increase risk. Don't do it.

Cost

To get your project back on track with the budget, see if you can find a way to reduce the resources you are scheduled to use. Go back to your team members to see if they put in any padding or cushion that you can take out. You may need to shop some competitors on supplies or equipment to see if you can find lower rates. Perhaps you can use supplies or equipment of a lesser grade, and therefore a lower price.

Other options include renegotiating contracts or contacting suppliers to see if you can get a discount for early payment. Some suppliers will take off 2% for payment within ten days.

Scope

If your product scope is not meeting its performance targets, you have a couple of options. You can go back to the stakeholders and talk to them about what they *need* and what is just nice to have. (Hopefully you prioritized your requirements when you collected them.) You may be able to loosen up some of the requirements. Sometimes talking with the team members and asking them if they can find a way to improve the process and/or performance will yield some good ideas. Team members know the most about both the processes and the product. If you don't ask, they may assume you don't really want to listen to any inputs.

Another option, and not one you want to pursue if you can avoid it, is to deliver what you can with the schedule and resources you have and then develop a phase 2 upgrade or a follow-on project to deliver the rest of it.

Another option is talking to your team members to see if they are **gold plating**. Gold plating means over-designing or make the product better than the client asked for. Some team members are perfectionists and really want the deliverables to be elegant. This is a nice trait, but it's not always appropriate. Sometimes good enough really is good enough. Testing can also sometimes be overdone. In an effort to cover all bases, there may be instances where extra testing is put into the mix. Look for places to combine testing. But don't take it out altogether or put the project at risk by shortening it too much. Shortening testing is a fine line to walk!

Finally, check your change control process. Make sure it is functioning the way you set it up. You may be having scope and schedule issues because people are sneaking in new requirements.

Monitoring and Controlling Risk

Project risk needs to monitored and controlled along with the scope, schedule, and cost. However, the process is a bit different. In risk monitoring and control, you look at project performance to see if the measurements you have taken add any new risks to the project and you look at the risk log to assess the status of previously identified risks. Looking at performance to see if you have new risks is a matter of seeing which variances fall outside the parameters established in the planning process. If there are any variances which indicate that project performance is at risk, then a risk is identified in the risk log and the risk management process is followed, as outlined in Chapter 10.

Monitoring risk is a matter of reviewing the risk register and seeing which risk events have passed—in other words, they either happened or they didn't. If they did not occur, you can close them. However, don't delete them from the register. You want to keep the identified risks there as part of the project documentation. If the risk did occur, see if it occurred the way you identified. If not, make a notation in the register comments section for the project documentation.

If a risk situation is active, then you should check the register for the planned response and implement the response. If the situation is not as planned, you may need to replan a more appropriate response and document it in the register.

Part of project close out and developing a robust lessons learned document is reviewing the risk register at the end of the project. A lot of learning can take place by looking at what risks did and did not occur and how accurate you were in predicting the risk outcome and behavior, as well as how effective your risk responses were in handling the situation.

Putting It All Together

In order to present concepts and information coherently, we break them into chunks, such as execution, risk management, control, and change management. However, in reality these things are all intertwined. While there are times when we perform formal change management (such as a change control board meeting) or formal risk management by reviewing the risk register, much of this is also done informally, just in the process of day-to-day project management.

For instance, someone may say, "Why don't we add this little bit of functionality to the component so it does XYZ. It will only take a few hours and it would be very cool." Your response is actually part of change management, whether you say, "No, nice idea," "That sounds interesting. How would it impact the other systems or components or work flows? Is there some justification for changing from the agreed-upon configuration?" or "Sounds interesting. Fill out a change request form." All of these answers represent change management.

Risk management can occur in response to project execution that is not going as planned. The discrepancies are noted in a variance report. If the performance falls outside the allowable parameters, performance is at risk. Thus a

Figure 13-14. Project Control Activities

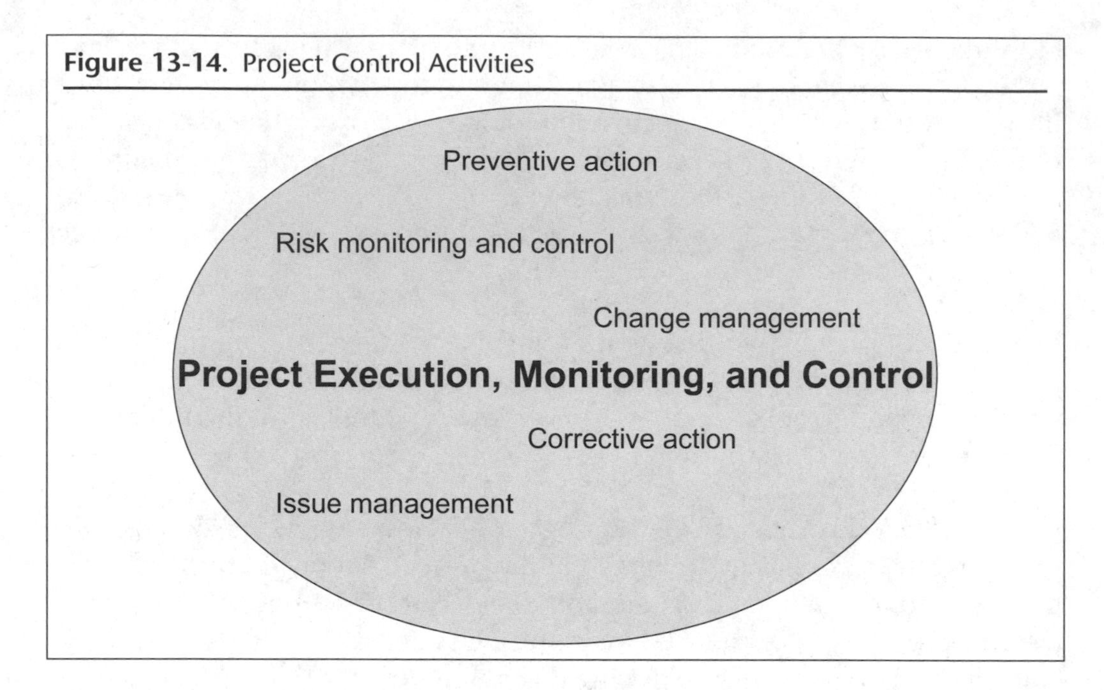

risk is identified, entered into the risk log (or the issue log as appropriate), an appropriate response is developed, and corrective action is implemented. If the corrective action requires some type of change, the change management process is initiated as well. As appropriate, a lesson learned is documented for future reference. You can see how all the component pieces are integrated to meet the project objectives.

Reporting Cycles

How often should you report status on a project? As always it depends on the project. Something to keep in mind is that formalized control takes time and resources, and therefore costs money. So it's important to balance the amount of control with the needs of the project and the risks involved with relaxing the amount of control. Figure 13-15 shows a graphic representation of the cost of control.

One thing to consider when establishing your reporting cycle and the amount of detail you need is how well the project is doing. If things are going well, on or ahead of schedule and on or under budget, you can consider reducing the detail and frequency of your reporting. If, on the other hand, the project is not performing well to plan, you may need to increase the level of detail you are asking for and the frequency of reporting.

Figure 13-15. Cost of Control

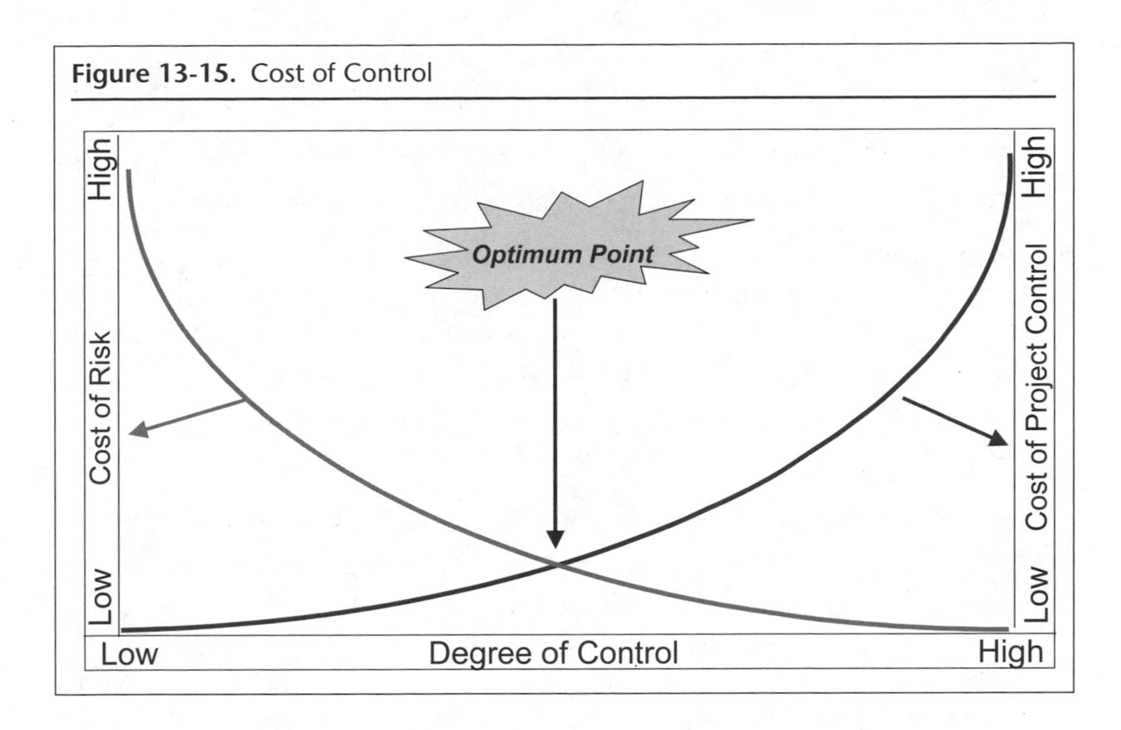

However, you would only increase the detail in the reporting for yourself, and possibly your sponsor if you need help. Remember that you will be looking at more detailed information than the customer and the sponsor. The sponsor will get summary information unless there are trouble indicators that he or she should be aware of. The customer will get only high-level milestone information.

Chapter Summary

- Monitoring is measuring and analyzing project information by comparing planned performance to actual performance, assessing trends, and developing forecasts.
- Controlling includes analyzing variances in performance, evaluating actions to bring performance in line with the plan, recommending preventive and corrective action, and managing those actions so they produce the desired result.
- Spend time in the planning process to define the items you want to monitor and control, and then set up your project baselines to reflect what you will be measuring.

- The baseline for measuring scope is the scope statement and WBS; the baseline for time is the schedule; and the baseline for cost is the budget.
- You can develop reports that show status, progress, and forecasts.
- Establish thresholds to determine which variances require corrective action.
- Use metrics to report progress. You can use variance metrics to discover how far off performance is according to plan, efficiency metrics to develop a ratio or performance for comparison to other projects, and forecasting metrics to determine the final outcome if performance remains the same.
- Charts and equations are better at presenting information than descriptions are.
- Before developing a corrective action plan, spend time discovering the root cause of the variance.
- Risk monitoring and control requires a different process than scope, schedule, and budget. In the risk monitoring and control process, you compare results to what was entered in the risk register. You consistently update the risk register to reflect new risks, changes to risks, and closure of risks.
- Project execution, monitoring, and control work together with risk management, issue management, change management, and corrective and preventive action. They all intersect and work together to create a successful project.
- Monitoring and control take time and money. Discover the point where you have enough control and the right level of detail without incurring too much risk or spending too much on control.

Key Terms

Monitoring
Baseline
Weighted milestone reporting
Variance
Status
Variance metrics
Forecast metrics
Cost performance
Control
Fixed formula reporting
Threshold
Progress reports
Forecasts
Performance metrics
Cost variance
Gold plating

Key Term Quiz

1. ______________ is concerned with developing corrective action plans to bring project performance in line with the project plan.

2. A ________________ is the approved plan, plus or minus approved changes.

3. Comparing the value you earned to actual cost will result in the ______________.

4. A measurement that helps you discover the amount that you are ahead or behind in your schedule or budget is a ______________.

5. A measurement that helps you understand how you are performing compared to other projects is a ________________.

6. A measurement that estimates what your final performance will be if future performance behaves like past performance is a ______________.

7. A ______________ is a parameter that sets the limit for taking action.

8. Reporting that is based on interim deliverables that add up to 100% is __________.

9. Comparing actual performance to planned performance is part of ______ ________.

10. Receiving 25% credit for starting a task and the other 75% for completing it is an example of _______________________.

Chapter Review Questions

1. What are the three components of monitoring?

2. What are the four components of control?

3. A change to the scope baseline would mean that you would update what documents?

4. Why should you start planning for the information you intend to collect during the planning phase of the project?

5. How can you get objective reports on the percent complete of a task?

6. This chapter discussed two specific types of reporting measurements. What are they?

7. What is the process for developing a forecast?

8. Not all variances require action. Explain why this is.

9. Describe the difference between a variance metric and a performance metric.

10. What are three areas of variance that you might find in the schedule?

11. If you planned for a task to take four days, and it starts on Monday the 11th and finishes the following Tuesday the 19th, what type of variance can you report?

    a. A variance in the start date

    b. A variance in the finish date

    c. A variance in the duration

    d. There is not enough information to determine

12. If you are looking to discover a cost variance, what should you compare your actual costs to?

13. How do you estimate what your final costs will be?

14. What is the best way to deliver information?

    a. A description

    b. An equation

    c. A chart or graph

15. When should you rebaseline?

14 *Project Audit and Closure*

After reading this chapter, you will be able to:

- Describe the purposes and the steps involved in an audit.
- Describe the activities needed to properly close out the project.
- Define how to obtain final acceptance of the project.
- Discuss closing out and archiving project documents and contracts.

How does management know how well the project is progressing? In most cases the reports we talked about in Chapter 13 are sufficient. However, there are times when a more objective review is appropriate. In some cases, this review is used for projects that are at risk. These reviews can help define all the troubled areas. In some cases, reviews are done after the fact to see if the project manager followed the appropriate procedures for managing the project. A formalized project review, conducted by an outside party, is called a project audit.

PROJECT AUDITS

Project audits, sometimes called **project quality audits,** are done to provide an objective review of how the project is being managed (or was managed if it is completed). Project audits are uncomfortable for project managers. We're judged by people who were not involved in the project and do not understand what we went through. Auditors are sometimes described as people who come in after the battle is over and shoot the wounded.

At the very least, audits take time and effort on the part of project managers and some team members. At the very most, audits will find out all the shortcuts you've taken to get the project accomplished! The best audits are done by people with no involvement in the project itself but with experience in the type of project and in auditing. The goal of auditing is to identify whether the project is being managed as expected, and if not, to identify causes and problem areas and make recommendations. If project audits are commonly done in your organization, then a history is built up showing organizational issues that cause problems on projects and solutions developed.

Audits are similar to **project reviews.** Reviews collect information and assess different parts of the project. For example, were the deliverables completed on time? If not, why not? Is the product successfully passing testing? If not, what are the reasons? The review can be done by anyone who is trying to come to a conclusion about some part of the project.

An audit, by comparison, is more formal and structured and specifically assesses how the project is being managed in comparison to the approved project management processes in the organization. This last part is important. The auditor will compare how you are managing the project with respect to the processes and standards that tell you how you are supposed to manage it.

For example, let's say your IT department's approved system development life cycle standard states that project managers will use a formal change control methodology for any change requests on their project. If the project is small, you may obtain a waiver against this requirement. On your project you have not gotten any change requests that you consider serious enough to require formal methodology, and you have not bothered to get a formal waiver because it's just more paperwork. Was your decision the right one? Maybe, maybe not. The auditors will come in and assess whether, in their opinion, change requests should have been done formally, and could write you up for not going through the change management process or write you up for not getting a formal waiver.

Audits can be scheduled or unscheduled. In the financial industry, typically an independent audit is scheduled ahead of time and the client knows when the audit will occur. A formal audit in project management should be done the same way. Formal audits can take weeks or months to complete, depending on the size and complexity of the project. Because audits take effort on the part of the project staff, they should be scheduled ahead of time so that the staff can fit the audit into their schedules. Surprise audits can also occur where the staff does not know the auditors are coming. Surprise audits tend to be shorter in duration and more focused on one particular aspect of the project.

Audits require a lot of preparation on the part of the project team and on the part of the audit team. If the auditors are from outside your organization, they will spend time learning your organization's project management processes, standards, and procedures. If the auditors are from inside your organization, they should already be familiar with those items.

The audit team members will identify the project documents they need to review and the personnel they will interview or survey. They will create a list of specific items that will be looked at in the documents and a list of questions that will be asked during the interviews and surveys. After they have gathered their information, they will spend time assessing and interpreting it. They will issue a final report stating their conclusions, outlining the reasons they arrived at those conclusions, and making recommendations when they feel something can be improved.

The information they obtain during their interviews and surveys is crucial to understanding the extent to which project processes are being followed. In order to obtain the most objective information possible, the answers the team receives from the project members must be as honest and as complete as possible. To ensure openness, all answers during interviews are kept confidential. The auditors will take notes on what the interviewees said, but names will be removed from the final report so that management has no idea who made any specific comment.

What kinds of questions are the auditors likely to ask? It depends on the goal of the audit. A general audit done to assess the overall status of the project is likely to ask a broad range of questions, with more detailed questions being asked later if the auditors find something they would like to pursue in more detail. The types of general questions that will be asked revolve around the overall status and processes of the project, including:

- Scope management
- Schedule management
- Requirements gathering and management
- Project team skills and experience
- Budget management
- Project communications

Figure 14-1 is a list of the types of questions that can be asked in an audit. Some questions might be yes-or-no questions. Some might involve ranking statements according to a scale. Free-form questions, such as "Tell me what problems you see on the project," give the auditor the most beneficial information.

Figure 14-1. Sample Audit

#	Question	Low — High					Don't Know
General project questions							
1	Are project deliverables clearly defined in the contract?	0	1	2	3	4	☐
2	Are the deliverables adequate and timely?	0	1	2	3	4	☐
3	Is there a clearly written statement of work (SOW)?	0	1	2	3	4	☐
4	Is the SOW defined in sufficient detail for the project?	0	1	2	3	4	☐
5	Do the project manager and the project sponsor have the same understanding of the SOW?	0	1	2	3	4	☐
6	Are assumptions clearly stated?	0	1	2	3	4	☐
7	Are project metrics clearly defined and reported on regularly?	0	1	2	3	4	☐
8	Is the Work Breakdown Structure adequate and accurate?	0	1	2	3	4	☐
9	Has the project been broken into reasonable phases?	0	1	2	3	4	☐
10	Are roles and responsibilities being fulfilled as defined?	0	1	2	3	4	☐
Communications questions							
1	Is there a project communications plan clearly identifying the stakeholders and how they will be communicated with?	No ☐ Yes ☐					☐
2	Is there a regularly scheduled project status meeting that discusses progress and issues with the team members?	0	1	2	3	4	☐
3	Is there a regularly scheduled project status meeting that discusses progress and issues with the client?	0	1	2	3	4	☐
4	Are minutes taken and published from the status meetings?	0	1	2	3	4	☐
5	Are project performance, progress, and issues being reported in accordance with the plan?	0	1	2	3	4	☐
Scope management questions							
1	Are the product's requirements clearly defined and approved by both client and contractor?	0	1	2	3	4	☐
2	Is there a scope management plan?	0	1	2	3	4	☐
3	How much do the project requirements change?	0	1	2	3	4	☐
4	Is the scope management plan being followed as written?	0	1	2	3	4	☐
5	Has the sponsor approved the scope management plan?	No ☐ Yes ☐					☐

Figure 14-1. Sample Audit (continued)

#	Question	Low — High					Don't Know
Team member questions							
1	Are all required team positions filled with people of adequate training and experience to do this job?	0	1	2	3	4	☐
2	Is the team familiar with the development tools being used?	0	1	2	3	4	☐
3	Does the project sponsor have a strong positive relationship with the project manager?	0	1	2	3	4	☐
4	Do you have a clear understanding of what your roles and responsibilities are?	0	1	2	3	4	☐
5	Is there any disagreement within the organization of the project's importance or priority?	0	1	2	3	4	☐

There are three main times to perform audits: randomly during the course of the project, when the project is having severe problems, and after the project is completed. This last audit serves as management's version of lessons learned—what was done, what was done well, and what could have been done better.

What Do You Think?

Think of a time you worked on a project that was in trouble. Would an audit by an outside expert have caught the situation before it got out of control?

For a project manager, the most useful audits are those that are done during the course of the project. Someone looking at the project from an objective standpoint can identify weak areas early enough that the project team can repair them before they lead to problems. Many project managers are so wrapped up in the day-to-day details of running the project that they can lose objectivity in identifying potential problems.

PM in Action!

Create an audit checklist for the types of project you are normally involved in.

CLOSING OUT THE PROJECT

No job is finished until the paperwork is done.

We have all heard that saying before, and it is especially true in project management. Closing out the project is more than just wishing everybody good luck and saying, "I hope to work with you again." Closeout processes are simple compared to much of IT project management. The two basic requirements are to conduct the post-implementation review and to perform the administrative closeout steps.

The post-implementation review has only two tasks:

- Prepare the post-implementation report.
- Solicit feedback through lessons learned meetings or surveys.

We often find ourselves in the position of closing out paperwork on one project while we are starting our next project, and starting a new project is always more interesting than closing out an old one. However, the organization does not grow and learn, and we as project managers do not grow and learn, unless we can learn from what we have done in the past.

OBTAINING FINAL PROJECT ACCEPTANCE

The first step in closing out a project is to make certain that the customer, client, or sponsor is actually happy with what you've delivered. The client has witnessed the user acceptance test and agreed that this is what it asked for.

There are two parts of final acceptance: validation and verification. When project managers talk about validation, they mean ensuring that the requirements meet what the customer expects. By verification, they mean that they are satisfying those requirements, as shown by testing, inspection, analysis, and other means.

The second step in closing out an IT project is transitioning the project to operations. Working hard to build a product that's not set up so it can be used effectively and maintained does no good. Part of our jobs as project managers is to make sure there is a clean turnover to operations.

Scope Validation

How do the people who requested the projects know they're getting what they wanted? The project manager may do everything correctly—gather the business needs and requirements, develop the solution that would satisfy those requirements, and test the final product against those requirements—and yet the project may still not be what the people who requested it had in mind. The assumption is that if the project manager completely satisfies the written requirements, the work will satisfy the original business needs. There are several reasons this might not be true:

- The written requirements may not satisfy the original business needs they were derived from.
- The translation of the requirements into detailed technical specifications may not be totally accurate.
- The product design may not satisfy those specifications.
- The product, as developed, may not satisfy the requirements.

The customer or client is not interested in the requirements. The customer is only interested in the final product. Requirements are just a means to transfer the original needs into the final product.

In a classic waterfall methodology, the customer doesn't see the final product until it is completed. If the customer doesn't like what is delivered, it is too late to do anything, and the project has failed by not delivering what was expected. In an iterative life cycle approach, the customer sees the product more often, although not in a fully developed form. If it is not what the customer expects, the customer can identify the problem early and the rework needed is not as extensive or costly. However, rework at any level can be avoided if the customer is continually involved in reviewing and approving the requirements and design.

Making sure that customers get what they expect at the end of the project is a matter of making sure they see what they are getting throughout the project. Make sure they understand the requirements thoroughly. Make sure they see the design before the development process starts. Get their feedback during the development process so they can see the product as it is created.

One good way to keep customers involved is to trace their high-level requirements to the product itself, and show how the requirement is being implemented. If a customer gave you performance requirements that, in the customer's mind, can only be met on a mainframe and you have designed the solution around clustered UNIX servers, you need to be able to show the customer how your solution satisfies the requirement.

Transitioning to Production

In most projects, having clients accept the final product is a matter of having them validate that the product meets their needs. This can be done by having the client witness the user-acceptance test, or by simply having the client sign an approval letter. Then the project manager can wash his or her hands of the project and go on to something else.

In IT, it is rarely quite so simple. Most IT projects (except in the case of IT consulting or services firms) are done for internal clients. In many companies, the development staff is different from the maintenance staff. The people who will have to maintain the system are often not involved in its development and do not understand the system as well as the developers and testers. Does your IT department want to be given a new LAN or a new software package in the production system and then have to fix problems at 2:00 A.M.? When problems occur in production (and they are guaranteed to occur), who can fix the problem faster than someone already familiar with the product? The maintenance team members will learn and gain experience, but they don't start out with that knowledge.

In Practice: Transfering Ownership

In the U.S. headquarters of a major overseas car manufacturer, the policy in the IT department is that the developers own the system until it has been in the production environment for two months. When the system goes down at 2 A.M., it's the developer on-call who has to wake up and fix it. The organization's experience was that after two months most of the bugs in the system have been worked out, and at that point the maintenance team accepts the system.

For other organizations, how does the organization tell when the system is ready for transition? Each time a bug occurs it is logged in the discrepancy log, and the specific module that caused the problem is identified along with the fix. After about two months of running in the production environment, the majority of the bugs have been worked out and the system is fairly stable.

The maintenance team will have to support the new system, so the team must determine what it needs to do the job adequately. The team certainly needs to know that the system will work in the production environment. If an operational-readiness test was not run during the project's testing phase, now is the time to ensure that the new system will work in the production environment. This is especially critical if the development work was done overseas, because the development environment is rarely the same as your production environment. Verifying that the system will work in the production environment is critical.

The maintenance team will need an operations guide showing how the system is expected to work in the production environment. The guide should include information on system backups and recovery, system interdependencies, upgrading the system, and system processes. A high-level system architecture and design description will help the maintenance team understand the system more thoroughly. In many IT departments, these documents are part of the normal project documentation.

The team also needs a maintenance and troubleshooting guide showing how to identify and fix problems in the system, as well as expected system performance so the team can identify system slowdowns. Other sections of the guide should include detailed troubleshooting procedures, a problem escalation guide, and a list of known problems identified during system testing.

Closing Out Project Documentation

Properly closing out a project involves gathering all the project documents, making sure any contracts have been successfully completed and can be formally closed and the final payments made, and making all the information available to other people who can learn from what you've done. This is called **administrative closure.** You can consider it the last piece of communications you need to do on the project.

Closing Documentation

Why should you even bother with closing documentation? This is a good question, especially when everyone is busy with the next project. The answer is simple: Without past information, you cannot do better in the future, and if there is a problem, you will not be able to track down the cause quickly.

What information should you gather? At the least, you should collect and organize the following documents:

- The project charter
- The project plan
  - Baselined project schedule
  - Baselined project budget
  - Risk management plan
  - Quality plan
  - Scope, schedule, and cost management plans
  - Configuration management plan
  - Communications plan
  - The project organization chart
- Risk and issues logs
- Test plan, test logs, and test results
- Status reports
- CCB meeting minutes
- Project presentations and reports
- Significant e-mails
- Change requests
- Major project decisions
- Contracts
- Lessons learned reports

You can see there's a lot to document, but you've been keeping it up all along and all these documents are necessary if you are going to learn from your projects and avoid repeating problems in the future.

Contract Closure

Of all the activities required to close out a project properly, **contract closure** has the most legal significance. A contract is a legal document between you and a supplier for goods and/or services provided in exchange for something of value, almost always money. All parties must agree before a contract can be closed. Most companies have contracting or procurement departments, which can be used to handle all the administrative details of ensuring the contract is closed out. However, you are the one who has to verify that all the work done by the contractor is completed satisfactorily, that deliverables were done on time to the quality expected, and work was within the contract budget.

If your company does not have a procurement department, you will be the one to take care of all of the administrative items. These include ensuring those just mentioned are done, that the contractor has received all payments due, and that there are no outstanding change orders to the contract. If the only contracts were for labor (hired programmers or testers who were paid an hourly wage), then there is usually little paperwork.

However, if you contracted a major part of the project or purchased components, then you want to make certain that the work is as expected. Let's say you bought 50 web servers from HP to create your new e-commerce web site. Would you just plug them into the production environment and expect everything to work perfectly on all of them? Not if you're smart. You would include time in the project for a burn-in test to drive out any initial problems. This might mean setting aside a weekend to let all the servers run and make sure they work as expected. Then, and only then, you would sign off on the contract to accept them.

Archiving Information

While the simplest approach to archiving is to just package up the project documents and store them somewhere, this is not the most effective way to archive. Almost nobody wants to dig through a lot of documents to see what can be learned from them, and even fewer of us have the time to do so.

The most effective way to archive **historical information** is in a database that can be searched. This is a form of a knowledge management system. Since most project documentation is in digital form, storing the documentation digitally is relatively straightforward and only requires a means of searching through the information that is stored.

Once a significant amount of information is available for searching, you can learn many things from the database. Wouldn't you like to be able to identify which team members consistently overestimate tasks? You can do that. How about being able to identify which contractors always deliver on time and to spec? Would management like to be able to identify project managers who consistently deliver their projects on schedule? It's possible to find out these things if historical information is captured and stored, and virtually impossible if it is not.

Checklists

The easiest way to complete the project closeout is to have a checklist of the things that need to be done and the process to go through so that nothing is overlooked. Figure 14-2 is an example of a **project completion checklist** that you might use as a template.

The Post-Implementation Report

Why should you write a **post-implementation report**? Nobody's going to read it, anyway, right? Three reasons: It's good for you, it's good for your company, and it's good for project management as a profession.

Let's say your project went well. Aren't you proud of that? Don't you want everybody to know? Would you like to do better next time? Learning from what went right and from what could be improved allows you to enhance your reputation as a successful project manager.

If the project did not go well, you need to write a post-implementation report to let other project managers know what happened so that they can avoid the same problems in future projects and so that you can learn to do better next time.

What goes into a post-implementation report? Your organization should have a standard for this. Being consistent with the standard is more important than capturing everything you can think of.

One part of the post-implementation report is that whatever categories you select are each rated on a scale of 1 to 10 as to how well the project did in this area. This gives an overall rating score to the project after it is over from your viewpoint as the project manager.

Figure 14-2. Sample Closeout Checklist

Item Description	Completion Date	Comments	Reason for NOT Completing
Solicit Feedback			
Prepare surveys			
Distribute or review surveys with appropriate participants			
Gather survey results			
Review and analyze survey results			
Summarize feedback for presentation at Project Assessment Meeting			
Prepare Post-Implementation Report			
Schedule Project Assessment Meeting			
Select and invite appropriate meeting participants			
Review and distribute survey summary results			
Gather notes and meeting results for inclusion in Post-Implementation Report			
Use survey feedback and meeting results to identify lessons learned and best practices			
Document each lesson learned			
Document best practices			
Develop action plans to implement lessons learned and best practices			
Gather summarized survey feedback, notes from Project Assessment Meeting, lessons learned, and best practices			
Distribute Post-Implementation Report			
Archive Project Information			
Gather all project information			
Archive information in project repository			
Locate hardcopy repository in designated documentation area			

Consider the following major categories as chapters, though you should feel free to add more:

1. Project effectiveness
   - Summarize how effectively the product or service met the needs of the customer, consumer, and the performing organization.

- Highlight specific product performance metrics.
- Identify and discuss outliers—specific stakeholder groups dissatisfied with the product or wildly enthusiastic about it.
- Identify and discuss specific issues.

2. Project management processes
   - Summarize effectiveness of the project management processes throughout the project.
   - Highlight significance of approved changes to the original project scope and how they were managed.
   - Compare the baseline versions of the project schedule and budget to the final versions and describe any discrepancies.
   - Summarize deliverables and compliance with defined quality standards.
   - Identify and discuss outliers—specific stakeholder groups dissatisfied with the management process or wildly enthusiastic about it.
   - Identify and discuss specific issues.
3. Risk management
   - Summarize effectiveness of risk management throughout the project.
   - Highlight significant identified risks that actually occurred and the effectiveness of the mitigation plan.
   - Identify and discuss outliers—specific stakeholder groups dissatisfied with the risk management process or wildly enthusiastic about it.
   - Identify and discuss specific issues.
4. Communications
   - Summarize effectiveness of the communications plan developed for the project.
   - Highlight significant communication activities that were particularly effective.
   - Identify and discuss outliers—specific stakeholder groups dissatisfied with the project communications process or wildly enthusiastic about it.
   - Identify and discuss specific issues.

5. Project implementation and transition
    - Summarize effectiveness of the project implementation and transition.
    - Highlight significant milestones of the implementation and transition and the effectiveness of the activities planned and executed for those milestones.
    - Identify and discuss outliers—specific stakeholder groups dissatisfied with the implementation and transition process or wildly enthusiastic about it.
    - Identify and discuss specific issues.
6. Performance of the project team
    - Summarize effectiveness of the project team within the context of this project.
    - Highlight significant responsibilities of the project team and the effectiveness of the team in accomplishing them.
    - Identify and discuss outliers—specific stakeholder groups dissatisfied with the performance of the project team or wildly enthusiastic about it.
    - Identify and discuss specific issues.
7. Organizational change management
    - Summarize effectiveness of organizational change management throughout the project.
    - Highlight significant change management impacts and the effectiveness of the organizational change management activities planned and executed for those impacts.
    - Identify and discuss outliers—specific stakeholder groups dissatisfied with the organizational change management process or wildly enthusiastic about it.
    - Identify and discuss specific issues.
8. Issues management
    - Summarize effectiveness of issues management throughout the project.
    - Highlight significant issues and the effectiveness of the issues management process for those issues.

- Identify and discuss outliers—specific stakeholder groups dissatisfied with the issues management process or wildly enthusiastic about it.
- Were issues resolved before change control was needed?

9. Key metrics (specific metrics depend on what you used during the project execution)

   Cost

   - Percent difference between the final cost, final approved baseline cost estimate, and the original cost estimate.
   - Number of approved changes made to the original budget.
   - Number of rebaselined budget estimates performed.

   Schedule

   - Number of milestones in baseline schedule.
   - Number of baseline milestones delivered on time (according to final baselined schedule).
   - Difference between elapsed time of original schedule and final actual schedule.
   - Difference between elapsed time of final baseline and final actual schedule.

   Scope

   - Number of baseline deliverables.
   - Number of deliverables delivered at project completion.
   - Number of scope changes in the post planning phases.

   Quality

   - Number of defects/quality issues identified after delivery.
   - Number of success measures identified in the business case that were satisfied or achieved at project completion.

Lessons Learned

Lessons learned is how we term the effort to understand how well things went on the project and what could have been done better. Ideally, you do this throughout the project, and formalize it at the end of each phase of the project. At the very least, go through a lessons learned process at the end of the project.

What Do You Think?

What areas of your projects is your organization most interested in assessing?

Capturing lessons learned is one of the easiest things to do, yet it is often overlooked and not done at all. Why? Usually because management sees no benefit in it, or because we have already started on our next project and we have no time. There's an old saying among experienced project managers: "What we learn from lessons learned is that we do not learn lessons learned." If we do not learn from what we and other people have done before us, we are doomed to repeat the same mistakes.

The biggest benefit to capturing lessons learned is that we learn how to do things better on the next phase or on the next project. We all make mistakes as we get caught up in the "busy-ness" of working on a project. Identifying these mistakes and learning from them helps us in the future.

A simple process identifies lessons learned:

1. Identify what went well and why.

2. Identify what could have been done better and how.

3. Did anything go differently than expected?

4. How could the project team have worked better together?

5. What serious issues were encountered during the project, and did you deal with them in the right way?

6. What improvements would you recommend for similar projects in the future?

7. What were the most valuable lessons learned?

Unlike many of the project meetings, the lessons learned meeting can be informal. In fact, it works best as an informal meeting. You want to get people to relax and not feel like they're going to be punished for telling you what went wrong. The best way to have a lessons learned meeting, in our experience, is to hold it right after work, and bring in pizza and refreshments. The refreshments can be anything within your company's guidelines. You should still prepare an agenda or a timeline, but there should be a loosening of the normal meeting structure so that people feel comfortable.

If you did the project for an external client, you may want to hold more formal lessons learned meetings during the day. However, if you have a meeting with only team members and internal stakeholders attending, make it loose and comfortable.

In most IT projects, members of the team start working on other projects as soon as their work on the project is done. This is especially true if you are using contractors to do part of the work. In this case, there may not be enough people left by the end of the project to hold a solid lessons learned meeting. In this circumstance, you can create an online form that people can complete as they start off-loading from the project. Collect responses to questions on what went well and what could be improved for each of the following areas:

1. Project scope and deliverables

2. Project sponsorship and overall direction

3. Project teams

4. Project management

5. Project logistics (facilities)

6. Project life cycle

7. Risk management

8. Other areas specific to your project

9. Overall assessment

The output of the lessons learned meeting should be placed in the archives. Sometimes the archives are known as the project library, the knowledge base, or by some other name. You want to ensure that other project managers can readily find the information and learn from what you did.

> ### *PM in Action!*
>
> Design a project close-out report that could be used in your organization. Do not use the information we presented. Use information specific to projects in your company.

*

NOTE

Lew Platt, when he was CEO of Hewlett Packard, was once quoted as saying: "If HP knew what HP knows, we would be three times as profitable."[1]

CHAPTER SUMMARY

- Project audits are used to ascertain if we have followed the company procedures in managing the process. Internal or external staff can do them, and they can be formal or informal. They generally require time to prepare and will involve project team members as well as the project manager.
- Project closure involves conducting a post-implementation review and performing administrative closure.
- Obtaining project acceptance means validating that the requirements are what the client expects and verifying that the requirements are met.
- When transitioning your project to maintenance, you should at the very least provide an operations guide and a maintenance and troubleshooting guide.
- Post-implementation reports are useful for you, your company, and other project managers. They can cover whatever your organization feels is appropriate. Some suggestions are: project effectiveness, project management processes, risk management, communications, project implementation and transition, project team performance, organizational change management, issues management, and key metrics
- Completing a lessons learned survey from project stakeholders helps you learn how to do things better in the future. You should cover what worked well in addition to what can be improved next time.

- Closing documentation is comprised of the project plan, logs, testing information, status reports, information on change management, significant project decisions and e-mails, and lessons learned reports.
- Contract closure entails making sure all contract requirements have been met, all disputes have been resolved, and the invoices have been paid.
- Project information should be archived in a method that makes it easy to retrieve in the future. One efficient way to archive project information is with a database.

Key Terms

Lessons learned

Scope validation

Project review

Project quality audit

Administrative closeout

Post-implementation report

Transition to production

Project audit

Project archives

Key Term Quiz

Match the terms in the table to the definitions in the table.

A	B
Project audit	The set of project documentation that will be filed in the historical repository.
Project archives	An examination of part of the project, focusing on a particular area to assess it in detail.
Scope validation	The final report summarizing the project, its processes, and results.
Historical information	The collection of documentation from all past projects, stored in such a way they can be accessed to learn what happened.
Administrative closure	A formal project review, resulting in a report describing how well the project is following approved procedures.

A	B
Lessons learned	Moving the delivered product into the production system.
Post-implementation report	The process of ensuring that the product meets the expectations of the users or client.
Contract closure	The process of formally closing out all legal contracts used on the project.
Project review	The capture of what happened on the project from the standpoint of the stakeholders.
Project completion checklists	The document that lists what the project manager has to do to close out the project.
Transition to production	The process of closing out the project and ensuring everything is complete.

Chapter Review Questions

1. Closing out a project means:
   A. Saying goodbye to the team members and the project sponsor
   B. Writing the post-implementation report
   C. Closing out all project documentation and contracts
   D. Both (b) and (c)
2. A project quality audit is:
   A. A way for management to criticize how the project manager did
   B. A formalized approach to assessing how well the project was managed compared to the approved processes
   C. A quick way to identify problem areas
   D. Part of the lessons learned process

3. Lessons learned meetings are:
   A. A way to capture what went right and what could have been done better on the project
   B. The formal process of gathering historical information for the archives
   C. Best done using online surveys
   D. A way for the project manager to get informal feedback on how he or she did
4. The post-implementation report includes:
   A. The schedule of project status meetings
   B. Details of the project's budget management process
   C. An explanation of the change management process used by the project manager
   D. None of the above
5. Contract closure includes:
   A. Ensuring that all project deliverables specified in the contract have been delivered
   B. Archiving the contract with the historical project information
   C. Meeting with the contractor to go over last minute issues
   D. Withholding the last 10% of the contract for 90 days
6. What are the four areas where disconnects can occur in scope validation?
7. What are some of the topics that are covered in an operations guide?
8. What are some of the topics that are covered in a maintenance and troubleshooting guide?
9. What are the three main times to perform audits?
10. When is the most useful time to get an audit for the project manager, and why?
11. List five categories that a post-implementation report might cover.

12. What are the key cost metrics that should be covered in a post-implementation report?

13. If you are conducting a lessons-learned survey for a virtual team, what are four of the nine topics we listed that could show up on your survey?

14. What is the difference between validation and verification?

15. In addition to the project plan, what other information should you collect for closing documentation?

END NOTES:

1. One of the authors originally heard this at the PMI EMEA 2004 convention in Prague, Czech Republic, during a seminar on HP's PMO approach, "Implementing a Global PMO," by Jake Stewart and Don Kingsberry. This quotation has been referenced multiple times in other articles.

APPENDIX *Answers to Review Questions*

CHAPTER 1

1. Scope, time, and cost
2. Depending on the organization, project managers may have full authority or very little authority when it comes to managing people and budgets.
3. Choose from:
   - Defined start and finish
   - Unique
   - One-time events
   - Customer focus
   - Project manager may lack formal authority
   - Temporary project team
   - Complex communications
   - Scope may evolve
   - Scope/cost/time constraints
   - Generally projects have high risk
4. A successful project is one that meets the triple constraints of scope, schedule, and cost. But to be a success the project must also be a strategic success, meeting the needs it was undertaken to address. Also, the team members should be satisfied with working on the project.
5. A project is a unique one-time endeavor. A program is a series of related projects that may have an element of ongoing operations. A portfolio is a collection of projects and/or programs that are managed as a single group to support business operations.

6. Choose from:
    - With IT projects, the project team is usually working on several projects at once and maintaining operations. On non-IT projects, people will usually only be involved in one project at a time.
    - The time span is shorter and priorities tend to shift more in IT projects than non-IT projects.
    - In technical projects, the technology itself is often a risk, and the risk on each project is different. Non-technical projects often have proven technologies without the risk and the risk is steady throughout the project.
    - Since IT projects are shorter in duration, there is no time for team development. On longer projects, team development can occur.
7. Time to market, customer satisfaction, alignment to strategic goals and meeting time, budget, and quality objectives.
8. Shutting down production for retooling
9. A portfolio of projects

CHAPTER 2

1. Strong matrix
2. Functional
3. Matrix
4. Center of Excellence
5. Administrative
6. The reason the organization exists
7. - The scope of the project office
    - Clear objectives
    - The budget to fund
    - Manage expectations
8. It can be an inefficient use of resources because highly skilled, and highly paid, resources may be on your project whether you need them now or not.

9. Goals are directions that the organization wants to head in to improve performance. Goals are generally qualitative in nature. Objectives are quantitative. They are specific targets to accomplish within a specified time frame.
10. All projects should be tied to an organization's **strategic plan**.
11. Values describe what is important to the organization. They may include how an organization treats its employees and shareholders, how it behaves as a neighbor, and how it behaves with respect to its environment.
12. Sarbanes-Oxley requirements necessitate upgraded software.
13. One of your customers, a municipality, has asked your organization to install software that can detect attempts to hack into the system.
14. 1) Complying with a new state regulation that requires your company to upgrade your security software 2) completing an upgrade to a financial package that your CFO needs 3) making an improvement to an internal process
15. Because there are limited resources to do all of them.

CHAPTER 3

1. Generally, the need for project management activities will be highest at the beginning and end of the project and fairly even in the middle.
2. A series of steps that will complete all parts of the project when done in sequence.
3. The waterfall model
4. Extreme programming
5. Tell the project sponsor that you're over budget and need more money
6. Makes the most effective use of resources while satisfying the product requirements

CHAPTER 4

1. Choose from:
   - Duration
   - Dollars

- Resource usage
- Criticality
- Risk
- Complexity
- Reporting requirements

2. Criticality
3. A category C project; it is small, neither complex nor risky, and not critical.
4. False. You should apply just enough project management to ensure the project is successfully completed, but no more.
5. Generally, the need for project management activities will be highest at the beginning and end of the project and fairly even in the middle.
6. Choose from:
   - Project life cycle information, including any phase gates, kill points, or sign-off points
   - Project charter
   - Project scope statement
   - Work Breakdown Structure
   - Milestones
   - Resource calendar
   - Schedule baseline
   - Cost baseline
   - Quality baseline
   - Risk register
   - Configuration management plan
   - Change management plan
   - The scope management plan
   - The schedule management plan
   - The budget management plan

- The risk management plan
- The quality management plan
- The communications management plan
- The procurement management plan
- The staffing management plan

7. Assumption log, issues log, risk log, action item log

Chapter 5

1. A project charter
2. To introduce the team to the project and to each other and to generate some excitement about the project. At the end of the meeting, all the team members should understand the scope of the project, their role in the project, how the project relates to the company's strategy, the planning process, and the next steps.
3. The scope of the project, their role in the project, how the project relates to the company's strategy, the planning process, and the next steps.
4. Choose from:
   - Requirements that satisfy customer, sponsor, or stakeholder needs
   - Business needs, high-level project description, product requirements
   - Project purpose or justification that ties to a strategic need
   - Business case justifying the project, including ROI
   - Summary milestone schedule
   - Summary budget
   - Functional organizations and their participation
   - Assumptions
   - Constraints
   - Stakeholder influences
   - Assigned PM and authority level

5. Choose from:
    - Project objectives
    - Product or services requirements and characteristics (including any technology requirements)
    - Project requirements and deliverables
    - Product acceptance criteria
    - Project boundaries
    - Initial project organization
    - Initial WBS
    - Configuration management
    - Approval requirements
    - Updates to:
        - Project milestones
        - Budget estimates
        - Assumptions
        - Constraints
        - Risks
6. The project charter is focused on how the project relates to the organization in terms of resources, strategy, and stakeholders. It also includes high-level information about scope, schedule, and cost. The project scope statement is focused on the scope of the project and the product.
7. The product scope defines only the end deliverable and its components. The project scope defines the work necessary to deliver the product scope.
8. 15%
9. A solution, not a requirement
10. They want to display all their charts.
11. The people who will be affected by the process change.
12. Affordable

Chapter 6

1. False. The WBS should be arranged however you want to manage the project. Unless your organization dictates a specific way, via a template, the decision is yours.
2. Top down and bottom up
3. True.
4. Finish-to-start
5. Finish-to-finish
6. Bottom up, approximate estimate, rough order of magnitude.
7. It is quick and does not take a lot of time.
8. It is accurate and the people doing the estimating buy into the estimate.
9. Parametric
10. Responsibility matrix
11. Mandatory dependencies are based on the nature of the work; discretionary dependencies are considered a best practice.
12. External dependency.
13. Probabilistic estimate
14. Triangular: 5.67 weeks. Beta: 5.3 weeks.
15. Give the decision-makers enough information to decide if the project should be approved

Chapter 7

1. Choose from: knowledge of project management methods and tools, technical and business skills, synthesis and analysis, balancing stakeholder expectations and priorities, holistic thinking, and explaining complex things in simple terms.
2. Choose from: leadership, team and people skills, team building and motivation, balancing their style to the situation, communication, and cross-cultural communication.

3. Choose from: supportiveness, being a risk taker, assertiveness, confidence, facilitation, flexibility, open mindedness, not panicking.
4. Monitor the project environment and keep the project manager apprised of changes to project prioritization, funding, and resource allocation. Buffer the project manager from internal uncertainty and conflict. Meet with the project manager on a regular basis to assess project progress. Assist in decision making and conflict management that is outside the project manager's authority.
5. They look for what is best for the project and the organization, not just their piece of the project.
6. Forming, Storming, Norming, and Performing.
7. Choose from: the need to be right, the need to look good in front of others, the need to be perfect, the need to protect egos, and the need to judge.
8. Choose from: communication, trust, participation, shared leadership and accountability, reflection on the team process.
9. Choose from: establishing the vision and goals for the project, allowing time for questions, clarification and discussion, listening and asking questions, sharing leadership, assessing the team process, varying leadership styles.
10. Choose from: name, mission, logo, communication, conflict management, team meeting roles
11. Trust.
12. • Hiring the people who can work within this challenging environment
    • Using the right technology tools to enable close and constant communications
    • Building the processes for communications and coordination
    • Building the trust required to work effectively across large geographic separations
    • Developing the right motivational approaches for each part of the team
13. Scope, resources, schedule, and priorities.
14. Accommodating, collaborating, compromising, avoiding, and competing.
15. Collaborating.

CHAPTER 8

1. Without a plan, there will be no specific, measurable efforts dedicated to ensuring that the project turns out a quality product.
2. An operational definition is that one you can measure against.
3. The customer or client determines the level of quality you need to achieve. For internal projects, this would be the project sponsor.
4. Product quality focuses on the product deliverables as they are produced. Project quality focuses on how well the project was managed.
5. The goal is to reduce product defects to 3.4 per million opportunities.
6. The five phases are define, measure, analyze, improve, and control.
7. The cost of conformance includes all those costs attributable to achieving the specific level of quality that is needed. The cost of nonconformance are all the costs associated with problems, defects, and bugs in the product.
8. Some metrics that help you understand project quality include: the number of change requests, the number of change requests against requirements, and the number of discrepancy reports written by testers.
9. An Ishikawa diagram helps identify the root cause of a quality problem.
10. The 80:20 rule was created when Pareto analysis results consistently showed that most problems are created by a small set of causes.
11. For most IT projects, the testing program forms the core of the quality effort.
12. The testing effort should be started during the design phase of the project in order to give the testers enough time to develop the testing program, set up the test environment, determine the expected test results, and create the testing documentation.
13. False. It is the goal to have the design satisfy the requirements, but testing should always be done against the requirements to ensure they've been satisfied.
14. False. It is never permissible to test on the production system. Testing should be done in a an environment as production-like as possible, but never on the production system itself.

15. When testing COTS software, two areas of emphasis are compatibility with existing systems and security, to ensure the new software does not cause security problems.
16. False. Users or their representatives should always be involved in the testing program so that they understand exactly how the product satisfies their requirements.

CHAPTER 9

1. Internal and external
2. Complexity, urgency, technology, technical skill
3. With 5 people, you have 10 channels. With 10 people, you have 45 channels.
4. The executives want to know what has been accomplished since the last report. They also want to know the current status and what is planned for the next report. They only want to know about the milestones. Executives also want to know about any new risks and any significant variances to the plan.
5. When information is pushed out, the project manager sends it or gives it or delivers it to someone. The PM is proactive in getting information distributed. When communication is based on pulling, the recipient has to take the initiative to receive the information.
6. The communication plan documents who needs what information, when they need it, how it will be given to them, and how to communicate under special circumstances, such as emergencies.
7. Choose from:
   - Jargon and slang
   - Ambiguous words
   - Superfluous information
   - Overly detailed information
8. Choose from:
   - Prepare, prepare, prepare.
   - State the objective of the communication.

- Use simple language and check for understanding.
- Allow questions and participation.
- Respond to verbal and non-verbal feedback.
- Summarize decisions and next steps.
- Be vivid, descriptive, and passionate (as appropriate).

9. - Stereotyping
   - Preconceived notions
   - Selective listening
10. Gestures, facial expressions, posture, eye contact, sighs, etc.
11. Choose from:
    - Make sure your objectives are clearly stated in the beginning.
    - Make sure there is a WIIFM in the first four slides.
    - Have something to grab their attention in the first four slides.
    - Put your points in a logical sequence.
    - Summarize your presentation at the end.
    - Have a clear call to action as appropriate.
12. - Have your notes in order.
    - Make sure your equipment functions.
    - Have your appearance and grooming be appropriate to the situation.
    - Check that your presentation can be seen from all seats in the room.
13. After the meeting, make sure you send out the meeting notes or meeting minutes. Follow up on any outstanding items, offline conversations, and action items.
14. - Avoid the use of slang.
    - Try not to use too many abbreviations (unless appropriately defined).
    - Avoided clichés, or at the very least, use with caution.
    - Avoid the passive tense where possible.

CHAPTER 10

1. A risk is an event that may or may not occur. An issue is something that has occurred that you now have to deal with.
2. Risk identification, risk analysis, and risk response planning
3. Team members, technical, project management, organizational, and external
4. Technology, technical requirements, testing, and vendors
5. 20%
6. Skills and experience, project management infrastructure, methodology
7. Reviewing project documents, interviews, checklists, risk breakdown structure
8. To document your risks
9. Preliminary risk analysis, probability-impact matrix, risk analysis form
10. Small projects with low technology have low risks. Large project with high technology in a low structure environment have high risk.
11. Avoid, mitigate, transfer, and accept
12. An opportunity
13. Exploit, share, enhance, ignore
14. A low probability and low impact risk
15. Using reserve

CHAPTER 11

1. Resource loading entails entering the percentage of time resources available into the schedule. Resource leveling means that anytime there is someone who is over allocated, MS Project will either split tasks or push completion dates out to keep the resources within the availability constraints assigned.
2. Fixed work, fixed duration, and fixed units
3. The duration will increase.

4. MS Project will either split tasks or push completion dates out to keep the resources within the usage constraints assigned.
5. It means we are looking for the best way to perform the project, taking into account our cost and time constraints, the scope requirements, and risk management.
6. Choose from:
   - A fixed deadline
   - Resources are promised somewhere else
   - A contractual constraint that requires the project be completed by a certain date
   - Bonuses tied to early delivery or penalties associated with late delivery
   - A promise to a client that it would have a completed product by a certain time and it is planning around the promised delivery date
   - An earlier deliverable may have fallen behind, and now we have to compress our part of the project to try and make up for lost time.
   - We have lost a resource and have fallen behind because we needed to bring in someone new and get him or her up to speed on the project and the tasks.
7. You may add staff, equipment, vendors, overtime, pay bonuses.
8. Shallowest
9. False. Only crash the critical path.
10. Slope = (crash cost – normal cost) / (crash time – normal time)
11. 75–80%
12. Because people who know what they are doing have to stop and educate the new people. Plus, you have more channels of communication, new team dynamics, and more confusion.
13. False. It takes time to stop working on one project and pick up working on another project.
14. Create a project master schedule.
15. To add schedule reserves, costs for risk responses, and cost reserves

CHAPTER 12

1. Two weeks
2. Preventive and corrective
3. Norming and Performing
4. Don't abdicate organizing meetings, collecting status information, resolving conflicts, following up on items from the meeting, and leading.
5. Choose from: establishing linkages between team members, managing vendor and consultant communication, and managing communication external to the project.
6. The details and significance can get lost if you wait until the end of the project.
7. Define, very clearly, upfront, what constitutes a change for all aspects of your project.
8. Project scope, schedule, processes, plans, requirements, approach, and resources
9. Error in defining the product, errors in defining the project, value added change, customer directed change, and external changes
10. The economy, competition, politics, or anything else outside the organization or the project.
11. Finding a way to do something faster, better, or cheaper
12. The work involved to assess the project impact
13. Configuration management
14. The baseline
15. The project manager, sponsor, technical leads, and ad hoc members as deemed appropriate

CHAPTER 13

1. - Comparing actual performance to planned performance
   - Assessing trends in the performance data
   - Developing forecasts of future cost and schedule performance

2. - Analyzing variances in performance
   - Evaluating alternative actions to bring performance in line with the plan
   - Recommending preventive or corrective action as appropriate
   - Managing the preventive or corrective actions to ensure they have the desired effect
3. Scope statement and WBS
4. It is easier to develop your planning documents in a way that is consistent with how you will collect and analyze information.
5. Establish how you are going to measure progress upfront.
6. Fixed formula and weighted milestones
7. Use information based on past performance and, assuming that performance will continue in the future, project the end result.
8. Only the variances that are outside the established thresholds require action.
9. A variance metric describes the amount of variance either in schedule or budget. It is project specific. A performance metric describes the efficiency with which you are performing on your schedule or budget. It can be compared to other projects in the organization.
10. Start date variance, finish date variance, duration variance
11. A variance in the duration
12. Compare them to what you earned, or actually accomplished. Do not compare them to what you planned to accomplish.
13. Take your budget at completion and divide it by your current cost performance factor.
14. A chart or graph
15. Only if there are extreme variances, the original estimates are far off the actual results, or if you are adding scope to the project.

CHAPTER 14

1. Both (b) and (c)

2. A formalized approach to assessing how well the project was managed compared to the approved processes
3. A way to capture what went right and what could have been done better on the project
4. None of the above
5. Ensuring that all project deliverables specified in the contract have been delivered
6.
   - How well the written requirements satisfy the needs they were derived from
   - The accuracy of the translation of the requirements into detailed technical specifications
   - How well the product design satisfies those specifications
   - How well the product as developed satisfies the requirements
7. How the system is expected to work in the production environment, including: system backups and recovery, system interdependencies, how to upgrade the system, and what the system processes are
8. How to identify and fix problems in the system, as well as expected system performance in order to identify system slowdowns, detailed troubleshooting procedures, a problem escalation guide, and known problems that were identified during system testing.
9. Randomly during the course of the project, when the project is apparently having severe problems, or after the project is completed
10. Those that are done during the course of the project itself. Having someone come in and look at the project from an objective point of view can identify weak areas in the project early enough that we can repair them before they lead to problems.
11. Choose from:
    - Project effectiveness
    - Project management processes
    - Risk management
    - Communications
    - Project implementation and transition
    - Project team performance

- Organizational change management
- Issues management
- Key metrics

12. - Percent difference between the final cost, final approved baseline cost estimate, and the original cost estimate.
    - Number of approved changes made to the original budget.
    - Number of rebaselined budget estimates performed
13. Choose from:
    - Project scope and deliverables
    - Project sponsorship and overall direction
    - Project teams
    - Project management
    - Project logistics (facilities, etc.)
    - Project life cycle
    - Risk management
    - Other areas specific to your project
    - Overall assessment
14. Validation is ensuring that the requirements meet what the customer expects. Verification is making sure that those requirements are satisfied, as shown by testing, inspection, analysis, and other means.
15. - Risk and issues logs
    - Test plan, test logs, and test results
    - Status reports
    - Configuration change board (CCB) meeting minutes
    - Project presentations and reports
    - Significant e-mails
    - Change requests
    - Major project decisions
    - Contracts
    - Lessons learned reports

Index

A

B

C

D

E

F

G

H

I

Q

R

U

V

W